Intergovernmental Relations in the American Administrative State

THE JOHNSON PRESIDENCY

An Administrative History of the Johnson Presidency Series

Intergovernmental Relations in the American Administrative State

THE JOHNSON PRESIDENCY

By David M. Welborn and Jesse Burkhead

 University of Texas Press, Austin

First edition, 1989
Requests for permission to reproduce material from this work should
be sent to:
    Permissions
    University of Texas Press
    Box 7819
    Austin, Texas 78713-7819
The paper used in this publication meets the minimum
requirements of American National Standard for Information
Sciences—Permanence of Paper for Printed Library Materials,
ANSI Z39.48-1984. ∞

Library of Congress Cataloging-in-Publication Data

Welborn, David M., 1934–
    Intergovernmental relations in the American administrative
state: the Johnson presidency / by David M. Welborn and Jesse
Burkhead.—1st ed.
    p.   cm.—(An Administrative history of the Johnson presidency
series)
    Bibliography: p.
    Includes index.
    ISBN 0-292-73849-8 (alk. paper)
    1. Economic assistance, Domestic—United States.
2. Intergovernmental fiscal relations—United States.   3. United
States—Politics and government—1963–1969.   I. Burkhead, Jesse.
II. Series: Administrative history of the Johnson presidency.
HC110.P63W43   1989
353.9′292′09046—dc20   89-31697
                                                                    CIP

Contents

Tables

Foreword

In this book David M. Welborn, Professor of Political Science, University of Tennessee, and Jesse Burkhead, Professor of Economics Emeritus, Syracuse University, examine the intergovernmental dimension of the Johnson administration's management of its Great Society programs. How the administration extended and sought to change intergovernmental administration of social programs and the consequences and implications of its actions for the American political system are discussed, illustrated, and evaluated.

This volume is one of several collectively designed to form an administrative history of the Johnson presidency and to discuss problems and methods in presidential management of the executive branch during the Johnson years. Some of the studies in the series, including the present one, deal with the infrastructure of presidential management—the structures, personnel, and operating arrangements for decision making and policy administration. This volume follows the publication of books on structuring and staffing the executive branch: Emmette S. Redford and Marlan Blissett, *Organizing the Executive Branch: The Johnson Presidency* (University of Chicago Press, 1981); Richard L. Schott and Dagmar Hamilton, *People, Positions, and Power: The Political Appointments of Lyndon Johnson* (University of Chicago Press, 1983); and Emmette S. Redford and Richard E. McCulley, *White House Operations: The Johnson Presidency* (University of Texas Press, 1986). These books are paralleled by another on the exercise of the appointive power for judicial positions: Neil D. McFeeley, *Appointment of Judges: The Johnson Presidency* (University of Texas Press, 1987).

Other studies in the series deal with the presidential management of the policymaking and implementation process in particular policy areas. These include W. Henry Lambright, *Presidential Management of Science and Technology: The Johnson Presidency* (University of Texas Press, 1985); James E. Anderson and Jared E. Hazelton,

Managing Macroeconomic Policy: The Johnson Presidency (University of Texas Press, 1986); Harvey C. Mansfield, Sr., *Illustrations of Presidential Management: Johnson's Cost Reduction and Tax Increase Campaigns* (Lyndon B. Johnson School of Public Affairs, 1988).

Yet other studies are underway that focus on presidential management of foreign policy, the Vietnam War, the implementation of civil rights legislation, and economic regulatory policies. A final volume will broadly analyze and appraise presidential management of the executive branch during the Johnson years and the lessons to be learned therefrom.

This series of studies has been financed by a grant from the National Endowment for the Humanities, with additional aid from the Lyndon Baines Johnson Foundation, the Hobitzelle Foundation, and the Lyndon B. Johnson School of Public Affairs of the University of Texas at Austin. Production of this book has also been aided by a grant from the Lawrence L. Durisch Fund, administered by the Department of Political Science, University of Tennessee, Knoxville.

The findings and conclusions in the various works in this series do not necessarily represent the view of any donor.

EMMETTE S. REDFORD
Project Director
JAMES E. ANDERSON
Deputy Director

Acknowledgments

Although not of the magnitude of the federal deficit, our indebtedness incurred in the preparation of this volume is of major proportions. For their stalwart support, a major part of it is owed to Emmette S. Redford and James E. Anderson, director and deputy director of the Lyndon Baines Johnson Administrative History Project. The contributions of Kay Hancock, Robert Blum, and Richard T. McCulley, research associates on the project, were likewise invaluable.

We are also indebted to the archivists at the LBJ Library. Claudia Anderson, Linda Hansen, Nancy Smith, and Robert Tissing not only provided expert assistance but also made the hours spent in the reading room sifting through red boxes of documents more pleasant than they might otherwise have been.

Syracuse University and the University of Tennessee were helpful in many ways. Both institutions provided academic leave as well as graduate assistants who made important contributions. At Syracuse they included Paul McDonald and Michael Fishback. At Tennessee they were David M. Dickson, David Duggan, and Peter R. Wiley. Secretaries at both institutions patiently typed and retyped manuscript drafts. Those at Syracuse were Virginia Halsey, Esther Gray, and Dee Ficarro. At Tennessee the word processors were manipulated by Irene Carney, Marie Horton, Debby Pierce, and Naina Pinkston.

Many colleagues shared their knowledge and critical capacities. Among them, Harold Seidman, on a visit to Austin at an early stage in this effort, was most generous with his time and comments. At the Brookings Institution, Joseph A. Pechman, Gilbert Y. Steiner, and, above all, James L. Sundquist read the manuscript and provided excellent critiques. At a later stage, Richard Leach of Duke University and Laurence O'Toole of Auburn University provided most useful reviews.

Acknowledgments

Thus, our indebtedness is great, but none of the above is responsible for any errors of fact or interpretation that might still linger in the book.

DAVID M. WELBORN

JESSE BURKHEAD

Intergovernmental Relations in the American Administrative State

THE JOHNSON PRESIDENCY

1. The Intergovernmental Mosaic

The precise effects of the presidency of Lyndon Baines Johnson on the politics and governance of the United States—and the world—will be debated far into the future. There is general agreement, however, that between late 1963 and early 1969, Johnson's driving leadership had a profound impact on national domestic policy. His ambitious initiatives in civil rights, education, health, economic opportunity, and other areas, presented under the banner of the Great Society, indelibly imprinted the lives of the American people.

Far-reaching alterations were made in the way in which political and governmental power was distributed. In the process, the multi-level mosaic of national and subnational governmental structures that dominates the American administrative state—the complex of bureaucratic structures and processes through which the bulk of governmental business is conducted—grew much larger and more intricate.[1] Perhaps the most important change was the enlarged scope and penetration of national power. A multitude of intergovernmental programs were enacted that thrust the national government into much closer and more intimate involvement in the operations of subnational governments. These programs were accompanied by new administrative structures, processes, and concepts of coordination marked by considerable variety, complexity, and innovation. In this period of development, the presidency played a central role in framing the policy initiatives that altered power relations. It also participated in shaping the new administrative arrangements, coordination devices, and other parts of the intergovernmental policy implementation apparatus.

Paul P. Van Riper has observed that "modern administrative development has been so complex or so much in the shadows as to be essentially anonymous."[2] There have been numerous studies of Johnson's Great Society and of "creative federalism," its intergovernmental dimension, that deal with particular programs and policies. Yet much of this interesting and consequential period of administrative development remains "in the shadows."

The basic purpose of this analysis is to clarify, through a comprehensive examination of the period, how and, especially, why the American administrative state changed as it did in its intergovernmental aspects during the Johnson years. It focuses on the proximate center of initiative during the period, the presidency, as it was affected in decision making by the external political environment, policymakers at other levels of government, administrators in established and new programs, and inherited models of policy and administration. Relying extensively upon White House memoranda and other materials employed in the processes of presidential decision making, the analysis concentrates upon one of a president's most important effects in governmental administration: shaping basic patterns in the allocation of governmental power and in administrative arrangements, not just within the national government itself, the president's primary domain, but also, under present conditions, through the whole of the governmental system. Before elaborating further upon the nature of this analysis, it is necessary to characterize national and subnational relationships as they were in 1961, then to outline in some detail the imprint of Johnson's presidency upon them.

The Federal Context

In the American system, questions of the appropriate balance of power and authority assigned to the national and subnational governments have been a sensitive issue and a staple in the nation's politics from its beginnings. They were, of course, a central point of debate in Philadelphia when the Constitution of the United States was forged. Out of the debate came adoption of the federal idea, manifest in a division of power between national and state governments. Some powers, such as taxation, were shared, to be sure; but others were placed in the province of one or the other component. The arrangement was such that in inception and during its early period of development, there was a limited concentration of authority at the center and tenuous and limited penetration of national authority into the work of state and local governments.

Quite a different organizational pattern was evident when the Democratic Party, led by John F. Kennedy and Lyndon B. Johnson, prepared to assume direction of the executive branch of the national government after the 1960 presidential election. The pattern was the product of almost two centuries of development. It was the residuum of numerous disputations over constitutional principles and a long history of pragmatic adaptation in policy and administration. At that time the federal system could be described by Arthur W. MacMahon as both mature and emergent, as having attained an essential character after decades of development while retaining a dynamic capacity for further change.[3]

The mosaic of the "mature" system was composed of three basic materials. Not wholly compatible in color or texture, they reflected a continuing ambivalence, if not division, in the nation concerning the allocation of power between the national and subnational governments. One major component was the "adversary, conflict-oriented pattern of national-state relations" associated with the concept and practice of dual federalism. As Deil S. Wright concludes, it remained politically significant even after its constitutional foundations were largely destroyed.[4]

Historic tensions about the degree of authority to be concentrated at the center and its controlling effects on other governments existed alongside a second component, one described by Morton Grodzins and Daniel J. Elazar. This is the historic practice of the shared exercise of power in the American governmental enterprise, involving pragmatic collaboration among national, state, and local institutions.[5] Following passage of the income tax amendment in 1913, major enactments, such as the Federal Aid Road Act of 1916, anticipated the collaborative pattern that would be accentuated dramatically in later years under new constitutional circumstances.

The new federal realities as they emerged in the 1930s in the form of a revised constitutional concept of federalism and associated innovations in policy and administration, conventionally characterized as "cooperative federalism," constituted the third component. The constitutional reformulation as ratified by the Supreme Court repudiated the concept of dual federalism and substituted for it, according to Edward S. Corwin, the principle that "the National Government and the states are mutually complementary parts of a *single* governmental mechanism, all of whose powers are intended to realize the current purposes of government according to their applicability to the problem at hand."[6] The practical effect of the new principle was to shift further the basis for the assignment of roles and responsibilities between national and state governments from the interpretation of constitutional language to the currents of politics and the pragmatic judgments of elected policymakers. Its basic effects were nationalizing. Indeed, in major part it was the result of purposive political efforts to that end.

Adjustment at the constitutional level was associated with a major reorganization in power relations. These had never been stable, of course, but, as Samuel H. Beer puts it, during the 1930s "the balance of the American federal system swung sharply toward Washington"[7] with dramatic extensions of national power. New programs in economic regulation preempted state power in certain spheres. A variety of new grant-in-aid programs radiated out from Washington through subnational institutions. Some of these further compromised the federal character of the system because of grant programs to local governments that bypassed the states. As a result of approximately thirty major grant-in-aid programs established during the Roosevelt, Truman, and Eisenhower administrations, both state and local governments found themselves to be "partners" with the national government in policy areas where previously they had been the premier figures. By 1960, according to David B. Walker, federal law contained 132 grant authorizations grouped under fifty-eight program headings.[8] During the 1930s, the new programs in the vanguard of cooperative federalism for the most part addressed major social problems, especially in health and welfare, that were propelled to the forefront of national concern by the Depression. Later, in the 1940s and 1950s, the major emphasis was on programs for public works and physical facilities in areas such as housing, urban renewal, airports, hospitals, and highways. Collectively, their effect was to make the administration of domestic programs much more distinctly intergovernmental in character.

The New Deal programs and subsequent additions obviously reflected an enlarged sense of national purpose in politics, which, in turn, resulted in an enlarged role for the national government in defining that purpose and in crafting and participating in programmatic responses. In the process the American administrative state became less federal and more intergovernmental in character. At the same time, however, choosing to work through subnational governments rather than using national program options indicated that considerable potency remained in the federal idea and in the political strength of subnational interests, constitutional reinterpretations notwithstanding. Regarding the New Deal experience, James T. Patterson observes, "For all the apparent nationalism of the 1930s, states rights . . . remained remarkably healthy."[9] Other indications are to be seen in the structure of the new grant programs and in their substantive and administrative characteristics.

With few exceptions, in which national grants went directly to local governments, the new programs involved the national government and the states. In either case, categorical formula grants were employed. These were largely stimulative in character, intended to encourage and assist subnational governments in attacks on conditions considered to be problems from both national and subnational perspectives. This suggests neither uniformity of purpose nor conflict-free relationships, but a compatibility of purpose and the restriction of national involvement to rather clearly focused and defined objectives. Major examples are establishing a public assistance program in each state, facilitating the construction of modern hospitals across the country, and developing an interstate highway system.[10]

Conditions were attached to the grants, and policy and administrative standards and specifications limited the discretion of recipients. Yet there was latitude. Program "mechanisms," according to Wright, "seemed to preserve local political control."[11] Flexibility was allowed in levels of effort and, in social programs, levels of benefits. National administrative requirements cutting across programs were limited and aimed principally at advancing the notion of "neutral competence" and in undergirding professionalism in the public service through insistence on merit systems, antipatronage prohibitions, and program administration by a single state agency.[12]

The character of administrative interactions in intergovernmental relations was shaped by a somewhat restricted sense of national purpose, focused program objectives, and the limited administrative requirements imposed by the national government. Implementation and coordination of effort were centered in vertical bureaucratic relationships typically involving professional administrators and functional specialists in discrete program areas at participating levels of government. Thus, political officials, particularly chief executives, were generally not key actors in program administration, and there was little emphasis on coordination of the various programs with one another either in Washington or at subnational levels. But because programs such as urban renewal, housing, and highways did have spillover effects on one another, the costs of their administration in relative isolation began to be noted in some quarters in the 1950s.

By 1961 within the federal system there had evolved an intricate web of working intergovernmental relationships among national, state and local governments. Yet the three levels of government retained high degrees of independence and possessed their own complex structural features and diverse political attributes. These relationships were complemented by some intrastate and interstate regionalism. Still there were extensive linkages and dependencies among and within the elements of the territorial configuration: national-state, state-local, national-state-local, among local governments, and in other ways as well. The American administrative state had come to follow no neat or tidy path. To the important extent to which it was intergovernmental in character, there was dispersion of functional authority, complex political relations, and necessity for intergovernmental cooperation.

From the perspective of the division of power, substantial concentration was apparent in the national government. Through its own and intergovernmental programs, there was also a substantial national penetration into the lives of the citizenry and into the operations of subnational governments. Yet substantial concentration and penetration stopped short of the all-inclusive and the pervasive. At the national level, power was relatively decentralized and located in the several bureaus administering intergovernmental programs and in the committees and subcommittees of Congress. Furthermore, in Washington, in the field, and in subnational instrumentalities, power was exercised largely by program specialists in the various functional areas, including, for example, public welfare, public health, housing, and highways. The dominant intellectual skills were those of the relevant profession or professions and those required for the operation of complex bureaucracies with unifunctional responsibilities and objectives. Coordination was basically secured by administrative rule and professional norms applied in narrow bands of interaction among professionals in and among the various levels of government involved in a particular program activity.

The federal system and the network of intergovernmental relationships as they existed in 1961 provided both constraints and choices for national policymakers. Established allocations of power obviously were constraints. But substantial opportunities for choice in the administration of new initiatives were provided in the organizational options that evolved over time. The choices made in the Johnson years, as has been noted, altered intergovernmental relations in a variety of ways and placed them under considerable stress.

The Johnson Imprint

Much of the avalanche of legislation in the 1960s that enlarged the national government's domestic role, though employing intergovernmental means, can be traced to Democratic congressional initiatives in the 1950s, as James L. Sundquist has shown.[13] These provided the basis of John F. Kennedy's legislative program in the Eighty-seventh Congress and the first session of the Eighty-eighth. Although his efforts met with only limited success, the number of major measures proposed and the smaller number enacted suggested the possibility of extensive and important changes in domestic policies under altered political circumstances. That alteration came, tragically, with Kennedy's assassination on 22 November 1963, followed by the Democratic Party's overwhelming victories in the 1964 presidential and congressional elections. In the aftermath, especially in the 1965 – 1967 period during the extraordinarily active Eighty-ninth Congress, the programmatic, fiscal, and administrative features of American federalism and intergovernmental relations were reshaped in profound ways.

The Program Dimension

It is difficult to avoid superlatives in describing the sheer volume of legislation enacted during the Johnson administration. Much of it was aimed at social problems and involved grant-in-aid programs. The magnitude of achievement was later summed by the Advisory Commission on Intergovernmental Relations. It found that by 1969, at the conclusion of Johnson's presidency, there were about 150 major grant-in-aid programs, almost a fourfold increase over the number in place in 1961. These programs included an estimated 400 separate legislative authorizations for grants. All told, approximately 1,300 activities were counted in which the national government provided some form of assistance to subnational governments.[14] Also during this period regulatory programs that partially preempted state authority were under development for protecting consumers and the environment and safeguarding health and safety.

That the Johnson presidency was to be an energetic one was clearly indicated in his first address to Congress on 27 November 1963. Stressing the importance of expeditious action on national civil rights legislation and the pending tax cut, he also mentioned, though not prominently, the fight against poverty, anticipating the public declaration of the so-called war to come a few weeks later.[15] The more important starting point for the ambitious initiatives to follow is the 1964 State of the Union message: "Let this session of Congress be known as the session which did more for civil rights . . . which enacted the most far-reaching tax cut of our time; as the session which declared all-out war on human poverty and unemployment." Johnson followed this reiteration of established themes with references to national needs in areas such as health and transportation policy reform, then challenged Congress "to build more homes, more schools, more libraries, and more hospitals than any single session of Congress in the history of the Republic."[16]

The substantial role to be played by state and local governments in Johnson's programs was underscored in his commencement address at the University of Michigan on 22 May 1964, in which the concept of the Great Society was put forth as the unifying theme of his presidency. Mobilization of the full resources of the American administrative state was inevitable in view of the complexity and intractability of the problems to be overcome in pursuit of the Great Society and the varied points of attack on poverty "in our cities, in our countryside, and in our classrooms."[17] The president continued in more explicit fashion: "The solution to these problems does not rest on a massive program in Washington, nor can it rely solely on the strained resources of local authority. They require us to create new concepts of cooperation, a creative federalism, between the National Capital and the leaders of local communities."[18]

Not clear at the time were either the exact forms of relations that would mark "creative federalism" or their collective meaning for the future form of the American administrative state. What was clearly foreshadowed was a succession of demanding legislative agendas offered by the president in the name of Great Society objectives. Congress responded in 1964 and through the remainder of Johnson's time in office by enacting many major measures that featured intergovernmental administration.

The second session of the Eighty-eighth Congress approved nineteen major measures with important implications for federalism and intergovermental relations. Collectively the enactments suggested the rather diverse bundle of program techniques that would be mobilized in the campaign for the Great Society, as a brief look at three of the most important shows. There was, first, the landmark Civil Rights Act of 1964, essentially an extension of national power of major proportions into the lives of state and local communities for the protection of constitutional guarantees against racial discrimination.[19] The Economic Opportunity Act of 1964, the legislative keystone of the war on poverty, similarly provided for the direct use of national power. Together with the Urban Mass Transportation Act of 1964, it also added to the roster of grant-in-aid programs but with a certain difference. In these two enactments the principal subnational partners were cities and, in the case of the former, new community organizations outside the bounds of established local governmental structures. At least in the program dimension, the events of 1964 suggested that the intergovernmental relations of the Great Society would be characterized by a diversity of approaches.

The initial pattern of legislative success and diversity in approach continued into the first session of the Eighty-ninth Congress, whose record was even more impressive than that of its predecessor. Thirty-two major domestic programs of intergovernmental significance were adopted. These included the Appalachian Regional Development Act, the Elementary and Secondary Education Act, Medicare-Medicaid, the Housing and Urban Development Act of 1965, the Public Works and Economic Development Act of 1965, the establishment of the Department of Housing and Urban Development, the Law Enforcement Assistance Act of 1965, the creation of the National Endowment on the Arts and the Humanities, and the Water Quality Act of 1965.

The pace of legislation slowed somewhat in 1966. In the second session of the Eighty-ninth Congress twenty-six major domestic programs were enacted, all with significant grant-in-aid features. These included important amendments to the Urban Mass Transportation Act of 1964, the Demonstration Cities and Metropolitan Development Act (Model Cities), the Clean Water Restoration Act of 1966, and the Comprehensive Health Planning and Public Health Services Amendments of 1966 (Partnership for Health). There were also significant program and authorization extensions in elementary and secondary education and for programs of the Office of Economic Opportunity.

The midterm elections of 1966 brought a setback for the Democratic Party and hence for the Johnson administration. Republicans scored above-average gains for an out-of-power party, increasing, for example, their members in the House of Representatives to the highest level since 1956. The Democrats lost forty-seven House seats, three Senate seats, and eight governorships.[20] The generally conservative swing in November 1966 was recognized by President Johnson as a factor that would make further congressional support of his Great Society program proposals more difficult.[21]

But there were other factors at work that appeared to slow the scope and pace of presidential initiatives. The State of the Union message in January 1967 emphasized the Vietnam War more than did the 1966 message: "Abroad, the question is whether we have the staying power to fight a very costly war, when the objective is limited and the danger to us is seemingly remote."[22] On domestic programs the tone was set more quietly: "Three years ago we set out to create these new instruments of social progress. This required trial and error—and it has produced both."[23] At a later point he noted, "There are mistakes and there are setbacks. But we are moving and our direction is forward."[24]

Despite the changed policy environment, the first session of the Ninetieth Congress enacted twenty-one major statutes providing for new or expanded domestic programs, again, all with intergovernmental dimensions. Among the most important new programs were the Public Broadcasting Act of 1967 and the Air Quality Act of 1967. The Office of Economic Opportunity's continuation was assured for two more years, and there were important reauthorizations for mental retardation and elementary and secondary education programs.

By January 1968 the Vietnam War was even more prominent in the State of the Union message: "I report to you that our country is challenged, at home and abroad."[25] A lengthy discussion of Vietnam and other aspects of foreign policy followed. There is no reference to the Great Society theme as such. Domestic programs were discussed, of course, but with even less emphasis on forward progress than in 1967.

During 1968, however, twenty-two new or expanded domestic programs were enacted, including such significant legislation as the Omnibus Crime Control and Safe Streets Act, the Juvenile Delinquency Prevention and Control Act, the Housing and Urban Development Act of 1968, a major extension of vocational education programs, and the Intergovernmental Cooperation Act of 1968. While the Vietnam War came to have a serious impact on funding for domestic programs, it is not unimportant that all five congressional sessions in the Johnson presidency adopted major social legislation with important consequences for the intergovernmental features of the American administrative state.

The Fiscal Dimension

The Great Society was not only a civil rights act, a war on poverty, a strengthening of public and private education, and many other measures; it was also a transformation in fiscal federalism. The very great increase in the number and volume of grants-in-aid altered the composition of federal outlay.

These changes may be summarized as follows: first, states, local governments, and nonprofit agencies became the grant recipients of funds for the administration of new programs that were initiated by the national government; second, the federal budget came to be increasingly characterized by grants-in-aid and transfer payments rather than by direct outlays for goods and services.

Appropriate fiscal data are set forth in Table 1. For those unfamiliar with fiscal year accounting as it was practiced at that time, some explanation is in order. The fiscal year (FY) 1960 serves as the base year. That period started on 1 July 1959 and ended on 30 June 1960—that is, before the election of John F. Kennedy in November 1960. So

Table 1. *The Federal Budget and Gross National Product, Selected Fiscal Years: 1960–1969*

Fiscal Year	GNP (billions)	Budget Outlays[a] (billions)	National Defense (billions)	As Percentage of GNP	
				Budget Outlays	National Defense
1960	$497.3	$ 92.2	$45.2	18.5	9.1
1964	616.2	118.6	51.5	19.2	8.4
1965	657.1	118.4	47.5	18.0	7.2
1966	721.1	134.7	54.9	18.6	7.6
1967	774.4	158.3	68.2	20.4	8.8
1968	829.9	178.8	78.8	21.5	9.5
1969	903.7	184.5	79.4	20.4	8.8

[a]Unified budget.

Source: Office of Management and Budget, *Budget of the United States Government, Fiscal Year 1980* (Washington, D.C.: GPO, 1970), pp. 577–578; Office of Management and Budget, *Special Analyses, Budget of the United States Government, Fiscal Year 1979* (Washington, D.C.: GPO, 1978), p. 102.

it is a "complete" Eisenhower budget. After presidential elections it is traditional for an incoming president to establish a transition team to work between November and the January inauguration on various policy matters, including the budget, which the outgoing president must send to Congress just before the inauguration of the incoming president. Thus the budget for FY 1962 is a combination of the last Eisenhower budget and whatever changes the Kennedy transition team could make in a two-month period at a time when the budget cycle was well advanced. After inauguration the incoming president modifies the budget of the outgoing president. President Kennedy started his modification, for example, with his State of the Union message on 30 January 1961 and a special message to Congress on the economy on 2 February 1961.

So it was with the first Johnson budget for FY 1965. This was a Kennedy budget plus whatever changes Johnson imposed between late November 1963 and January 1964. And, of course, there are always changes in the budget before all appropriation acts are completed, which in those years was typically in August or September following a January submission. Such changes may be initiated by the president, and the president's budget is always subject to considerable modification by Congress. As a further complication, for purposes of reviewing the historical record, it is necessary to examine budget outcomes, not proposals. Therefore, Table 1 is presented in terms of fiscal year outlays, roughly equivalent to expenditures.

Fiscal years, calendar years, presidential elections, and congressional budget actions are not well phased to facilitate fiscal analysis. Therefore, in Table 1, and somewhat arbitrarily, FY 1960 is an Eisenhower year, FY 1965 a Kennedy-Johnson year, and FY 1969 the last Johnson year, since that budget was presented in January 1968 and action on it completed before Nixon was elected in November 1968, even though the fiscal year closed on 30 June 1969 after Nixon had been in office for five and one-half months.

Column one in Table 1 exhibits in current dollars the economic base for the Great Society programs—and for the Vietnam War. The first important legislation that the Johnson administration secured from Congress was a tax reduction measure in 1964, which had been previously proposed by Kennedy. This act provided a major fiscal stimulus to the economy in 1964 and 1965. By 1966 the rapid increases in defense expenditures, as shown in column three, provided a further stimulus. In consequence, the gross national product (GNP) in current dollars increased by 46.7 percent between FY 1964 and FY 1969. Total budget outlays increased even more rapidly—55.6 percent. National defense outlays also increased more rapidly than GNP—by 54.2 percent between FY 1964 and FY 1969. Inflation rates in the calendar years 1965–1967 averaged only 2.7 percent per year. Inflationary pressures began to intensify in the later years of the Johnson administration; the consumer price index increased by 4.2 percent in 1968.

The budget increased as a proportion of GNP during these years. The increase between FY 1964 and FY 1968 was 2.3 percentage points, or 12.0 percent. National defense outlays peaked in FY 1968 at 9.5 percent of GNP, then receded a bit in FY 1969 to 8.8 percent. Therefore, in the FY 1964–1969 period the increase in budget outlays as a proportion of GNP was 1.9 percentage points, or 10.3 percent. As the figures show, these were years of rapid economic growth, low unemployment, rising per capita incomes, and only modest inflation. The rapid expansion in budget outlays contributed to the GNP growth, and in turn the GNP growth made possible the acceleration in outlays with a modest increase in relation to GNP.

That this was a period of substantial economic growth was, of course, well understood by the president and his advisers. Official statements could be cited almost endlessly. The president's economic report of 28 January 1965 stated:

I am pleased to report
—that the state of our economy is excellent;
—that the rising tide of prosperity, drawing new strength from
  the 1964 tax cut, is about to enter its fifth consecutive year;
—that with sound policy measures, we can look forward to unin-
  terrupted and vigorous expansion in the year ahead.[26]

Further positive results were reported in 1966 and 1967.[27] The
president's economic report of 1 February 1968 began: "Most Americans see the economy in terms of a particular job or farm or business. Yet the welfare of each of us depends significantly on the state
of the economy as a whole. . . . For, as a people, we face some important choices."[28] The choices, of course, were between military and
domestic programs at a time when the Vietnam War was generating
both inflation and balance-of-payments difficulties. Many supporters of the Great Society came to feel that Vietnam War outlays severely constricted the resources that otherwise might be devoted to
the new domestic programs.

Table 2 exhibits data that describe the changes in fiscal intergovernmental relations that occurred in these years. In FY 1950 national grant-in-aid outlays were $2.3 billion, or 5.3 percent of total
outlays. Data for FY 1960 and FY 1964–1969 show that the amounts
of grants-in-aid doubled in the Johnson years, but, as with the GNP
comparisons in Table 1, when related to other magnitudes, the increase in aid is somewhat less startling. As a proportion of total outlays, the increase is 2.4 percentage points, or 27.9 percent from FY
1964 to FY 1969. As a proportion of nondefense outlays, the increase
is 3.4 percentage points, or 19.0 percent. And since state and local
expenditures from their own resources were growing rapidly during
this period, the increase in the last column of Table 2 is 2.8 percentage points, or 19.2 percent.

During the Johnson years, then, the amount of monies funneled
through subnational governments approximately doubled. But expenditure of their own dollars also rose significantly, resulting in a
modest rise in dependency on grants-in-aid. These aggregate patterns are important in their own right, but they tend to understate
the true fiscal impact of the Johnson presidency on subnational governments. One concomitant effect was the tremendous enlargement
of the range of subnational activity that was supported in some degree by grants by 1969. Perhaps of even greater importance were the
trends in fiscal federalism set in motion by the commitments made
in the Johnson years and by the more specific out-year authorizations contained in much of the legislation enacted during that time.

Table 2. *Federal Aid Outlays and Federal Expenditures, Selected Fiscal Years: 1960–1969*

Fiscal Year	Federal Aid (millions)	As Percentage of		
		Total Federal Outlays	Domestic Federal Outlays[a]	State-Local Expenditures
1960	$ 7,040	7.6	15.9	14.7
1964	10,141	8.6	17.9	14.6
1965	10,904	9.2	18.4	14.6
1966	12,960	9.7	19.2	15.6
1967	15,240	9.6	19.5	16.3
1968	18,599	10.4	20.9	18.2
1969	20,255	11.0	21.3	17.4

[a]Excludes defense, space, and international programs.

Source: Office of Management and Budget, *Special Analyses, Budget of the United States Government, Fiscal Year 1974* (Washington, D.C.: GPO, 1973), p. 217.

By FY 1978, federal aid outlays were 17.3 percent of total budget outlays, up from 11.0 percent in FY 1969; and as a percentage of state-local expenditures, grant-in-aid outlays were at 26.4, as compared with 17.4 percent in 1969.[29]

The Administrative Dimension

The tremendous sweep of intergovernmental program development and alterations in fiscal patterns were associated with basic changes in administrative structures and processes. State, local, and regional officials were brought into new, intimate, and demanding relationships with the national government. National administrators, in pursuit of program objectives framed in new statutes, were required to confront the intricacies and idiosyncrasies of thousands of subnational jurisdictions to a much greater degree than before. Administrative adaptation was not easy in Washington, in state capitals, or in local governments.[30]

The principal means of association was the familiar categorical grant-in-aid. But as employed in the Johnson years, the device was given innovative twists that, together with the sheer increases in the number of programs, had several immediate consequences for intergovernmental administration. These twists and their effects were further magnified by a small but important number of departures from the categorical theme. These included block grants to states in health and law enforcement as well as target grants for Appalachian regional development, for combating poverty, and for urban development through the Model Cities program.

One major administrative consequence was the substantial increase in complexity produced by the rapid and radical extension and diversification in administrative interactions among and within levels of government. The proliferation of program initiatives was a major contributing cause, made more acute by a tendency to subdivide them into narrow bands of activity, each with its own grant mechanism. For example, the administration's 1964 proposal for enlarging the supply of well-trained nurses included four separate grant programs aimed at nursing schools. They provided for the construction and rehabilitation of facilities; improved instruction; planning for nursing services; and training nursing supervisors and teachers. This particular example of separately funding small parts of a larger endeavor is a modest, not an extreme, one. Furthermore, as was the case with programs established before 1964, there were considerable differences from program to program in matching, eligibility, and other requirements, including those of an administrative nature.

With proliferation came diversification in two important respects, both adding to complexity. First, there was diversification in eligible recipients of grants-in-aid. Some programs were aimed specifically at states or cities. But in many instances eligibility was conferred on a range of prospective participants, including state governments, several varieties of local government, and private, nonprofit institutions. Diversification in grantor agencies also contributed to complexity, as recipients often found themselves in relationships with a number of federal agencies and bureaus, each with its distinctive interests, perspectives, and requirements. This new diversification of grant recipients was most prominent in the federal-urban subventions. This was not a new feature in intergovernmental grants—federal support for airports, hospitals, and public housing in urban areas dates back to the 1930s and 1940s. But the magnitude of federal program and fiscal ties to the cities was sharply increased by Great Society programs in mass transportation, in the poverty programs, and, of course, in Model Cities. Such programs bypassed state agencies and state governors, often to their consternation.

A second major consequence was increased national control over subnational administration as national problems were projected onto state, local, and regional agencies. New programs enlarged Washington's realm of involvement and supervision. Furthermore, control over content, according to James L. Sundquist, became in-

creasingly "close."[31] The resort to narrow categorical grants was itself an instrument of control. And many of the new ones were of the
project, not the formula, variety. Donald H. Haider estimates that
150 new project grant programs were authorized between 1964 and
1966.[32] In such programs, awards are made on the basis of the discretionary judgments of Washington and federal field-office officials,
not legislative entitlement based upon meeting certain minimal requirements. Funds were distributed to a select group of "winners"
among a pool of applicants after a detailed scrutiny of proposals.
This approach allows grantors more leeway to exert control over
program content than is the case with formula grants.

The conditions written into categorical grants of both types increasingly became more demanding, especially as to the administrative practices and processes of recipients. Among the more popular
of these were requirements for program, areawide, and regional planning as a basis for program activity and for the systematic evaluation
of program effects. Novel requirements were introduced that in later
years were applied more extensively. Mandated citizen participation, of course, was an important feature of the war on poverty's
community action program, where it became a precedent for application in other areas. Also beginning to appear with some frequency
were conditions related to national purposes that transcended particular programs, such as the prohibition of racial and other forms of
discrimination and the advancement of environmental protection.
In addition to more conditions, review and control for compliance
were more rigorous than in the past. All in all, the national government was becoming a more demanding senior partner in the administration of intergovernmental programs.

The proliferation of intergovernmental programs and the nature of
the policy objectives and strategies associated with building a Great
Society combined to place a considerable premium on the integration
and coordination of governmental efforts, the third major administrative consequence of Johnson's initiatives. Integration requires the
conceptualization and articulation of purpose transcending discrete
lines of activity and, at least in the broad sense, indicating how they
relate to one another. The task of integration is to provide coherence
to governmental effort and an overall framework and guide to coordination. It wrestles with the problem, in Martha Derthick's words,
"of defining federal purposes so as to guide executive behavior down
common or compatible paths and to circumscribe the scope and intensity of interagency differences."[33] Coordination involves contending with problems of duplication and overlapping and developing structures and processes that actually link related lines of

activity, whether vertically through hierarchy or laterally through formal or informal processes of communication, consultation, and negotiation.[34]

The integration and coordination of large-scale governmental efforts are difficult to obtain under most circumstances, especially when the jurisdictional boundaries of departments, agencies, and levels of government are crossed. But the challenge during the 1960s was of extraordinary proportions, in part due to the nature of Johnson's policy objectives. They were, of course, unprecedented in their sweeping ambition—to erase racial discrimination, to end poverty, to remove barriers to education and raise its quality, to improve the nation's health, and to rebuild the cities. The various objectives were not mutually exclusive. Efforts in pursuit of one could advance or impair efforts focused on others. The challenge at this level, in short, was to harmonize broad streams of governmental activity and to manage their interrelationships and their rippling and reciprocal effects.

Within these broad streams of activity, the program strategies that were employed, in addition to being substantially intergovernmental, were typically multiprogram and multifunctional. Take, for example, the Economic Opportunity Act of 1964, the centerpiece of the war on poverty. It was a multiprogram strategy in that eleven programs were authorized. Six of them were intergovernmental in that they involved grants to subnational units, while five were to be administered directly by national agencies. (In one of the latter group, the Job Corps, state and local governments were eligible to receive contracts for the operation of training centers.) Although the act placed administrative authority in the director of the Office of Economic Opportunity, in fact, in addition to the OEO, the functions to be deployed in fighting the war were those of the Departments of Agriculture; Health, Education, and Welfare; Labor; and the Small Business Administration. The coordination problem was exacerbated in that many other programs—some old, some new, some national, some intergovermental, but differing in their particulars and administrative arrangements—also dealt with the societal conditions addressed by the Economic Opportunity Act. These programs were factors in what was purportedly to be a coordinated war on poverty, but there were many impediments to blending their resources and efforts into an integrated and coordinated mix.

There were three major foci of coordination efforts. The first was set in Washington and involved relations between the Executive Office of the President and departments and agencies as well as among departments and agencies—an intragovernmental dimension at the national level. The second was set in the vertical relationships among governments at different levels, including the field offices of federal departments and agencies in their transactions with subnational governments. The third was again in horizontal relationships among federal agencies that attempted to cooperate with one another and with other jurisdictions at the regional, substate, or local level. Our intergovernmental administrative structure is complex, and the Great Society's programs added greatly to its complexity.

The fourth major consequence was increased stress and conflict in the intergovernmental administrative system. The tremendous growth in programs in a few years' time and the added complexity enlarged national control, and problems in coordination were themselves important sources of discomfort.

There were others. One was that the enlarged responsibilities of subnational governments were often "new and unsought," according to Harold Seidman, even requiring hazardous experimentation. These responsibilities were "thrust" upon them almost without warning and often extended into sensitive areas of social and political relationships.[35] The limits of subnational resources and capacities to respond were tested and, in many instances, exceeded. Washington and its field units faced similar challenges and experienced similar limitations in the translation of new legislation into effective intergovernmental programs. Local priorities did not necessarily square with those established in Washington. A related troublesome factor was that soon the flow of fiscal resources into Great Society programs began to fall below the level of governmental and public expectations. In addition to contributing to general frustration, competition among prospective recipients of federal funds became more acute. Mayors and governors grew anxious about their roles in program administration and about the political implications of those programs for their constituencies. In short, it was a time of flux and movement, a time of unsettling and, not uncommonly, unwanted changes in intergovernmental relations that were made all the more difficult later in the decade by an increasingly acrimonious political climate stimulated by the Vietnam War.

The Great Society and State Development

The awesome and complex initiatives of Johnson's presidency are of such proportions as to make it quite difficult to grasp with confidence their collective meaning for the developing character of the American administrative state. Stephen Skowronek supplies an interesting and useful basis for examining the question in his analysis of American state development. He suggests that three basic features define the essential character of any state. First, and most important, is how power is organized, especially the extent of "the concentration of authority at the national center of government" and the extent of "the penetration of institutional controls from the governmental center throughout the territory." Also important are the degree to which authority is centralized within the national government and the degree of specialization in the performance of institutional tasks and official roles.[36] The other features are the manner in which the actions of officials are coordinated and "the kinds of intellectual skills and human talents integrated into government."[37]

Skowronek's study of reform in civil administration, army reorganization, and national railroad regulation concludes that between 1877 and 1920 a fundamental shift occurred "from a state organization that presumed the absence of extensive institutional controls at the national level toward a state organized around national administrative capacities."[38] A powerful national bureaucracy had come to the forefront as a result of progressive reform efforts, a bureaucracy that in Skowronek's view defied authoritative control and direction."[39]

Skowronek is among those who think that the changes spawned by the Johnson administration were extensions of a "reconstitution" of power relations that occurred before 1920, then solidified in the 1930s. Theodore J. Lowi is of a similar mind, asserting that "a large, positive, interventionist national state is finally and forever the central feature of the American political system."[40] Although the Great Society enterprise contributed to this condition, he says, the foundations for the "national state" were laid before its time. Other scholars, including Wright, Daniel J. Elazar, and Richard Leach, are in essential agreement with the proposition that the American administrative state was not changed in any fundamental sense in the 1960s.[41]

There are opposing views. Beer, for example, emphasizes two phenomena that he argues are fundamental breaks from the precedents of the New Deal. Both were first apparent in war on poverty programs, then spread to others. One was "the increasing introduction into politics and government of ideas originating in the social sciences which promise to bring about social change through manipulation of . . . the hidden processes of society." In addition to determining who gets what, politics increasingly became "a process that also seeks to affect such outcomes as who *thinks* what, who *acts* when, who *lives* where, who *feels* how." The other was the countercultural call for participation, its advocates "personalistic, egalitarian, participatory in their message, cultural rather than economic in their concerns."[42]

Walker is the most fervent proponent of the proposition that there were changes of truly basic import. Focusing on recent developments in intergovernmental relations that are rooted in the 1960s, he argues that "to contend that these trends are merely logical extensions of the intergovernmental pattern of the New Deal is to ignore the stark contrasts between the simpler, more sorted-out, less expensive features of the earlier one and the widely pervasive, highly intrusive, hyperintensive traits of today's."[43] Walker is particularly concerned with their implications for program implementation. He fears that the intergovernmental system now is "overloaded," with its capacities so taxed that its ability to function must be questioned.[44]

Contrasting views such as these prompt curiosity about the intentions of Great Society policymakers. Did they consciously seek "reform" in intergovernmental power relationships in any fundamental way? Clearly they were driven by a strong sense of national purpose, as the next chapter will show, but what vision of the American administrative state animated their efforts? Questions such as these are especially interesting in light of the administrative consequences characterized in the preceding section.

Wright expresses a commonly held view when he asserts that there was no coherent vision—there was an "absence of an organizational philosophy."[45] Supporting evidence is found in flawed administration that suggests inattention to questions about implementation in developing and operating programs. It is also found in variety and incongruity in program arrangements, especially in regard to the distribution of power. For example, although a strong sense of national purpose was clearly evident, intergovernmental programs in almost all instances were the means chosen to advance the administration's policy interests. The fate of ambitious national policy objectives was tied to intergovernmental administrative mechanisms that many national policymakers felt to be inadequate to the task. New categorical programs varied considerably in their particulars. Many of them featured project grants in which national bureaucratic power was enhanced. Yet there was also movement in a different direction. Certain initiatives seemed to challenge national bureaucratic power. Prime examples include community action arrangements in poverty programs, new regional development programs, and block grant programs.

A penetration of the inner workings of the Johnson presidency to examine choices affecting the development of the American administrative state requires pursuit of several related lines of inquiry. One involves explaining incongruities, especially why, in an overall pattern of action that emphasized expanding the role of the national goverment, intergovernmental programs were featured and why some initiatives, such as block grants, were promoted that had the potential for constraining national power. Another line of inquiry focuses on program implementation. It involves determining how questions of implementation strategy were approached, identifying the major sources of problems in program implementation, and profiling the responses of the Johnson administration to them. A third line of inquiry centers on the institution of the presidency and, in a sense, subsumes the first two. It focuses on presidential execution of two related executive leadership tasks: management of the processes of policy and program development and management of administrative adaptations required by policy and program innovations. Studies of management or executive leadership at the presidential level often emphasize a fundamental tension at work. It is between the requisites of seeking unity, consistency, and coherence in the operations of government and of dealing with the immediate political interests of presidents as well as with the pluralistic political pressures that converge upon the office.[46] How management and political imperatives interacted in affecting presidential choices is an important aspect of the analysis.

A final line of inquiry pervades the entire analysis. In concluding his frustrated search for "the federal principle," S. Rufus Davis observes that we now know a tremendous amount about federalism. "Only the more we have come to know about it," he notes, "the less satisfying and the less reputable has become almost the whole of our legacy of federal theory." Further, "the greatest disenchantment has come with the discovery that, throughout history, the repeated mix of culture-bound, time-bound theorems of constitutional rationalism and political sentiment have not prepared statesmen and electors for the facts of federal life, nor have they explained their experience as they lived it."[47] In the broadest sense, the chapters to follow aim to chronicle the experiences of public officials facing "the facts of federal life" during an interesting and consequential time.

It could be argued that policymakers in the United States have not lived an authentic federal life for some time. A relatively simple federal arrangement has been replaced by what Wright describes as "multiple, complex and interdependent interjurisdictional relationships."[48] Yet federalism persists as a set of values and as a contributor both to the evolution of the governmental system over two hundred years and to the shape of its institutions. In a very careful review of the evidence, Harry N. Scheiber describes "how residual elements of older stages of federalism—doctrines, structures, or policies—have survived in succeeding epochs, including the present."[49] Thus, although generally Great Society policymakers may not have been federalists, federalism helped form the institutional and political context in which they worked during the Johnson presidency. In making decisions allocating power in a system that is not unitary, Great Society policymakers did, then, face "the facts of federal life" despite the absence of generally accepted federal principles to apply and the weakened condition and appeal of the concept in many quarters.

A Glimpse Forward

As a basis for exploring the intricacies of intergovernmental change during the period, this chapter has provided an overview of what Great Society policymakers produced. Chapter 2 examines the Johnson presidency at work in order to reveal the sources and dynamics of policy and program development. Particular initiatives of special significance in the Johnson presidency are explored in chapters 3 through 6. They deal with the war on poverty and those of its programs authorized by the Economic Opportunity Act of 1964, with Model Cities, with the concept of regionalism and substate and multistate regional institutions as devices for integration and coordination of effort, and with block grants and other alternatives to categorical grants-in-aid. Attention centers on the origins and nature of the initiatives, their distinctive features, and the role and impact of the presidency in carrying them forward. Chapter 7 focuses on presidential response to systemic problems in the administration of intergovernmental programs. The final chapter places the experiences of federal life during the Johnson presidency into historical perspective and considers them in relation to the purposes and fate of the Great Society's administrative arrangements and in the context of the ongoing development of the American administrative state.

2. Policy Nationalization and Subnational Administration

In the White House on the evening of 18 March 1967, President Johnson offered a toast in concluding his third set of remarks of that one day to the nation's governors: "Our Federal Union: May we build on its past to lift the quality of life in the future. May we build a land where the least among us can find contentment and the best among us will find greatness. Ladies and gentlemen, to the Union."[1] As the previous chapter indicated, the union celebrated by Johnson in 1967 was quite different from that of November 1963.

If queried in the early days of his presidency, neither Johnson himself nor the governors could have imagined the magnitude of the alterations in policy and in the American administrative state that would come in the next three and one-half years. Changes in the roles and responsibilities of national and subnational governments during this period, touching numerous areas, were not truly planned nor were the attendant administrative wrenches. Rather, they were more the spontaneous products of a policy environment that allowed nationalist policy entrepreneurs in Washington a unique opportunity to address a raft of problems they perceived to be national in character. Policies and programs that were nationalist, centralizing in some respects, and reformist in spirit and purpose were cast, with limited exceptions, in intergovernmental forms.

The purpose of this chapter is to provide a broad view of the Johnson presidency at work in framing Great Society initiatives, especially those of an intergovernmental character, and in coping with their immediate effects. After characterizing the policy environment, the discussion turns to policy development processes, the dispositions of policymakers, and the politics of policy and administrative change.

The Policy Environment

In assessing the achievements of Johnson's presidency and the programs of the Great Society, Doris Kearns observes that "special circumstances produced a blend of interests, needs, convictions, and alliances powerful enough to go beyond the patterns of slow, incremental change."[2] The special circumstances of the moment, however, were rooted in the historical circumstances of national development. These circumstances constituted an important part of a policy environment that was conducive to the nationalist and centralizing policy thrusts that marked Johnson's efforts. They include, especially, the agglomeration of changes experienced by the American society that, over time, enhanced its national character; the political and policy innovations associated with the New Deal; certain political developments in the 1950s culminating in John F. Kennedy's legislative program; and the political circumstances arising in the aftermath of his assassination.

Commentators generally emphasize the connection between societal changes and the political and policy innovations of the 1930s and 1960s. James L. Sundquist points to a steady "coalescing into a national society" that "destroyed the isolation of states and communities."[3] Martin Landau, in examining the sources of the Supreme Court's 1962 reapportionment decision in *Baker* v. *Carr*, asserts, "From a collection of loose, uncentralized or decentralized units, the United States . . . has evolved into a highly centralized, integrated community" to the point at which, he argues, its federal characteristics are lost.[4] Samuel H. Beer emphasizes the processes of modernization, driven by "the advancement of science and technology and . . . the democratization of wants" that cause increased differentiation and scale of activity in the economy and elsewhere in society. These interact to generate "ever larger and more complex networks of *interdependence*."[5] Interdependence, in turn, is the necessary condition for the movement of modern society toward greater centralization, if the proper political conditions are present. From an economic perspective, in a growing and complex industrial economy externalities in both benefits and costs become increasingly prominent over time. Air pollution does not honor state boundaries. With extensive interstate population migration, an inadequate education of children in Mississippi generates welfare and dependency problems in other states. The concentration of poverty in urban areas receives national attention. That which was once perceived as a local or a state problem is perceived by the citizenry, affected interest groups, and their elected representatives as a national problem. And once a problem is perceived, the oft-noted American genius for pragmatism suggests that something ought to be done about it, particularly if fiscal resources are available for that purpose, by the extension of national policy and administration.

In the 1930s, economic emergency created a demand for national action that, as Theodore J. Lowi puts it, "established a strong national state as politically feasible and constitutionally acceptable."[6] According to Beer, during this period there was a "centralization of government authority and the nationalization of political action."[7] In the aftermath of World War II, during the late 1940s and the 1950s, the nationalistic policies and politics of the New Deal persisted, despite President Harry S. Truman's difficulties in extending its scope and President Dwight D. Eisenhower's coolness to its philosophy. The idea of ambitious national action in response to national problems was kept in the forefront even in Truman's losing battles with Congress, as well as in Eisenhower's rare ventures into policy activism, such as the National Defense Education Act of 1958. It was further advanced by Supreme Court decisions, especially in the civil rights area, as well as in the passage of the Civil Rights Act of 1957. In his valuable work on domestic policy development, Sundquist describes the emergence in Congress of a Democratic policy agenda in the 1950s.[8] It reflected a growing view that "there need be no limitation upon the extension of federal responsibility except those imposed by fiscal and administrative circumstances that may prevail at any given time."[9] This agenda became the basis of John F. Kennedy's legislative program. "The climax and symbol of the philosophy" developed in Democratic circles during the 1950s "was President Johnson's concept of the Great Society."[10]

Kennedy's legislative agenda, then, influenced the environment in which the policymakers of the Johnson administration worked. Some of his proposals were enacted and became important elements in the Great Society enterprise. Opposing forces in Congress blocked passage of a significant part of Kennedy's program. Proposals still pending when Johnson assumed the presidency became part of his agenda.

Several distinctive points stand out in regard to Kennedy's efforts.[11] Despite the strong sense of national purpose that drove the Kennedy administration's major initiatives, almost all of them involved subnational governments in implementation. There were major exceptions. Proposals were forwarded and enacted to increase social security benefits, to raise the minimum wage and expand its coverage, and to refine various other national programs. In only three instances were there proposals to create major, new, and distinctly national programs that did not require some form of cooperation with subnational governments. These were health insurance for the elderly, civil rights protection, and a Youth Conservation Corps to combat unemployment among young people. None were enacted during Kennedy's time in office.

Three types of intergovernmental programs made up the bulk of Kennedy's legislative initiatives. One type expanded upon previously established programs, such as federal aid for highway and airport construction, urban renewal, public health, public assistance, and vocational education. In reaction to what was judged to be the penury of the Eisenhower administration, authorization levels were raised, the scope of programs was expanded, and benefits were liberalized.

The second type consisted of a substantial number of new grant-in-aid programs structured, for the most part, along traditional lines. Of the seventeen that became law, ten dealt with health problems. Among the failures, the most notable were aid for elementary and secondary education and urban mass transportation, although a small demonstration program for the latter was enacted.

The third type of program combined in integrated conceptual fashion direct national effort and complementary efforts by subnational governments supported by grants-in-aid. The Area Redevelopment Act (ARA) of 1961 and the Manpower Development and Training Act (MDTA) of 1962 are the prime examples. When the Kennedy administration's manpower proposal was being drafted, there was considerable support among those involved for a truly national program because of dissatisfaction with existing state vocational education efforts. The political situation did not allow this, however, and the program structure that emerged provided for programs managed by the Departments of Labor and Health, Education, and Welfare (HEW) with significant state participation.[12]

Kennedy's political position was improving when he was struck down in November 1963. The Democrats had done reasonably well in the 1962 mid-term elections, losing only four seats in the House and gaining three in the Senate. Prospects for Kennedy's reelection in 1964, together with substantial gains in Congress, appeared to be favorable. Tension in relations with the Soviet Union had eased. Economic conditions were improving, and the pending tax cut was expected to strengthen economic performance. Events on the civil rights front and the administration's shrewd handling of them added luster to its overall standing in many quarters and increased the likelihood that Congress would soon act on major legislation in this sensitive area.

In the first months of Johnson's presidency, these factors, joined with the nation's shock at Kennedy's death, created a unique environment for action on an ambitious policy agenda. The new president was prepared to act. No ideologue, he began his political career as a New Deal liberal, but he adopted more conservative stances with changes in the political climate and after being elected to the Senate from a conservative state. As vice president, however, he easily took on the more liberal and nationalist coloration of the Kennedy presidency.[13] Not long before becoming president, he spoke to the American Municipal Congress. His major theme was interdependence. "What we must not forget . . . is that levels of government must function interdependently if they are to succeed independently. Ours is a system of interdependence. Authority is divided not to prevent action but to assure action."[14] It was clear he meant that in a system of interdependency, the national government had a major, even leading, role to play. As president, according to Kearns, Johnson's view of the role was shaped by his sense that "none of his fellow citizens' desires were . . . wholly beyond his ability to satisfy."[15] In confirmation, he said in retrospect, "At the heart of it, I thought of the Great Society as an extension of the Bill of Rights. . . . In our time a broadened concept of freedom requires that every American have the right to a healthy body, a full education, a decent home, and the opportunity to develop to the best of his talents."[16]

The new president's leadership in pushing such objectives during the traumatic period of transition was critical in exploiting the opportunities presented by a favorable policy environment. Constantly pressing for the enactment of Kennedy's legislative program as a memorial to the slain president, he pried open the congressional doors in 1964 and produced a considerable record of legislative achievement. Further momentum was supplied by the 1964 elections. The campaign provided the country with a clear choice between Johnson's vision of the Great Society and the conservative alternative presented by the Republican candidate, Senator Barry Goldwater of Arizona. The clash in policy positions was clear in the campaign, and the result was unambiguous. Johnson won 61.4 percent of the popular vote and carried the electoral vote by a 486 to 52 margin. The Democrats increased their majority in the House by 38 votes, giving them a 295 to 140 advantage; and their control of the Senate was cemented by a gain of 2 seats, making the partisan balance there 68 to 32. For most of the next two years, Johnson, with the aid of various public and private interests that saw possibilities for policy and programmatic gains, exploited his political advantages to the hilt. And, as noted in chapter 1, this was a period of rapid economic expansion, an expansion that was both supported and reinforced by the growth of the public sector.

By late 1966, however, the favorable environment for Great Society programs was turning sour, and the process of curdling continued to the end of Johnson's presidency. Although new programs continued to be established, they tended to be smaller in scope and considerably less dramatic in their impact than the landmark victories of the 1964–1966 period.

Several factors were involved. Certain aspects of the war on poverty, a cornerstone of the quest for the Great Society, received extensive negative publicity. There were critical reactions from some state and local officials to the multitudinous new Washington initiatives. Riots and lesser forms of unrest in the cities were gripping signs of weakness in the social fabric, of unrealized popular expectations, and, to some, of the harmful consequences of Johnson's policies. There were sixty-seven ghetto riots in the summer of 1967 alone.[17] Criticism of the Vietnam involvement rose, accompanied by upheavals on college campuses. Though weakened by the 1964 elections, Republicans seized the opportunities presented by these developments to mount a political comeback in the 1966 mid-term elections.

At about the same time that the 1966 election results showed a change in the general political climate, the fiscal environment weakened and budget problems began to confront Washington policymakers. Three years or so before, the prospects seemed good that funding at increasingly higher levels for social programs would be readily available far into the future. Because of the number of new programs established, rapid growth in the domestic budget, and the need to finance the war in Vietnam, those prospects proved to be wrong. From 1966 onward, the need for budget restraint was accentuated by the constant prospect of budget deficits and creeping inflation.[18] Intergovernmental programs were affected in a number of ways. There were, for example, cuts and delays in the release of funds to the states for highway construction in that year and into 1967.[19] A number of other grant programs were similarly affected.[20] But the most important consequence was that funding could not be increased sufficiently to meet the expanding needs of the programs that had been erected with such fanfare.

The bleak fiscal situation was sharply and fully delineated for the president's benefit in a memorandum from Charles L. Schultze, director of the Bureau of the Budget (BOB), on 7 November 1966. The key problem was "simply that *we are not able to fund adequately the new Great Society programs.* At the same time, States, cities, depressed areas and·individuals have been led to expect immediate delivery of benefits . . . to a degree that is not realistic." He continued, "This leads to frustration, loss of credibility, and even deterioration of State and local services as they hang back on making normal commitments in order to apply for Federal aid which does not materialize."[21] Schultze went on to note the typically large gap in many program areas between authorizations and what could actually be provided in the budget. He argued forcefully that extreme selectivity be exercised in proposing even modest new programs.

Assessments of budget directors, of course, do not deter continuing pressures from within and without the government for new programs and for generous funding all along the program front. Dashed hopes and competition for resources exacerbated conflict among administration officials. In Congress, among state and local governments, and among interest-group claimants, budgetary disappointment contributed to weakened political support for the administration.

Arrangements for Domestic Policy Development

In the first phase of Johnson's presidency, the activist external policy environment meshed with an internal environment for domestic policymaking that also stimulated policy activism and innovation. Preparation of the legislative program was the vital center of domestic policy development. In this area, as in the performance of various other presidential functions, Johnson was assisted by a "subpresidency." Emmette S. Redford and Marlan Blissett define this concept as including "all those who served the president—continuously or ad hoc, in an institutional capacity or otherwise—in the exercise of his responsibilities. This included, on occasion, individuals in departments or independent agencies who had separate official responsibilities but whose loyalties to the president led them to look at problems from a presidential perspective."[22] Thus, at any given time individuals in a variety of official and nonofficial positions might be involved, but at the center of a particular subpresidency is "an inner circle of White House aides" devoted to safeguarding the president's interests.[23]

The subpresidency that provided legislative proposals changed in character from year to year, but initially it was dominated by new, nontraditional structures and processes closely tied to the White House and staffed by a novel mix of participants. Just as there was a measure of continuity from Kennedy to Johnson in the substance of policy pursuits, there was a measure of continuity in the processes employed for developing major policy initiatives. Task forces, used by Kennedy during the transition period in 1960, then in certain circumstances afterward, became the central element in the yearly policy reviews. Out of these came not only Johnson's legislative program, which was their prime focus, but also policies for administrative implementation. In 1964 the linkage between a favorable policy environment and the task forces was clear in the president's mind. In remarks outlining the task force approach made in a cabinet meeting in the summer, he said, "From an economic standpoint we can afford to move boldly where new programs are called for . . . from a budget standpoint we can afford to introduce new programs . . . from a political standpoint we can afford to think in bold terms and to strike out in new directions."[24]

From 1964 through 1968, roughly 135 presidential task forces were established, almost all of them dealing with domestic policy questions. These task forces have been analyzed extensively by other scholars.[25] Here attention will be restricted to key features that help to understand policy and program choices bearing on intergovernmental relations.

The first feature to note is that the task forces were the cornerstone of a highly centralized method for policy development. Processes were directed, as Hugh Davis Graham puts it, from "the cockpit of the presidency."[26] Task forces were established by the White House, membership was determined and charters were drafted there, and their recommendations were reviewed and analyzed by presidential aides. In 1964 Bill D. Moyers coordinated the task forces. When he became press secretary in 1965, responsibility shifted to Joseph A. Califano, Jr. With the help of a small number of assistants, who, like himself, were young but talented, he directed domestic policy operations through the remainder of Johnson's presidency. Presidential aides served as liaisons with task forces and were also active participants in their deliberations. An important element in the control exercised by the White House was the secrecy that cloaked both the existence and activities of the task forces. The president insisted that his options not be limited by the political pressures that would be precipitated by public awareness of particular policy deliberations.

A second important feature was the emphasis placed on searching for new policy ideas beyond the standard bureaucratic and clientele group sources. Indeed, enriching the pool of ideas for consideration was the central purpose of the task force operation. In early planning for 1964, the heads of the Bureau of the Budget and the Council of Economic Advisers (CEA) jointly emphasized this aim when they suggested to Moyers that the task forces "be composed mainly of technical experts who possess the gift of originality and imagination."[27] Johnson told the cabinet that he expected the task forces "to be imaginative, and not . . . bound by timid, preconceived notions."[28] The first group of task forces, organized in 1964, carried through on the commitment to enlarge the sources of policy ideas. All of them were external or "outside" task forces, so designated because most of the membership came from outside the government. A total of 153 members served. The largest group, 35 percent, came from universities. The next largest group, 25 percent, were policy-level U.S. government officials. The remainder were drawn from research organizations, business firms, and foundations, among other sources. Only 5 percent of the membership came from state government and 2 percent from local government. Representatives of clientele groups were notably absent.[29]

A third and related feature was that the task force operation underwent adaptations over time. Perhaps the most significant change involved the increased use of interagency task forces composed primarily of high-level policy officials. The shift to interagency groups in part may be related to changes in the policy environment and an interest in consolidating early legislative successes. In 1965 twelve interagency task forces, compared with four outside task forces, reported to the president. From 1965 through 1968, ninety interagency task forces were established, far more than the twenty-seven external groups. During this period, in the major domestic program spheres of greatest importance for state and local government, there were forty-seven interagency and ten outside task forces. Patterns of representation on the latter type did not change, however. The largest source of membership remained the universities, and state and local officials were rarely asked to serve.[30]

Each year the legislative program development process became more elaborate and systematic, and in 1967 it reached a certain maturity. The search for ideas and suggestions started in May. White House aides visited a number of academic centers. Ideas were solicited from White House personnel, the Bureau of the Budget and other executive offices, and particular individuals in government judged to be thoughtful and imaginative. Responses were joined with the recommendations of presidential commissions and committees and with other material relevant to the legislative program, such as the list of expiring legislation compiled by the Bureau of the Budget. In August the mass of material was organized and subjected to study and review by White House and other presidential aides. This was followed by organization of the appropriate task forces. Usually they were given a lengthy list of policy ideas or problems to consider. After task force reports were submitted in late fall, they underwent intensive review at both the departmental and presidential levels. In the process of review, the legislative program was forged in meetings involving White House and other executive office staff and top-level department officials.[31]

Although their contents were influential, the acceptance of task force recommendations was far from automatic. For example, in the preparation of the 1965 program, a number of important proposals were altered or rejected. The Task Force on Education's general aid program for elementary and secondary education was dropped in favor of a grant program targeted at disadvantaged students. Other notable proposals falling by the wayside were block grants for urban services and public assistance, grants to the states for nursing home care, and an income tax allowance for the children of lower-income families. The reports of the two task forces in the natural resources and environmental areas were viewed quite critically by administration officials. The Department of the Interior found the report of the Task Force on the Preservation of Natural Beauty to be "stimulating and replete with ideas. But many of these are poorly organized and not thought through." In addition, "Leadership is placed almost wholly with the Federal Government."[32] Although the proposals that later went to Congress were ambitious, they were far less extensive than the menu provided by the task force. Officials of the Departments of the Interior and HEW were dissatisfied with the report of the Task Force on Natural Resources in the environmental control area because it did not go far enough. The departments did not like its central proposal, to employ interstate regional agencies and user charges as the main means for water pollution control. Instead, "If a truly vigorous attack on pollution is going to be launched, it will have to be done by Federal authority and under Federal administration."[33] Subsequently, authority for a "vigorous attack" along these lines was requested and enacted in 1965.

A final feature was the important role that Johnson played at critical stages in the policy development process. In late summer he reviewed proposed task force charters and membership. On rare occasions he conferred with task forces, but his involvement usually began when their reports were submitted. Just before the first of the year, after departmental and executive office assessment of task force reports, Johnson was an active participant in extensive sessions to set the legislative agenda. In them, he had an opportunity to judge the appropriateness of policy directions, consider budgetary implications, and assess political factors related to the issues at hand. Then, as Congress returned to work, he reviewed policy decisions again as the State of the Union, budget, and special legislative messages were put together.

Although the process became increasingly systematic and produced a multitude of policy ideas, it was not without its limitations. The work of task forces was not always of high quality nor were their reports always fertile compendia of new ideas. Even the reports of external task forces in 1964 and 1965 were often burdened by conventional thinking. In later years task forces were inclined to focus on incremental adjustments and extensions of established programs rather than on bold new departures. The process moved at a frenzied pace, especially from the time task force reports were received until messages and bills were dispatched to Congress. Integrating and coordinating the various parts of the effort and giving thorough consideration to policy proposals were constant challenges that often were not fully met. Part of the problem was in the basic structure of the process whereby a number of task forces worked independently, drafting programs within their particular charters on a case-by-case basis and shaping them according to limited policy objectives and special political circumstances. Furthermore, the task forces tended to work at a fairly high level of generality. The secrecy injunction cut them off from one another, even when there were overlapping concerns, and often from the expertise of program specialists at operating levels within the government. When it came time for proposals to be reviewed, elaborated into detailed program schemes, and integrated into the budget, resources were taxed to the limit. Much work had to be done in a very short time. Califano and his small staff were overwhelmed. The Bureau of the Budget and other participants did not have time to analyze proposals thoroughly. Program specialists in the departments and agencies could give the reports only scant attention. The budget process was disrupted in its last critical stages. In short, the demands of the policy development process and the resources available to manage it and provide comprehensive and thorough central review of the entire set of proposals were out of proportion in the legislative program subpresidency.[34] The limitation had special implications for program implementation.

In the Policy Forge: Preparing for 1965

With Johnson in the White House, 1964 was a demanding year for Congress. At his urging, it approved, among other measures, the Economic Opportunity Act, civil rights legislation, an urban mass transportation program, and a major housing and community development bill. At the same time, it was debating other sensitive proposals that would be carried over to the next session. Well before legislative activity was concluded in 1964, work was underway on planning an even more extensive program for 1965, which as much as any, defined the course of Johnson's domestic policies.

Concerted action began in late May 1964 when Kermit Gordon, director of the Bureau of the Budget, and Walter Heller, chairman of the Council of Economic Advisers, identified for Moyers a number of subjects that task forces might investigate. Just a few days before, President Johnson had set forth the Great Society theme in the University of Michigan speech. Gordon and Heller included on their list three topics specifically mentioned there by the president. They were metropolitan problems, education, and environmental preservation, all areas, of course, in which state and local governments had substantial interests. Other suggested topics that touched upon their interests included transportation, income maintenance, area and regional development, water resources, and intergovernmental fiscal relations.[35] The final task force roster followed the Gordon-Heller suggestions almost exactly. Ultimately, there were fourteen in the domestic sphere.

During the summer BOB and CEA staff members drafted issue papers for use by task forces and attached to them the names of persons who might be considered for membership. The papers provide useful insights into the eclectic, nationalist, and pragmatic policy dispositions of key actors in the Executive Office of the President.[36] In general, the papers shared a common perception that there were substantial unmet national problems requiring central action along a broad domestic policy front. In education, there were "still many areas in which the Nation's educational system fails to perform at an adequate level."[37] Serious gaps were seen in the provision of income maintenance assistance and health services for the disadvantaged. The paper on metropolitan and urban problems noted the increased isolation of minority and low-income populations in central cities as a result of migration to suburbs. Its major focus, however, was on the general governmental disarray and the poor public services characteristic of metropolitan areas. The paper on natural beauty and the environment noted the unfortunate absence of comprehensive national policies in these spheres. Most of the papers contained rather lengthy lists of concrete program proposals for task forces to ponder.

All of the papers dealing with major domestic policy areas were quite critical of state and local governments and saw them as sources of many of the problems that the task forces were to address. At the same time, no real challenges were mounted to existing intergovernmental program arrangements. Nor were there calls for many distinctly national programs that would bypass state and local governments or threaten established patterns in intergovernmental program arrangements.

The fiscal aspect of national-state-local relations was addressed directly in a paper on intergovernmental fiscal cooperation, but not in a prescriptive way. It pointed to the prospect of increasing federal revenues, even budget surpluses, and to the growing demands pressed on state and local governments for more services and increased taxes. The paper discussed various means for the transfer of federal tax revenues to subnational governments and related policy considerations.

Overall, the desirability of an expanded role for the national government was not subjected to critical analysis in the papers; it was assumed to be inevitable. In discussing outdoor recreation, for example, the paper on natural resources said, "As in many other areas the pressures are invariably toward augmentation of the federal role."[38] There was no sense of limits. Nor was there a sense that in any of the policy areas there were serious problems that appropriately or necessarily ought to be left to the ministrations of state and local governments.

The tone of the task force reports that followed was much the same as that of the staff papers. A nationalist disposition was clearly evident. In education, the task force took its cue from the president, who, it said, had determined "that education is at the top of the Nation's agenda."[39] The Task Force on Metropolitan and Urban Problems asserted that up to that time there had been no "genuine national response to urban development."[40] According to its chairman, Robert C. Wood, it reached "a decision that there was an urban crisis."[41] The task force report started from the premise that "new Federal efforts . . . are . . . necessities of modern community building."[42] Near the end of the Johnson presidency, Wood, then under secretary of the Department of Housing and Urban Development, observed, "We've put in national goals, national policies."[43] The 1964 task force was an important contributor to that effort. In its report it sought "new approaches to the dramatically new kinds of urban communities that are now evolving and suggested new ways in which the national government might produce them."[44] The basic theme of the Task Force on Health was that the national government had a positive duty to advance "the right of every individual to adequate health services."[45] The Task Force on Income Maintenance saw in existing circumstances an opportunity to build "a fuller measure of security for every American" through improved benefits supplied by the national government.[46] Charles Haar, a member of the Task Force on Natural Beauty, said of his group, "We were all activists. We all believed in government action." Its report recommended a broad range of national initiatives.[47] Of a similar mind was the Task Force on Environmental Pollution. It urged that the national government accept increased responsibilities in this area. In its view, it should be "our national policy to shield our nation's air, water, soil and living resources from pollution and its consequences and . . . to take such measures as may be necessary to protect these priceless heritages for the benefit of one nation as a whole."[48]

Recommendations for new and extended intergovernmental programs dominated all of the task force reports, even though, like the authors of the background papers, the task forces generally judged state and local governments to be unable and perhaps unwilling to correct deficiences in education, health, public assistance, and other program spheres. For example, regarding state and local governments, the Task Force on Metropolitan and Urban Problems observed that "limitations of resources and authority have prevented a comprehensive, consistent attack on major urban problems."[49] On the Task Force on Education, according to Francis Keppel, its chairman, many "felt that the state departments of education were the feeblest bunch of second-rate, or fifth-rate educators who combined educational incompetence with bureaucratic immovability."[50] Their views on local educational establishments were not much more flattering.

A limited number of proposals for direct national action were built upon established programs, including financial assistance to students in institutions of higher education, social security, home mortgage financing, and natural resources conservation. Only four major, distinctly new national programs were put forward. The most prominent of these was medical assistance for the elderly. A network of national research and demonstration laboratories affiliated with universities was a central part of the Task Force on Education's plan to enlarge the educational opportunities for disadvantaged youth and to dilute the influence of the established state and local educational bureaucracies and of traditional thinking about education. New concepts and methods in education were imperatives, according to the task force, because "the old ways of doing things will not solve our problems."[51] The Task Force on Metropolitan and Urban Problems put forward the idea of rent supplements or rent subsidies for low-income families paid directly by the national government to landlords. Finally, the Task Force on Income Maintenance proposed a tax adjustment allowance for the children of poor families. Several members, in fact, favored an income allowance for all persons falling below a minimum income level.

Neither in consideration of national programs nor in exploring the dimensions of new and expanded intergovernmental programs did the task force reports indicate the application of explicit criteria to guide the assignment of roles and responsibilities among levels of government. For the most part, established intergovernmental program structures served as models to be elaborated upon. If there were general criteria applied, they were these: in existing program relationships, the national role should be expanded; and in new relationships, it should be substantial. And there was no sense that there were necessary, fundamental limits to the national role if intergovernmental forms were employed. Furthermore, political limitations to the expansion of national powers generally were not recognized. There was one exception. For sound political reasons, based upon historical experience, the Task Force on Education urged that care be taken to retain "the Federal-State-local balance which is so crucial to our educational future. And State, local, and private efforts should continue to be the predominant forces in American education."[52]

The intergovernmental program proposals of the task forces were numerous and wide ranging. The most important recommendation of the Task Force on Education was for general aid to elementary and secondary education tied to a distribution formula that would favor poor areas. Rivaling it in significance was the recommendation for supplementary education centers at the local level to aid schools in educating disadvantaged students. The task force also suggested several new programs in support of public and private institutions of higher education.

The report on metropolitan and urban problems was distinctive for its comprehensive and systematic exploration of the urban landscape. Its recommendations covered, among other things, the development of new communities, urban transportation, housing, economic development, and government organization. Among its major new intergovernmental program ideas were block grants for the provision of urban services and a demonstration cities program that two years later would emerge as a major legislative initiative.

The health group proposed a major set of new programs for the education of health professionals and for health facilities in communities. It also suggested grants to the states of up to 50 percent of the costs of nursing home care for the needy and grants for community, regional, and state health planning. Although in general the Task Force on Income Maintenance preferred a social insurance approach to the existing complex of assistance programs, it recognized that a radical shift in policy was not then possible. Alternatively, it proposed that a number of categorical public assistance grants be converted into a block grant program. To be eligible, states had to meet minimum benefit standards and eligibility criteria that would expand the recipient population and raise levels of assistance in many of them. It also recommended much more generous community service grants and less state discretion in administration of the unemployment compensation program.

The ambitious Task Force on Natural Beauty touched upon almost every conceivable way in which the national government, in its own program efforts and in working with state and local governments, could advance the cause of environmental quality. It even contemplated national involvement in maintaining and managing city parks.

The Task Force on Natural Resources was the most restrained of the groups. Giving most of its attention to national programs, it made only one recommendation with intergovernmental implications. That was for river basin organizations established by state and local governments to administer water pollution control programs based upon effluent charges. In the absence of state and local action, the national government was to fill the gap.

By and large, the task force reports focused on basic program goals and outlines and did not delve into the particulars of program implementation.[53] With the exception of the natural resources report, however, all contained portions that suggested an awareness of a relationship between program characteristics and effective administration. The emphasis on planning found in a number of reports was, in part, in the interest of program coordination. A certain awareness of the administrative complexities associated with numerous categorical grants was reflected in the recommendations for general aid, income tax allowances, and block grants by the education and income maintenance task forces. Effluent charges for water pollution control were, in the view of many, a more efficient administrative approach than the alternative method of regulation based upon water quality standards.

The most extensive treatment of the implementation dimension was by the Task Force on Metropolitan and Urban Problems. It was especially concerned with structural questions, and throughout its report it emphasized the importance of "coherent forms of public organization to help shape the city at all levels of government with the help of additional resources for research, planning, and development."[54] There were several proposals directed at the national government. One was for a new Department of Housing and Community Development that Congress had proved reluctant to establish. The task force also recommended strengthening the HEW secretary's office and creating an Urban Affairs Council in the Executive Office of the President for coordination purposes. Regional offices dealing with urban-oriented programs were to be strengthened and authority was to be decentralized to enable them to provide more effective support to state and local governments. National officials at the regional level were to serve as planning and program coordinators for particular states and metropolitan regions. At the local level, planning requirements were emphasized in several grant programs proposed by the task force. Along with other devices, these requirements were intended to strengthen political leadership in state and local government by bringing activities then administered separately "into a comprehensive strategy."[55] New organizations were proposed to bring public and private resources together in urban development. Involvement of colleges and universities in urban extension programs and training programs for state and local officials were also intended to enlarge administrative capacities.

Dominating Characteristics

The major portion of Johnson's legislative program for 1965 went to Congress early in the year in seven special messages. Four were based substantially on task force reports. The others dealt with voting rights, economic development, and law enforcement. The major domestic proposals were dominated by two characteristics: the nationalization of government policy and intergovernmental administration in which subnational institutions played important roles in program implementation. As precedents, they defined the direction to be followed in subsequent years.

Nationalization of Government Policy

One emphasis, of course, was the need for a more active national government, but throughout Johnson's presidency it was an activism tempered in two ways. Obviously, state and local interests were taken into account in framing proposals. Temperance was also evident in rhetoric. In 1965 and thereafter, extreme care was taken to envelop proposals in language designed to ease apprehensions that state and local government officials might have about the expansion of national power. When reviewing message drafts, Johnson was especially attentive to this aspect of content. For example, the education message stated, "Federal assistance does not mean federal control. . . . The late Senator Robert Taft declared: 'Education is primarily a state function—but in . . . education, . . . the federal government has a secondary obligation to see that there is a basic floor under those essential services for all adults and children in the United States.'"[56] In regard to cities, the message declared, "Whatever the scale of its programs, the federal government will only be able to do a small part of what is required. The vast bulk of resources and energy, of talent and toil, will have to come from state and local governments, private interests and individual citizens."[57] The law enforcement message was even more emphatic. Although it recognized crime as a national problem, "That recognition does not carry with it any threat to the basic prerogatives of state and local governments."[58] In area and regional economic development, the president's message declared, "No Federal plan or Federal project will be imposed on any regional, State or local body. . . . The initiative, the ideas, and the request for assistance must all come *to* Washington, not *from* Washington."[59]

At times, such self-effacing language was difficult for policymakers to bear, as in the case of the 1968 education message. One draft contained a section called "Improving the Education Partnership." The language characterized Washington as a "junior partner" whose responsibilities in recently initiated programs would be shifted to state and local levels "as rapidly as they can bear." Other references to the primacy of states followed. The Bureau of the Budget did not like the language. It struck out all the deferential phrases, and its revision made clear that "the Federal Government should share in the decision-making process and not just dispense checks." Ultimately, the entire section was dropped from the message.[60]

In the nationalization of government policy, there was a dual emphasis on aid for the poor and disadvantaged and on enhancing the quality of life of all citizens. Although rural areas were not ignored, an urban preoccupation was evident. Enactment of the Economic Opportunity Act, civil rights legislation, and other measures advanced in 1964 anticipated other initiatives in 1965 and future years intended to benefit the less fortunate. The president recommended and Congress enacted measures protecting civil rights in voting and housing in 1965 and 1968. In fact, most of the major legislation enacted in 1965 was targeted basically at the needs of the poor and disadvantaged, including the Elementary and Secondary Education Act, the Higher Education Act, the Appalachian Regional Development

Act, and the Public Works and Economic Development Act. Several measures were passed that expanded access to health care for the elderly, the poor, and the mentally ill. Access to low-cost housing was expanded. As in the case of civil rights, in future years there were efforts to build further on these foundations to increase services and opportunities for the less affluent.

As urban unrest mounted in the latter part of Johnson's presidency, there was a pressing sense of urgency in policy deliberations, especially in regard to the disadvantaged in society and the urban environments in which so many of them lived. Clearly reflecting this mood were the 1967 task forces on cities, chaired by Paul N. Ylvisaker, commissioner of New Jersey's Department of Community Affairs, and on education, chaired by William C. Friday, president of the University of North Carolina. In the view of the cities group, "A dangerous confrontation is building in most of our metropolitan areas between white and Negro, rich and poor, growing suburb and declining central city." Neither "'natural' forces" nor "current programs at present scale" were sufficient correctives. It urged a Lincolnian "venture in national leadership."[61] The education task force saw substantial barriers remaining to equal opportunity and overall quality in education.[62] Both groups produced wide-ranging recommendations for new and expanded programs, but a changed policy environment limited possibilities for adoption.

The emphasis on the overall quality of life was pervasive, but it was especially apparent in the interrelated areas of environmental quality and public health and safety, where national action typically involved a partial preemption of state authority.[63] Important steps were taken toward building a complex of intergovernmental programs in 1965. At first, objectives were not sharply focused. Charles Haar, who served on the 1964 Task Force on Natural Beauty, commented on conversations with White House staff members. "There was this thing they were trying to put together. They weren't quite sure what it was. It was the environment, it was the quality of life, it was beauty, and it was a very amorphous and difficult subject."[64] Specification began to develop in 1965 with the enactment of three especially significant measures. The Water Quality Act provided for a major expansion of the national government's role in combating water pollution. The Highway Beautification Act, a measure of considerable personal interest to the president and Lady Bird Johnson, established new programs for the control of billboards and junkyards. The Law Enforcement Assistance Act was intended to strengthen the protection of the public against crime and violence. Also in 1965 the administration requested and Congress approved new intergovernmental programs in water resources planning and solid waste disposal and a national program to regulate automobile emissions.

Other actions followed. Legislation strengthening the water pollution control program was passed in 1966, and a major air pollution control law was enacted in 1967. Additional areas in which Johnson proposed and Congress approved new or strengthened programs included aircraft noise, motor vehicle and highway safety, hazardous consumer products, surface and deep mine safety, meat and poultry inspection, fire safety, radiation from consumer products, and gas pipeline safety. In many of these, national and state efforts were joined. However, the administration was unable to secure passage of some of its proposals, especially those that first came to Congress in 1968. These included programs focusing on agricultural chemicals, boat safety, occupational health and safety, fish product inspection, and drinking water standards.

Intergovernmental Administration

The second dominating feature of Johnson's domestic proposals was a major reliance on intergovernmental programs and a limited use of new, exclusively national programs in the pursuit of substantive policy objectives. Nevertheless, the intergovernmental means employed were centralizing in their intent and effects. The principal one, of course, was the categorical grant-in-aid, usually narrow in scope and often of the program rather than the formula variety. Charles J. Zwick, who succeeded Schultze as director of the Bureau of the Budget, captured what seemed to be the disposition of many policymakers when he said of his agency, in regard to education, "The bureau would always be in the role of producing a tough set of federal standards. We always would be pushing for project grants rather than automatic formula grants, so that you could reward and punish."[65] On occasion, however, alternative approaches were considered and in some instances chosen. One was to draw categorical programs together in unique ways to fashion multifunctional approaches to problems. The major examples are in the Economic Opportunity Act and the Model Cities programs. Another approach was to establish new area or regional agencies to plan and administer programs in an integrated fashion. Yet another was the creation of broader and more flexible bundles of financial assistance for state and local governments through grant consolidation, block grants, and revenue sharing. These alternatives are discussed in later chapters.

Another intergovernmental program mechanism came to prominence in the 1960s in the environmental, health, and safety areas, first in water pollution control and later extended to other areas in which there was partial preemption of state authority. Although there were variations from program to program, the central idea was for state agencies to regulate on the basis of standards set or approved in Washington. If states did not elect to regulate or did so poorly, national agencies were to assume regulatory responsibilities. Often categorical grants to states for program support and related purposes were associated with regulatory authority.

Despite major reliance on intergovernmental programs, national programs had a part to play in the Johnsonian domestic policy scheme. Established programs, including minimum wage requirements, social security, housing, and others in areas such as consumer protection, law enforcement, and natural resources, underwent adaptation congruent with major policy themes. Many of the new intergovernmental programs were accompanied by national components, frequently involving research and demonstration activities. In addition, there were several new, quite significant supplements to the national program roster because the nature of the problems addressed were unsuited to an intergovernmental approach. Civil rights protection and Medicare are prominent examples. Others include the regulation of both automobile safety and emissions, oil pollution in coastal waters, and aircraft noise.

It was rare for national and intergovernmental options for attaining a particular policy objective to be assessed systematically, but this did appear to happen at times. One case was urban development, including its low-income housing dimension. In regard to urban development generally, the major new national program, which was first proposed by Johnson in 1964, enacted in 1966, and enlarged in 1968, provided loan insurance and guarantees to aid in the construction of new communities on the periphery of urban population concentrations.[66] Other ideas calling for direct national action were rejected. In 1966 a task force recommended establishing a public-private corporation under federal charter to build new cities. Administration officials judged the corporation proposal to be "most extreme and . . . politically impossible."[67] Task forces in both 1966 and 1967 suggested the creation of a public-private development bank, again under federal charter, to finance public facilities in urban areas. The bank idea was rejected, and grant programs remained the major means for the national government's participation in these matters.

The adequacy and affordability of moderate—and, especially, low-income—housing were of continuing major concern.[68] When Johnson became president, two basic approaches were employed: mortgage insurance was provided for home ownership and for rental units, and grants-in-aid were provided for public housing supplied by local housing authorities. Although the number of public housing units increased during Johnson's tenure, there was some dissatisfaction with the intergovernmental approach. One problem, an aide told the president, was "the lack of readiness of the local housing authorities to move quickly."[69] Housing was an aspect of the Model Cities program that will be discussed in chapter 4. Additionally, two new national programs were established. The first, recommended by the 1964 task force on cities and enacted in 1965, was rent supplements. The other, passed in 1968, was mortgage subsidies for low-income rental housing. Also in 1968 the president's Committee on Urban Housing, chaired by Henry J. Kaiser, Jr., recommended without success an experimental program in which housing allowances would be paid directly to low-income recipients.[70]

Manpower training was also a high priority in the Johnson presidency, and, as shown in the following chapter, there was a good deal of intergovernmental program development. The ultimate objective, of course, was not training per se; rather, it was moving people into jobs *through* training. In the White House there was persistent frustration based upon the view that the employment objective was not being adequately met and that the various grant programs were in part to blame. This frustration finally produced a new national program in 1968 that essentially was the creation of the White House. It was labeled Job Opportunities in the Private Sector (JOBS). Coordinated by the National Alliance of Businessmen and chaired by Henry Ford II, JOBS bypassed existing training programs by providing for the national government to contract with businesses in the fifty largest cities to supply on-the-job training to the hard-core unemployed. Participants were guaranteed jobs upon completion of training. By 1971 it was hoped that there would be 500,000 training slots.[71] The JOBS program was an addition to, not a substitute for, intergovernmental programs, although it drew funds away from them.

Probably the most radical proposal for a new national program was to replace wholly or partially the hodgepodge of public assistance and social service programs with some form of guaranteed annual income. Many, including Gardner Ackley, chairman of the Council of Economic Advisers, thought that the existing system of aid to the poor was fundamentally flawed. At one point he told the president, "Our Federal-State public welfare system is a mess."[72]

Among the problems were program fragmentation, low benefit levels, eligibility gaps, and variations among states in benefits and eligibility requirements. Public assistance programs were thought to cause the breakup of families and to provide disincentives to seek employment. In the minds of some, the interests of the poor would be better served if money spent for social services were given to them in the form of cash transfers.

Beginning in 1964, several task forces considered the matter. In that year, as noted previously, an external task force suggested an income tax allowance for children, but the idea was not put forward for congressional consideration. The following year, 1965, two task forces considered the question of a guaranteed annual income. A task force on public assistance, chaired by Wilbur J. Cohen of HEW, was cool to the idea. It preferred to increase benefit levels and expand eligibility, in part through tightened standards governing state programs.[73] A task force on income maintenance headed by Ackley was quite positive toward some form of guaranteed income level.[74] No action was taken on the basis of either report at that time.

A major decision point was reached in late 1966 in anticipation of the expiration of a number of public assistance authorities in 1967. Proposals had to be submitted to Congress, and several groups were put to work preparing them. Johnson, however, appeared to resolve the policy debate between the advocates of assistance and income approaches even before receiving the final recommendations of his advisers. Apprehensive that Republicans would steal the initiative on social security benefits, he announced in a Baltimore speech on 12 October his intention to seek generous increases.[75]

Nevertheless, debate on options continued within the administration. On one side, HEW strongly favored improving public assistance and social service programs, expanding social security coverage, and increasing benefit levels as the preferred routes. On the other side, although not in complete agreement, CEA, BOB, OEO, and the Labor and Treasury departments tended to favor an income strategy. In regard to public assistance, the Task Force on Income Maintenance, chaired by Ackley of CEA, was "uncertain whether the defects of the present state-Federal system can be overcome."[76] However, it concluded that "it is politically infeasible to overthrow the present . . . system in favor of an entirely Federal program, however preferable the latter form may be."[77] Ackley made the point in a slightly different way in a memorandum to the president a few days after his task force report was submitted. "In the long run we must choose between trying to patch up the existing system (through Federal standards for benefits and eligibility), or an all-Federal system."

The national alternative could be "a universal system of income guarantees."[78]

The matter of a guaranteed annual income was discussed in a White House meeting on 29 November. Politics aside, the budgetary situation precluded radical policy change. It was agreed, however, that "it would be desirable to take a crack at neg. income tax for children. Try out the system and reaction."[79] Despite this agreement among the president's principal advisers, a proposal did not go forward to Congress. On the social security issue, CEA, BOB, and others felt, according to Zwick, that "the Social Security program is fairly regressive. . . . We were arguing that the . . . increases were eating up our fiscal elbowroom for other programs." Zwick and his allies were not sufficiently persuasive. An emphasis on social security increases, he continued, was "dictated by the President and Califano and Wilbur Cohen over the dead bodies of those of us in the Bureau and the Treasury and the Council of Economic Advisers. . . . There was just always great political sex appeal to this because all those old people vote."[80]

Two related messages went to Congress early in 1967. The first, on 23 January, had social security benefits as its centerpiece.[81] The second, focusing on children and youth, came a few days later.[82] In addition to social security items, proposals were included for tightened standards governing public assistance benefits, expanded child welfare programs, and new work incentive and voluntary work-training programs. But the social security message did not end discussions of alternatives to existing systems of income support. In his January 1967 economic message, Johnson announced his intention to appoint a commission to study proposals for guaranteeing a minimum income as Ackley's task force had recommended.[83] Although OEO began a small negative income tax experiment soon after announcement of the commission, its members were not named until the conclusion of a year-long battle over social security in Congress.[84] The commission was composed of a number of distinguished citizens and was chaired by Ben W. Heineman, chairman of the board of the Chicago and North Western Railway Company. The commission was charged by the president to examine the welfare system, to explore all alternatives "however unconventional," and to make recommendations for improvements.[85] The commission did not report until after Johnson left office, and despite vigorous importunings from the Council of Economic Advisers during 1968, no further serious discussion of variants of the guaranteed annual income idea took place at the presidential level until it was taken up by the Nixon administration.[86]

The Implementation Dimension

The Johnson administration's domestic policy development process has been criticized for giving insufficient attention to implementation questions in intergovernmental programs.[87] That criticism is too broadly stated. More precisely, implementation, especially in the context of particular programs, typically was a matter of concern in task forces and other places. Absent were the means for assessing the overall, combined administrative impact of policy and program proposals, their interrelationships, and the problem of central coordination.

Even in 1964, when persons outside the government played such a prominent role, there were signs of considerable sensitivity to the implementation dimension. Over time, as policy and program development became increasingly dominated by administration officials, there evolved a repertoire of instruments associated with the facilitation of effective implementation. They were attached to particular intergovernmental programs almost as a matter of course. Perhaps the most important were the requirement for program plans and the requirement that program activities be coordinated with plans. Closely associated with planning requirements were incentives for areawide or regional program implementation. Other instruments included grants to state and local agencies to support planning, program administration, and personnel training; the provision of technical assistance; research, development, and demonstration projects to find and test means for improving program effectiveness; and program evaluation requirements.[88] Attention was also given to special implementation problems in the context of particular programs. As will be shown in chapter 7, especially from 1966 onward, other improvements in implementation were sought through administrative and legislative actions.[89]

Problems in program interrelationships within and between all levels of government were acutely felt and often addressed with varying degrees of success, particularly in the aftermath of initial efforts to implement new policies and programs. Five task forces were established with charters bearing on aspects of intergovernmental program administration: the Task Force on Government Reorganization, chaired by Donald Price of Harvard University, reported in November 1964; the Task Force on Intergovernmental Fiscal Cooperation, chaired by Joseph Pechman of the Brookings Institution, reported in December 1964; the Task Force on Intergovernmental Program Coordination, chaired by Stephen K. Bailey of Syracuse University, reported in December 1965; the Task Force on Intergovernmental Personnel, chaired by William Carmichael of Cornell University, reported in December 1966; and the Task Force on Government Organization, chaired by Ben W. Heineman, reported in June 1967. These and other broadly conceived efforts to come to grips with and alleviate implementation problems through systemic adjustments cutting across programs are treated in subsequent chapters.

Policy Politics

A striking feature of the nationalization of government policy tempered by the use of intergovernmental administrative arrangements was the absence of basic, sustained discord among the principals involved in the executive branch, in Congress, and in various constituencies across the country. Uniformity in basic dispositions was particularly striking in the executive branch. The major architects of the president's initiatives were policy professionals in and out of government, supported, if not led, in all cases by officials at political levels in the various departments and agencies. The immediate impetus for their efforts came from the president and his staff. Congress, state and local officials, and other affected interests did not challenge the basic course charted by the executive, although there were occasional disputes over particulars, usually precipitated by Republicans.

In the overall process of policy development, the influence of the executive branch was preeminent. Within it, the absence of serious conflict makes it difficult to weigh the influence of the various participants. It is possible, however, to make some general distinctions. Clearly, the public policy professionals exercised the greatest influence over the particulars of policy and program content.[90] Executive office staff, including those in the White House, played key roles in setting the agenda and then in filtering and adapting recommendations in the process of formulating the president's proposals. Johnson's own broad policy interests and objectives provided the general context within which his subordinates worked and thus were diffuse but certainly potent factors in the process.

The president typically did not tinker with the specifics of policy and program proposals. Robert C. Wood, as professor and task force member and later as administration official, was at the center of urban policymaking throughout Johnson's presidency. He says that the president "supported and took most of the recommendations on most of the legislation."[91] This also appears to be the case in other policy areas, although, as Wood indicates, there are some instances on record in which Johnson did balk on specific matters. Charles Zwick provides one example concerning food programs. He reports: "The President was always quite skeptical about these as either being (a) politically unacceptable, and (b) attempts for interference and intervention in properly state and local affairs. . . . He went out of office without a big feeding program, and that had at various times the Secretary of Agriculture, Orville Freeman, Charlie Murphy, who was a close confidant, Joe Califano and the whole staff, me, all of us, just beating on him continuously. And we didn't win."[92] Usually, however, the president's major involvement was in providing the political leadership required to move measures through Congress and to secure their acceptance by state and local officials and others whose support was important.

As has been documented in numerous places, Johnson gave a great deal of attention to preparing the best possible congressional reception for his proposals. He reviewed them from the standpoint of legislative politics, insisted on head counts and consultations with key members, and was especially attentive to timing and packaging. During the course of congressional consideration, he was kept informed about major developments and actively participated in devising and putting into play legislative strategies and tactics.[93] Although relations with Congress were not always harmonious, usually the president got most of what he sought.[94] Committees in the House and Senate tinkered with specifics, added components to their particular liking, and revised budget authority, timetables, and appropriation levels, but usually they did not make major substantive alterations. In addition, Congress exercised a policy leadership role in several areas, including environmental and consumer protection regulation, housing, and economic development; but in such instances the administration often adopted the congressional perspective as its own and willingly joined in legislative initiatives.

There were occasions, however, in which perceived state and local interests were guarded by Congress, creating some difficulties for the administration. Congress acted to strengthen program control of local public officials in several of the president's proposals, including rent supplements, the Teacher Corps, and the community action segment of the Economic Opportunity Act. It was cool to persistent requests to tighten standards governing state administration of public assistance and unemployment compensation programs. It did not give the administration all the authority it sought over state programs in air and water pollution control and gas pipeline safety. Although highway beautification legislation passed, its impact on state highway programs was rendered largely ineffective by the refusal of Congress to fund it. There were some close calls on items of major importance. One came in 1967 during reauthorization of the Elementary and Secondary Education Act of 1965. A strong drive was mounted in Congress, spearheaded by House Republicans, to construct a substantial block grant component out of categorical elements, but it was beaten back.[95]

In congressional proceedings, state and local governments and related clientele groups were more involved than in executive processes. By and large, they were much more inclined to urge favorable congressional action on intergovernmental program proposals than to oppose them, notwithstanding whatever questions they had about an expanded national role. Although not disposed to be nationalists, state and local representatives exhibited behavior that was usually in concert with a nationalist policy orientation in Washington. Among other factors, the lure of new dollars was an important consideration. At times, however, they resisted controls or strings in Congress with mixed results.[96]

From the standpoint of the presidency, state and local governments were not major political factors in formulating the basic outlines of domestic policy in the 1964–1966 period. It was not necessary to struggle for their support. They did become a major concern, however, as the impact of Johnson's first initiatives on state and local governments began to be felt. In response to negative reactions, a political strategy was developed to deal with the concerns of governors and mayors. It was, in a sense, a compensatory effort to secure political acquiesence in the absence of a comprehensive and sustained strategy to deal directly with problems in intergovernmental program administration.

Implementation Politics

Interactions between the White House and state and local governments were complex but can be characterized as eventually comprising two related systems. One was the policy and program system in which specific issues were raised on an ad hoc basis by state and local officials or department and agency officials and brought to presidential attention.[97] The second involved systematic presidential liaison with state and local officials. At times the two effectively merged, as in the case of the implementation of the Economic Opportunity Act, which is discussed in the next two chapters.

Presidential liaison with governors and mayors was conducted on a loose and irregular basis in 1963 and 1964. Although the governors, who were in Washington to attend Kennedy's funeral, were one of the first groups Johnson addressed as president, future contacts were limited until early 1965.[98] At that time a systematic liaison effort emerged. Former Tennessee governor Buford Ellington was appointed to serve as director of the Office of Emergency Planning (OEP), and general liaison with state governments was included in his portfolio. Vice President Hubert H. Humphrey was assigned responsibility for liaison with local governments. Humphrey continued in this role until the conclusion of Johnson's presidency. Ellington left in March 1966 to seek and win another term as governor. He was succeeded by Farris Bryant, formerly governor of Florida, who was followed in early 1968 by former Texas governor and U.S. senator Price Daniel.[99]

A number of core functions were performed by Ellington and his successors and by the vice president. Probably the most important was to explain and build support for all of Johnson's domestic and foreign policies. Another function was to facilitate the resolution of problems between state and local governments and Washington. A third was to keep Johnson informed about the moods and thoughts of the officials with whom they were in contact.

Several types of activity were involved. Bryant's monthly reports to the president are indicative. They show numerous telephone conversations with governors, personal meetings, attendance at conferences and other formal gatherings, and a large number of written communications. For the most part the activities were carried out in fairly routine fashion, but there was drama from time to time. In the summer of 1965, for example, Ellington was at a governors' conference in Minneapolis. There, he later recalled, he "saw that there was some trouble brewing" in the form of a feeling that federal officials "were stepping over the bounds in states, this wasn't the South, this was all across the country." Sensing that the basic problem was a lack of communication, he called Johnson and asked him to come to the conference. That was not possible. Instead, Air Force One flew to Minneapolis, brought the governors to Washington for dinner and a presidential "massage," and returned them to the conference the same evening.[100]

The president was personally involved in liaison efforts on a fairly impressive scale. Between his meeting with 41 governors on 25 November 1963 and December 1966, there were eighty-eight meetings with individual governors in his office, participation in twenty group sessions with a total attendance of 269 governors (some obviously were repeaters), and 193 telephone conversations with state chief executives.[101] On other occasions, he met with state legislative leaders. White House staff members also saw state officials from time to time.

The vice president took his liaison responsibilities quite seriously. His periodic reports to the president show a range of activities much like Bryant's. He attended and, in addition, sponsored numerous meetings and conferences in Washington and across the country with mayors, city managers, and county officials, among others. He and his staff worked on the problems of individual local governments and distributed vast amounts of material to them to enhance their understanding of federal programs and procedures. As with governors, the president and his aides met with or addressed local officials fairly frequently.

On the surface, the tone sought by the president and his aides in their relationships with state and local officials was one that suggested a sober search for mutual understanding and for the resolution of problems in the implementation of intergovernmental programs. They were largely successful in maintaining this tone, but underneath there were always charged political currents. All the participants had important political interests at stake. Johnson wanted the active support of all Democrats and as many Republicans as he could attract for his policies and programs, domestic and foreign. Beyond support, he wanted an absence of public criticism that might threaten his general political standing. Democratic governors and mayors were mindful of their own political fortunes, independent of the president's. Republicans, of course, had their own partisan political agenda to pursue.[102] In these complex relationships, the president had two major problems. The first was to maintain the support of Democrats, even when loyalty was strained by policy disagreements and administrative frustration in intergovernmental program implementation. The second was to prevent Republicans from using White House contacts for their own partisan purposes. The problems were interrelated in that the nonpartisan approach adopted by the president in official relationships—one that allowed him to work with Republicans—caused difficulties at times with members of his own party.[103]

Although there were stresses and strains and on occasion sharp public conflicts, Johnson was relatively successful in realizing his objectives. The mayors of most large cities were Democrats, and, despite periodic disagreements, they persisted in backing the president. Republican governors on the whole were cooperative within normal partisan limits. Ironically, it was Democratic governors who caused the greatest public flap. The executive committee of the National Governors' Conference met in White Sulphur Springs, West Virginia, in mid-December 1966. The Democrats had a private session to review the political situation in the aftermath of the previous month's elections, in which their party had suffered serious losses. Various complaints were vetted about the Johnson administration.[104] A candid press briefing resulted in extensive coverage of "the revolt of the governors." Johnson moved quickly to deal with the situation. Three days after the story broke, he had a group of the dissidents to the ranch for some strong talk and a public demonstration of mutual regard and support for Johnson's efforts.[105]

The matter did not end there, however. During the next few months, presidential attention to the governors was intense. The message "The Quality of American Government," sent to Congress on 17 March 1967, addressed various problems in intergovernmental relations. The fact that all the governors were invited to meet in the White House the following day, during which Johnson spoke to them no less than three times, indicates that their concerns were an important factor in producing the message. The president subsequently met with Republican and Democratic leaders of the governors' group on ways to smooth relations, and he spent a day with New England governors in May and a day with Democratic governors in early July for general discussions of problems in intergovernmental relationships and to demonstrate his personal interest in gubernatorial views.

Johnson's personal efforts supplemented an ambitious campaign conceived in the White House to deal directly with the specific problems and concerns of individual governors and top state officials.[106] Early in 1967, Bryant, accompanied by a group of high-level Washington officials, began a series of visits to state capitals. The first was to Dover, Delaware, on 26 January, and the fortieth and last was to Austin, Texas, on 6 June. In the meetings, problems were identified and were either resolved on the spot or referred to an appropriate place for resolution. Bryant's detailed reports to the president on each meeting indicated that, in his view, the visits were highly successful in both political and administrative problem-solving terms.

The visits were the high-water mark of the liaison effort. After they were concluded and once the sense of crisis abated, Bryant and then Daniel continued routine liaison activities, as did Humphrey. However, after Johnson withdrew as a candidate for reelection and Humphrey entered the race, the pace of activity slackened, but there were no further major upheavals in relationships.[107]

Conclusions

Domestic policymaking in the Johnson presidency was nationalist, and eclecticly so. There was scarcely a problem of any significant proportion that was viewed as inappropriate for inclusion on the agenda of the Great Society. Yet the intergovernmental option for program administration was almost always chosen. The question arises of why national policy objectives were not more often joined with national administration. Henry J. Aaron addresses this question in the important area of aid to the poor. During this period, he was associated with the Office of Economic Opportunity, an agency that very strongly supported an income policy for the poor, relegating public assistance and social services to a supplementary role. An income policy, if successful, obviated the need for a host of intergovernmental programs. However, he asserts, "The officials of the Johnson administration obeyed the long-standing, if unspoken, rule of American politics, not to make income redistribution an issue." In his view, the refusal "to rely primarily on cash transfers" was a fatal flaw in the war on poverty.[108] But there is a more general explanation. Policymakers labored within an institutional context in which, because of precedents set over the years when federalism was a more important influence than in the 1960s, intergovernmental administration was the generally accepted norm for the execution of national domestic policy in many spheres. Bureaucrats at all levels and members of Congress had vested interests in the continued use and expansion of intergovernmental programs. Though reformers might rail against their limitations, direct national administration simply was not a realistic option in most instances.

Although national administration was rejected, indeed frequently not considered, there was a strong commitment to the protection of national policy interests fueled by perceptions of inadequacy and even bad faith at subnational levels. These interests were protected by restrictions on state and local program discretion. Although, in the process of expanding national power, the purest means were not employed for the concentration of governmental authority at the center and for a deeper penetration of that authority into subnational levels, these objectives were still sought in intergovernmental program administration.

Related issues were less thoroughly addressed in the substantive policymaking activities of the Johnson presidency. Two of the most important were how authority for the administration of Great Society programs would be organized in Washington and how they were to be coordinated. In the legislative program subpresidency, task forces worked independently of one another and were subject to reconstitution each year with shifting charters and membership. Another subpresidency focused on implementation. It was very loosely organized, if not amorphous, but included, among other elements, the task forces that looked at general questions of government organization and broad issues in intergovernmental relations, the two tenuously connected liaison systems, and the Bureau of the Budget. Although the president and his aides were fairly adept in handling administrative changes in political terms, performance of the management function was impaired. Despite the beleaguered efforts of the BOB and the White House staff, the legislative program and executive direction subpresidencies were not effectively linked. Thus there was, at best, limited joint consideration of basic substantive and administrative policy issues on an ongoing basis. This condition and the persistent problems it produced in attaining unity, consistency, and coherence in program administration were very much at the heart of the Johnson administration's experience with the Economic Opportunity Act, one of its premier legislative achievements.

3. Administrative Arrangements for Attacking Poverty

Two of the most publicized initiatives of the Johnson presidency were the Economic Opportunity Act (EOA) and the Model Cities program. They were related in several ways. Both were conceived as important weapons in the war on poverty. To a certain extent, Model Cities was a response to perceived flaws in the EOA; its organizational design was intended as a partial corrective for those flaws. More important, the two initiatives shared a common conceptual foundation. In pursuit of the closely related objectives of expanding economic opportunity and stemming the decline of central cities, a multifunctional approach was employed. New programs and established older programs previously administered in relative isolation were to be meshed. This required new institutional arrangements at the local level in addition to new patterns of relationships among and within governments at all levels. Both initiatives, but especially the Economic Opportunity Act, challenged existing power arrangements, intergovernmental as well as intragovernmental, in some fundamental ways. It is not surprising that the administrative innovations contained in the act and in the concept of a coordinated attack on poverty proved to be quite difficult to implement.

The Economic Opportunity Act

The message to Congress rang with purpose, confidence, and certainty. "Because it is right, because it is wise, and because, for the first time in our history, it is possible to conquer poverty, I submit . . . the Economic Opportunity Act of 1964."[1] It was, the message later promised, "a total commitment by this President, and this Congress, and this nation, to pursue victory over the most ancient of mankind's enemies."[2] Thus on 16 March 1964 the president unveiled the programmatic legions to serve in the vanguard of the war on poverty.

Congress responded promptly. After twenty-five days of committee hearings, the Economic Opportunity Act was adopted with only minor changes and signed by the president on 20 August. The initial budget authorization was $947.5 million, and the first-year appropriation was $800 million. Johnson approved the appropriation bill on 7 October, and the next day the Office of Economic Opportunity (OEO) began operations.

At the time the law was enacted, many saw it as a landmark in domestic policy development. Despite strong, although not unanimous, support for its objectives, implementation efforts were soon surrounded by controversy. The act received substantial congressional attention in 1965, 1966, and 1967. Some legislative adjustments were made, but at the conclusion of Johnson's presidency, the statutory foundations of EOA programs were much as they were laid in 1964.[3]

On the surface the act's most distinctive features were its sharp focus on the problem of poverty and its suggestion of a comprehensive and integrated approach to alleviating the causes of economic misfortune. Except for the community action component, about which more will be said later, the specific programs packaged in the act and displayed in Table 3 were actually not especially new or inventive when taken individually. Most of them had been proposed to Congress previously or had antecedents in prior governmental initiatives. Certainly this was true of the major expenditure items, which were the five manpower and training programs established in Titles I, II, and V. Furthermore, most of the programs of an intergovernmental nature were expected to employ conventional grant-in-aid implementation mechanisms.

The Genesis of the Act

The emergence of poverty as a conspicuous item on the national policy agenda in early 1964 was principally a result of the efforts of a rather small group of individuals, including two presidents, who defined the problem in national terms and determined that a large-scale national response was required. Daniel P. Moynihan, a major participant in designing the war on poverty, locates its origins in John F. Kennedy's assumption of the presidency. According to Moynihan, "His election brought to Washington . . . a striking echelon of persons whose profession might justifiably be described as knowing what ails societies and whose art is to get treatment underway before the patient is especially aware of anything noteworthy taking place."[4] In the early 1960s there was no vocal constituency in states

Table 3. *Major Economic Opportunity Act Program Components*

Program	Activity
Youth (Title I)[a]	
Job Corps	Agreements with federal, state, or local agencies or private organizations to operate conservation and training centers.
Work Training	Grants to state or local agencies for youth work-training programs.
Work Study	Grants to institutions of higher education for student part-time employment.
Community Action (Title II)[b]	
General Community Action	Grants to public or private nonprofit agencies for action programs to mobilize community resources to combat poverty.
Adult Basic Education	Grants to states to increase literacy and employability.
Rural (Title III)[c]	
Rural Poverty	Loans to low-income rural families and cooperatives.
Rural Workers	Grants to state and local agencies and other entities to assist migrant and other low-income agricultural workers and their families.
Employment and Investment (Title IV)[d]	
Small Business	Loans and loan guarantees.
Work Experience (Title V)[e]	
Training for Welfare Recipients	Grants to state and local agencies and nonprofit organizations.
VISTA[f]	
Volunteers in Service to America	Volunteers for state and local agencies and private and nonprofit organizations.

[a]FY 1965 authorization: $412.5 million.
[b]FY 1965 authorization: $340 million.
[c]FY 1965 authorization: $35 million.
[d]FY 1965 authorization included in Title III.
[e]FY 1965 authorization: $150 million.
[f]No specific authorization.

or communities demanding a war on poverty. There were no interest groups demanding action. Congress was not ready and waiting for an ambitious initiative. As Moynihan puts it, "The war on poverty was not declared at the behest of the poor: it was declared in their interest by persons confident of their own judgment in such matters."[5]

This is not to suggest a complete absence of public attention to poverty prior to 1964. The term "war on poverty" was used in a speech by Kennedy commemorating the Social Security Act at Hyde Park, New York, in August 1960. There were references to poverty in the Democratic Party platform written earlier that summer. And in his inaugural address, Kennedy said, albeit in connection with foreign assistance, "If a free society cannot help the many who are poor, it cannot save the few who are rich."[6]

Although the markings are rather faint, the path to a poverty program began in the early days of Kennedy's presidency. A number of his legislative initiatives, largely developed by Democrats in Congress in the 1950s, addressed problems of economic development and employment, although they did not focus sharply on the problems of the very poor. The path began to take a more certain form in late 1962 when Kennedy told Walter Heller, chairman of the Council of Economic Advisers (CEA), "Now look! I want to go beyond the things that have already been accomplished. Give me facts and figures on the things we still have to do. For example, what about the poverty problem in the United States?"[7] The precise sources of Kennedy's interest in poverty are unknown. Speculation generally includes his exposure to the grinding poverty in West Virginia as a candidate in 1960 and to several recently published books and articles on the topic.[8] His interest, according to James L. Sundquist, another participant in developing the poverty initiative, joined with "an attitude . . . in Washington . . . —a feeling that the 'New Frontier' was made up mainly of old frontiers already crossed, and that . . . all of the innovations conceived over the course of a generation and written into law would not, singly or collectively, change the gray face of the 'other America.'"[9] Further, according to Sundquist, there was the feeling that dealing with social problems piecemeal was "striking only at surface aspects of what seemed to be some kind of bedrock problem, and it was the bedrock problem that had to be identified so that it could be attacked in a concerted, unified and innovative way."[10]

Some also doubted that existing governmental institutions could be relied upon in attacking poverty "in a concerted, unified and innovative way." State and local governments were deeply suspect, as were the departments and agencies of the national government. For example, when, at a later date, the Department of Health, Education, and Welfare (HEW) made its bid to lead the fight against poverty, prime promoters of a poverty initiative, according to an analyst close to the situation, "condemned" the department's "stodginess, its nearly exclusive reliance on counterpart functional bureaucra-

cies at the State level, and its poor reputation for coordination of related activities—in Washington, in its field structure, and between
its functional State and Local counterparts."[11]

Following Heller's talk with Kennedy, CEA staff members and an
informal interagency staff group began work on a poverty initiative.
In October, departments and agencies were asked to make specific
program proposals. On 19 November 1963, Kennedy told Heller un-
equivocally that he wished to send a poverty program to Congress.[12]
Then came Dallas and 22 November. The very next day Heller briefed
the new president and in the process asked whether the poverty
project should go forward. Johnson was as forthright in his response
as his predecessor. He told Heller, "That's my kind of program. . . .
Move full speed ahead."[13]

During the next few months the poverty effort evolved through
several stages. In the three weeks following Johnson's positive reaction, Bureau of the Budget (BOB) staff continued to analyze the sub-
mittals of departments and agencies. There was little if anything in
them that was novel or striking; many of the specifics had been put
forth previously and did not get at the "bedrock problem." There
were no departures from the piecemeal approach to dealing with
poverty or threats to established intergovernmental arrangements.
BOB staff members were discouraged; breaking out of the established program mold appeared to be a remote prospect. According to
one of them, William B. Cannon, meetings in the White House in
October and November showed that a coherent poverty initiative
was not in sight.[14] Sundquist says, "Well into December the bureau
was still 'floundering' . . . in search of a theme and a rationale that
would distinguish the new legislation . . . from all that had gone
before."[15]

Finally, in mid-December the process was energized by the emergence of community action as a core concept around which to build
a poverty program. The idea of community action came to BOB from
the staff of the President's Committee on Juvenile Delinquency and
Youth Crime and from the Ford Foundation. Both had recently ex-
perimented with community improvement projects. In the group
struggling to develop a program, Cannon became the prime advocate
of community action.

On 12 December, a joint memorandum was prepared by the bureau, CEA, HEW, and the Justice Department's juvenile delinquency
group. The key idea presented in it was to authorize state and local
governments to establish development corporations with broad authority to found and fund antipoverty activities. The poor would be
among the participants. The use of many program approaches was an-

ticipated. Authority was to be given to the president to divert funds from other government sources to the development corporations.[16]

Community action's appeal for Cannon, as he later stated, was based on his view that "existing state and local structures of government were inadequate for the Great Society's poverty agenda because they were typically insensitive to the nature and identities of communities and because they inhibited participation in civic affairs."[17] In contrast, community action provided a means "to bridge the basic gaps in the national system of government between local neighborhoods and local government, and between the public and private sectors."[18] Furthermore, it resonated with an ethos of localism that he still felt to be a powerful, though muted, component of the nation's political ideology.[19]

At the operational level, according to Harold Seidman, another BOB staff member, community action was attractive to its advocates "as a unifying force to meld together the resources of Federal, state, and local governments and the private community in the war against poverty."[20] It would facilitate attacking poverty in a comprehensive and coordinated manner.[21] And, as Moynihan put it, community action held out "the alluring, intoxicating possibility of doing it from the *bottom*."[22]

The Bureau of the Budget's first concrete proposal to the president was a cautious one. It called for a demonstration program that would empower ten local development corporations with broad discretion to plan, spend, and coordinate antipoverty efforts. The coordination mandate extended to the activities of federal departments and agencies. Johnson went over the proposal with Heller and Kermit Gordon, director of BOB, at the LBJ Ranch in late December. He made two critical decisions at that time. First, he rejected a small-scale, experimental program. He later said, "I was certain that we could not start small and hope to propel a program through the Congress. It had to be big and bold and hit the whole nation with real impact."[23] Money on the order of $1 billion would be sought from Congress to dramatize the effort.

The second critical decision was to retain community action as a core program concept. Cannon says that Johnson "vacillated" on the point but suggests that in the end he was persuaded to approve it by arguments cast in terms of localism.[24] Questions remain as to whether he was aware of the uncertainties attached to the concept and of its potential for launching challenges to existing institutions. C. Robert Perrin, who became an assistant director of OEO in 1966, thought not. "I don't think he ever understood what community action was about, in the sense that it was going to be controversial and that it was not going to be smooth."[25] In his memoirs, however, Johnson indicates that he was aware of the risks. "I realized that a program as massive as the one we were contemplating might shake up many existing institutions, but I decided that some shaking up might be needed to get a bold new program moving. I thought that local governments had to be challenged to be awakened."[26] Moynihan asserts that Johnson was indeed aware of the risks and did not relish them. "His attitude toward community action appears to have been one of instant suspicion and dislike. He appears to have judged that it would encounter exactly the political troubles it did run into."[27] Jack Conway, who came out of the labor movement to help plan community action and get it underway, also reports that at the ranch in December Johnson was concerned about community action and quotes the president as saying, "In Texas, we realize that our civilization is very thin." Johnson then went on to discuss instances of violence precipitated by governmental action in his native state, concluding, "I am always aware of the fact that government and relationships are very fragile."[28] Despite this awareness, he gave his approval, but it was one tempered, according to Moynihan, by a clear indication that he wanted no disruptions.[29]

Johnson introduced the poverty initiative in his State of the Union message and amplified it in the budget message of 21 January 1964. The president's economic report, released at about the same time, contained a chapter on poverty. The approach outlined in the budget message was along the lines of the Bureau of the Budget's proposal. It was now, after revision, a national rather than a demonstration program. The president announced that he would seek an appropriation of $500 million for community action and $500 million for other unspecified programs.

Both before and after the budget message, internal debate persisted on several issues. One was whether the president should propose new legislation with only a community action title, or whether other titles should be added to include the additional programs that were to receive funding. Multiple titles were pushed by Labor, HEW, and Agriculture in particular; this approach was favored by certain White House staff members as an easier route to higher appropriations, but it was opposed by BOB. Another issue still unresolved was the location of administrative and coordination responsibilities in Washington.

Late in January the president decided that a new arrangement was required to resolve the various lingering disagreements. R. Sargent Shriver, director of the Peace Corps and later to be designated head of OEO, was asked to lead a new task force to develop a program in final form. At this point, community action came under strong attack. According to Cannon, Shriver was quite skeptical about it and was biased toward reliance on national programs. Cannon suspects that community action might have been lost if one of its supporters had not prevailed upon Attorney General Robert Kennedy to intercede with Shriver, his brother-in-law.[30]

Community action stayed, and it was decided to add other titles. Questions about other programs to be included and about administrative arrangements dominated the task force's agenda. There were several key decisions in addition to the content of the various titles. The first decision was to establish a new agency to run the poverty effort. Several related decisions could not be resolved within the task force and went to the president. It was Johnson who determined, over the Bureau of the Budget's objection, that OEO should be located in the Executive Office of the President. He also decided that HEW and Labor would operate several EOA programs through delegations and that OEO would have both operating and coordinating responsibilities.[31] According to Moynihan, preoccupation with these matters caused community action to be "somewhat lost sight of" in the work of the task force.[32] Its potential role as the organizing principle for the entire effort was forgotten for the moment, Cannon says. The concept was "too elusive."[33]

The final task force product was a negotiated accord that reflected a nationalist perspective on public policy, the political and policy interests of the president, the entrepreneurial interests of Shriver, and the programmatic interests of various departments and agencies. Although focus had shifted away from the Bureau of the Budget's reformist interest in institutional innovation at the local level, a community action title remained in the bill. The bureau's search for new concepts of coordination was not closed completely.

The Economic Opportunity Act and the American Administrative State

In part, the new poverty law was compatible with existing intergovernmental and intragovernmental power arrangements and can be seen as reinforcing them. Reinforcement came principally through guaranteeing to "old line" departments and agencies and their state and local extensions a share of the antipoverty effort. But in various ways it also challenged established interests and forms. That it both challenged and reinforced proved to be the source of considerable tension in implementation.

In introducing the war on poverty in his State of the Union message, Johnson said, "Poverty is a national problem, requiring improved national organization and support. But this attack, to be effective, must also be organized at the State and the local level and must be directed by State and local efforts."[34] These remarks suggest a facilitative, not controlling, national role similar to that found at the time in numerous other program areas. The completed version of the act, however, provided for a greater concentration of authority in the national government and more extensive penetration of the national government into subnational levels than promised earlier in January. Through both direct national involvement at the community level and intergovernmental programs, the national presence and impact would be enlarged. Furthermore, the role to be played by state and local governments in the poverty effort was not clear. Sar A. Levitan notes that the act was intentionally designed to give OEO considerable flexibility in dealing with state and local governments.[35] Thus it challenged the presumption that they were entitled to play important roles in the administration of social service programs.

The law assigned significant responsibilities to the states only in the adult basic education and work experience programs. Both were to be implemented by HEW through established national-state networks. In most of the other program areas, states were included among the various institutions that were eligible to compete for grants and contracts. Provision was made, however, for grants or contracts to state agencies to supply technical assistance to community action programs. Finally, governors were given a veto power over community action projects and Job Corps centers in their states and over the use of VISTA volunteers.[36]

General- and special-purpose units of local government were guaranteed even less involvement by the statute. The only specific designation was that local schools would organize and administer adult basic education efforts. Like the states, local governments were eligible to propose projects in most of the program areas.

The nationalist cast of the legislation and the uncertainties about the roles to be played by state and local governments were accentuated by the eligibility of private, nonprofit agencies to serve as instrumentalities of the national government in the implementation of several programs, including neighborhood youth corps, community action, migrant worker, work experience, and VISTA programs. Furthermore, the act did not bar profit-making enterprises from seeking Job Corps contracts. Grant and contract arrangements between the national government and nongovernmental entities are at times lumped under the term "private federalism," but there is no governmental federalism in them. They are nationalist in character and transfer into the social arena the techniques used to secure goods and services from the private sector in defense, space, and other distinctly national enterprises. They involve direct program administration from Washington.

The greatest unknown in the equation and the greatest potential challenge to established arrangements was community action and what it might become. Neither during the development of the legislation nor during congressional consideration was its meaning truly specified. The act basically stated that community action programs "shall be focused upon the needs of low-income individuals and families and shall provide expanded and improved services, assistance, and other activities, and facilities necessary in connection therewith." Examples of program activities were given, but none were mandated.[37] Vagueness also marked the associated requirement that there be "maximum feasible participation" of those to be served by community action programs, although there was an understanding within the task force that the requirement was to guard against racial discrimination. Beyond that, according to Moynihan, "It was taken as a matter beneath notice that such programs would be dominated by the local political structure."[38] Nor was there further clarification as the legislation moved through Congress. Robert Perrin, then a staff aide to Senator Patrick McNamara (D-Mich.) who worked on the measure in that capacity, recalls:

> The phrase maximum feasible participation . . . never really became a subject of much discussion during the legislative process. In my own recollection "feasible" was the key word. Every time you use the word "feasible," you have the option of going as far as you want to or stopping as short as you want to. And I always considered it in that context, that the idea was good—participation obviously was good, but feasible would control how far you had to go. So I think that was one of the reasons we never considered it an all-powerful tail that was going to start to wag a dog one of these years.[39]

When time came to implement the Economic Opportunity Act, according to Richard Blumenthal's analysis, advocates of three concepts of community action competed for ascendancy.[40] All shared the view that existing state and local institutions and intergovernmental program arrangements were seriously deficient, but they differed in other respects. One concept originated in the Ford Foundation's community development experiments and was quite close to that adopted within the Bureau of the Budget in December 1963. Community action was a device for planning and coordinating diverse public and private activities at the local level. Changes in the conduct of local affairs would be stimulated, if not forced, by national authority exercised by local community action agencies. Although not foreordained, under this concept a further centralization of power in Washington over communities might possibly emerge as local agencies were subjected to OEO direction.

The other two concepts of community action were more radical in their implications. In them national authority would be dispersed among communities, not concentrated; it would be used to empower the poor. One emphasized bringing about change by entrusting program planning and administration to the poor themselves. Program content would be shaped by the poor, not by officials in Washington, state capitols, or city halls. The other envisioned community action programs as institutional bases for expressing dissent and for confronting the established order.

Despite differences, all three concepts of community action challenged the existing distribution of political and governmental power at the local level and the character of national-local relations through the application of national authority from the center. It can be argued that all were reconstitutive in purpose. Cannon, an advocate of the conservative version, seems to agree. He felt that even this version was "a new approach to government."[41] It was an attack on the "federalizing, centralizing and nationalizing nature of the New Deal programs."[42]

Established power relations in Washington were also challenged by the notion of an integrated, multifunctional attack on poverty. This required broadly based collaboration in both intergovernmental and intragovernmental dimensions in order to be effective. Consequently, it was a clear threat to the independence and prerogatives of specialized social service establishments that had matured in the three decades since the New Deal. Furthermore, the coordinating role given to OEO threatened to create much stronger presidential-level control over important domestic programs than they had experienced in the past.

A final challenge to the existing order implicit in the Economic Opportunity Act concerned the complex of intellectual skills and human talents needed to fight a successful war on poverty. The dissatisfaction with existing efforts aimed at the economically deprived included dissatisfaction both with traditional ways of thinking about the poor and with the intellectual resources employed in addressing their problems. In Washington, to a certain extent, the war on poverty was seen as an experimental project in applied social science launched on a national scale, transcending traditional disciplinary boundaries and the conventional "expert" thinking of education, health, welfare, and other specialized professions. The stereotypical risk-aversive, unimaginative, and narrowly focused bureaucrat in Labor, HEW, and other agencies and their counterparts at state and local levels were seen as part of the problem.

Devising new and different approaches to alleviating poverty required a different mix of skills and talents. Those identified with the social sciences were one important set.[43] Community action, especially its more radical variants, called, in addition, for expertise almost never found in established bureaucracies at that time. One was community organization, or knowledge about how to mobilize and organize persons not accustomed to participating in governmental affairs and to aid them in articulating their interests and concerns. Another was the set of raw intellectual skills and interests honed by actually experiencing the circumstances of poverty; these were thought by at least some to be vital ingredients in community action decision making.

In summary, the Economic Opportunity Act at the least suggested the possibility that it might alter the American administrative state in important ways. Whether or to what extent this might occur would be determined in the implementation phase as administrators struggled to give detail to the act's broad outlines. The answer would be the product of political and administrative conflict precipitated by the act.

Intergovernmental Politics

Although the Economic Opportunity Act could be read as a potential challenge to certain prerogatives of state and local governments, those governments offered no meaningful opposition to its enactment. In fact, several mayors testified in favor of it. Negative reactions were soon heard, however. These were of major concern to the White House. Pacification of state and local officials, especially governors and mayors, was one of the more important ways in which the presidency was involved in the intergovernmental strains and institutional adjustments caused by the war on poverty.

The Cities React

As implementation of the act began in late 1964 and early 1965, indications of mayoral distemper were heard in Washington. In part, its sources were located in the initial disarray often associated with new programs and were exacerbated by administrative pressures spawned by other fledgling Great Society programs. From his listening post as director of the Office of Emergency Planning, Buford Ellington cautioned the president in mid-1965: "Something has got to be done to eliminate the confusion regarding the administration of the poverty program." He continued, "In my opinion, Mr. Shriver and his staff are doing a good job. . . . However, there seems to be a lack of understanding at the local level as to which department or agency is responsible for each individual program."[44] But administrative deficiencies were not quickly rectified, as was indicated in a critical study by the U.S. Conference of Mayors that was pointedly brought to Johnson's attention by the vice president in late 1965.[45]

More, of course, was involved than administrative problems. In his analysis of the war on poverty, John C. Donovan observes, "Stated crudely, mayors as a group would like to maximize the flow of federal anti-poverty dollars into their cities while minimizing the degree of federal interventions in local customs."[46] It was not long before many city officials became aware of community action's radical potential to threaten "local customs."

The prime difficulties in the relationships with mayors turned on two related issues. The first was the composition of the boards established by mayors to govern community action agencies organized under city auspices. Such boards were very likely to be appointed in the manner to which mayors were accustomed—composed of the mayor's political supporters, representatives from established interest groups, and a sprinkling of civic-minded, upper-middle-class citizens. Mayors had not been accustomed to appointing to advisory boards such persons as might be representative of poor neighborhoods. Yet OEO required this to be done. Even before OEO was funded, in October 1964 the Philadelphia poverty agency was disestablished because of an unrepresentative board. As one OEO official later put it, "Actually, Mayor Tate was only guilty of doing business as usual. Nobody told him the rules had been changed."[47]

Strong pressures from OEO to secure representation of the poor quickly drew a response from influential mayors. On 20 January 1965, Mayor Theodore R. McKeldin of Baltimore wrote Johnson in the aftermath of a meeting attended by fifteen mayors representing, among others, the cities of St. Louis, Cleveland, and Philadelphia. McKeldin reported, "There was an extremely strong and almost unanimous feeling that your plans are being hindered at the Federal level by individuals who insist on unrealistic requirements and who do not understand the problems and operations of local governments."[48] The president instructed Bill Moyers, then his key assistant in the domestic sphere, to have Vice President Hubert H. Humphrey and OEO director Shriver "work it out." Shriver's response was to characterize the letter as "an excessive overstatement," to defend OEO's actions, and to suggest that the problem was limited to a very few cities.[49] Shriver's downplaying of the mayors' discomfort notwithstanding, the participation issue did not immediately die.

A second and perhaps more serious source of friction with the mayors emerged from OEO's funding patterns. In many communities funding went directly from OEO in Washington to newly created private, nonprofit community action agencies.[50] Funding on occasion was also provided for the community projects of independent groups when a city had established the "official" community action agency. In both cases, antagonism toward city hall often accompanied an independence of it. The consequences were disruptive. For example, early in OEO's history there was direct funding of a Syracuse University project for training community organizers.[51] The training went beyond classroom lectures to include organizational experience. As a part of their assignment, the trainees organized the tenants of public housing projects to press for improved facilities. They also initiated a voter registration drive in poverty areas. More Democrats than Republicans were registered, and the mayor was a Republican. The mayor later testified: "Lost was the original purpose of the program—to teach people how to combat poverty. In its place they were taught how to attack city hall, and Albany and Washington. The program . . . was funded directly without any member of the Syracuse administration knowing anything about the program until the grant was announced."[52]

Extreme forms of confrontation associated with the war on poverty were experienced in only a few cities, most of them among the nation's largest and most volatile. But a few dramatic situations served as warnings to others where adversarial relationships had not actually developed or had been kept in bounds. Because of the existence of community-oriented, nationally funded activities that were outside the control of local governments, a general uneasiness was unmistakable in city halls.

Uneasiness peaked in June 1965 when the U.S. Conference of Mayors came very close to adopting a resolution submitted by Mayor Samuel Yorty of Los Angeles and Mayor John F. Shelley of San Francisco, both Democrats. It stated in part: "No responsible mayor can accept the implications in the Office of Economic Opportunity Workbook that the goals of this program can be achieved by creating tensions between the poor and existing agencies and by fostering class struggle."[53] The resolution was sidetracked by an alternative proposal that a committee of mayors, chaired by Richard Daley of Chicago, carry the views of the conference to the vice president and OEO officials.

The mayors' reaction to community action "got the President pretty damned upset," according to Robert A. Levine, then a top OEO official.[54] Furthermore, Johnson was bothered by the events and incidents that caused the mayors' discontent. Bernard Boutin, Shriver's deputy, knew Johnson's views on situations such as Syracuse. "He was very unhappy with some of those things. He voiced them to me."[55] The president's initial apprehension about community action had quickly become a reality.

As the months passed in 1965, political controversy centering on the war on poverty came to include more than the mayors' complaints about community action. On the other side, community activists hurled charges of "boss rule" at mayors who resisted their claims. Critics pointed to "excessive" salaries paid to OEO officials and community action staffs. There was extensive negative publicity about both Job Corps and Neighborhood Youth Corps operations. In Congress, lengthy reauthorization hearings provided a forum for adverse assessments. The explosion in the Watts area of Los Angeles during the summer of 1965 underscored the stark problems of the inner cities and intensified the public spotlight thrown on the poverty program and the allegations of its critics.

It is against this backdrop that the Bureau of the Budget attempted to use the mayors' complaints to alter the course that OEO was setting for community action and to enlist Johnson's support in its effort. The bureau's basic point, director Charles L. Schultze told the president in mid-September 1965, was that OEO's operative concept of community action was ill-conceived. The mayors were correct in their assertion that the proper role for the poor was working in antipoverty programs; community action should not sponsor the political organization of the poor or give them policymaking responsibilities. OEO, his memorandum continued, should be told to deemphasize the policy role of the poor and to emphasize program planning and coordination efforts in cooperation with local officials.[56]

Despite the president's indication of agreement with the bureau's position and some fairly substantial initiatives on its part, the effort to bring community action back to something resembling BOB's original conception had little effect. The precise reasons are unclear, but at least three factors appear to be of some significance. One was that OEO staff stoutly resisted the bureau's intrusion. Another was that the bureau's prime constituency for changing direction, big-city mayors, was small and already in the process of eroding. The final factor was that the press learned of the matter and printed stories depicting BOB as threatening budget sanctions to force changes in community action. This created problems with civil rights organizations and related groups, elicited denials that community action would be throttled, and erected an insuperable obstacle to the attainment of the bureau's objectives.

In the midst of the publicity, Shriver vigorously defended OEO. He told Johnson, "The question of 'maximum feasible participation' was a controversial point at the beginning of the war against poverty, but for the last two or three months we have been successful in getting this problem almost wholly resolved."[57] This perhaps was a bit of an overstatement. About a month later, the vice president passed on to Johnson word that Mayor Daley of Chicago and several other Democratic mayors were to meet soon "to go over the poverty program. Daley was particularly upset and critical."[58] But OEO did not yield. The workbook it issued in 1966 stated: "Involving the poor at the administrative levels of CAAs is a *condition of funding*. . . . It is required that the poor and the advocates of the poor occupy positions of evident influence."[59]

Humphrey had concluded his December 1965 memorandum to Johnson by noting that most mayors now strongly backed most aspects of the poverty program. Mayors were writing the White House in support of OEO programs and protesting any cutbacks in funding. On 1 January 1966, Joe Califano, who now had Moyers's domestic portfolio, reported to the president that the mayors of Atlanta, St. Louis, Milwaukee, and Detroit had sent such letters. A similar letter came from John Gunther, executive director of the U.S. Conference of Mayors.[60]

Other evidence of mayoral support was continually relayed to Johnson. In August 1966, as Congress was considering appropriations and amendments to the Economic Opportunity Act, Shriver wrote to the president:

One year ago this month Mayor Naftalin (Minneapolis) was giv-
ing OEO h——.
This year he has written every Minnesota Congressman and
Senator and has endorsed OEO's programs without exception.
The U.S. Conference of Mayors has officially endorsed OEO's leg-
islative stance, and supports the Administration Bill 100%.
Both of these are complete changes from last year.[61]

In November and December 1966, mayors were also communicating with the White House and protesting against rumored transfers of programs from OEO to Labor.[62]

Undoubtedly, the efforts of the president's personal agents, the vice president, Buford Ellington, and Farris Bryant, Ellington's successor as director of the Office of Emergency Planning, played an important part in the turnabout. But there was also mayoral self-interest. Community action was a source of funds for many. In addition, after programs were established and some, such as Head Start, became quite popular, it was advantageous to continue them. Perrin observed that as 1967 approached, although many mayors still "weren't completely happy" with community action, "they had come around to accept this as a price . . . for new federal money . . . ; and they . . . agreed generally that the community action agencies were a going thing and a necessary thing."[63] Moynihan saw "an adaptive process" at work in which community action agencies were incorporated "into the structure of civic governance." Many mayors found them to be useful. "Of a sudden they realized it might be difficult to live without them," especially in dealing with minority populations.[64]

This is not to suggest that community action suddenly gained universal political favor. It did not. In particular, it remained a sore spot for many in Congress. Legislation in 1966 imposed several administrative restrictions on community action operations. Of greater significance, Congress limited OEO's funding discretion in community action and, consequently, the program discretion of local agencies. The method chosen was to earmark a substantial portion of community action funds for specific programs, including, among others, Head Start, legal services, and neighborhood health centers.[65] In part the action can be explained by the appeal of the programs selected for earmarking. But it was also stimulated by objections to the more radical possibilities of community action revealed in some settings. Restricting program discretion was a step toward limiting radical impulses. Other steps would be added in 1967.

The States React

Stimulated by the technical assistance grants contained in the act, state governments promptly began to establish central institutional foci for war on poverty involvement. By 1966, poverty offices existed in forty-nine state governments. Most of them were a part of the governor's office, and many were assigned broad program coordination responsibilities.[66]

Although there was not the trauma experienced by some cities, EOA implementation at the state level was not problem free. Certain governors felt the sting of community action protests. There were early controversies over administrative practices and the governor's veto. Early in August 1965 Ellington reported to Johnson on the recently concluded National Governors' Conference. In regard to poverty, he said, "All are in favor of the program, but I didn't talk with a single Governor who approves of the way it is being handled in Washington and at the State level."[67] Jake Jacobsen, another presidential aide, passed along a second report on the conference from a longtime political agent of the president. "The problem most discussed which affects State-Federal relations is the operation of the Office of Economic Opportunity and the various poverty programs handled by Labor and OEO." The most pointed complaint of governors involved the direct dealings between national and local officials in areas such as vocational education. State officials were being bypassed.[68]

Administrative problems of this type, aggravating though they might be, received little public attention and did not cause any serious problems for the president until the end of 1966. In the interim, national-state administrative relations in the antipoverty enterprise were, on the surface, not marked by serious acrimony. However, during this period the veto issue was sharply defined and received considerable attention. Specifically, the issue was whether the veto power of governors provided in the 1965 legislation should be maintained or diluted.

In the first eighteen months of OEO's existence, governors often threatened vetoes but used the power only five times.[69] Some of the vetoes were quite controversial. Alabama governor George C. Wallace's veto of a countywide biracial community action group precipitated heated controversy in Congress when OEO legislation was considered in 1965. A proposal to allow the director to reverse a governor's veto was a lively issue throughout the entire summer. A very large volume of mail from governors was addressed to the White House; the OEO was at pains to prepare careful responses for the president's signature. Such a reply, for example, sent to Governor John Connally of Texas on 10 June 1965, extended to three pages and argued, as forcefully as possible, that limiting the governors' veto authority "closes an avenue for possible abuse that exists under the law as now written. It provides a method of review of vetoes which are arbitrary, capricious or discriminatory."[70] As might be expected, however, the National Governors' Conference in July 1965 adopted a resolution expressing "firm opposition" to "any diminution of the power of a Governor to veto proposed projects and programs under the Economic Opportunity Act."[71] These petitions notwithstanding, in 1965 the director was authorized to override gubernatorial vetoes within thirty days.

It is uncertain whether the battle over the veto should be seen in symbolic terms or as an issue with real implications for national-state power relations. From passage of the EOA to the end of Johnson's presidency, there were approximately fifty vetoes by governors out of 30,000 or more opportunities.[72] Governors George Wallace of Alabama and Ronald Reagan of California were responsible for a large portion of them. In a 1966 study, the Advisory Commission on Intergovernmental Relations (ACIR) found not only miniscule use of veto authority but also little use of the threat of veto to influence program decisions.[73] Furthermore, OEO exercised restraint in responding to vetoes. According to Perrin, OEO allowed many to stand or made program changes that caused them to be withdrawn. "So in practice it has not been a serious break either in our ability to proceed nor has it . . . given the governors a feeling that we would simply ride roughshod over them."[74]

As 1966 drew to a close, the veto issue was all but forgotten. Yet the deluge of change experienced since 1964 was taking its toll on gubernatorial morale, especially among Democrats disappointed in 1966 election results. The governors' discontent became public in the mid-December meeting at White Sulphur Springs, West Virginia, and the poverty programs were major factors. After his meeting with several of the disgruntled governors at the ranch a few days later, the president commented that some of the governors "have had grave questions about the poverty program and its administration." In particular, "I think they have been disappointed on occasions in decisions that were made—in guidelines, in administration, or in personalities that they had to deal with."[75] There would be a concerted effort to ease gubernatorial anxiety in 1967 and to address the concerns of mayors.

The 1967 Reauthorization

The central event in the war on poverty in 1967 was reauthorization of the Economic Opportunity Act. In preparation for the legislative struggle, a systematic effort was initiated at the presidential level to deal with problems raised by the governors. The 1967 visits to state capitals by teams of federal officials were generally described in the previous chapter. An OEO representative was a team member, and on many trips it was Perrin. He found, in fact, that many governors were poorly informed about the poverty program. A major concern of most of them and their economic opportunity staffs was "money coming into their states over which they had no real controls. And they indicated interest in distributing the money."[76] As to the complaint "that they didn't have enough power over the programs in their states . . . I couldn't argue with them too much, because they didn't have that power and they weren't intended to have that power."[77] Nevertheless, the simple fact of the visits appeared to have a positive effect on national-state relations in poverty matters.

In the midst of these trips, two important presidential messages were dispatched to Congress. The poverty message was sent on 14 March, followed on 17 March by a broad set of proposals to improve the quality of government in the United States. At a White House briefing for governors the next day, the significance attached to the poverty program for the overall tenor of national-state relationships was indicated by the placement of Shriver as the lead speaker and "flak-taker" ahead of the cabinet secretaries, who later spoke and responded to questions.[78]

Six months later, in the midst of the reauthorization struggle in Congress, Bryant reflected on his nine months as presidential liaison with the governors. Looking back to late 1966, he recalled for Johnson the "dismay" that marked the mood of the governors "over the confusing proliferation of programs, bypassing of the Governors by Federal agencies, distortions of State budget priorities to meet Federal grant requirements, delays, red tape, and growing Federal domination in areas traditionally reserved to the States." Since that time, attitudes had changed. "The Governors had been made aware in tangible fashion of your concern with their problems, and they have reciprocated fully."[79] The governors had been brought into the fold.

In the poverty message Johnson disclosed his intention to seek legislative changes in the community action program that addressed some of the criticisms of state and local officials. Changes included a more explicit definition of the relationship between community action agencies and state and local governments; tighter personnel and other administrative specifications; required representation of local public agencies on community action boards; and a strengthened role for the states in rural community action.[80] By and large, these alterations were not controversial and stayed in the legislation.

Considerable support for reauthorization was provided by governors and mayors. For example, in mid-October, when the bill was moving from committee to the House floor, Shriver wrote to Johnson about a message he had just received from Governor Warren P.

Knowles (R-Wis.). In the governor's view, "a $2 billion investment for community action alone is none too much." Shriver continued, "This is just one more example of the fact that the people who are closest to poverty, Mayors and Governors, regardless of party, are *for* OEO. The Republicans . . . in Washington are the only ones against us." To this he attached an endorsement by twenty-two Republican mayors.[81] Notwithstanding this support and the changes proposed, strong congressional opposition arose. Community action continued to be the major problem, especially programs administered by nonprofit organizations. To secure additional support for reauthorization, particularly from southern Democrats, an amendment was proposed by Representative Edith Green (D-Oreg.). It provided that local governments would have the option of establishing the community action agency or of designating the private agency to perform community action functions. In either case, the agency would be governed by a board equally composed of public officials, representatives of poverty areas, and representatives of business, labor, and charitable groups. After inclusion by the House, the amendment was reluctantly accepted by the Senate in exchange for a higher level of funding than the House had favored.[82] Several minor provisions were also included to give the governors somewhat more authority.[83]

As finally adopted, the OEO reauthorization was for two years, not for the one-year period preferred by the House. Although underfunding continued to be serious, given the original intent of the OEO charter and the expectations of the new constituencies that had been created, there were no further major congressional conflicts over OEO during the remainder of the Johnson presidency.[84]

Observers close to the scene attribute much of the 1967 reauthorization to the political skills of Shriver in dealing with Congress.[85] Some in OEO felt that the agency received little, if any, help from the White House during this critical time.[86] Johnson's dissatisfaction with OEO and his view that it was "run by 'kooks and sociologists'" were well known in Washington.[87] In 1967 he told one of the senators involved with poverty legislation that although "this was hardly his favorite program," "he was prepared to stick with it."[88] In fact, he and his staff were deeply involved throughout the year in the fight to continue the program.[89] Presidential attention to the reactions of the states and cities to the poverty enterprise before and during consideration of the legislation was an especially valuable supplement to Shriver's efforts and an important contribution to a reasonably successful outcome.[90]

Administrative Politics

At the end of Johnson's presidency, the struggle to enlarge economic opportunity still drew substantial support from governors, mayors, other public officials, and the general public, but administrative deficiencies continued to plague the effort.[91] In an understated reflection of this, in his last State of the Union message Johnson said, "I believe the Congress this year will want to improve the administration of the poverty program by reorganizing portions of it and transferring them to other agencies."[92] Reality was more accurately portrayed in a review of OEO programs just nearing completion by the General Accounting Office (GAO). Its release came in March 1969 when the Nixon administration was in the initial phase of its assault on the Democratic poverty initiative.

The GAO report stressed from the outset the serious administrative difficulties that OEO had encountered—the urgency in initiating new programs, problems in developing a new organization and staffing it effectively, delays and uncertainties in congressional authorizations and appropriations, and the problems of working out new and different relations with states and local governments. However, after pointing out that GAO had been charged by Congress to look at deficiencies and not achievements, the report catalogued a variety of flaws. Overall, it asserted that although there had been progress, "The administrative machinery is still in need of substantial improvement."[93] A fundamental and persistent problem was the inability of OEO to exercise its coordinating role. The administrative stress in the war on poverty that was stimulated by coordination difficulties in Washington and at subnational levels persisted to the end of Johnson's presidency.

The Challenge of Coordination

The coordination challenge was immense. Its magnitude is illustrated by a brief review of manpower programs, which constituted only one segment, but a key one, in the war on poverty. The program structure in 1968, as outlined in Table 4, is not much different from that of 1965.

With programs divided among Labor, HEW, and OEO, fragmentation in program responsibilities was substantial, accentuated by even further divisions of administrative authority within the two departments. A multitude of state and local agencies and private nonprofit institutions were involved in execution. With varying program

Table 4. *Major Manpower Programs, 1968*

Agency	Programs
Labor	United States Employment Service
	Apprenticeship and Training
	Manpower Development and Training Act
	Institutional Training
	On-the-Job Training
	Experimentation and Demonstration Program
	Work Incentive Program[a]
	Job Opportunities in the Business Sector[b]
HEW	Vocational Education
	Vocational Rehabilitation
	Adult Basic Education
	Work Incentive Program[a]
OEO	Neighborhood Youth Corps[c]
	Job Corps
	Operation Mainstream[c]
	New Careers[c]
	Special Impact[c]
	Community Action Manpower Program
	Concentrated Employment Program[c]

[a] Administered in part by Labor and in part by HEW.

[b] In collaboration with the National Alliance of Businessmen and the Department of Commerce.

[c] Delegated to the Department of Labor.

objectives, standards of eligibility, and levels of assistance and procedures, competition for resources and clients was often the norm.

A 1966 paper prepared for the President's Task Force on Government Organization spelled out some of the consequences. After noting extensive overlap and duplication, it stated: "Most programs tend to use separate and uncoordinated means of recruiting people . . . leading to confusion, misunderstanding and inadequate service to the applicant population. Likewise, with 12 different programs supporting job development efforts . . . and over half a dozen programs supporting on-the-job training, the employer complaints about multiple agency contacts are justified."[94] Furthermore, the paper continued, "Respective roles and functions of agencies and programs are unclear, leaving prospective clients as well as program administration confused."[95]

In the same year, a presidential task force looking at urban employment opportunities described the situation as follows:

When the various manpower programs are translated into action at the local . . . level there are from eight to fifteen public agencies and an even greater number of private [organizations] administering programs with Federal funds. In a particular city the State supervises the local Employment Service; the County Welfare Department might administer a work experience program; the public schools establish the vocational training under the MDTA; the Community Action Agency might run independent programs to recruit, counsel and perhaps train and employ individuals from poverty target areas; and the Urban League, the YMCA, and various labor organizations might administer on-the-job training programs. Generally no single organization has had a large enough piece of the action to exercise any effective overall planning, integration and coordination.[96]

These comments clearly underscore the two closely related administrative problems that were the source of continuing pulling and hauling among administrators. One was to coordinate the programs established by the Economic Opportunity Act. The other was to mesh these with other programs addressing the plight of the poor.

Arrangements for Coordination

Anticipating a broadly orchestrated attack on poverty, the authors of the Economic Opportunity Act included in it a very general set of arrangements for coordination. Coordination in communities was addressed obliquely in the community action title. The capacity of community action agencies to pull together a wide range of program resources in the elimination of poverty was buttressed by the inclusion of two "preference" provisions. One directed all federal agencies to give preference, if feasible and lawful, to the applications of approved community action agencies for assistance or benefits.[97] The other called for preference to be given to community action agencies in awarding grants for EOA programs, including those administered by other departments and agencies under delegations from OEO.[98]

The major focal point for coordination in Washington was the director of OEO. Ultimate responsibility, however, was vested in the president, who was given a redundant grant of authority in the act to direct "that particular programs and functions . . . shall be carried out, to the extent not inconsistent with other applicable laws, in conjunction with or in support of programs authorized under" the EOA.[99] The director was empowered only to secure information from other agencies. However, the act instructed agencies to cooperate with the director and to "carry out their programs and exercise their functions in such manner as will, to the maximum extent permitted by other applicable laws, assist in carrying out the purposes of the Act."[100]

An Economic Opportunity Council was established by the act to serve as a forum for interagency coordination. Chaired by the director of OEO, its membership consisted of the heads of departments and agencies whose work bore on the poverty problem.[101] It was given no authority, and its functions were not articulated clearly.

Midcourse Assessments

Serious problems in coordination began to surface as implementation of the act began. Even when extraordinary presidential attention was given to a situation, deficiencies in coordination were difficult to overcome. The cataclysmic riots in the impoverished Watts area of Los Angeles between 11 and 15 August 1965 sharpened awareness of administrative limitations. The report of the task force dispatched by Johnson to deal with the situation underscored the difficulties involved in mobilizing the resources of government to address effectively the immense social problems concentrated in such areas. The task force went so far as to recommend the designation of "a principal federal officer for the Los Angeles area" to coordinate federal programs with state and local programs.[102] Johnson rejected the recommendation, but other steps were taken to improve the organization of the poverty program in Los Angeles. They were not wholly effective. Not long afterward, Under Secretary of Commerce LeRoy Collins reported to Califano regarding two recent OEO grants in Los Angeles that had not been cleared at the local level in violation of understandings reached after the riot. This, Collins wrote, seriously impaired the "attempt to resolve the ongoing fight for control of the anti-poverty program" and "undermines much of the effort we made in Los Angeles."[103]

Early in 1965 a cabinet committee on education and training programs identified a wide range of coordination and organization issues in the war on poverty and pointed to the close relationship between problems in interagency relationships in Washington and poor coordination at subnational levels. In response, officials in the Bureau of the Budget began to work on a proposal for an extensive internal study and review.[104] Instead of this approach, in the aftermath of the August disruption in Los Angeles, Schultze established an external task force to examine issues in intergovernmental program coordination. It was chaired by Stephen K. Bailey of Syracuse University. Although the task force did not focus exclusively on the poverty program, its December 1965 report highlighted the occurrence there and in other areas of "too many instances of confusion and contradiction" in complex networks of intragovernmental and intergovernmental administrative relationships. Its major prescription was strengthened presidential-level machinery "to keep in proper relationship all of the Federal programs having an impact on communities and to initiate prompt action to correct administrative conflicts and hiatuses."[105]

Critical scrutiny was not restricted to official Washington. Approximately three weeks before the Bailey task force submitted its report, Vice President Humphrey forwarded to Johnson a study produced by the U.S. Conference of Mayors. It dealt exclusively with the administration of EOA programs. Several critical observations were set forth based upon a series of consultations with officials at all levels of government. Two stood out in importance. The first was that the performance of community action agencies was frequently deficient. They too often failed to establish solid working relationships with existing public and private agencies that would allow them to serve as "a single, broadly representative coordinating agency acting as a program umbrella" for their areas.[106] The second was that a major barrier to realization of the umbrella concept was "a serious and continuing lack of coordination at the federal level." The report continued, "Most of the CAA Directors reported that they had not encountered meaningful coordination between OEO and the so-called delegated programs operating through the Department of Labor, the Department of Health, Education, and Welfare and various other departments. Neighborhood Youth Corps Projects, work-study programs, work-experience programs and others have frequently been approved by federal agencies without any involvement of the local CAA."[107]

The pace of authoritative criticism quickened in 1966 as administrative problems were dissected in Congress, by the Advisory Commission on Intergovernmental Relations, and by additional presidential task forces. Senator Edmund S. Muskie (D-Maine), from his position as chairman of the intergovernmental relations subcommittee of the Senate Committee on Government Operations, began his persistent effort to address fundamental issues in national-state-local relationships. In speeches and hearings, he developed the theme of "too much tension and conflict rather than coordination and cooperation all along the line of administration—from top Federal policy makers and administrators to the State and local professional administrators and elected officials."[108] Muskie's general campaign to focus attention on problems in intergovernmental relations, supplemented by more hostile criticism from some Republicans, reinforced other efforts to address questions about the administration of war on poverty programs. Many of the critical themes enunciated in the mayors' study and articulated by Muskie were elaborated in an April 1966 ACIR report. The report carefully examined the intergovernmental dimensions of OEO programs; gave special attention to the role of states, effects on local governments, and coordination at the local level; and highlighted numerous areas for improvement.[109]

External criticism was joined by still more criticism from within. Late in 1965 Secretary of Labor W. Willard Wirtz, Secretary of Health, Education, and Welfare John W. Gardner, BOB director Charles L. Schultze, and Bernard Boutin of OEO met with Califano to review a number of coordination issues. One was that the various agencies were handing out money to states and cities in areas of overlapping responsibility without knowing what others were doing. Wirtz advocated a program control system to provide information about funds flowing to particular recipients.[110] At about the same time the ACIR report was released, a manpower task force described weaknesses in coordination in that area, especially at the community level.[111] In mid-summer 1966, Schultze, reflecting BOB's views, complained to Califano and Moyers, "Right now, no one person has the real authority to settle major coordination problems in the poverty program. When conflicts arise agencies bicker among themselves and nobody can settle the dispute."[112] Several months later, in September, the president formed the Task Force on Government Organization with Ben W. Heineman at its helm. Its first report examined the war on poverty and OEO. The topic, Heineman says, was of great interest to Johnson. "One of the first matters that the President asked us to take up out of order was what should be done about OEO. So we studied and reviewed OEO very carefully and made a special report."[113] It went to the president in December 1966.

The report was directed almost entirely at OEO's mix of operating and coordinating functions at the national level. The state of coordination at subnational levels received limited attention. Nonetheless, the task force analysis found serious problems in coordination in both Washington and in communities. "We have been depressed," the report stated, "by the inadequacy and malfunctioning of existing arrangements for program co-ordination, conflict resolution, and resource allocation in the War on Poverty." Consequently, "Many lower-echelon federal bureaucracies and counterpart functional departments in the states and cities . . . continue to sanction and practice 'business as usual.' 'Business as usual' frequently excludes services to the poor, and skirts the toughest problems."[114]

The foregoing critical assessments should not be taken to suggest utter administrative chaos and a complete absence of coordination. Rather, they indicate flawed operations in an effort whose success in the minds of many of its architects was premised on attaining a high level of coordinated effort. The challenge inherent in the conceptualization of the antipoverty drive was to reach a degree of coordinated activity rarely sought, much less obtained, in the American administrative state. The critiques of the Heineman task force and others made clear that at least by the end of 1966 the challenge had been met with considerably less than complete success.

Impediments to Coordination in Washington

In addition to a rapid proliferation of programs and the sheer complexity of program structures, a number of other factors impeded intergovernmental and intragovernmental program coordination. Clearly one was the absence of a comprehensive and substantive policy on poverty based upon a working understanding of its nature, its causes, and the relationships among them. Shriver captured the situation in a September 1965 comment to *Newsweek*. "We are the first to admit we don't have all the answers. This is a war that is going to require social inventiveness, just as we needed military inventiveness when we plunged into World War II."[115]

Lacking a true policy or governing orthodoxy, the antipoverty effort took on an experimental character that invited the relatively free play of a hodgepodge of concepts and approaches. In this context, the varied and conflicting institutional interests and attitudes of participants found full opportunity for expression. Turf struggles were especially intense in the manpower sphere. OEO had to contend with established and politically potent bureaucracies in Labor and HEW, both of which pressed extensive and overlapping jurisdictional claims. The Department of Labor's view that "manpower is Labor and Labor is manpower" was a challenge to both OEO and HEW.[116] John Gardner, while secretary of HEW, once observed at a meeting, "There is simply no getting away from the fact that the expansion path of the Labor Department, which is very small, is right through the heart of HEW."[117] Samuel Hughes of BOB characterized the situation for Califano this way: "Each agency wants the key role in job programs. Labor claims all manpower programs belong to it. HEW claims all that involve health, education or welfare, or its clients—e.g., the aged. OEO claims all poverty jobs."[118]

More was involved than simply turf. The ambitions of each contending department or agency were animated by its distinctive concerns and approaches. Hughes's comment indicates a sense of different constituencies. In addition, Labor placed great value in on-the-job training, while HEW emphasized a classroom approach. OEO believed that both approaches were defective when applied to the truly poor.

Competition was intensified by budget pressures. Late in 1966, as noted in an earlier chapter, Schultze warned the president that "*we are not able to fund adequately the new Great Society programs.*"[119] Vietnam was the major reason. From that time onward, the struggle for resources was a constant factor, as was an insistence on the development of still more new programs. To Stanley C. Ruttenberg, who was responsible for manpower programs in Labor, "The most frustrating experience . . . was being continually told by the White House people that you had to come up with new programs and new ideas, or even implement the new ideas . . . they had, and being simultaneously told there's no more money."[120]

When interests clashed, both Labor and HEW could call upon powerful support. In the case of Labor there were the AFL-CIO, professional associations such as the Interstate Conference of Employment Security Directors, and influential members of Congress. HEW had its own congressional supporters as well as the backing of professional educators at state and local levels and any number of vocational training and rehabilitation groups. Although OEO could draw upon some support from cities, civil rights groups, and certain other interests, it could not match the reservoirs of external political resources at the disposal of the two cabinet departments. The power imbalance was reflected in the president's early decision to delegate administration of important EOA programs to others, including Labor and HEW.

Interagency differences were quite evident when OEO and the departments worked out the specifics of the administrative delegations. According to OEO's administrative history, "Meeting after meeting was held and great differences of opinion and approach between sovereign agencies were discussed at great length and compromised. . . . This was a complicated process, and brought totally different concepts together from a variety of agency backgrounds toward the common goal of eliminating poverty."[121] The result was "a series of complex administrative relationships, each different and demanding a novel set of dealings between OEO and another agency."[122]

Jousting among OEO, Labor, and HEW over programs was a continuing factor in the evolving war on poverty. For example, in late 1965 OEO and Labor clashed over the form a new community work program should take, requiring mediation by BOB.[123] Competition peaked in 1966 and 1967, and some program alterations were made. In 1966 Congress transferred the adult basic education program to HEW. Also in that year Labor won a partial victory in its effort to claim the work experience program, later renamed the work incentive (WIN) program for welfare beneficiaries. Congress divided responsibility for the program between it and HEW.

During this period Labor locked horns with OEO over the delegation of four new manpower programs. They were the concentrated employment program, which was designed to focus resources from a number of programs in selected areas where employment problems were especially severe; the new careers program, which addressed manpower shortages in health, education, welfare, and public safety; the special-impact program, which emphasized job creation in poverty areas; and the operation mainstream program, which targeted problems in rural areas and among the elderly. This time OEO resisted delegation because it feared that administration by Labor through state employment services would not carry the programs to the poor.[124] Ruttenberg observes that the basis of OEO's opposition "was the feeling, 'Well, maybe they just wouldn't be able to run them in an intelligent, modern way and turn it over to that bad old Employment Service to run and it would be very bad.'" Labor won, he says, "after great stress and strain and only after strong support from the White House."[125]

When submitting the initial delegations to Johnson for his approval in late 1964, presidential aide Myer Feldman told him, "Of course, the Director of the Office of Economic Opportunity will continue to be responsible for the policies which will govern the delegated programs."[126] In all of the delegations, which totaled nine from 1964 to 1969, OEO was expected not only to work out initial arrangements with other agencies but also to monitor outcomes. Since one agency has difficulty in supervising another agency, even when it has control over funding, these arrangements were marked by friction, and they were often renegotiated annually. Although OEO retained a monitoring capacity, in truth it did not "govern" the delegated programs. According to Perrin, whose office in OEO was generally responsible for liaison with delegatees, results were mixed. Some influence was exerted. On the other hand, initially "we probably were too busy taking care of Community Action and the programs we were running to spend as much time as we should have spent on these other programs. It got out of hand. I think Shriver's view was: well, just let Labor and HEW run these things, and don't bother me with that; we've got enough problems of our own."[127]

In contrast to HEW and Labor, the Department of Agriculture was guaranteed only a minimal role in implementing the Economic Opportunity Act. Still it experienced significant conflict with OEO. The nub of the problem was not Agriculture's discomfort in collaborating with OEO; rather, it was OEO's lack of interest in Agriculture's participation in the war on poverty.

A part of the problem was that many thought of poverty as an urban phenomenon. Sundquist says that most of those on Shriver's task force viewed rural areas as "backwaters" and rural people as "unenterprising and hardly worth saving, because if they had any gumption they'd get up and leave." Discussions of rural poverty were always an "afterthought."[128]

Officials in Agriculture struggled continually against the emphasis placed on the larger cities in the poverty program and sought to highlight poverty's rural dimension and to play a role in carrying antipoverty efforts into rural areas. Evidence of rural poverty was outlined in some detail by the president's 1964 task force on agriculture. It noted, for example, that "while only 29 percent of all families live in rural areas, 46 percent of those with cash incomes under $3,000 (accounting for 50 percent of the individuals in such families) are rural."[129] Rural poverty themes were amplified the following year in the report of a presidential task force on agriculture and rural life.

Agriculture's initial strategy was to try to work with OEO while, at the same time, strengthening its own programs that affected the economic well-being of rural communities. The Forest Service ran several Job Corps training centers. Some linkages were established between Agriculture's food distribution programs and certain OEO operations. Researchers in Agriculture developed the methodology for calculating the poverty income line, although OEO was reluctant to supply the department with research funds for an extensive exploration of the characteristics of poverty.[130]

The core point of conflict was community action in rural areas. Agriculture offered OEO the use of its extensive field structures in organizing community action agencies. However, OEO was not responsive. In late 1965, Secretary of Agriculture Orville L. Freeman asked for the vice president's help in improving relations with the poverty agency. He commented to Humphrey after an aborted meeting with Shriver: "It has been our feeling, as you know, that the Department's facilities could be used effectively by the OEO. A little seed money to get more people out in the field, using resources al-

ready there, will bring more results I'm confident than the OEO setting up a whole new field staff for that purpose. Nevertheless, Shriver
does not see it that way."[131]

Subsequently, a second strategy was employed. One part involved
highlighting the fact of rural poverty. Freeman attempted with some
success to push the cause of rural poverty in the White House and to
publicize it through that medium. Johnson discussed it in his 1966
message on agriculture, announcing that he would establish a commission on rural poverty. The 1967 poverty message gave extensive
attention to its rural aspects. The rural poverty commission reported in late 1967 with considerable fanfare, and this was followed
a short time later by a message to Congress on agriculture that focused on securing increased prosperity in rural America.

Another part of the strategy was to extend the department's independent efforts. Its state and local field offices were used to aid rural
communities in their search for federal development funds and to
provide them with technical assistance.[132] New institutions called
community development districts were established to promote rural
development. The districts were suggested by a task force on agriculture and rural life.[133] In a message to Congress from Johnson in
January 1966, the president proposed a pilot program of multicounty
districts. They were both to plan and coordinate the planning of
other local agencies in order to form the basis for "a comprehensive
attack on rural community problems." The jurisdiction of the districts was to include "planning for all public services, development
programs, and governmental functions" within their boundaries.[134]
Later that year legislation passed the Senate, but it was stymied in a
House committee.

The following year there was a change in approach. The Department of Housing and Urban Development (HUD) agreed to amend
section 701 of the Housing and Urban Development Act of 1954 to
authorize the creation of planning agencies in nonmetropolitan
areas. HUD was to dispense grants and consult with Agriculture
prior to certification. Agriculture was to serve as a source of technical assistance. When the measure was being considered in the
White House, William D. Carey of BOB predicted to White House
aide Harry McPherson, "OEO will dissent strongly, arguing that
everything we want to do can be accommodated within the Economic Opportunity Act. In particular, Shriver is disturbed by the
thought that rural community action . . . might be sidetracked rather
than made the principal operating vehicle."[135]

Carey's prediction proved to be accurate. When the 1967 poverty
message was being drafted, Shriver's basic argument to Califano was

that "new structures" were not needed. "What we do need is to use the existing community action structures and to increase their numbers."[136] Freeman's response was that rural community action was usually too narrow in focus and that these agencies were often hostile to working with local officials of other agencies.[137] Despite OEO's protestations, the president recommended and Congress enacted the legislation. Implementation began in 1969. Thus, the inability of Agriculture and OEO officials in Washington to agree upon a plan of action for rural America limited the effects of the poverty program there and added to institutional complexity at the local level.[138]

Two underlying factors exacerbated OEO's difficulties in its relationships with other departments and agencies. These involved certain administrative characteristics of OEO and the attitudes of at least some of its staff. OEO began its operations with unbureaucratic rapidity and a great deal of administrative ingenuity. Civil service requirements were waived in the interest of rapid organization. "Chaos" was a word often used to describe the state of OEO administration. Shriver believed the characterization to be apt and, furthermore, seemed to like that condition. He later observed, "OEO was real hurly-burly. . . . We were creating as we went, and . . . government people don't like that—they like clean, bureaucratic charts, they wanna know where everybody is all the time, who's reporting to whom."[139] He continued: "So a lot of criticism came onto me, came onto OEO, saying that they were chaotic, that it was disorganized, that I was a great guy, I could think of a lot of things, but, brother, was this place confused! You know. It never bothered me a bit—because frankly I'll take whatever you call confusion and it can actually create and help poor people, that's what our job is."[140]

Shriver's comments give some insight into his administrative style. For a considerable period of time, he continued to serve also as head of the Peace Corps and lacked a strong deputy in OEO. His style and split responsibilities bred administrative confusion in OEO. That, in turn, confounded relations with other departments and agencies. Perrin described Shriver's "peculiar way of operating. He did it more by personal assistant than he did by program mechanisms. . . . This always creates problems in an organization. Or his assigning a problem to whoever he happened to run into in the men's room or thought of on the spur of the moment . . . no matter how many . . . administrative lines it crossed."[141] Basically, Perrin felt, "Shriver just wasn't interested in administration."[142] Bernard Boutin, Shriver's first deputy, echoed Perrin's assessment. "Sarge, once he got something going would lose interest . . . and wanted to jump on to something else. Yet, as deputy, I was limited as to what I could do without his stamp of approval and we had some very violent disagreements on that." [143]

In this lax administrative environment, according to Perrin, various program officers were engaged in activities that impinged on other people, who, in turn, would be unaware of that engagement. Bertram H. Harding, later deputy, then acting director, perceived a great deal of staff independence during the first two years of OEO's existence. "They were difficult to manage. They were continually going off in their own private directions with their own private agendas." [144] Their independence and intensity won them the appellation "poverty warriors," but it was a disorganized war they were conducting.

The second underlying factor that exacerbated OEO's interagency difficulties was clashing perspectives on poverty programs. Perrin, for example, attributed coordination problems in part to "the very parochial attitude that a lot of departments had. They had been running their programs for all these years; they didn't want this upstart agency involved." He saw Labor and the others as operating "their programs on behalf of those who were not the poorest of the poor. And this was the way they had been operating for years." [145] The clash in perspectives was real. A report on an interagency conference on the pilot neighborhood facilities program held in 1967 is illustrative. Labor representatives saw the solution to the core poverty problem as jobs; for HEW representatives, it was developing healthy and productive individuals; and for HUD representatives, it was improving the physical environment. OEO representatives saw the problem in terms of citizen involvement. [146] The distinctive perspectives of HEW, Labor, and HUD were locked into complex intergovernmental administrative arrangements that differed in important respects. HUD's ties were principally with cities. Those of HEW and Labor were with states. In each department there was a strong tendency to be responsive to its own subnational clienteles.

Perrin's attitude toward the old-line departments, critical as it was, was a moderate one. Many of his colleagues held more extreme views. According to Sundquist, who served in Agriculture, "the basic difficulty" in relationships "was that the OEO had a complete and thorough and unshakable distrust of the Department. . . . They thought we were a department of racists and that the best thing we could do for the program was to get out of it." [147] Harding saw a general set of hostile attitudes at play that soured relations. "Sarge was having a lot of external Executive Branch problems. Caused more by his people than by Sarge, I must say. That is an almost overriding contempt and arrogance. Contempt for and arrogance toward bureaucracies in Labor, HEW, Bureau of Indian Affairs, all the rest of them. These people—I never have really seen anything as arrogant as I encountered with the staff in meetings with these other people."[148]

The strong centrifugal forces swirling in and about the poverty program, ranging from competition over turf to the hostile attitudes of government officials toward others, were foreshadowed in the competition and tensions of late 1963 and early 1964 when the poverty program was being developed. Their administrative implications were not seriously considered, however. According to Sundquist, "very little attention" was paid to coordination issues.[149] He was convinced that OEO would fail as a coordinator when Shriver announced to the planning group that he had won the right to run the Job Corps. "My reaction . . . was, 'Oh God! Here goes the concept of an Executive Office coordinating agency.'"[150] For Sundquist, operations and coordination were in fundamental contradiction.

His premonition proved to be correct. OEO's involvement in operations heightened a sense of competition among the various agencies and distracted it from its coordination responsibilities. Furthermore, Shriver was uninterested "in being anybody's chief of staff for an internal government-wide coordination role."[151] In fact, OEO did not have the capacity to serve successfully in a coordinator's role. Its franchise to coordinate was not an exclusive one. In late 1966 Shriver forwarded to Califano a memorandum from Perrin with the annotation, "Here's a glimpse of reality in the bureaucracy!" Perrin's basic point was that the growing emphasis on improved coordination was imperiled by "too many coordinators and too many conflicting mechanisms." He noted that since 1964, in addition to the Economic Opportunity Council, the following had been established: the President's Committee on Rural Poverty, chaired by the Agriculture secretary; the President's Committee on Manpower, chaired by the Labor secretary; and the Department of Housing and Urban Development's convenor order, which authorized its secretary to initiate meetings on urban problems and to take a lead in framing coordinated responses. (Soon there was to be a similar order for rural problems vesting convenor authority in the secretary of Agriculture.) Perrin also noted increased coordination efforts on the part of BOB.[152] Indeed, Perrin's list was incomplete. It did not include, for example, a cabinet committee on employment established in 1963, the coordination role of the Commerce secretary in economic development, and the role in coordinating summer youth programs played by presidential task forces, the vice president, and later a cabinet group on urban problems again led by Humphrey. He also might have mentioned a host of lower-level interagency committees that linked OEO and other departments and agencies.

When Perrin wrote his memorandum, it was clear that the presumptively premier instrument for coordinating the war on poverty, the Economic Opportunity Council, was not working. Its chairman, Shriver, did not become a "coordinator of the coordinators."[153] Although President Johnson joined the first meeting of the council, he neither met with it thereafter nor took steps to make it an effective force. The council met about twenty times through 1966, but departments and agencies began to send third- and fourth-level representatives rather than principals. Although OEO prepared the agenda, other agencies were to bring their poverty program problems to the council for discussion. They did not do this.[154] Whatever early vitality the council attained appears to have been contributed by Vice President Humphrey, who attended regularly. The administrative history of OEO states: "The council was not an unalloyed success, largely because of the lack of full-time permanent staff and the reluctance of agencies and departments to commit problems to such a forum."[155] For all practical purposes, the EOC ceased to function in 1967.

Shriver's own assessment was less qualified. "In my judgment," he wrote in late 1966, "the Economic Opportunity Council has been a rather complete failure to date. . . . It was doomed to failure from the beginning. . . . Coordination and direction by a superior is feasible. Coordination and direction by a peer is possible. Coordination and direction by a subordinate is not possible. Since I am not a cabinet officer it was ridiculous to think that I could be the chairman of a group of cabinet officers and expect that this group would ever . . . be a productive mechanism."[156]

His inferior status undoubtedly was a limitation on both the EOC and on OEO's own capacity to coordinate. Another factor of considerable importance was the absence of effective fiscal sanctions that could be applied to recalcitrant departments and agencies. Although the funds appropriated for Economic Opportunity Act programs were theoretically under the control of OEO, in fact they never were. According to Frederick M. Bohen of Califano's staff, Congress in 1966 "torpedoed" OEO's budgetary leverage over employment and adult education programs by making changes in the act.[157] Finally, it should be stressed that the OEO budget was a very small part of the total resources involved in the war on poverty. The estimates in

Table 5. *Estimated Federal Funds for Programs Assisting the Poor, Selected Fiscal Years: 1961–1970 (in billions)*

	Actual			Estimated	
	1961	1964	1968	1969	1970
Education					
OEO			$0.6	$0.5	$0.5
Other agencies	$0.1	$0.1	1.7	1.7	1.9
Manpower training and employment					
OEO			0.8	0.7	0.7
OEO/Labor			0.1	0.4	0.5
Other agencies	0.1	0.2	0.7	0.9	1.2
Health					
OEO			0.1	0.1	0.1
Other agencies	0.7	1.0	4.0	4.9	5.7
Financial assistance and maintenance					
OEO					
Other agencies	8.3	9.8	12.4	12.9	13.5
Other assistance					
OEO			0.5	0.5	0.5
Other agencies	0.5	0.7	1.2	1.8	2.6
Total Federal Assistance	9.8	11.9	22.1	24.4	27.2

Note: Totals may not add, due to rounding.
Source: General Accounting Office, *Review of Economic Opportunity Programs,* Report to the Congress of the United States, 91st Cong., 1st sess., 1969, p. 22.

Table 5 suggest that OEO provided less than 10 percent of federal assistance to the poor in fiscal year 1968. The GAO report estimated that this was about 5 percent of the total in that year when state, local, and private resources devoted to the alleviation of poverty were counted.

Impediments to Coordination in Communities

By late 1966 and early 1967 it was quite clear that, in general, community action agencies were not effectively performing the coordination function at the local level. There were several reasons. Impaired coordination in Washington was one. Another was the context in which the agencies were first established. When implementation of the Economic Opportunity Act began, OEO maintained a fast, even frenzied, pace in approving them. Congress had removed statutory language that came close to requiring local planning before funding. In OEO little initial attention was given to local concepts and plans for coordination. The mood at OEO was tempestuous, and the inclination was to move full steam ahead. The mood is suggested by Shriver's description of the first-round processing of community action applications. Top staff met two or three evenings a week working through stacks of forms submitted from around the country. The atmosphere was tense, and anger often grew out of disagreements, causing staff members to stalk out. "They'd be so goddamn mad at another guy they couldn't stand to be in the room." As arguments grew more intense, Shriver

> sat at the other end of the room and . . . frankly . . . enjoyed it. I thought it was good because people felt so deeply about what they were doing. . . . You never saw such zeal, or such objectivity, or such dedication to the needs of the poor. . . . They were fervent, they were emotional, they were dedicated, they worked like hell, they were strained to the breaking point. Sure, they had fights. I thought that was a tremendous manifestation of the whole élan, or the whole desire, what produced the goddamn results.[158]

Administrative complexities, including the matter of local coordination, did not receive careful attention in this atmosphere.

Another contextual factor impeding coordination was the taxed administrative capacities of state and local governments. As Eli Ginzberg and Robert M. Solow put it retrospectively, "The sorry fact is that most state and local governments . . . are poorly structured and poorly staffed to carry out new and innovative tasks. They have a hard time even meeting their routine commitments."[159] At the state level poor coordination of state programs had implications for coordination at the community level. A paper prepared for the Heineman task force drew the connection. "Institutional barriers to program integration and coordination by CAAs at the local level often trace back to rigidities in administration introduced at the State level by education and health departments, welfare agencies, and the State employment service."[160] It concluded, "A powerful coordinating, noncategorical agency at the state level may be indispensable to effect local coordination of Federal programs funded through State agencies."[161] At about the same time, Wirtz made a similar observation to Heineman in reference to programs for which he was responsible. He commented, "There is a *minimum* of working relationship between the *state* Employment Services and Vocational Education agencies, and a *maximum* of 'vested interest' approach on the part of these agencies at the state level."[162]

The state employment services were particularly difficult to deal with in both state capitals and in communities, even though they were intended to play a major role in the new and reoriented manpower programs. According to Ruttenberg, many state program administrators felt that it was not "their job to deal with welfare recipients, or to deal with the long-term unemployed, or to deal with . . . those individuals who have been less fortunate in receiving education and training."[163] Their preferred clienteles were employers and workers who had the skills sought by employers. There was strong resistance to working with community action agencies and the unskilled.

The very existence of community action programs clearly challenged the state employment services and numerous other established programs. To the extent that the new agencies were perceived as competitors, coordination under their auspices was an especially unappealing option for these programs. It would be even less attractive to the extent that mobilization of the poor and social protest activities were prominent on the community action agenda. As Bohen put it, "Established agencies, ranging from Boards of Education to Welfare Departments, the Employment Service and United Fund agencies, were not prepared to be told that their programs were failures; they found it difficult to accept attack graciously, or submit to coordination by a new, untried agency."[164]

In the face of such reactions, community action agencies often lacked the institutional capacity to assert themselves effectively. In Sundquist's words, they suffered from "multiple disabilities."[165] One was the conflicting goals of concurrently striking at "political poverty" and remedying "economic poverty."[166] A balance in emphasis was struck at different points from community to community, but to the extent that programmatic success was emphasized, political objectives suffered. To the extent that political objectives were emphasized, performance of functions such as coordination was hampered. In addition, many agencies lacked administrative capacity and program expertise. Staffing limitations not only made it difficult to undertake complex coordinating tasks but also gave excuses to those wishing to stay away from the community action umbrella. The nature of the guidance and assistance provided to local agencies from national and state levels was also a source of weakness. Bohen reported that only two state poverty agencies, despite quite visible needs, productively assisted in planning and coordination at the local level.[167] At about the same time, Shriver also complained of a lack of state assistance to local agencies.[168] According to community action agency officials, OEO itself was the source of substantial administrative problems at the local level, further hampering coordination efforts. They complained of red tape, delays in processing applications, poor communication of requirements, and inconsistency and instability in regulations.[169]

OEO and other agencies, according to local officials, were also inattentive to preference requirements, which were potentially among the more effective instruments for coordination of diverse programs at the community level. The U.S. Conference of Mayors' study found that OEO's failure to implement the preference provision for projects approved by local agencies as part of their comprehensive programs "has caused serious concern among those who have worked hard to develop umbrella-like agencies."[170] OEO was neither inclined nor able to force Labor and HEW to support projects of community action agencies out of the EOA funds they administered. The departments preferred to deploy funds independently of the community action umbrella through their own channels.[171] Nor did the preference requirement work outside the EOA program structure. Bohen found "that only about 35 community action agencies out of the 1000 in the country have attracted funds from sources outside the Economic Opportunity Act of 1964."[172]

OEO itself emphasized program operations in communities, not the coordination function. As early as January 1965 a BOB memorandum noted, "The original concept of the local CAP agencies . . . was that they would plan and coordinate. To the extent they become operators it seems . . . we have merely confused organization and multiplied competition among local agencies, rather than providing a mechanism for planning and coordination."[173] They did become operators, principally of national-emphasis programs conceived and promoted by OEO in Washington. Viewing the situation from a staff position, Levine judged that top leadership in the agency thought that "national emphasis programs were a good thing and should be encouraged."[174] As Perrin noted, OEO's encouragement was buttressed by "congressional interests and effort." Such encouragement was basically precipitated by "the inability of many Community Action agencies to truly effectively handle large-scale programs" on an independent, self-initiated basis.[175]

In 1965 four national-emphasis programs were developed by OEO: Head Start, Upward Bound, legal services, and foster grandparents. Head Start was especially popular. The increasing support it gained at the community level was reflected in Congress. In 1965, with OEO's approval, funds were specifically designated for Head Start. Subsequently, all communities receiving OEO funds were required to establish Head Start programs. Other national-emphasis programs were specifically mentioned in the act by Congress in 1966: legal services, comprehensive health services (neighborhood health centers), emergency loans to individuals, and subprofessional training programs. For the first time, Congress earmarked funds for specific community action programs. In 1967 the legislation listed eight such programs, and although some discretion in funding was allowed, OEO continued to earmark on its own.[176] What started out in 1964 as essentially a block grant with considerable local autonomy increasingly developed into categorical grants through earmarking. The second annual report of OEO, in 1966, stated: "We have slowly evolved out of the New Deal philosophy of welfare into a new federalism whereby the work of a democratic government is not of finding things to do for the people, but to let the people do things for themselves."[177] The national-emphasis programs, in fact, went in a different direction. Many of the officials in Washington, in the regional offices, and in the communities who were responsible for community action matters felt that earmarking greatly hampered innovation and experimentation and did not allow people to make their own choices.[178]

It is not possible to ascertain the degree to which community agencies would have had a different mix of local programs in the absence of earmarking by Congress or encouragement from OEO to undertake national-emphasis programs. But the earmarking exemplifies the way in which Congress and sometimes grantor agencies, after authorizing a considerable degree of local autonomy, subsequently proceeded to whittle it away. There is nothing inexplicable about this behavior. Members of Congress can secure more constituency support from categoricals than from block grants. Interest groups tend to coalesce around specific issues; support for research on cancer, heart disease, or stroke, for example, is easier to mobilize than support for general "health research." Nor is it certain that community action agencies would have been stronger coordinators without the national-emphasis programs. Nevertheless, the easy ac-

cessibility of the programs early in OEO's history provided a rationale for neglecting the coordination dimension.

Conclusions

The Economic Opportunity Act was partially the product of a reconstitutive and nationalist reform impulse shared by certain policy
professionals in the Kennedy and Johnson administrations. These
reformers were suspicious of established national bureaucracies and
their state and local counterparts, bureaucracies that principally had
their roots in the New Deal and the precepts of cooperative federalism. The administrative state contemplated by the reformers was
quite different from the one then in place. In early planning, they
sought an approach to attacking poverty backed by national power
that bypassed or subjugated these bureaucracies. However, the power
of entrenched institutions precluded this, and they were assigned
prominent places in the poverty effort. Something of a reconstitutive spirit remained in the act nevertheless. It is reflected, among
other ways, in the idea of a multifunctional attack on poverty, in the
implicit challenge to old-line departments and agencies to change
government thinking by placing a high priority on the problems of
the neediest in society, and in creating the possibility of redistribut-
ing power in communities through the participation of the poor
themselves in program implementation.

Serious political and administrative problems were encountered
in implementing the act. The political problems were managed with
considerable success, as in the visits to governors, due in no small
part to presidential effort. Administrative problems were less trac-
table as established institutional interests clashed with reform ideas.
In part they were caused by the president's political decision to give
old-line agencies a share of the action. His equally political decision
to place OEO in immediate presidential orbit did not provide it with
adequate means to establish order. Nor could the Economic Opportunity Council perform a central presidential management function.
The Bureau of the Budget was unable to fill the gap, as the collapse
of its effort to redirect the community action program in 1965 at-
tests. The political reaction to its initiative was too strong. Even
after this experience, Bailey's proposal for strengthened central management in late 1965 was set aside. In coordination, then, "partisan
mutual adjustment" seemed to emphasize partisanship more than
adjustment.[179]

As the next chapter will show, substantial effort was invested in
improving cooperation and coordination in order to advance the

basic purposes of the war on poverty. Problems were not ignored, but what appeared to be a key problem—a weak capacity for providing program unity, consistency, and coherence at the presidential level—was not resolved. In the end, the power inherent in established intergovernmental and intragovernmental administrative arrangements appeared to be a major victor in the war Johnson declared in 1964.

4. The Halting Search for Administrative Order in Poverty and Related Programs

Administrative conflicts and coordination problems generated by the Economic Opportunity Act were persistent irritants in the Washington executive complex and at subnational levels. Officials in presidential offices received a constant flow of information about them. Attention to problems, however, was more spasmodic and groping than sustained and systematic. Although there was keen awareness of deficiencies, only modest and piecemeal corrective steps were taken. President Johnson confronted administrative issues on occasion, usually without decisive results. White House aides and Bureau of the Budget (BOB) officials were involved more frequently, often prompted by task force reports that underscored implementation problems and coordination breakdowns. By and large, the day-to-day struggle to smooth operations was left to the departments and agencies themselves.

Focus on Washington

To the extent that a search for administrative order was undertaken by Johnson and his staff, the focus was almost always on the Washington dimension, although the implications of problems there for subnational levels and intergovernmental relations were usually recognized. The presidential response to administrative problems took several forms. They included mediation by presidential agents, promotion of administrative changes in departments, direct presidential coordination in special circumstances, and development of options for major organizational changes.

Mediation and Promotion

White House staff and BOB officials were frequently involved in resolving disputes within the government. Bertram M. Harding, an

Office of Economic Opportunity (OEO) official, felt that, beyond what the departments and agencies did on their own, "Any real coordination . . . is effectuated by Califano and his minions."[1] According to C. Robert Perrin, also of OEO, starting in late 1966 the Bureau of the Budget was "becoming more and more active in the coordinating role," though not always with positive results.[2] One mechanism was an annual, wide-ranging interagency manpower program review.[3] The bureau's actions were not necessarily welcomed. Early in 1967 Joe Califano received a complaint from Secretary of Labor W. Willard Wirtz. As Califano told the president, "He believes the coordination problems of the Federal Government are severe . . . but does not believe the Budget Bureau should play such a strong role in trying to work them out."[4]

The bureau and the White House also sponsored administrative changes in OEO, Health, Education, and Welfare (HEW), and Labor. In the case of OEO, two particular problems were general administrative disorder and the role of regional offices. In February 1966 the BOB director commissioned Harding, then deputy commissioner of the Internal Revenue Service, to do a management survey of OEO. After it was completed, Harding became deputy director, then acting director when R. Sargent Shriver was named ambassador to France in 1968. Perrin concluded that Harding brought "more stability to the administrative operation, not only here but in the regions." Harding emphasized delegation of authority to the regions "to minimize . . . the red tape involved and confusion in bringing things here to Washington."[5]

OEO established seven regional field offices in 1965, and these offices, to an extent, helped to smooth administrative relations with the governors and the state economic opportunity offices. They were impeded in dealing with departments such as Housing and Urban Development (HUD), HEW, and Labor because of differences in regional boundaries and field headquarters locations.

The OEO regional offices were conceived as the major linkage between the community action agencies and OEO in Washington. They were to serve as providers of budget and programmatic assistance to the local agencies. OEO gave the regional offices considerable autonomy and responsibility for assuring that the national-emphasis programs were properly integrated into local budgets.[6] The regional offices, as defenders of the community action agencies, were also involved in reducing the processing time for funding; they had authority to approve local agency budgets. Regional officials did not regard themselves simply as interpreters and enforcement officials for regulations forged in Washington. They reported directly to the deputy director and director of OEO, and they also consulted with the assistant directors in charge of specific programs.

The major administrative change affecting regional offices was to give them additional authority continually from 1965 through 1968, often over the opposition of officials based in Washington. The Bureau of the Budget was a major supporter of decentralization. In sending forward a set of delegations for presidential approval in 1968, a BOB memorandum stated: "The decentralization of authority embodied in these delegations is long overdue; it has been the cause of a great deal of controversy within the agency. The greatest objection has come from program directors."[7] Many issues with respect to funding, monitoring, and other aspects of regional office operations remained to be clarified at the end of Johnson's presidency.[8] Nevertheless, it was Perrin's view that overall "the regional system worked reasonably well and frictions were at a minimum."[9]

In HEW and Labor, the problem was to adapt departmental organization to handle the new responsibilities imposed by both the spirit and the programs of the Economic Opportunity Act. In HEW the major step was to consolidate all social and rehabilitation services into one administrative complex. In Labor there was an effort to transform a number of highly independent old-line bureaus into an integrated manpower unit. The Labor initiative was especially challenging.

A Wirtz memorandum circulated in the White House in late 1967 noted a number of central considerations that drove his past and future organizational efforts. "The increasing number of training and work-training programs involving Federal financing *require* that there be a *single* strong central point through which all such programs are administered." Furthermore, "This is particularly essential in connnection with the increasing importance of projects in which resources of various authorizations are brought together and in which various agencies (Federal, D/L, State, local; and public and private) are frequently involved."[10]

With presidential support, especially from BOB, Wirtz was able to make considerable progress toward a muscled Manpower Administration in Washington and to make inroads into regional arrangements.[11] Completion of the reorganization effort by subjugating the U.S. Employment Service and its state extensions to departmental authority was foiled in late 1968, however. As Califano stated in a memorandum intended for the president, Wirtz's plan was that "the Manpower Administration . . . will be unified and greatly strengthened by merging the Employment Service and the Bureau of Work Training Programs, which now have overlapping functions and duplicative staffs, and by establishing a single line of authority from the Manpower Administrator to the Regional Manpower Administrator."[12]

Because of prior presidential statements and the backing of BOB and White House staff, Wirtz thought he had Johnson's personal support for completing his reorganization project. But when Califano asked the president if an announcement could be made, he refused permission. Nevertheless, Wirtz issued the reorganization order, precipitating a tense conflict between Johnson, who wanted the order rescinded, and his Labor secretary, who was determined to go forward. Precisely why Johnson objected to the order is unknown, but it probably had more to do with timing than substance. The organizational changes proposed by Wirtz were sure to draw strong objections from the states, thus generating political controversy in the midst of a presidential election year. In fact, a White House directive was under preparation stating that no action should be taken that might complicate the presidential transition that would come several months later. After an awkward period of maneuvering, it was announced that the reorganization was deferred pending consultation with the governors. Completion of manpower reorganization would have to wait until the Nixon presidency.[13]

Presidential Coordination

In addition to support for certain organizational changes and limited interventions to resolve disputes, there were a number of initiatives that directly addressed interdepartmental coordination problems. Some of them, such as the President's Committee on Manpower and the Housing and Urban Development and Agriculture convenor orders, were not a great success and, as noted in the previous chapter, may have aggravated problems. The effort to coordinate summer youth employment programs aimed at the disadvantaged was an exception.

It began in 1965 when Johnson asked the vice president to chair a cabinet committee on employment. Other members were the secretaries of Defense, Commerce, and Labor and the head of the National Aeronautics and Space Administration. In mid-May of that year Johnson received the committee's outline of a campaign that was conceived in Washington but was to be implemented at the local level. The purpose was to provide public and private summer jobs for young people.[14] The campaign was announced by the president on 22 May. Characteristic of the times, the specifics of the campaign were still being debated by BOB, Labor, and others in the middle of June when many prospective enrollees were already out of school.[15]

A special summer effort to employ disadvantaged youth between the ages of sixteen and twenty-one was to be an annual event for the remainder of Johnson's presidency. Seen as a key element in the war on poverty, each year it received special presidential attention. The 1966 program was planned by an expanded task force again chaired by the vice president. It pulled together resources from Labor, HEW, Commerce, and OEO and included an explicit scheme for field coordination.[16] Although work began earlier than in the previous year, program plans were perceived, especially by state and local agencies and others responsible for implementation, to be the product of another crash undertaking. Subsequently, coordination and planning became more systematic. Responsibility for the 1967 program was given to a task force headed by Shriver. It completed its work at a meeting in Califano's office in December 1966. One outgrowth of the task force's work was an executive order that established the President's Council on Youth Opportunity and a summer program staff structure.[17] The council, chaired by the vice president and made up of the heads of ten departments and agencies, came into being on 9 March 1967. Although task forces supplemented the council's work in planning the 1967 and 1968 programs, the council and its staff were the main focus for coordination. Its December 1968 report described considerable improvement in planning, evaluation, and liaison with state and local governments.[18]

Unfortunately, the incremental development of a fairly strong device for coordinating summer activities was not matched in the overall coordination of the poverty program.[19] Although there were numerous proposals and some formal changes in arrangements, no real headway was made. As early as December 1964, Shriver attempted to overcome the weaknesses in the Economic Opportunity Council (EOC) scheme. According to White House aide S. Douglass Cater, Jr., at that time he sought "a sweeping mandate from the President to coordinate all 'poverty-related programs.'"[20] Failing to elicit a positive response, Shriver returned several weeks later with a proposal to amend the Economic Opportunity Act to give the OEO director "positive authority to coordinate and direct specified poverty-related efforts through a programming system."[21] Again, no action ensued.

The coordination issue arose again toward the end of 1966 when Ben W. Heineman's Task Force on Government Organization looked at the war on poverty. Shriver was now arguing, without success, for a Social and Economic Development Council built along the lines of the National Security Council. Its membership would be the same as the EOC's, but the chairman would be named by the president. An executive secretary, also a special assistant to the president, would direct a small staff. OEO would be released from its general coordination responsibilities.[22] The Heineman task force concurred in the proposition that OEO's role should be changed. At that time it favored assigning coordinating responsibilities to a special assistant to the president and removing OEO from the Executive Office of the President.[23]

The Heineman approach was not accepted. One possible reason is suggested by a memorandum the president received from Lawrence F. O'Brien, then postmaster general and before that head of congressional liaison in the White House. Johnson asked O'Brien to look at the Heineman recommendation from a congressional perspective. O'Brien did not like it because presidential coordination would "involve the White House publicly in every OEO tangle."[24]

Instead, it was decided to seek statutory changes in the Economic Opportunity Council in conjunction with reauthorization of the Economic Opportunity Act in 1967. The changes proposed were similar to those suggested by Shriver, and Congress accepted them. In revised form, the director of OEO was the only EOC member designated by law. Others were to be named by the president, as was the chairman. Another provision authorized an independent staff for the council. It was to be headed by an executive secretary, also appointed by the president. Although enacted, the changes came to naught. Prodded by OEO, in April 1968 Califano finally prepared materials to send to the president for establishing the new EOC. Harding was to be named chairman, and James Gaither, one of Califano's assistants, was to be executive secretary.[25] But revival of the EOC became enmeshed in other related schemes for altering the poverty program, and the legislative revisions were never put into place. Another probable factor was the president's lack of interest; in reviewing one draft of the 1967 poverty message, he struck out the EOC language, but it was later reinserted.

It might be useful to pause at this point and consider the sustained and serious presidential attention given to coordinating summer programs in contrast to the half-hearted concern for coordination in the broader sense. In reviewing Shriver's 1964 request for a stronger coordination mandate, Cater cautioned presidential aide Bill Moyers. "Unless I miss my guess, there is fodder for a first-class bureaucratic war in this proposal."[26] Strong, overarching coordination of the entire poverty enterprise was a major threat to other departments and agencies and was potentially quite disruptive.

Another factor concerns the political interests of the president. In the case of summer programs, there was a strong interest in minimizing, if not precluding, summer unrest and disorder in the cities by providing jobs for young people. Public concern commanded presidential involvement, and to the extent that government action produced positive results, there would be political credit. Conversely, urban unrest would impose political costs. The prominent role played by the vice president was only one indication of the importance the White House attached to the summer programs.[27]

In contrast, many thought that the president had a good deal to lose politically by maintaining too close an association with certain poverty program operations. Some also thought it would not be good for the programs. At one point in 1966 Schultze provided Califano with a rationale for presidential restraint in regard to community action programs (CAP). In discussing coordination problems, he noted that OEO had not had close enough contact with the president to allow it to be an effective coordinator. But, he continued, "If CAP is close to the president, he loses by his association, and CAP will lose its freedom of action because of the sensitivity of its relationship with the president."[28] From this perspective, a strong presidential investment in coordination at the top, which was a precondition for successful coordination in the field, was questionable for both programmatic and political reasons.

Organizational Changes

Whereas amelioration of administrative complexity through a strengthened capacity for central coordination was at issue from time to time, amelioration through lessening the need for strong central coordination was an option more seriously and frequently entertained. The means usually considered was devolving program responsibilities from OEO through limited or comprehensive reorganizations. The underlying idea was to pack related programs "into a single institutional box."[29] To the extent this was done, as one assessment of the prospective liquidation of OEO claimed, "It would have the virtue of reducing some problems of coordination in Washington and the field, and of lowering the temperature, or eliminating some long-standing institutional feuds."[30]

In fact, almost from the start the concept of "spinoff" figured

prominently in discussions of the poverty effort's organizational future. The idea was that OEO would serve as an agent for innovation.
As innovative programs matured, they would be transferred to other
parts of the government, freeing the poverty agency from routine
responsibilities and facilitating a continuing creative role for it.
Whether the rationale was to improve coordination or to protect
OEO's role as innovator, however, the poverty agency generally
tended to resist any diminution of its authority.

Head Start, a prominent case in point, illustrates how budget considerations, constituency, and other political concerns become intertwined to influence organizational choices.[31] Head Start, from its beginning, was one of the most popular OEO programs, emphasizing
as it did nutritional, educational, and health objectives in the summer program for preschool children. Organizational machinery and
staffing were planned even before the Economic Opportunity Act
was adopted by Congress. Its first-year enrollment, which was anticipated to be 100,000, actually exceeded half a million. As soon as
budget appropriations were in hand, OEO sent letters to superinten-
dents of schools and public and private welfare agencies inviting
their application for grants. Early in 1965 Lady Bird Johnson hosted a
White House tea for the wives of all governors to enlist their cooperation and support. A committee of congressional wives organized support in their districts. Federal management interns volunteered their
weekends to work with small communities in the preparation of
grant applications. Community action agencies, where they were organized, made Head Start a priority in the first years. (Later, there
were intraagency conflicts on this point because community action
agencies felt that they were deprived of funds as OEO appropriations
were earmarked by Congress for Head Start efforts operated outside
their jurisdiction.)

Initially it had been planned within OEO to transfer Head Start to
HEW after five years. With its early success, however, many, including Republicans in Congress, concluded that an earlier move was
justified. There was White House attention to the question early in
1965, but OEO opposed a change.[32] The widespread support that
Head Start received offset some of the "scandal" stories about the
Job Corps and community action that were in the news columns.
Head Start, on the other hand, was receiving favorable reviews. In
accordance with the original plan, Jule M. Sugarman, assistant director of OEO for Head Start, pursued the possibility of delegation to
some other department or agency, focusing on the U.S. Office of Education. Others, however, were not anxious to transfer the program

there, claiming that Head Start served multiple objectives and was not merely an education program. At that point a decision was made by the director of OEO to retain Head Start, believing that it would help the agency's other programs in appropriations committee hearings, especially among members from the South, where the program was very popular. Other justifications for retaining Head Start in OEO were that it would aid in organizing community action agencies in the South, promote their integration, and counter the power of "racist" Southern school boards.[33] It was not until Nixon became president in 1969 that Head Start was moved to HEW.

Perhaps the sharpest sustained struggle over spinoff concerned manpower programs; it was fought from late 1963 to 1969. Experts who examined the programs favored relocation more often than not. In 1967 the Heineman task force recommended their consolidation in HEW. At about the same time, a study by Sar A. Levitan and Garth Mangum urged their placement in Labor.[34] However, a presidential task force chaired by George P. Shultz, then of the University of Chicago and later a cabinet officer in the Nixon and Reagan administrations, opted to retain them in OEO.[35] In the aftermath of these assessments, as the legislative program for 1968 was being developed, Labor made a concerted effort to bring the EOA manpower programs under its immediate jurisdiction. OEO successfully resisted, and no major changes were proposed to Congress.

Perrin cites several reasons for OEO's stout opposition to spinoffs. It was felt that the agency could not survive the loss of its popular programs; special concerns for the poor might be lost if OEO were not in the picture; and opportunities to draw more programs under the community action umbrella would be lessened.[36] Harding added an additional consideration, the Shriver factor. "Sarge was very ambivalent about . . . spinoff," he said. "He would constantly reiterate the fact that this agency was set up to innovate, to develop, to mature, and then to hand programs over to the existing agencies of government. The only problem was that in Sarge's mind these programs never really reached that point. . . . He'd kill me if he ever thought I had characterized him as a bureaucrat, but he really was; it tore his soul out to take one of these pieces and give it away to somebody else."[37]

Many in OEO, including Perrin, felt that the White House generally supported it on the spinoff issue. Staff there "was quite protective. . . . They helped us resist raids from other departments." He might have added that the White House staff also helped OEO to resist shifts in program responsibility to HEW and Labor that were recommended by the Heineman Task Force on Government Organization.[38]

Protective though the White House might have seemed, at several points its occupants gave serious consideration to abolishing OEO. That option first arose in late 1965 as organizational plans for HUD were being prepared. Heineman and Walter P. Reuther, head of the United Auto Workers, suggested that community action be placed in the new department and that other OEO programs also be relocated. Califano was enthusiastic about the plan as he described it to the president.[39] Apparently Johnson was not opposed. Subsequently, the necessary delegations were drafted, and a reorganization order was prepared for his signature, but action was not taken. Kermit Gordon, director of BOB, was opposed, and news of the pending changes leaked to the press.[40]

White House interest in abolishing OEO surfaced again in the summer of 1966. Moyers and Califano asked Schultze of BOB for his views on the future of the agency. Harding's management review was underway at the time. Schultze's preference was for a comprehensive spinoff of programs, including a transfer of community action to HEW.[41] Work in the White House on massive organizational changes proceeded during the next few days. Moyers, in a memorandum to Califano on the topic, noted, "As you know, the President is pressing on this."[42] Again, prospects for change were dimmed by leaks. *Washington Post* columnist Marianne Means revealed, "President Johnson has secretly ordered the Budget Bureau to begin a quiet survey that may be the first step toward the dismantlement of the anti-poverty program as it now exists."[43] The disclosure came at a crucial time in congressional consideration of amendments to the Economic Opportunity Act. Moyers reported to the president that in Congress "the opponents of the War on Poverty are making hay" with the Means column.[44] The administrative review by Harding continued, but the reorganization option lost currency for the moment.

It resurfaced again in early 1968. In February, at the direction of the president, Califano and Charles J. Zwick, now the BOB director, prepared a redistribution of EOA programs along the lines suggested by Schultze in the summer of 1966.[45] Adding to the movement to make major changes, a short time later Wilber J. Cohen, acting secretary at HEW, proposed to the president that all or most of OEO's responsibilities be shifted to his department.[46] By early April the White House had received a brief from the Department of Justice on the legal methods to be used in effecting program transfers.[47] There were no leaks this time, but any chances of change were killed by the president's decision not to seek reelection and by his opposition to making major alterations in governmental arrangements during the remaining months of his administration.

Focus on Communities

There were relatively few initiatives mounted in Washington that directly confronted problems in the coordination of war on poverty efforts at the community level. One, the establishment of neighborhood centers, received strong presidential backing. Others, mostly concerning manpower programs, in general were departmental initiatives.

In a speech given in Syracuse, New York, on 19 August 1966, Johnson announced, "I'm going to ask Secretary Weaver [of HUD] to set as his goal the establishment, in every ghetto of America, of a neighborhood center to service the people who live in that area." Shriver was also directed to increase the number of neighborhood legal service centers.[48] The president's instructions had their origins in the report of a task force on public assistance that completed its work in the fall of 1965. Schultze, commenting on its recommendations, said in a memorandum to Califano, "At the present time the provision of many social services is highly fragmented. The 'one stop' center is aimed at concentrating and coordinating responsibility for these services in one location so that poor families are not bandied from one place to another." He suggested that HEW, OEO, and Labor be asked to prepare a joint plan.[49]

It quickly became clear that, although improved access and coordination were relatively uncontroversial objectives, there were competing ideas about exactly what the centers should be.[50] OEO claimed that its developing network of neighborhood service centers should be the vehicle for drawing social programs together at the community level. Labor and HEW thought it would be better to experiment with different types of centers before opting for a particular approach.

According to Califano, the president's Syracuse remarks precipitated a "bureaucratic Donnybrook."[51] When Johnson spoke, staff from BOB, HEW, HUD, OEO, and Labor were grappling with the specifics of the neighborhood center concept. In the aftermath of the speech, another interagency group led by HUD was established at the president's direction to work on a plan.[52] In the process, departmental and agency interests in promoting client access to their own programs overpowered the coordination objective. Warfare continued through the development of the legislative program for

1967. One part of the problem was that, like OEO, a number of departments already had their own community outposts to be defended. Labor had approximately 140 youth opportunity centers scattered about the country, for example. Another part of the problem was that additional programs were promoting the center concept in their own behalf. In January 1967, when a special message to Congress on older Americans was being drafted, Shriver dashed off a personal note to Califano. Responding to language in the draft message, he remarked: "All we need is another set of 'comprehensive centers'—OEO now has 600. Ellen Winston wants a whole set of 'Comprehensive' Social Service Centers. The educators want Comprehensive Community Schools replete with health & welfare services. The MDs have got 60 comprehensive Health Centers in the works, etc.!"[53]

Similar disputes over language about neighborhood centers arose during the preparation of the poverty and health messages.[54] After much debate, two directives were announced in the 1967 poverty message. One instructed the director of OEO, in cooperation with the secretary of HUD and other departments, "to expand and strengthen the development of Neighborhood Multi-Service and Multi-County Centers in the coming fiscal year." The other instructed the director of OEO to cooperate with the secretary of HEW to encourage communities to establish neighborhood health centers.[55]

Comments of administration officials on drafts of the message indicate that, despite a certain surface clarity in language, great disagreement, even confusion, remained. For example, at one point Robert C. Weaver, the HUD secretary, lodged a very strong objection with Califano. "The discussion of neighborhood centers . . . remains unclear. Not only does it fail to acknowledge the full variety of centers now being established, but it also divides authority between HUD and OEO in the model program. As now written, it contradicts the President's assignment of responsibility to me, and more important, would confuse the operation of the present program."[56] Although Weaver's position produced some changes in message language, the underlying problems persisted.

The "centers now being established" mentioned by Weaver numbered fourteen and constituted a pilot program developed by an interagency group operating under fairly close presidential scrutiny. They were to house a variety of poverty programs. The effort floundered. One assessment found that "Federal and local officials were . . . confused, or in disagreement, over what type of neighborhood center would be supported, where the funds would come from," as well as on other points.[57] Beset with bureaucratic conflict and funding problems, according to Califano, "few" of the centers "were ever put in operation."[58] In 1968 the pilot program was folded into the Model Cities undertaking.

In addition to efforts to attain better coordination through physical proximity, a miscellany of rather modest steps were taken that had some broad implications for facilitating program coordination at the local level. Provisions referring to coordination with community action programs were included in the Elementary and Secondary Education Act of 1964, the Housing and Urban Development Act of 1965, and the Public Works and Economic Development Act of the same year. As required by section 613 of the act, OEO published the *Catalog of Federal Programs for Individual and Community Improvement* in 1965; responsibility for it shifted to BOB in 1967. In 1966 OEO was authorized to make grants to states and communities to establish information service centers. No grants were made because of community action budget problems. However, OEO provided technical assistance to several state centers in 1968.[59]

Of greater potential significance, a "checkpoint" procedure was introduced in 1966. OEO negotiated agreements with HUD, HEW, and Labor to give community action agencies a review role in local poverty projects funded by those departments. Under this procedure the local community action agencies could at least comment in advance on the relation to their programs of projects carried out by other agencies. In addition, other departments and agencies and local officials were to comment on community action projects.[60] The procedure was to provide a device that community action agencies might use to give at least partial meaning to the preference requirements. Although the procedures were observed in at least some communities, they had little effect in broadening the scope of community action programs or in enlarging their coordinating capacities.

Because of the number and significance of manpower programs, coordination of them at the local level received rather focused and sustained attention. An important step was taken in October 1965 when the principals of the President's Committee on Manpower established an interagency task force on coordination at the local level. Its initial analysis revealed extensive problems, including program overlaps, duplication, and the failure of agencies in the field to communicate with one another.[61] Subsequently, teams of Labor, HEW, and OEO officials were dispatched to several localities to work on coordination deficiencies.

By late August 1966, teams had conducted field surveys in twenty-eight urban and two rural areas. The results were quite promising. According to a participant, one of the teams' most important functions was to bring "all the various state and city government people together who worked in these programs—and in many cases we introduced them to each other for the first time."[62] Essentially, the teams "negotiated and mediated disputes and abrasions, . . . unclogged a few channels to Washington, and . . . provided clarification in policies and programs."[63] Despite a strong start and a vigorous recommendation from the parent committee that the effort be continued and expanded, other priorities prevailed, and the team approach to ameliorating manpower coordination problems at the local level came to a sudden halt.

One of the priorities that intervened was the concentrated employment program (CEP). During 1966, sparked by Johnson's strong interest in giving special attention to areas where unemployment was very high, Labor began to develop a plan for attacking unemployment in the worst city slums. Consolidation of manpower authorities in the 1967 reauthorization facilitated the establishment of special programs in twenty cities and two rural areas.[64] The idea was to create an "integrated delivery system designed to eliminate, in specific target areas, the problems of diffusion of resources, fragmentation of programs, lack of interprogram cohesion, inadequate social services, and minimal involvement of private industry in the rehabilitation of the severely disadvantaged."[65]

All manpower programs in a community were to be brought together in a unified administrative scheme. Labor and OEO worked out an agreement whereby community action agencies, the presumptive sponsors of the programs, would subcontract them to the Employment Service, the presumptive supplier of manpower services. As the Task Force on Urban Employment Opportunities observed, this approach "moves the CAA (community action agency) closer to its intended role of coordinator and evaluator of programs. It likewise puts the pressure on the Employment Service to deliver manpower services to the poor."[66] In each target area, leadership responsibilities were placed in a representative of the Manpower Administration supported by an interagency team of Labor, HEW, and OEO officials.[67] After the agreement was forged, Washington applied strong pressure on the Employment Service to be more cooperative with community action agencies.[68]

A BOB program review in mid-1968 found "that CEP is better than what went before (the scattering of Federal project grants throughout a community)." It appeared that "the CEP concept has proven to be at least moderately successful: institutions are in place, people are being trained, program linkages have been improved—*and, as a result, institutional changes are occurring in the ES, city governments and other local institutions."* It was not clear, however, whether there was potential for the concentrated employment approach to "emerge as *the system* for the delivery of manpower services."[69] Despite generally favorable reviews of the CEP, the resources available for the program shrunk as a result of central budgetary decisions. It proved impossible to sustain fully, much less expand and improve, this promising experimental effort.[70]

Although there were problems in implementation, the concentrated employment program preserved at least a nominal role for community action agencies in coordinating manpower programs in selected cities.[71] But even as the concentrated employment program was being put into place, a new coordinating scheme was being developed that did not provide a place for community action organizations. The scheme was the cooperative area manpower system (CAMPS). Initiated by Labor, the system was to link manpower program planning at national, state, and local levels in order to prevent duplication and to improve effectiveness. An early BOB evaluation concluded, "CAMPS has provided a good start in pulling together the Federal manpower effort especially at the local level."[72] Initially established through voluntary interagency arrangements, the system was formalized by an executive order signed by Johnson on 15 August 1968 that directed relevant departments and agencies to participate in the system.[73] Because of objections registered by HEW and HUD, the final version was without a provision that, in the words of Secretary of HEW Cohen, would "require each Federal department or agency to invoke sanctions such as withholding approval of State plans or the withholding of funds in the absence of approved CAMPS plans."[74] Thus, the order was more an exhortation than a forceful device for planning and coordinating action.

Despite continuing bureaucratic conflict over coordination, observers noted significant shifts in the attitudes of program administrators toward the poor that helped to mute conflict. One witness is James C. Gaither, an assistant to Califano. He says, "Despite all the pressure from the White House, the Poverty Program did more to turn the Labor Department around from an organization that served the high school graduate son of the union man to minorities who were disadvantaged; the same thing in Student Aid and HEW; the same thing in the Office of Education."[75] Such shifts had promising implications for coordination, but they were not sufficient to offset the complex of impediments that plagued the war on poverty.

Model Cities

As administration officials continued to confront problems of coordination in Washington and in communities more than two years after the Economic Opportunity Act was passed, a related major effort in the war on poverty was enacted—the Demonstration Cities and Metropolitan Development Act, signed on 3 November 1966.[76]

The Model Cities program benefited from the early experience and mistakes of OEO, especially the difficulties encountered by the community action agencies in their coordinating and community mobilization efforts. It was also in part intended to compensate for the deficiencies of Economic Opportunity Act programs. James C. Sundquist asserts that the most important influence of OEO was "as the forerunner and trial balloon for what was designated as the ultimate flowering of the Johnson Administration's intergovernmental system—Model Cities."[77] In Model Cities, there was provision for community participation, but funds were to be controlled by local public officials. In addition, Model Cities was structured with an intent to better coordinate interagency relations in Washington and interagency relations in the communities.

Origins

Model Cities, as the nomenclature indicates, was to be directed toward urban problems. It was first suggested by a pre-1964 election task force chaired by Robert C. Wood, then on the faculty of the political science department of the Massachusetts Institute of Technology. The report of the Task Force on Metropolitan and Urban Problems was sent to the president on 30 November 1964. Sweeping in its scope, it recommended programs for block grants for urban services, assistance contingent on local preparation of social renewal plans, assistance for city planning and code enforcement, renewed emphasis on urban transportation, and the creation of an urban affairs council within the Executive Office of the President. The report's final two paragraphs, under the rubric "The Demonstration City," stated:

> We believe there is need to accelerate the impact of the varied human development programs by dramatic demonstration of ongoing and newly conceived urban aids in one or more especially chosen cities. Such a demonstration would involve long-range and short-term planning both for city-wide renewal and a

comprehensive program of human services. The city would be of typical size and present typical problems of urbanization.

The selection of the cities could take place through procedures established by the White House. The recipient should be assured of federal funds sufficient to develop the model program for urban America.[78]

Consideration of the idea continued through 1965. In late spring of that year, Reuther, United Auto Workers president, became a prime mover when he wrote a memorandum to Johnson urging major central-city rebuilding. "We must go to the core of the problem literally, with a few large-scale demonstrations in depth and totality and not medicate around the edges in bits and pieces." He urged "a crash program" to construct new neighborhoods for 50,000 residents in each of several large central cities.[79] According to Charles Haar, then a Harvard law professor and later both a member of the task force that proposed Model Cities and a HUD official, it was a "typical Reutheresque letter." It was one of "those marvelous, charging-forward letters which say, 'Let's do something, for Christ's sake.' . . . He said, 'Here we are, this great country. Let's put some money. Let's put some energy.'"[80] Reuther followed up his letter with several conversations with people in the White House on what might be done.

In August 1965 the president indicated interest in the organization of a task force to consider Reuther's suggestion. This was followed by a letter from Califano to Weaver asking for the establishment of an inside task force on urban affairs and housing. "To plan our next steps toward the Great Society, it is desired to secure out of the deliberations of your task force concrete proposals and goals toward which the Great Society can move."[81] A report was not forthcoming from this group, but in September Wood was asked to serve as chairman of an outside task force to prepare a legislative program on urban problems for the following year.

Its first meeting was held in the White House, as were several subsequent ones. Califano told the group, according to meeting notes, about "the president's conviction that urban affairs represented his most urgent domestic problem." The task force was to focus on Reuther's plan and on a broader suggestion of a Marshall Plan for cities to combat urban blight and crime. The theme of the meeting was the general importance of actively stimulating localities to confront deteriorating conditions and to improve the living environment of the poor and nonpoor alike. Breaking up segregated neighborhood patterns was a distinct subtheme. The notes of the meeting reveal

that "Wood stressed the point of the innovative quality of demonstrations as an alternative to national administration of national
programs and thereby escaping the present economic and political
organizational handicaps and bottlenecks."[82]

The president was continually informed of the work of the task
force, which also came to have the organization of the new Department of Housing and Urban Development as part of its responsibilities. Harry McPherson, who served as White House liaison, reported
in a memorandum to the president on 9 December 1965: "The cities
group is coming down to the wire. Its two most important recommendations will concern HUD organization and the Reuther-inspired
Demonstration Program. . . . This is the hardest working group of
volunteers I have ever seen. All have contributed. Heineman has been
outstanding; he and three professionals, Wood, Haar, and Rafsky,
wrote the organizational chart. Reuther . . . supplied the vision,
drive, and sometimes . . . rhetoric that has kept this moving."[83]

A report was filed with the president on 21 December 1965.[84]
Among its numerous recommendations, the most controversial was
that community action be transferred to HUD in order to build into
the new department a sensitivity to the plight of the poor in cities. It
was rejected. The task force was generally critical of existing urban
programs. In urban renewal especially, it saw little concern for the
housing and other needs of the poor. Programs were too rigid; consequently, many problems were ignored. Federal spending was inadequate and poorly coordinated. The report emphasized the need for a
large increase in the supply of low-cost housing, a planned and comprehensive approach to dealing with urban problems, and flexibility
and innovation in programs and their administration.

The demonstration cities proposal was the principal means for re-
orienting urban policy. The report anticipated the selection of sixty
to seventy demonstration cities in a national competition. Choices
were to be made by a special presidential commission on the basis of
rigorous criteria. In this way the national government could define
the general direction to be taken in the demonstrations but leave
room for adaptations at the local level. Flexibility in funding was a
key element. Demonstration cities would be given priority in the
distribution of grants from existing programs. Funds would be placed
in a single account. To assist in consolidating a pool of resources, a
federal coordinator was to be named for each city. This coordinator
was also to certify the withdrawal of funds from the account. Such a
funding arrangement required that the conditions, rules, and regulations tied to particular grant programs be relaxed. Supplemental
grants would be provided for 80 percent of project costs not covered by

other programs. Program responsibility would be placed in the mayor's office, although there might be alternative arrangements under certain circumstances. Residents of demonstration neighborhoods were to be involved. In Washington, a cabinet-level council chaired by the HUD secretary would be the prime vehicle for coordination.

Johnson discussed demonstration cities in both the State of the Union and the budget messages in January 1966; a special message to Congress followed on 26 January. It touched upon a number of urban problems and issues. Appropriations were requested for mass transportation and rent supplements. Congress was urged to provide means for the construction of new communities and to bar racial discrimination in housing. Heaviest emphasis was given to metropolitan planning and demonstration cities.[85]

The president's proposal for a new program was set out in the context of the flaws evident in urban renewal and other established housing and urban development efforts. To attain "the prize" of "cities of spacious beauty and lively promise, where men are truly free to determine how they will live" would require experimentation and varied approaches, of which the demonstration cities was one, the president asserted.[86] This approach, he continued, was built around several requirements indicated to be necessary by three decades of experience. The resulting program would "concentrate our available resources . . . to improve the conditions of life in urban areas; join together all available talent and skills in a coordinated effort"; and "mobilize local leadership and private initiative, so that local citizens will determine the shape of their new city—freed from the constraints that have handicapped their past efforts and inflated their costs."[87] The message did not spell out program particulars in great detail, although it did say that social programs would be combined with physical reconstruction and rehabilitation. The number of projects to be funded and the costs were not specified. The major item of expenditure would be federal grants for planning and implementing elements of demonstration programs.

The basic intentions driving the new program were to focus more explicit attention on the poor in urban programs and to establish an innovative means for intergovernmental program coordination. As in community action, there was to be coordination from the bottom up. Communities were invited to package federal programs in distinctive ways and to mesh them in implementation. There was a basic difference in that responsibility for the architecture of program complexes was more emphatically placed in local officials, particularly the mayor, rather than community and nonprofit "amateurs," although citizen participation was an important ingredient.

After the message, when the task force report was transformed into draft legislation, several changes were made. Participating cities were to be selected by the secretary of HUD. They were not given explicit priority in existing grant programs. Whereas the task force indicated that a development authority might serve as the demonstration agency, the bill restricted eligibility to city governments or local public agencies. No mention was made of a cabinet-level coordinating council; instead, the secretary of HUD was instructed to consult with other officials.

The measure was not received with great enthusiasm in Congress. Major urban legislation had passed in the previous year. The civil rights implications of the new initiative were a source of apprehension for some. There was concern, particularly among Republicans, about program costs and increased federal control. Other members were uneasy about a program that would benefit a limited number of cities and the possibility that money might be directed to them from others. The big-city focus was also a problem. Urban renewal interests felt threatened.

Intense lobbying activity and some adjustments were required before eventual passage of the legislation in November.[88] The program concept and organizational framework proposed by the administration emerged largely unchanged, but Model Cities unofficially was substituted for demonstration cities as the name of the program. HUD was given major administrative responsibility for the program, and at the community level responsibility was vested in elected government officials—mayors or county executives. The administration suffered a defeat in the rejection of its proposal for an Office of the Federal Coordinator, to be appointed by HUD for each demonstration city.[89]

There were few guidelines in the statute to assist HUD in the selection of the model cities and few guidelines delineating the types of programs that these cities might undertake. The legislation was dominated by such phrases as "coordination," "participation," and "innovation" without operational content. This gave great leeway to HUD to determine program guidelines.[90] Congressional intent on one point was very clear, however. The chief executives of cities and counties were to be relatively free to establish their own program priorities. But this feature was joined by acceptance of the community participation provisions in the administration's proposal. Balancing the roles of local officials and community representatives would become a source of problems in implementation.

The number of demonstration cities was not specified in the law. Reuther's initial idea was for less than 10. When legislation was submitted to Congress, 60 to 70 participating cities were contemplated. By the time Congress completed action and implementation began, the number had risen to approximately 150, despite limited funding. Johnson originally asked for a six-year program and an authorization of $2.3 billion. He got instead a three-year program. The law authorized $12 million in planning grants for both FY 1967 and FY 1968 and $400 million in FY 1969 for implementation.[91] Congress added $250 million for urban renewal projects in demonstration areas started after FY 1968.[92] This was to protect urban renewal funds for nonparticipating cities. Appropriations were even less generous. For FY 1967 Congress made $11 million in planning funds available.[93] For the next year, although it provided the full $12 million for planning, it appropriated $300 million for implementation, including $100 million in urban renewal funds.[94] Subsequently, Johnson's $1 billion request for FY 1969 was pared to $625 million, half of that for urban renewal.[95] According to HUD, "The program has been tragically underfunded from its inception, and the total appropriation has been spread thin as the number of participating localities has increased."[96]

Limited funding and the conclusion of Johnson's presidency only two years after enactment meant that the promise of the Model Cities approach would not be fully tested. Nevertheless, Model Cities, whether viewed as an offspring from OEO experience or as a new and different approach that attacked urban poverty, urban decline, and the problems of intergovernmental program coordination, did at least represent a major effort to equip the federal government to respond to local needs that varied from community to community. It was an effort to inject a national urban policy, very general though it might be, with a considerable degree of local autonomy and simultaneously bring into concert the implementation of a number of fragmented grant programs.

Modus Operandi

Cities that wished to participate were required to prepare a comprehensive demonstration plan (CDP). HUD's program guide required that physical and human resource programs be "developed into integrated systems. Each component should be comprehensive so that projects and activities within each component reinforce each other, and inter-relationships between components should be developed so that projects and activities in one can provide reinforcement and support to those in others."[97] This was to be done in the context of preparing a comprehensive plan for development after a probing examination of needs. The guidelines listed about fifty programs administered by seven departments and OEO as possibilities for addressing identified needs.

At the local level, program responsibilities were to be in a city demonstration agency that was an integral part of ongoing governmental operations. The agency was to focus on planning and coordination. Unlike its community action counterpart, it was not to administer programs. Although preparation of a CDP was the responsibility of local officials, the act required "widespread" participation by citizens. But as in the case of the EOA, it did not define exactly what that meant. The formal guidance given by HUD for the development of plans was only slightly more specific.[98]

In the first round, planning grants were awarded to 63 of the 193 applicants in November 1967; in March 1968, more were approved. The second round, in September 1968, increased the number by 33 cities. Local plans were carefully reviewed by regional interagency committees and in Washington. Many deficiencies were found. These included weak specification of program linkages, inadequate citizen involvement, and an absence of innovative approaches to urban development. The awards were made by the secretary of HUD based upon evaluations prepared by the Model Cities Interagency Review Committee which met as often as twice weekly. It had been established by Califano in May 1967 with representation from HUD, Labor, HEW, Transportation, Commerce, and OEO.[99] This was actually a subgroup of a Model Cities Coordinating Committee established by Secretary Weaver under his convenor authority.

When the Model Cities applications were approved, the funding pattern was as follows: grant funds were available from HUD to cover 80 percent of planning costs; and grant funds were available for administering approved components of the CDA programs up to 80 percent of the total nonfederal contributions required for all projects or activities under existing federal aid programs. Special urban renewal add-on funds were also available. The basic idea was that established programs should be used to the maximum extent in financing the execution of a comprehensive plan, but, in Wood's words, the local community would receive "a supplemental grant to use at its own discretion to fill in the chinks."[100]

Intergovernmental Politics

The intergovernmental tension and the turf conflicts precipitated by Model Cities were considerably less tempestuous than those associated with the Economic Opportunity Act. Mayors generally favored

the Model Cities proposal and continued to support it after enactment. It touched far fewer communities. Consequently, whatever
problems arose did not attain the national visibility or have the general political impact of community action programs. Although citizen participation became an issue in some places, the fact that model
city efforts were under the control of local officials was beyond debate. And because of community action, mayors and others at the
community level were now somewhat experienced in dealing with
the citizen participation phenomenon. States had no administrative
responsibilities or approval authority in the selection process, although in a few instances state support was given to local efforts.

Having learned from OEO's experience and aided by the fact that
only a small number of cities was involved, HUD made a significant
effort to work closely with prospective and successful applicants and
took pains to keep the White House informed. For example, in February 1967, in the first stage of implementation, HUD hosted meetings
on the program in six cities for 3,500 officials.[101] The assistant secretary in charge of the program traveled the country extensively. In
August 1967 a conference of professionals in urban affairs reviewed
HUD's guidelines and caused the department to make changes in
them. The major complaint about the guidelines in their original
form was that they forced planners to emphasize categorical program matters rather than a comprehensive conceptualization of urban problems.[102] Between November 1967 and December 1968, interagency teams visited all the demonstration cities.[103] Attention
was also given to the concerns of individual cities. For example, in
March 1967, HUD and OEO staff went to Baltimore to help with
planning and organizing a program.[104] A team was dispatched to Los
Angeles to meet with the mayor and others to explain why that city
was not selected.[105]

The citizen participation requirement was the principal source of
strain in national-local relationships. HUD took these requirements
seriously. According to its administrative history, "Viewing citizen
participation as an important element, the Model Cities Administration was determined to enforce it. All but one of the cities approved were required to alter extensively this aspect of their proposals during the planning stage."[106]

A varied pattern emerged. In cities with strong established neighborhood representation, a "bicameral" system often developed in
which the poverty population organized a group to work with the
official group designated by the mayor. In other cities there was
a "unicameral" approach whereby neighborhood representatives

served on the official board. HUD would approve either organizational arrangement. However, in 1967 and 1968 HUD came to favor
the bicameral option.[107]

In Model Cities, as in the community action program, the community participation requirement always presented a contradiction.
If neighborhood residents were to have final authority over model
city plans, their views on resource allocation were likely to differ
from those of city hall, producing inevitable antagonism and chanc-
ing limited accomplishment. Alternatively, if the community demonstration agency was to be an integral part of municipal government and accountable to elected officials, neighborhood views would
often have to be ignored, and the decisions of the "establishment"
would thereby be imposed on the neighborhoods. Sundquist and
Davis, in their field investigations from 1967 to 1969, found that in
some cities this contradiction was resolved reasonably well. In other
cities, particularly where community action agencies had developed
strong community participation devices, the contradictions were
never resolved, and indeed they often threatened the funding and administration of the CDP.[108]

Coordination in Washington and in Communities

While the first model city grant recipients were being selected, John
Gardner of HEW sent a memorandum to the president in which he
observed, "No assignment immediately ahead offers a more interesting opportunity for collaboration among Federal Departments than
the Model Cities Act. But it's not only an opportunity," he continued, "it will be a very severe test for all of us. And we can't afford
to flunk it."[109]

The White House did not disagree. Despite its heavy workload,
Califano's office took a major interest in the coordination problem.
He and his aides were not only instrumental in organizing the process for reviewing applications, they monitored the participation of
the various departments and agencies involved. For example, early
in May 1967 Califano asked each of them to report to him on the
staff resources they were contributing to Model Cities activities.[110]

Not long thereafter, in early July, a supplement to the report of the
Task Force on Cities highlighted difficulties to be expected in coordination at the local level and their relationship to central coordination. These difficulties involved the limited resources of mayors,
restrictive program regulations that hampered innovation, the necessity for separate negotiations with grantor agencies, different program timetables, and administrative delays in federal agency opera-

tions. Administrative innovation was required to surmount these difficulties, and this in turn required strong central coordination in the Executive Office of the President.[111]

That was not to be provided. Despite Califano's interest, developing a continuing mechanism for coordination was left to HUD, HEW, Labor, and OEO. Guidelines governing Washington and regional office relationships were completed in December 1967. The interagency memorandum of agreement began with an emphatic recognition of the overall importance of coordination in Model Cities and the special importance of effective coordination in Washington for success at regional and local levels. In the body of the agreement, however, the commitment to coordination was somewhat compromised by the recognition that cooperating agencies would retain "full authority and responsibility for conducting their own programs."[112]

Arrangements in Washington that were specified in the agreement were already in place. Agency heads designated officials at the assistant secretary level to provide overall leadership and direction on Model Cities matters. Collectively, those designated constituted a Model Cities policy group. They were responsible for naming staff members to serve on a working group to give detailed attention to the program. The plan that was specified for regional offices followed the same basic approach.[113]

An interagency agreement could describe structures and processes for coordination, but it could not guarantee special funds for projects in model city neighborhoods. Generally frustrated by the budget stringency imposed by the Vietnam War, grantor agencies were not generous in their contributions to the program.[114] As Weaver later explained, "The . . . problem that we have not gotten over is how to get the funds from the other departments which are involved."[115] In recognition of this problem, the note on Model Cities in the 1967 cities task force report suggested that certain appropriations of participating agencies be earmarked for model cities and that HUD be empowered to spend them. This, of course, was not acceptable to those agencies. However, there was some pressure from the White House for the voluntary commitment of funds. Califano's calls to HEW, Labor, and OEO in April 1968 asking for allocations had little effect. In August 1968 he directed that agencies specify for him "within about a week" the funds they were setting aside for Model Cities as well as their general plans for program implementation, including relaxation of requirements.[116] There were no meaningful results.

Not long after Califano's memoranda were sent, he and BOB director Zwick received several similar letters from model city mayors detailing a number of problems. The level of funding was not one of them, but coordination was. The mayors' fundamental complaint was the disjunction between the comprehensive planning requirement and the innovative programming imperative inherent in the Model Cities idea, on the one hand, and the categorical grant system on the other.[117]

For Model Cities officials, a primary wedge for penetrating and reshaping the categorical grant system and improving coordination at the local level was mayoral approval of all grant projects affecting model neighborhoods. At the time, mayors typically had authority over only a small portion of the grant funds channeled into their cities. After a difficult struggle, urban renewal officials agreed to abide by the approval procedure. Less success was achieved with HEW and Labor. HEW was hampered in its ability to comply by the fact that most of its grant programs were administered by the states and were governed in part by state law. It had only limited control over a highly decentralized set of programs. Labor was preoccupied with establishing the concentrated employment program, its own response to particularly troubled neighborhoods. Labor was willing to include model city neighborhoods in CEP areas, but it would agree to do no more than consult with mayors. OEO was also reluctant to subject its programs to mayoral review.

The mayors' letters prompted another round of admonishing memoranda to participants directing them to "promptly take the steps . . . necessary to assure that the promises of this Administration to the cities are kept."[118] By this time the end of the Johnson administration was clearly in sight, and it was unlikely that major actions would be taken without more prodding by the White House. This was done in selected instances. There was a follow-up on the relationship of crime and manpower programs to Model Cities in the latter part of 1968.[119]

Greatest attention was given to problems in relationships between community action and model city demonstration agencies. Sundquist and Davis found these relationships frequently to be "strained and sometimes downright hostile."[120] The basic reasons were that the two types of agencies were in competition for resources and influence and were guided by different philosophies. The issue came to the White House in August 1968 when HUD proposed that mayors be given approval authority over OEO programs in model city areas. OEO strongly opposed the idea.[121] Under sponsorship of Califano's office, however, a compromise was struck. Project review and conciliation processes were designed to mesh the two program operations, but the more basic thrust of the agreement was to move toward arrangements that would effectively conjoin the two programs in model city neighborhoods at some point in the future.[122] The outcome was a positive step toward improved coordination at the local level produced by a coordinated effort in Washington. It was late in coming, however, and overall the challenge posed in Gardner's memorandum to Johnson was not fully met. Nevertheless, there had been progress. According to Sundquist and Davis, "Despite the tensions and conflicts engendered within the communities by the struggle for control of the model city organization, the plans that emerged at the end of the planning year 1968 represent a remarkable achievement in coordination."[123]

Conclusions

At various points in this and the preceding chapter, several sources of problems encountered in the administration of Economic Opportunity Act programs were identified. One major problem, so perceived by many of the officials involved, was defective coordination of intergovernmental programs at and among all levels with negative consequences for program effectiveness. Although it seemed that scarcely a day passed that pressing problems in the American administrative state did not come to the attention of the White House, the search for correctives at that level appeared to lack persistence, determination, and system. Many factors were involved, but two were of prime importance.

One factor was the absence at the presidential level of a sufficiently strong basis for action on questions of administration. OEO, despite its location in the Executive Office of the President, could not play the role of a strong central coordinator or be accepted as an objective and honest broker on administrative issues. The amorphous, complex, and harried subpresidency for executive direction was able to give only thin and spasmodic attention to questions of administration. Furthermore, there was no coherent strategy to apply at either the national or subnational levels, at least during the initial period of EOA implementation. Community action programs did not benefit from strong presidential backing. Support was given to Model Cities agencies with limited results. Basically, decision makers at the presidential level allowed a variety of competing schemes for coordination to thread through the intergovernmental system. As for Washington, at times officials thought in terms of curing deficiencies by regrouping programs. Reorganization to lessen the necessity for presidential management seemed to be the Bureau of the Budget's natural response. At other times, though less frequently, they thought in terms of strong central coordination.

The second factor was the ability of established bureaucratic institutions to deflect policy initiatives that challenged their discretion and administrative customs and to discourage the imposition from above of significant administrative change. It must also be noted that OEO, a major challenger, was motivated by its own interests in program and organizational matters. Bureaucracies at subnational levels were equally difficult to redirect, particularly in connection with the coordination function of community action programs. There were signs that Congress was wary of power redistributions, especially in communities. This is indicated by the Green amendment and the rejection of the local federal coordinator idea in Model Cities.

It is useful to view the Johnson administration's experience with the implementation of the EOA and Model Cities programs in the larger context of the presidency and the politics of broad governmental change. The reform objectives of these initiatives of the 1960s challenged established institutions in a way that the programs associated with cooperative federalism did not. Indeed, the national bureaucratic complexes that were threatened were the products of cooperative federalism. At the local level, especially in regard to the Economic Opportunity Act, there was reason to perceive the national government as more intrusive and potentially directive than facilitative. That substantial tension developed is not surprising. As Paul E. Peterson argues, in both community action and Model Cities the national interest in the redistribution of power tangled with local developmental interests.[124] An accommodation of sorts was worked out in the play of intergovernmental politics in which the president was a prime participant, along with governors, mayors, and Congress. Nevertheless, Washington's ability to require substantial alterations in the operations of states and communities, especially in a short period of time, was shown to be quite limited.

In part this was because the government in Washington was poorly equipped to play the role of a unified national government. The mechanisms for concerted, as opposed to fragmented, national action were not available. The power and independence of established departmental and agency bureaucracies, though challenged, were not actually diminished by the EOA or by Model Cities legislation. The feeble efforts to develop effective mechanisms for coordination floundered in the administrative politics engendered by the two programs, a politics in which the president and his aides were reluctant to engage. The efforts made to secure administrative order of the sort

required if the reform objectives of the two programs were to be realized in communities were usually ad hoc and tentative. When opportunities for decisive action arose, they were not taken.

The experience of the Johnson presidency suggests that when presidents seek major changes in national-state-local relationships, they
place themselves simultaneously in two political environments.
One is intergovernmental (and public), involving political leaders at
subnational levels, certain organized interests, and Congress. The
other is administrative, involving relations within the national government and with state and local bureaucracies. Johnson's basic
problem was that it was difficult to be successful in both political
arenas. For example, to have waded forcefully into administrative
politics and brought order into EOA programs and Model Cities
through strong presidential-level management would have been
costly in and of itself, even if the various centrifugal forces at work
had been overcome. Substantial presidential energy and political resources would have to be spent. The political costs could be considerable. But success itself in this area would be threatening to state
and local interests if a basis for truly unified and potent national action was thereby created. That is, if creation of an authentic administrative capacity to act forcefully as a national government produced
such action at state and community levels, the president's position
in intergovernmental politics would be uncomfortable, to say the
least. There would be additional political costs and grave risk to his
overall political standing as a result of public conflicts with subnational officials, Congress, and affected interests over intergovernmental program issues. The risks to presidents inhering in con-
flictual intergovernmental politics may cause a reluctance to play
administrative politics with purpose. In fact, these risks appear to
have had this very effect in the Johnson presidency.

5. Experiments in Multistate Administrative Regionalism

Among the distinctive administrative themes associated with Great Society programs was regionalism—multistate and substate. New institutions at both levels were created to complement, if not transcend in some respects, the activities of established national departments and agencies and of state and local governments. Three sets of joint national-state regional commissions were authorized in a single year, 1965. One consisted of river basin commissions for water resources planning. The other two were established to spur economic development, first in Appalachia and then in other parts of the country where economic progress lagged. For the Advisory Commission on Intergovernmental Relations (ACIR), establishment of the commissions was "a turning point of historical and practical significance in the growth and application of regionalism to serve governmental programs and policies."[1] This has proved to be an overstatement, but during the 1960s considerable significance was generally attached to their creation.

Regionalism was also important at the substate level. Numerous laws passed during Johnson's presidency encouraged or required the establishment of areawide governmental entities and processes overlying the jurisdictions of local governments and, in some sense, standing between them and state and national governments. By 1973, according to an ACIR calculation, approximately 4,000 geographic program areas across the country had been spawned by twenty-four federal programs.[2] Not all of these originated in Johnson's presidency, but many did. Among them were the local development districts authorized by the Appalachian Regional Development Act of 1965 and the Public Works and Economic Development Act of 1965. In these two laws, multistate and substate regionalism were joined.

Administrative Regionalism

Region, of course, is a word with many meanings. Definitions range from the deceptively simple, such as "an area exhibiting homogeneity in one or more of its aspects," thus representing "an area or spatial generalization," to the highly complex.[3] That generalization, depending upon the regional aspects emphasized, may be cast in a variety of terms, three of the most common being geographic, cultural, and economic.

Another form of regionalism, administrative regionalism, grows out of a more general concept of region. In basic terms, it is areal organization for government activity on the basis of geographic, cultural, economic, or other commonalities. It expresses concepts of regionalism through governmental structures. According to the ACIR, administrative regionalism "has been a persistent if not always persuasive part of the American political tradition."[4] Its principal purpose is "to reconcile government area and function"—that is, to set the performance of a governmental function in an appropriate areal context.[5] In general, multistate and substate administrative regionalism arises when, for one or a combination of geographic, economic, cultural, or other reasons, the established boundaries of state and local governments are judged not to provide an appropriate areal context for action. Thus, administrative regionalism has frequently had a reform connotation.

An economic perspective on problems of regionalization has been particularly influential in thinking about administrative arrangements. Regardless of the precise form that it assumes, the perspective suggests that three considerations must be examined. The first is economies of scale. A larger organization may be more efficient, in a technological sense, than a smaller organization. The marginal cost of providing additional units of water or sewage treatment may be lower if several jurisdictions—municipalities or even states—can organize a cooperative regional effort.

A second economic consideration that may influence attempts at regionalization is income distribution, broadly defined to include differentials in economic growth. With changing technologies and changing patterns of resource utilization, some areas (regions) may fall behind while others advance, inviting efforts to narrow the growth differentials through regional undertakings.

A third economic consideration is externalities. An upstream jurisdiction that fails to purify its sewage may impose costs on a downstream jurisdiction. An economically efficient solution can be obtained only by regionalizing sewage treatment with an equitable cost-sharing arrangement.

An interdependent and advanced industrial economy undergoes constant change. New technologies emerge; patterns of resource use change, regional income levels are altered with resulting regional controversies, exemplified by the contemporary Sun Belt–Snow Belt tensions. And a changing economy certainly generates new externalities. Yesterday's chemical manufacturing is today's source of carcinogens. Today's air pollution will require new regional air pollution abatement districts in the next decade. As a consequence, organization, reorganization, and experimentation are constantly necessary; regional administrative patterns cannot be expected to remain invariant over time.

Application of "the science of the region" to administration is an imposing task, confronting as it must the difficulties in defining, measuring, and relating commonalities and overcoming political forces antithetical to regional approaches.[6] Furthermore, administrative institutions that transcend conventional governmental boundaries may arise for reasons other than considerations of region in the full meaning of the term. These reasons might include the need to counter governmental fragmentation, to improve coordination of related functions, or to attain economies of scale. There are, to be sure, institutions that are clearly regional in their foundations, such as the Tennessee Valley Authority and river basin planning agencies. But many, if not most, regional administrative institutions seek coherence in government activity through institutions that are imperfectly regional in character in the sense that the complex, comprehensive, and organic perspective of regionalism is not manifested strongly in their structure or operations. Though informed by the idea of regionalism, their identity is strongly shaped by nonregional factors.

In the United States the most distinctive feature of administrative regionalism is its frequent association with planning and the coordination of planning, as opposed to the coordination and administration of program operations, though there is clearly a relationship. This is not to suggest the complete absence of program operations in regional form. There are, for example, the regional offices of federal departments and agencies; the Tennessee Valley Authority; units such as the Port Authority of New York and New Jersey, established by interstate compact; numerous water, sewer, school, and other special districts and authorities at the local level; and even integrated governments in a few metropolitan areas. But except for special districts, the incidence of such enterprises is limited.

Indeed the first major manifestation of administrative regionalism focused on planning—regional planning at the local level, given impetus by the City Beautiful movement in the early part of the century. The idea of regional planning gradually spread through the country and was spurred further in the 1930s by the promotional efforts of the National Resources Planning Board.[7]

During the 1940s and 1950s the regional planning phenomenon continued to gain momentum. There was a considerable amount of river basin planning with joint national-state participation on an informal basis. Several proposals were made to formalize such relationships, and in 1961 a joint compact created a regional body with national and state membership to plan and regulate water resources in the Delaware River basin. A number of interstate compacts were established to plan and promote regional economic development.

At the substate level, local regional planning initiatives were stimulated particularly by housing legislation enacted in Washington. The 1949 act introduced substate, regional, and metropolitan planning as criteria for assistance. Planning as a requirement for aid was emphasized more strongly in 1954 amendments to housing legislation. Furthermore, section 701 was added to the 1949 act that year to create a grant-in-aid program to assist state, metropolitan, and regional agencies to plan on a metropolitan basis.

At the conclusion of Johnson's presidency, administrative regionalism was a more pronounced feature of the American administrative state than at the beginning. The most pervasive and dramatic effect was the explosion of substate regional organizations, which will be examined in a subsequent chapter. Less dramatic in their effects, though conceptually more profound in their constitutional and administrative significance, were the joint multistate commissions.

The Multistate Commissions

Multistate regionalism does not fit easily into a federal system. Budgetary and executive functions have been allocated over time to national and state institutions, and working ties have been established around grants-in-aid and other interrelationships. Inherent in these allocations and relationships are concepts of institutional prerogatives, such as the power of the president, the national government's control of its budget, and the ultimate authority of federal departments and agencies over program matters assigned to them. Regional proposals may challenge these established power arrangements. The prerogatives of various state officials may also be challenged. Thus, multistate regionalism conflicts with some very strong and deeply rooted elements in the complex of the American administrative state.

The Advisory Commission on Intergovernmental Relations underscores these complexities:

> Regionalism has, for the most part, been approached on an *ad hoc* basis. This, of course, is to be expected, given the tenuous political base of regional governmental agencies and instrumentalities. Thus, regionalism presents a dilemma for the American Federal system. For on the one hand, there are definable regional phenomena that demand the formulation of suitable multistate policies. Yet, on the other hand, regional institutions lack the broad-based authoritative character of Federal and State governments. . . . It . . . remains a delicate task to fit regional institutions into a political system that is not organized along regional lines.[8]

That "delicate task" was at the forefront on 9 March 1965 as President Johnson signed the Appalachian Regional Development Act in the Rose Garden. Of it he said, "Originated by the Governors of the Appalachian States, formed in close cooperation with the Federal Executive, approved and enacted by the Congress of all the people, this is the truest example of creative federalism in our times."[9] As he spoke, other multistate arrangements were under active consideration. A water resources planning bill was nearing passage in Congress. Final decisions on economic development legislation were being made in the White House. Both proposals would become law within the next few months. The nearly simultaneous emergence of three sets of multistate institutions, all involving national participation, in the fabric of the American administrative state raises interesting questions about their origins, the forces that brought them into being and gave them shape, and their relationships to established institutional arrangements and power relationships.

River Basin Planning Commissions

In the long history of intergovernmental administration, there are few experiences in regionalism that are truly unprecedented.[10] Regional organizations that are sometimes described as new or innovative may, in fact, have many antecedents. This is very much the case with organizations for water resources planning and development. Since the nineteenth century, the national government, state governments, substate regions, and local jurisdictions have all been involved in the development and regulation of navigable waters, the control of flood damage, and the provision of water supplies, often in a regional context. However, it was not until the 1930s, largely as a result of the efforts of the National Resources Planning Board, that a joint national-state approach to comprehensive river basin planning and water resources administration began to emerge. During the 1940s and 1950s, the idea of more closely coordinated water resources planning on a regional basis gained momentum, as did the idea of joint national-state involvement in it; and there were experiments in voluntary efforts sponsored by the national government. Furthermore, several interstate compacts were negotiated among states to deal with water problems, and two state proposals to establish joint national-state interstate compacts were put forth but rejected.

The legislative background of the Title II commissions for water resources planning starts in the Eisenhower administration with a report by the Advisory Committee on Water Resources Policy, a cabinet-level body. It recommended that "regional or river basin water resources committees be formed with a permanent nonvoting chairman appointed by the President and with membership composed of all Federal departments and states involved."[11] In 1959, water resources legislation, including provisions for river basin commissions along the lines suggested by the advisory committee, was drafted by the House Interior and Insular Affairs Committee. The Bureau of the Budget (BOB), while supporting the idea of river basin planning, objected to other parts of the bill, and it languished in committee.

In January 1961 the bureau forwarded to Congress new legislation to establish river basin commissions. Soon thereafter the Senate Select Committee on Water Resources issued a major report based on forty studies covering the gamut of water resources activities in the country. The report endorsed a more active role for states in water resources planning. In mid-1961 the Kennedy administration framed still another bill that included the river basin commission proposal, called for the establishment of a Water Resources Council, and recommended authorization of grants to the states for planning. But controversy over the commissions was to delay enactment until 1965. The dispute involved a clash between national prerogatives and state interests in multistate regionalism, and it carried over into the Appalachian and economic development initiatives.

The nub of the controversy was whether the commissions would be national bodies or joint national-state bodies. The bureau was strongly committed to the first approach and to the proposition, as Martha Derthick puts it, that "none but a federal official might make plans or policies for the federal government."[12] In the bureau's version, the president established the commissions and appointed the state members. The commissions reported to the Water Resources Council, which was composed of federal officials, and were subject to its authority. Acting through the Interstate Conference on Water Problems, associated with the Council of State Governments, the states objected and proposed a number of changes that would enhance their role on the commissions.

The state position was strengthened by another 1961 event, the formation of the Delaware River Basin Commission as a joint national-state interstate compact. This commission was given a broad and potent charter to plan, approve, regulate, and manage water resource projects in the Delaware River basin. The four states involved, New York, New Jersey, Pennsylvania, and Delaware, sought national participation, which initially the Bureau of the Budget and federal departments and agencies strongly opposed. There were constitutional reasons and a fear that in the arrangement national power would be subordinated to that of the states. A series of reservations, including one giving veto power to the single national representative on the commission, and evidence of strong support in Congress and in the Kennedy White House overcame resistance and opened the way to the compact's approval.

In the Water Resources Planning Act of 1965, Title I designated the Water Resources Council (WRC) as the coordinating agency at the cabinet level for water resources. The secretaries of Interior, Agriculture, Army, and Health, Education, and Welfare (HEW) and the chairman of the Federal Power Commission were members. The president named a chairman. The council had previously existed as an informal coordinating body. Title II of the legislation authorized the president to establish joint multistate regional commissions upon request by the WRC or on petition of a state with the concurrence of other states in the river basin. Commission members were drawn from interested federal agencies and from states and interstate compact organizations within the region's boundaries. Their basic function was to prepare and maintain comprehensive and coordinated plans for water and attendant land resources that would serve as a guide to development. Each commission was to have its own staff. Title III authorized grants-in-aid to states for water resources planning. Before the Water Resources Council could provide assistance, states were required to submit a program for comprehensive water and related land use planning. A major purpose of this title was to increase the quality of state participation in the work of the multistate commissions.

Under this legislation Johnson established four Title II commissions in 1967: the Pacific Northwest River Basins Commission, the Great Lakes Basins Commission, the New England River Basins Commission, and the Souris-Red-Rainy River Basins Commission. Other Title II commissions were subsequently created.

In the new law, issues that had provoked controversy since 1961 were compromised. The Water Resources Council retained authority to prescribe "principles, standards and procedures" for project justification (cost-benefit analysis). The WRC was authorized to review the plans prepared by Title II commissions, submit them to governors for their review, and then submit them to the president for review and transmittal to Congress with recommendations for federal project authorizations. However, the WRC did not acquire a veto authority over the plans and projects of Title II commissions. Although the president retained the power to appoint chairmen, they were denied authority to veto commission decisions. The states were given authority to appoint vice-chairmen and state members. In her study of multistate regionalism, Derthick notes three reasons for the concessions made by BOB on these points. First, conceding to joint membership in the Delaware River Basin Commission, which had strong powers, made it difficult to deny such membership in commissions involved only in planning. Second, national autonomy was threatened less by Title II commissions than by the joint compact device and provided an alternative to such compacts. Third, denial of a veto to chairmen was softened by a provision in the legislation stressing that agreement on all issues should be reached by consensus.[13]

Derthick concludes that "Title II was negotiated by the governments and the governmental agencies whose interests would be primarily affected."[14] Among these, there appeared to be no great controversy over the concept of the act; indeed, it seemed to reflect a professional consensus of what was necessary. It was a reform that filled a generally recognized need. Disagreements over some particulars were grounded in differences in the perceived institutional interests of the participants. The most important of these was between the states, seeking the greatest possible weight for their views in commission operations, and the Bureau of the Budget, trying to defend the prerogatives of the national government. An ambiguous, shared power relationship in commission governance was produced by allowing state members to be selected by the states and limiting the ability of presidential appointees to control planning by the commissions. Perhaps ambiguities in governance are inherent in the multistate regional form. They were certainly present also in the case of the Appalachian Regional Commission (ARC), a new regional organization that was also the product of negotiations involving varied state and national interests.

The Appalachian Regional Commission

The genesis of the Appalachian Regional Commission also precedes the Johnson presidency. In fact, the first initiatives began in the fall of 1956 when a president of the Kentucky Junior Chamber of Commerce organized a multicounty regional development council in eastern Kentucky. National attention centered on Appalachia when disastrous floods struck eastern Kentucky in January 1957.[15] In the aftermath, a regional planning body was established in the area, and John D. Whisman, the junior chamber president, was named its executive director. The origins of the ARC idea are to be found in the planners' study of the area's problems completed in 1959. The study, according to Monroe Newman, "produced a far more sweeping idea than the usual catalog of desirable acts to ease the effects of the disaster. The basic points it made were that the fundamental problems of the area were beyond the ability of the localities or the state to remedy, that these problems were not unique to eastern Kentucky but were shared by neighboring areas, and that a regional approach to them was essential."[16]

The concept of a regional approach was attractive to a number of governors, and they organized the Conference of Appalachian Governors in 1960. After the 1960 election, the conference adopted a resolution calling for "a special program of regional development" with national participation.[17]

At approximately the same time, Senator Paul H. Douglas of Illinois, at Kennedy's request, headed a task force on area and regional development. Douglas and other Democrats in Congress had urged a major development assistance program for several years. Among other things, the task force recommended regional development commissions in the most depressed areas of the country, beginning in Appalachia.[18] Soon after the new Congress convened, it passed the Area Redevelopment Act.

When the Appalachian governors met with President Kennedy in May 1961, the idea of an Appalachian regional effort confronted the reality of the recently passed redevelopment act, which offered assistance to all depressed areas. Because much of the region would be eligible for aid under this law, it seemed impolitic for the president to endorse immediately another program of assistance for one part of the country. A negotiated compromise established a special office in the Department of Commerce's Area Redevelopment Administration (ARA) to concentrate on Appalachian affairs in consultation with the governors.

There the matter rested until early 1963, when floods again ravaged parts of Appalachia. Once more the governors sought assistance. This time they had two years of experience with the Area Redevelopment Act on their side. Its programs were beset with numerous problems and limitations, providing a basis for an argument that it was simply not a sufficient vehicle for attacking Appalachia's distinctive problems.[19] After meeting with the governors who sought emergency aid and long-term assistance, Kennedy responded in April 1963 by appointing a committee to plan for the comprehensive development of the region. This committee, which became known as the President's Appalachian Regional Commission (PARC), was composed of national officials and the governors of nine states. It was chaired by Under Secretary of Commerce Franklin D. Roosevelt, Jr. The director of the small staff was John L. Sweeney, who formerly worked for Senator Patrick McNamara (D-Mich.) as a staff aide on the Senate Committee on Education and Labor. The executive secretary was John D. Whisman, now the Washington representative of the Conference of Appalachian Governors.

PARC's efforts were funded by the Area Redevelopment Administration and supported by a consulting team from the University of Pittsburgh. The commission searched broadly in developing its proposals. According to Sweeney, "We had about one hundred people in various departments of the federal government as the staff."[20] There were at least as many state officials working on approximately twenty study teams and subteams.[21] "We spent from June '63 until November '63 developing the solutions. We then took them around the region, made a swing of it to each state capitol explaining what we thought the answers would be in getting unanimous support."[22] The last meeting at the state level was in Hagerstown, Maryland, on 22 November 1963, the day Kennedy was assassinated.

Kennedy's strong support for an Appalachian program was quite clear, but the position of the new president was not. On 13 December, Johnson met with the new governor of Kentucky and his predecessor to discuss an emergency economic relief program initiated by Kennedy a month previously for the eastern portion of the state. A statement issued by the White House announced the continuation of the emergency program and made a terse, noncommital reference to the larger effort.[23] In the next months there were other brief references in the State of the Union address and the economic and poverty messages to Congress, but there were no indications of specific proposals or great enthusiasm for a regional initiative in Appalachia. As the Bureau of the Budget and PARC continued to work on refining the Appalachian program, those involved, such as Sweeney and William L. Batt, Jr., the head of the Area Redevelopment Administration, sensed only lack of interest on the part of Johnson and his White House advisers.

In early March 1964, Roosevelt and others were pushing Johnson to meet with the Appalachian governors to receive PARC's report. He seemed agreeable but was in no great rush to do so, first wanting "to see a summary of the report and a summary of our proposals to Congress."[24] In the next weeks the president's interest quickened. Batt gives the credit to Roosevelt:

> When President Johnson became president and didn't show any interest in this program, Frank told me that he talked to him one night at a party at the White House making a suggestion that the President was missing a good bet. At this point we all thought that the Appalachian program was dead, and Frank tells me that he persuaded President Johnson that here was a good way for him to get into the South, a way to find common ground with Southern governors and do something for the South, completely outside the racial issue. Right afterwards, President Johnson exhibited a great interest in this thing, it got his solid backing.[25]

Governor William W. Scranton of Pennsylvania, who was deeply involved in the Appalachian effort and a potential candidate for the 1964 Republican presidential nomination, was also a factor. In briefing the president on progress in drafting the PARC report early in February, presidential aide Lee C. White passed along the Department of Commerce's view that "Scranton would use a watered-down version to his political advantage."[26] A month later, on 2 March, White encouraged Johnson to meet with the governors on the report, noting, "We are advised that there would be considerable political gain from a personal meeting. . . .—on the other hand, any lack of interest may well be the subject of criticism from Governor Scranton."[27] In Sweeney's judgment it was a remark of Scranton himself that precipitated action. He says: "One day absolutely without any planning whatsoever he [President Johnson] ran into Governor Scranton at some function . . . , and the Governor said to him, 'You know, we spent a lot of time on Appalachia, and we sure hope you will give it your attention.' That was all he said to him. The next thing I knew,

Bill Moyers was on the phone saying, 'John, the President would like to meet with the governors. Can you set the meeting up?'"[28]

James L. Sundquist, who contributed to the PARC effort as an official of the Department of Agriculture, mentions rumors that Johnson at the time "was opposed to the regional approach to development." But, in Sundquist's view, he was "trapped."

> Had the commission [PARC] been composed solely of federal officials, it could have been controlled and directed. Had it been made up of private citizens, it could have been repudiated. In either . . . case, the report might even have been, if necessary, suppressed. But a mixed federal-state commission, launched in a glare of publicity, operating in the open, and backed by the political and official leadership of nine states, could not be subjected to any of these forms of discipline. President Kennedy, it turned out, had given away part of the administration's power to make its policy and budget decisions.[29]

If Johnson, in fact, was in a trap, he soon set about making it one from which he could derive some benefit. By mid-March 1964, program details had been worked out for the most part, and the report was released on 9 April. Johnson's positive response came approximately two weeks later on 24 April.

The president began that day in Chicago, where the evening before he had spoken at a meeting of the Cook County Democratic Party. After speeches at South Bend, Pittsburgh (two), and Paintsville, Kentucky (two), the long-awaited meeting with the Appalachian governors was held in Huntington, West Virginia. According to Sweeney, "We got into the session down at Huntington and he said, 'Now, I'm here to listen,' and Governor Wallace Barron of West Virginia . . . outlines why they thought this was a far better program than economic development or anything else. He said, 'Thank you very much,' and we all climbed on the plane."[30] But before embarking, Johnson spoke at the airport on the problem of poverty both in the country and the region, and he commented on the meeting with the governors and the PARC report. He said, "The Governors have again tonight renewed their interest in that report and again indelibly stamped their approval on it. I have gone over it in some detail with them and I will have an announcement to make in a very few days concerning further implementing . . . or supplementing it."[31]

That note of caution quickly evaporated.

"A very few days" turned into the next day. Again, according to Sweeney, when Johnson was aboard Air Force One:

> He called Frank Roosevelt and myself back into his part of the cabin and said, "Can you have the bill ready for me by Monday morning?" Frank reached in his briefcase and pulled out the draft bill and gave it to him. And he said, "Has this been cleared?"
>
> And we said, "Yes, the Budget Bureau has cleared it. It is all just waiting for your submission."
>
> He said, "All right, I want you both over at the White House . . . tomorrow at ten o'clock because I am going to announce the Appalachian program."[32]

There was a press conference the next morning, a Friday, and the bill went to Congress on Monday, 28 April.

The measure passed the Senate easily in 1964; the House was not ready to vote on the matter until too late in the session, and the bill was not brought to the floor. Reintroduced in 1965, it quickly passed both houses with relative ease and was signed by the president on 9 March.

Prior to the Appalachian Regional Developmental Act, "this country had never attempted a multi-program approach to the problems of relatively low income areas that addressed these areas as an inter-related, contiguous group," according to Newman.[33] The act authorized just over $1 billion in aid. The largest portion by far was $840 million for construction of highways and access roads through June 1971. The other authorizations were for two years. They included grant-in-aid programs for the construction and operation of demonstration health facilities, soil and water conservation, strip mine reclamation, vocational education facilities, water pollution control facilities, and local development districts. For the most part, emphasis was on enlarging existing programs in the region. The most innovative part of the program structure was the authorization of $90 million to increase the national share of grant programs in the region, a recognition of the financially strapped condition of its state and local governments. The remaining two elements in the legislation were a $5 million loan program for improving timber production and a regional water resources plan that was to be prepared by the Army Corps of Engineers.

Governance arrangements for the Appalachian effort were fairly complex. The act established the Appalachian Regional Commission, whose membership included the federal cochairman, who was appointed by the president subject to Senate confirmation, and the governor (or his representative) of each state covered by the act. One of these served as the states' cochairman. Supported by a small staff, the commission's basic responsibilities were for planning and coordination. It had only two programs to administer. One was a small research and development effort. The other was a program of grants to assist development districts at the local level. Thus, its own budget was small.

Two points about governance arrangements stand out in importance. One is the joint national-state composition of the commission, in which national authority over the commission's activities was safeguarded by giving a veto power to the federal cochairman in all matters decided by the commission. The other is that money for highways and other programs was authorized not for the commission but for the Departments of Commerce, HEW, Agriculture, Interior, and Defense. Of the more than $1 billion authorized, only $7.9 million was under commission control. This arrangement caused serious problems for the commission during its early years. ARC could develop and approve plans for spending, but ultimate authority for decisions on funding projects was retained by the departments receiving the authorizations and appropriations.

With its origins in the initiatives of the region's governors, the act was the product of a sequence of negotiations, first within PARC, then between PARC and the Johnson administration, which was represented principally by the Bureau of the Budget, then between the administration and Congress. In order to understand why ARC took the form it did, it is important to understand the underlying negotiations. Those within PARC are the most difficult to describe. Donald N. Rothblatt concludes that PARC's initial proposals were the product of several elements. They included the recommendations of the teams and subteams that studied the problems of the region and two tours of Appalachia by PARC members in which they elicited the views of citizens and state and local officials as to needs. Finally, according to Rothblatt, there was "a series of bargaining sessions among the states" in which "each member of PARC acted as a partisan for the needs of his state or locality and a series of incremental shifts . . . among the programs was made until an equilibrium position . . . was reached."[34]

In Washington, negotiations began late in October 1963 when PARC's draft report was ready for review within the government. There was much about it that officials in the Bureau of the Budget did not like. From then until the eve of submission to Congress, there was a struggle over the final content of the report and the proposals to be recommended by the president. All the participants seemed to be in general agreement that the two should be in close conformity. Those with the president's interests in mind wanted to appear responsive to the governors and to ensure their full support for legislation. Those sensitive to the interests of the governors wanted to spare them the embarrassment of having their publicly endorsed proposals rejected by the president.

The bureau's initial review of the PARC proposals was sent on 18 December 1963 to Ted Sorenson and Lee White in the White House. Upon Sorenson's departure, White became the presidential aide in charge of Appalachian matters. The review recorded a number of "serious reservations," the most serious being the basic justification for doing anything at all at that time.[35] After noting that the consultant's economic plan for the region would not be completed for several months, the review observed, "The program proposed is largely a massive augmentation or acceleration of existing Federal programs with no assurance that it will lead to permanent long-term economic development."[36] Another general reservation argued, "The program is not in proper balance between human and physical resources—only 6% is proposed for human resources as contrasted to 33% for highways and airports and 21% for timber, agricultural and water resources." The bureau was particularly concerned that only 1.6 percent of the funds was to be spent on education.[37] The states were strongly committed to the emphasis on physical resources, especially on highways that would ease access to remote areas. Despite BOB's stance, allocations remained essentially unchanged through the negotiations. Passage of the Economic Opportunity Act and other Great Society programs focusing on human resources served to dilute the force of the bureau's objections on this point.

The bureau also perceived a basic organizational problem in PARC's initial concept of a mixed ownership national-state corporation to run the Appalachia program. Harold Seidman, then acting assistant director for management and organization in the bureau, after reviewing the corporation concept in November 1963, defined the problem in the following way: "Apart from the constitutional questions raised by the proposal, and these are very serious, we believe that the recommended arrangements are organizationally unsound and would diffuse and confuse authority and responsibility for the conduct of a number of ongoing Federal programs." He communicated his views to the director of the bureau, Kermit Gordon, noting, "We expressed our concerns to PARC staff and suggested a number of alternative courses of action. Our advice and suggestions have been almost completely ignored."[38] Not long afterward, Seidman's views were adopted by the bureau. Among the objections to a mixed ownership corporation were these: its use was inappropriate as this form of organization was reserved for programs that at some point would become entirely private; it impeded presidential and congressional control; it placed governors in a position of directing and controlling federal authority and funds; it violated constitutional provisions for the appointment of officers; it added to administrative complexity and might impair rather than facilitate efforts in Appalachia; it relied mainly on federal appropriations and federally guaranteed bonds, and sufficient financial contributions were not required from the states to ensure their cooperation in holding down costs; and it violated established financial policies in several respects.[39] In short, the corporation would alter national and state power positions in unprecedented ways.

An alternative, originating with Seidman, was suggested by the bureau. It was "a joint Federal-State development planning commission along the lines of the joint river basin commissions . . . now pending before the Congress."[40] Seidman further suggested that research and demonstration responsibilities be placed in a consortium of the region's universities, and that any new operating programs be placed in the appropriate departments or be combined in a special Appalachian office in Commerce.

In addition to pushing the option of a joint regional organization for planning and coordination, the bureau attempted to deflect PARC's thrust for ambitious action with two additional recommendations. One was to augment or accelerate some existing programs for FY 1965, but not "highways, timber, coal, and major water resources projects." The other was to await completion of the consultants' studies, do additional planning within the government, and aim to put together "a carefully designed program" by October 1965.[41] The White House, however, elected to move ahead immediately in the development of a more ambitious program.

Since a sizable program proposal now seemed likely despite its reservations, the bureau next began to concentrate on shaping the PARC report into something that would be minimally acceptable and would not commit too much. Sundquist says that PARC's final report was "uncensored."[42] That may be, but the bureau did have an impact on its content. Sweeney reported to the president in January 1964 that the bureau was exerting strong pressure to ensure "that the PARC report should conform to existing policy determinations." As a result, Sweeney acknowledged, "some substantive recommendations have been revised."[43] More specifically, the idea of a mixed ownership corporation was modified and presented as a supplement to the commission idea.[44] The bureau managed to cull requests in the report for FY 1965 appropriations by a substantial amount. In the process several program elements were eradicated altogether or drastically reduced. BOB was also successful in deleting a proposal giving special advantages to the region in the matching formulas for all the grant programs included in the package. This victory was later upset when Congress approved a bundle of supplemental funds to state and local governments in the region to help them meet matching requirements. The bureau partially succeeded in blocking inclusion in the report of long-range estimates of "necessary" federal spending that might then be taken as public commitments.[45]

The most sensitive spending issues had to do with transportation—airports, parkways, and highways. As to airports, the bureau's position was that no particular improvements should be specified in the report.[46] In the end, the report called only for a review of Appalachian airport facilities in the context of economic development objectives.[47] A $127 million proposal to tie parkways such as the Blue Ridge and Allegheny to the region's system of highways was excised.[48]

The bureau was more successful in fighting parkways than in molding the highway portion of the report, the most important element from the perspective of the governors. PARC sought 500 miles of secondary feeder roads and 2,150 miles of through highways. The total cost was estimated to be $1.2 billion over five years. Four basic points of advice were given to the White House by BOB in response to PARC's highway proposals: the report should not contain an estimated cost for the five-year period; it should not specify construction mileage or location; PARC's cost-per-mile estimates were far too high, making the total cost figure too high; and the fifty-fifty matching ratio should be retained, except for Kentucky and West Virginia, where there were special circumstances.[49]

Sweeney vigorously defended PARC's positions. He told the president, "The Governors have gone along with all suggestions on tailoring the report to meet Presidential goals. But now we would in effect, ask them to completely revise the one recommendation they consider essential. Such a demand by the Federal establishment would also ignore the basic political problems they face."[50] For the most part, Sweeney prevailed. The final report contained the $1.2 billion figure as the total cost of the highway package. However, the governors were made to understand that the president's message and the legislation would ask for a lower authorization. Roosevelt assured Johnson in early February 1964 that "the Governors are aware of your budget decisions and will enthusiastically accept your revision when you present it to the Congress."[51] Subsequently, the legislation requested an authorization at the bureau's level. PARC also succeeded in breaching the fifty-fifty matching formula for highways, although it was retained as a facade. Roosevelt explained to Johnson the means by which this would be done. "You would propose that the basic formula be 50-50. However, recognizing the relatively [sic] inability of the Appalachian States to pay a 50 percent share, you would recommend that the Federal Government provide an additional $170 million to be added to its 50 percent share of $420 million and subtracted from the states' share."[52] This would result in an effective ratio of seventy-thirty. Also, proposed highway routes were shown in the report, and a total mileage figure appeared, albeit tucked away in an appendix.

Although subject to severe criticism by Republicans in Congress, the act that passed in 1965 did not differ drastically from the legislation proposed by the administration. There were modifications, however. As the bill moved through Senate passage to the edge of the House floor in 1964, the Appalachian Regional Corporation, to have been capitalized at $50 million, was stricken, as was a grant program for pasture land improvement. Based upon PARC's estimated highway program costs, the national budget authorization for the program was raised substantially. Also increased by a large amount was the discretionary supplemental fund for grants-in-aid. This was a compromise offered by the president to dissuade the House committee from adding a special accelerated public works program for Appalachia in place of the development corporation.[53] After Congress adjourned in 1964 with action still pending in the House, Sweeney made minor changes prior to reintroduction, and with them the bill was quickly enacted in 1965.[54]

The Appalachian Regional Commission and its programs were the product of extensive and complex negotiations among a variety of influential actors. Congress had a limited role in shaping the act. The negotiations that truly counted were those within PARC and among PARC, the Bureau of the Budget, and the White House. The White House role was basically that of mediator. On one side were officials in the government such as Sweeney who had a sincere interest in Appalachia and who were critical of customary approaches to the problems of economically deprived areas. With the backing of influential governors, they attempted to expand the flow of resources into the region by a considerable amount. They also promoted organizational arrangements that significantly limited the power of national bureaucracies over the deployment of these resources and increased the power of states. On the other side, the Bureau of the Budget was a stout defender of the established order. Although not able to block action, it did protect presidential prerogatives, its own authority in budget matters, and departmental command over expenditures. Despite the participation of states, when it was established, the ARC appeared to be under national control.

Economic Development Commissions

If Appalachia was to be singled out for special national attention, why not other depressed regions? Certainly the political logic is unassailable; members of Congress are understandably anxious to channel resources into their districts and states. And it seems generally agreed that this was the trade-off that President Johnson made in return for senatorial support of the legislation for Appalachia.[55] In consequence, the Public Works and Economic Development Act of 1965 was proposed by Johnson on 25 March 1965.[56] Enacted in August, Title V authorized the president to establish new multistate regional development commissions. Five such commissions were established in 1966–1967: New England, Ozarks, Upper Great Lakes, Coastal Plains, and Four Corners (Utah, Colorado, Arizona, New Mexico). The Old West and Pacific Northwest commissions were created in 1972. Title V commissions, known formally as regional action planning commissions, were loosely modeled after the ARC in their administrative structures and planning responsibilities, but there were significant differences in regard to programs and access to funding.

The new law in large part was an outgrowth of experience with the Area Redevelopment Act of 1961. The 1961 legislation contained four major program elements for areas meeting rather loose eligibility criteria for economic development assistance: long-term loans to industrial and commercial enterprises; grants and loans to communities for public facilities; training assistance for the underemployed and the unemployed; and technical assistance in economic development planning. Considerable controversy surrounded its implementation. There were accusations of maladministration.[57] In Congress, area redevelopment programs had to compete for funding with the Accelerated Public Works Act of 1962. The latter authorized funding at both national and subnational levels for public works to alleviate unemployment. It was more flexible and simpler to execute than the redevelopment law and quite popular in Congress. Portions of the Area Redevelopment Act came up for reauthorization in 1963, but in part because of a preference on the part of some in Congress for more accelerated public works, the legislative process stalled.[58] The struggle in Congress continued on into 1964, with the Area Redevelopment Act due to expire on 30 June of that year.[59]

The area redevelopment approach also encountered problems within the economic development fraternity. The most prominent manifestation was the publication in 1964 of Sar A. Levitan's critical evaluation of ARA's first two years.[60] There were three key criticisms, as later summarized in a Bureau of the Budget paper: too many areas were eligible, thus diluting program impact; "areas," typically counties, were inappropriate units for economic development activity as defined under the act; and economic development activity under the act was not adequately informed by planning.[61]

It was against this background that officials of the Bureau of the Budget sparked a review of policy options in the fall of 1964. As a result, by 19 January 1965 Commerce had written a bill for a revised economic development program. It was prepared after extensive discussions involving the White House, and it had received initial clearance. The legislation provided for development facility grants and loans to depressed areas, technical assistance to them, and a new program of aid for economic development centers, or communities that, while not depressed themselves, could have a positive economic effect on areas that were. Encouragement was given to economic development planning on a multicounty or regional basis rather than a county basis. All of the elements subsequently included in the legislation to be submitted to Congress, which then enacted it with little change, were there except for Title V, authorizing the multistate commissions.[62] Although a bureau paper of 12 November 1964 contained a vague reference to the desirability of planning across state lines, there is no indication that serious consideration was given to this dimension in the policy development process.[63] But within a week after the Commerce bill seemed set to go without provision for the commissions, Title V was added.[64]

By including Title V, the bureau was attempting a preemptive strike against a bill just introduced by the chairman of the Senate Public Works Committee and thirty-two cosponsors that followed closely the language of the Appalachia bill. It authorized the president to establish multistate regional commissions, to provide liaison between them and the national government, and to appoint a high-level, full-time federal member with veto authority. Commissions were to prepare plans for development and submit them to Congress.

Alarmed at the prospect of Appalachia-like commissions throughout the country that would be "lobbies for large new public works programs," the bureau proposed a restrained, less threatening version more in line with its organizational principles.[65] The model was PARC, not ARC. Regions were to be established by the Commerce secretary, under whose general authority they were to operate in their only activity—planning. There were to be no authorizations of grant funds or of any program activities. The language was such that the president was not required to appoint a federal member, and provisions for compensation suggested that if there were one, service would be on a part-time basis.

Before the economic development bill was introduced and while the Appalachia bill was moving toward passage in the House, Sweeney was concerned about the possibility of efforts to add ARC-like multistate commissions to the former. Several changes in the economic development bill would reduce the risks of harm, he told Lee White of the White House. These changes would, first, empower the president instead of the Commerce secretary to establish the commissions; second, include a $20 million authorization for planning in Title V rather than lumping funds with other categories of planning in another part of the bill; and, third, increase national participation in administrative costs from 75 percent, as proposed by BOB, to 100 percent, as in the Appalachia bill.[66] In the final version of the administration's bill, authority to designate commissions remained with the Commerce secretary, but the other two changes recommended by Sweeney were incorporated in the measure.[67]

The bill moved through Congress with relative ease. A number of amendments were added in the Senate that brought the economic development commissions closer in concept to that of the Appalachian Regional Commission and away from the bureau's concept. The administration, however, was able to get most of them removed in the House.[68] The major exception was the provision in the law for a high-level, full-time federal cochairman appointed by the president with the advice and consent of the Senate. Despite this, the economic development commissions differed from ARC. Their subjugation to the Department of Commerce was clear, and there was no commitment of funds in the legislation for program action in the regions. The initial emphasis was solely on planning.

The Presidency and Commission Operations

Essentially, the laws establishing the three multistate commission arrangements were very loosely drawn charters for the integration and coordination of governmental efforts along regional lines. Organizational arenas were established. Key actors were identified and assigned responsibilities with varying degrees of specificity, then exhorted to plan and coordinate through such means as review and consultation without specification of precisely how coordination was to be obtained. This was to be worked out in the interplay of national and state power in the processes of implementation.

In these processes, presidential involvement beyond routine actions on budgets and appointments was modest and episodic. Water resources planning received almost no attention, the Appalachian Regional Commission received a greater amount, and the economic development commissions fell somewhere in between. The high point of presidential concern for commissions came in 1967 when the Appalachian program was up for reauthorization. Problems were confronted in relationships between the commission and the departments and agencies that controlled program funds. Also at issue were renewed congressional efforts to assign program responsibilities and funds to the economic development commissions. At the base of most conflicts were the competing claims of state interests and national interests as they were perceived by officials of the national government.

Establishing the Commissions

Presidential lack of interest was illustrated early in 1966 when the Department of Commerce was ready to announce the designations of the first three economic development commissions. W. Marvin Watson, who handled appointments for the president, asked him, "If there is good Congressional representation and if Governors have good attendance, do you want to attend?" His response was no, but it would be "O.K. for V.P."[69] Toward the end of the year Commerce tried again when it was time to designate the Four Corners and Coastal Plains regions. Once more the invitation was declined. "I don't care about participating in this," the president said.[70] Subsequent to the Huntington session when he was urged to support their proposal, Johnson met briefly once with the Appalachian governors after rejecting staff recommendations that he do so on at least two other occasions.[71]

Presidential aloofness stemmed from a variety of factors. The most important evidently was the limited substantive and political significance, from a presidential perspective, of the three regional enterprises. Furthermore, the water resources and economic development commissions were within the immediate provinces of cabinet secretaries.

Among the more important presidential decisions affecting program implementation were those naming the Commerce officials who would lead the economic development program and the Title V and Appalachia cochairmen.[72] Sweeney, who was at the center of PARC activity, was told by the White House well before the act passed that he would become Appalachian cochairman.[73] When he moved to the new Department of Transportation in 1967, he recommended that Joe W. (Pat) Fleming II, his special assistant, replace him. Johnson was reluctant at first, but not, he said, because of Fleming's prior work for his foreign policy nemesis, Senator J. William Fulbright (D-Ark.). The president's position was that "Pat Fleming is a young man that I don't know. It has nothing to do with Fulbright. I'm not going to employ somebody I don't know."[74] Not long after this comment, however, the appointment was made.

Even before legislative action on the Public Works and Economic Development Act was completed, White House decisions on personnel were being made. On 12 June 1965, Marvin Watson, who also handled political matters, expressed his thoughts about the situation to the president. Noting that the bill called for a new organization to replace the Area Redevelopment Administration, he wrote: "I have concern over the new personnel that will be utilized. I do not think that the people heading up the ARA program are the type and/or quality that you will desire. This includes the Director, the deputies and even several of the field men that I have known for the past few years." It should be noted parenthetically that Watson often found himself handling inquiries from members of Congress and others about ARA and, later, EDA grant and loan applications. In his experience with ARA, he continued, "I have not recognized much, if any, political strength from [sic] Commerce Department." Consequently, "I trust that we could interest ourselves in this one division." He asked for and received presidential permission to discuss the matter with Secretary of Commerce John T. Connor, Commerce's personnel director, and Civil Service Commission chairman John Macy, who was also Johnson's principal aide on presidential appointments.[75]

The two key appointments in Commerce were assistant secretary of economic development and administrator of the Economic Development Administration. On 17 August 1965, even before the president signed the law, Macy was ready with a recommendation for the assistant secretaryship. After setting forth a number of rigorous qualifications, he surveyed the credentials of seven "outside" and two "inside" possibilities. His choice was one of the latter, Eugene P. Foley, head of the Small Business Administration.[76] Foley was appointed a little more than a week later. After just a few months in office, he informed the White House that he wished to leave, but he was persuaded to stay until Congress adjourned.[77] His resignation was announced on 5 October 1966. He quit, he said, "because I could see the way the wind was blowing. Commerce was cracking down on EDA—the White House had decided that EDA should not be spending money in cities. Vietnam was eating everything up."[78]

The administrator's position was not filled until several months after it was created and after Foley revealed his desire to leave. Macy recommended Ross D. Davis, who was the choice of Foley and Connor. He was Foley's top aide at the Small Business Administration and ran the agency after Foley left.[79] The president accepted the recommendation and later made Davis assistant secretary after Foley departed. The administrator's position was left vacant.

The relative care with which these appointments were approached apparently did not carry over to the economic development commission cochairman. In early 1966 Schultze told Joseph A. Califano, Jr., now one of Johnson's top domestic aides, that the Bureau of the Budget felt a need from the start for "a strong hand in . . . program planning as it develops." Without it, "regional commissions are likely to turn into a very powerful lobby for expensive public works, increased grants, etc." The bureau's initial plan for keeping the commissions under national control was to name Foley, the assistant secretary, as federal cochairman in each region. This idea was discarded for political reasons and because members of Congress, according to Schultze, "already have, in many cases, their own candidates for these jobs. It would be difficult to turn them down."[80] Nevertheless, Commerce officials initially set high professional standards for the cochairman positions. Persons professionally qualified to lead complex planning efforts through uncharted terrain were sought. But the political pressures channeled through Congress, and perhaps from Watson, for a different type of appointment were strong. In the end, Derthick reports, appointments were used for patronage purposes, and selections were made on political grounds.[81]

Delay in designating regions and selecting cochairmen contributed to a slow start for the economic development commissions. Other parts of the act, such as the designation of substate regional development districts, were understandably viewed by Commerce officials as more important and received priority attention. Problems in getting underway were exacerbated by continuing ambiguity about the mission of the commissions, and neither the statute nor Commerce dictates were able to resolve them. According to Fleming, this ambiguity was quite evident in the Title V officials who visited ARC seeking assistance. "Guys came into office without any clear ideas about what was expected of them, or what they were supposed to produce, or when they were supposed to produce it."[82] Indeed, the end of Johnson's presidency was in sight before the commissions began to function.

In contrast, the Appalachian commission was operational almost immediately. An administrative structure of sorts and leadership were in place even before passage of the act. Its boundaries and mandate were clear, and it did not have to await the initiatives of bureaucratic overseers in a department. Without the benefit of external guidance, it seems, several important administrative and program decisions were soon made within the commission that shaped the basic character of its operations. The position of states' representative was created administratively. Funded by the states, the representative and a small staff were located in the commission's Washington office for the purpose of amplifying the states' voice in commission activity. Also established was an executive committee, which evolved into a prime center for decision making. It consisted of the federal cochairman, the states' representative, and the executive director, a nonvoting but still influential member.[83]

In the program sphere perhaps the most important decision made was that commission approval of projects to be funded by line departments would be based on state plans rather than on a regional plan. In planning, except for somewhat restrictive guidelines for the identification of growth centers, states were allowed rather wide discretion. Furthermore, because Congress failed to specify how funds were to be divided among the states, the commission developed allocation formulas for most sections of the act. Consequently, Derthick finds, there was little in the way of authentic regional planning or action. The commission did not become an "organizational breakthrough that would transcend the states."[84] Operationally, the major difference between commission programs and normal state-federal grant relationships was that the states, through the commission, participated in drafting some of the guidelines that regulated their use of federal funds.[85]

While the commission was developing its mode of operations under conditions of substantial independence, presidential authority was invoked in defining its relationships with funding agencies and the role of the federal cochairman in those relationships. The mechanism was Executive Order 11209, signed on 24 March 1965 shortly after the act was approved. It established the Federal Development Committee for Appalachia.[86] The arrangement was conceived by Sweeney and BOB.[87] Headed by the federal cochairman, the committee consisted of members designated by and representing the heads of nine departments and agencies that were the principal sources of grant funds.

The stated purpose of the order was to coordinate planning for Appalachia at the national level. It delegated to the cochairman the president's authority to provide liaison between the national government and ARC as well as authority to secure a coordinated review of commission proposals by interested departments and agencies. But in its substance the order did not provide the cochairman with the means to be an active central coordinator, nor did it provide departments and agencies with incentives to adapt their programs to regional development purposes as they might be articulated by the commission. The order did underscore the point that the cochairman represented the national government to the commission and its state members. Although the cochairman's positions bound the national government, they were first to have the consent of affected departments and agencies. Thus, this authority was circumscribed by that of the departments and agencies to which the act allocated funds for the region.

Interagency Relations

Serious difficulties in meshing the commission's aspirations for Appalachia with those of other parts of government were foreshadowed for Sweeney and others even before the act was passed. A crisis arose threatening the demise of ten hospitals, seven in Kentucky, two in West Virginia, and one in Virginia, built in the 1950s by the United Mine Workers (UMW) Welfare and Pension Fund. Because of operating deficits, they were sold in 1962 and 1963. Purchasers, with the aid of questionable area redevelopment loans, were the Board of Presbyterian Missions and Appalachian Regional Hospitals, Inc.[88] The hospitals were about to go under in early 1965 because there was no money to pay the notes coming due to the mine workers' fund and an insurance company.

Sweeney was in the forefront of efforts to save the hospitals. ARC, of course, had no program funds of its own. To solve the problem of hospitals, as in the case of any ARC-approved project, funds would have to be provided by someone else. He and others, including Daniel Patrick Moynihan, then at the Department of Labor, put together a rescue plan. Two key elements were a $500,000 grant from the Office of Economic Opportunity (OEO)—grants from other agencies were also anticipated—and agreement by the note-holders to a gradual amortization of the debt.[89]

The first stumbling block was OEO. After consultation with R. Sargent Shriver, its general counsel informed the White House that such a grant would not be legal and would set a dangerous precedent.[90] Sweeney and Moynihan argued rather weakly a counter position on the legal point to Harry McPherson, who had become the White House mediator, and added strong policy justifications for action.[91]

On 11 March 1965 McPherson summarized the situation for the president. Though clearly in favor of saving the hospitals because of the prior loans, the purposes of Appalachian development, and political considerations, he objectively presented OEO's reservation. He proposed to Johnson the outlines of an approach that included persuading OEO "to take a step they do not want to take." The president's response was to the point: "OK. Go ahead and get it done and get credit with gov [the governor of Kentucky] and UMW."[92] McPherson transmitted this "directive" to Shriver.[93]

By early April OEO had acceded to the directive, but a new problem emerged. Sweeney reported to McPherson that all parts of the plan were in place save one. The head of the mine workers' fund, Josephine Roach, refused to cooperate. "The only alternative," Sweeney said, "is to ask OEO to increase its grant from $500,000 to $1.2 million. OEO will resist this to the hilt."[94] McPherson proposed to try again, personally, with the UMW. After McPherson asked the president to speak to John L. Lewis, head of the union, "telling him that I am coming to see him and that you hope he can be helpful to us on a matter of great urgency and importance," a meeting was held.[95] He described the outcome for Bill Moyers. "Appalachia took a body blow last Tuesday at the hands of . . . the frantic spinster who runs the UMW welfare fund. She turned us down cold when we requested a delay in the July 1 deadline for repayment of the . . . debt. It was a bitter meeting, like a dark page from Dickens . . . John L. Lewis was gracious and understanding and no help. Neither was Tony Boyle. The old woman has them all crawling." The only recourse was OEO. "As a consequence," he continued, "I've asked Ramsey Clark to render an opinion on whether OEO can make a $1.2 million grant to pay off the welfare fund and various other debts. John Sweeney is convinced it can be done. Don Baker of OEO is sure it can't. . . . It will look pretty bad if we let these facilities go under just as the Appalachia program gets under way."[96]

OEO finally caved in. On 8 June 1965, McPherson informed the president that it had made a grant of $1.2 million to the Appalachian Regional Commission, which immediately passed the funds along to the hospitals. "OEO had and perhaps still has doubts about the propriety of the grant." Although apparently no formal opinion was given, he assured Johnson that "the Justice Department has no such doubts." However, he continued, "The grant is for the establishment of regional hospital centers in Appalachia," a purpose compatible with OEO's interpretation of the law. "In actuality," he confided, "it will be used to pay off the hospitals' debts," which is precisely what OEO said could not be done. Thus, it appears that the stated purpose of the grant was legitimate, but its actual purpose was subject to serious question. In any case, McPherson concluded, "The grant has avoided what might have been a thoroughgoing political and social disaster for us."[97]

In general, ARC had mixed success in coordinating programs for Appalachia and in enlisting the cooperation of departments and agencies that controlled appropriations. The Federal Development Committee for Appalachia was never effective. Monroe Newman, at the time an economist on ARC's staff, notes a consistent record of failure in relations with the Federal Aviation Agency but, for the most part, harmonious relationships at the program level with Agriculture; Health, Education, and Welfare; and the Federal Highway Administration.[98] Derthick finds that when the commission shared responsibility with an operating agency, the arrangement tended to work adequately when the grant program was established and the ground rules were clear. Problems arose, however, in new programs, such as child development and health care demonstration, because of uncertain lines of responsibility, limited resources, and a low level of interest on the part of the operating agency.[99]

Commission relationships with the Office of Economic Opportunity and the Economic Development Administration were especially troublesome. Despite the Appalachia hospital experience, initially ARC and OEO appeared to work well together. Active contacts were established between the federal cochairman and OEO's directorate and at the staff level. But soon, according to Newman, the two agencies were "walking separate paths" because of a clash in philosophies.[100] ARC was committed to the idea of seeking progress through established political and economic power centers. For OEO, these centers were the obstacles to progress.[101]

The commission's difficulties with EDA arose primarily from the fact that much of Commerce's budget authority for Appalachia programs, including funds for supplemental grants, was delegated to the agency. ARC was provoked by the close and detailed review by EDA of proposals that had been approved by its own staff. Newman concludes that constituency differences were also an important contributing factor to tension in the relationship. ARC was oriented to the states and EDA to local governments. Furthermore, the two agencies differed in their approaches to economic development. According to Newman, "The staff of each agency thought the other's strategy so misguided that the intellectual basis for respect needed for cooperation was eroded."[102]

Overall, from ARC's perspective the greatest operating impediment was the control of program funds by others. According to Sweeney, "There was a real problem in getting federal support for a number of the programs . . . because the guy could say, 'Look, the money's mine, and I don't give a damn how you recommend it, you are going to spend it my way or it is not going to be spent. . . .' I was going around with my hat in hand a whole lot of the time."[103] Not infrequently, he said, "when I would reach an impasse with HUD or Commerce or anybody, I would then have to go to the Bureau of the Budget and the White House and say, 'Now you guys tell them, I've exhausted myself.'"[104]

In addition to difficulties in guiding the expenditures of department and agency appropriations, dependency also created problems for ARC in the appropriations process itself. In many departments, according to Fleming, funding for Appalachia was not a high priority. "When it came time to take cuts in the budget, either with the Budget Bureau . . . or in making agreements with appropriation subcommittees, this was one of the first things that they'd be glad to drop or reduce. . . . You had people testifying on programs who didn't understand them, and it just wasn't a very healthy situation."[105]

With custody over a number of programs of vital interest to Appalachia, the Department of Commerce was a chief culprit in ARC's eyes. In the development of Commerce's budget for FY 1967, the second year of commission operations, the ax fell hard on programs for Appalachia, which were funded at almost $309 million the first year. Based upon Commerce's request, the budget bureau's tentative figure for FY 1967 was $172.55 million. Three programs received no funding at all. Almost all the others suffered severe cuts. Highway funds went down 44 percent, and grant supplements declined 33 percent.

Sweeney appealed to the president through McPherson. He was especially upset by the secretary of Commerce. In fact, McPherson told Califano, "He is boiling with Connor." "Connor 'could care less' about the program, as he has responsibility for it; so when the boss asked Commerce to stay level Connor reached out and decapitated Appalachia." Sweeney sought to limit the reduction of funds to an overall 23 percent.[106] Ultimately, as Table 6 shows, he was unsuccessful.

Table 6. *Appropriations for Appalachia (in thousands)*

Fiscal Year	Highway	Nonhighway	Administrative Expense	Total
1965–1966	$200,000	$105,550	$1,290	$308,840
1967	100,000	57,850	1,100	158,950
1968	70,000	56,700	746	127,446
1969	100,000	73,600	850	174,450
1970	175,000	107,500	890	283,390

Source: Advisory Commission on Intergovernmental Relations, *Multistate Regionalism* (Washington, D.C.: GPO, 1972), p. 34.

Such experiences led the commission to promote the idea of direct appropriations to ARC during the following year. According to Fleming, in the Bureau of the Budget and the White House "The attitude . . . was that they were sympathetic to your problems, but were reluctant to have money appropriated to any agency that wasn't strictly federal in character. We had the state governments involved." [107] State involvement was both a source of strength and a source of weakness for the Appalachian Regional Commission.

Reauthorization and Its Aftermath

The commission's budget aspirations became an issue in its 1967 reauthorization and, with them, its place in the governmental structure. Similar issues bearing on economic development commissions were also raised in connection with ARC reauthorization.

In Congress

At Sweeney's urging, with Califano's backing, and over the strong objections of the Bureau of the Budget, a draft reauthorization bill was not sent to Congress. [108] Instead, the president asked in a letter for an extension of the law "in substantially the same form as it was enacted in 1965." [109] Absence of an administration bill meant that the vehicle for extension, as Sweeney no doubt knew, would be legislation drawn by Senator Jennings Randolph of West Virginia, a senior Democrat and influential supporter of the Appalachia program. His bill, Schultze wrote the president with some alarm in early 1967, "would make major and highly undesirable changes" in the law. Among other things, it shifted program and project approval authority to the commission and empowered it to direct departments and agencies to carry out its decisions, did away with the provisions for prior approval by the president or a designee—the federal cochairman—of commission recommendations, and provided for appropriations directly to the commission.[110] The effect of the changes was to give state members almost complete control over the Appalachia effort.

Working with the congressional committees, presidential agents were able to excise the most objectionable features in Randolph's bill. The appropriations issue was compromised. Henceforth, funds would be appropriated to the president, not to the several departments. The act explicitly authorized the president to transfer appropriations for supplemental and local development district grants to the commission, and it was understood that funds for highways and other program elements would be treated the same way. Supplemental grants, local development district grants, and certain research and development grants would now be made by the commission. Others, such as for highways or vocational education, would still be made by the relevant department, though the funds were now the commission's, subject to its approval authority. The commission was vastly strengthened in its say in program activities and in the appropriations process. One other change was made which, though apparently of no great practical significance, was a departure from the organizational principles asserted by the Bureau of the Budget. That change was the requirement of state approval of all federal projects in that state. In other words, states now had veto power over grant-in-aid relationships between the national and local governments in the region.[111]

Congressional efforts to attach to the Appalachian bill changes in economic development commissions were at least as vexing for administration officials as were the issues bearing on Appalachia itself. Members from Oklahoma, Arkansas, and Missouri opened the fray in October 1966 when they submitted to the president a $681 million development program for the Ozark region. At this time the Ozark commission had no staff and no planning in process.[112] Pressures for program funds from this and other regions, demanding consideration equal to that given to Appalachia, ultimately resulted in the Bureau of the Budget's reluctant acceptance of a small grant supplement authorization in the legislation.[113] Following the Appalachian precedent, these funds were to help grant recipients meet matching requirements. Although there was no appropriation for this purpose for FY 1968, the Economic Development Administration provided almost $9 million of its own funds to the commissions for supplements.[114]

Other issues concerned congressional efforts to shape administrative arrangements in order to give the Title V commissions some of the independence and stature of the Appalachian commission and to give the states a prominent role in the supplemental grant program. As in the case of Appalachia, the legislation, enacted over BOB objections, gave the states veto authority over grants to their localities.[115] Although the act contained a stronger planning requirement for grant approval than the bureau expected to get, national authority was weakened by denying the Commerce secretary discretionary authority to judge the compatibility of grant proposals with plans.[116] But administration officials were successful in thwarting efforts to have appropriations for supplemental grants go to the president and those for administrative expenses directly to the commission rather than to the Commerce secretary.[117]

The Problem of Commission Governance

The centrifugal pressures attending the 1967 legislation once again underscored dilemmas in the governance of joint multistate regional institutions. The pressures substantially freed the Appalachian Regional Commission from the power of departmental bureaucracies; at the same time, Commerce's authority relationship to the Title V commissions became ambiguous at best. There were real prospects of growing disarray in national administration and of expanding the power of states in grant allocations and program determinations involving federal funds.

Pre-1967 efforts to deal with governance problems in some systematic way were flawed. As noted above, the Federal Development Committee for Appalachia never became operational, and the idea of naming an assistant secretary of Commerce to serve as federal cochairman of each Title V commission was quickly abandoned. In 1966 the Department of Commerce proposed an executive order to give the secretary control over the votes of Title V federal cochairmen, but it was not promulgated.[118] In its place, on 17 June 1966 the president wrote to the secretary and the cochairmen. The secretary was instructed to supervise and provide leadership for cochairmen who, in turn, were to elicit the views of the secretary on matters before their commissions and to be guided by them and by established national policy in making decisions. The secretary, according to the

Bureau of the Budget, did not implement the president's directive.[119]

While the 1967 legislation was being framed, the status of all the commissions was caught up in planning for a reorganization that would combine the Departments of Commerce and Labor. The president's early 1967 letter requesting that Congress extend the Appalachian program said that the new department would coordinate regional economic development activities. It would, he said, "have the basic responsibility for the Federal government's efforts in all of the regional commissions that have or soon will be established, including the Appalachian Regional Commission."[120]

When it was clear that the proposal for a new department was floundering, James Gaither, a member of Califano's staff in the White House, asked both Ross Davis, the assistant secretary with economic development responsibilities in Commerce, and the Bureau of the Budget to think in the long term about commission governance. A paper subsequently prepared by BOB and cleared by Davis proposed two alternatives. One was legislation that would place all functions and responsibilities of all economic development cochairmen and the Appalachian cochairman under the authority of the Commerce secretary. The weaker alternative was an executive order that would vest the president's Appalachian authority in the secretary of Commerce to complement the secretary's existing authority over Title V commissions. Sweeney and Fleming of ARC opposed the statutory route, and there would be strong congressional reservations. BOB director Schultze was also inclined to favor the less ambitious course, according to Gaither.[121] Further discussion produced the outline of an executive order by the time Congress completed action on the 1967 legislation. It was then fleshed out and signed by the president on 28 December 1967 in a form that closely followed the bureau paper's recommendations.

The major stumbling block in securing agreement on the order was the Appalachian commission. Gaither later characterized Fleming's position during this period as preferring "autonomy and one big pork barrel for the Regional Commissions."[122] Appropriations were a key problem. According to Fleming, even after the understanding was reached about their transfer from the president to ARC, Commerce lobbied to have the appropriations go to it instead. At a White House meeting, Schultze and Califano told him "they wanted to do this." In his view they "were legitimately, and I think the President was legitimately, concerned about the precedent that this program established for these other regional commissions. . . . I'm very sympathetic to that problem. Because if the same form and structure were applied in these others, you'd have six independent agencies with separate line items in the budget, and it just gets to be an administrative nightmare." Despite his sympathy for their concerns, Fleming argued successfully that the appropriations should go to his commission as planned. It would be "an absolute breach of faith" with Congress if they did not, he told the White House. "Besides that, these governors would come storming down on them, mainly because the Commerce Department is about the most incompetent bureaucracy in Washington. They really are."[123]

Another problem in securing agreement on the order concerned the president's authorities in the act to conduct liaison with the Appalachian commission and to secure a coordinated review of its proposals by other agencies. The authorities were delegated to the cochairman when the Federal Development Committee for Appalachia was established in 1965. When Califano secured Johnson's approval for the executive order idea early in October 1967, hoping the president could sign the act and the order together, these authorities were to go to the Commerce secretary with Fleming's consent, Califano said.[124] The act, but not the order, was signed on 11 October. The reason for not signing the order was strong opposition from certain senators who, Califano reported to Johnson, "do not want the Federal cochairman for Appalachia to have to take orders from the Secretary of Commerce."[125] In view of congressional opposition, Schultze and Califano were "inclined to drop this," wait until 1969, and in the meantime try to control the Appalachian commission through the budget process. The president did not wish to give in so easily. He instructed Califano to "try to sell" the order to dissident senators.[126] Apparently the selling effort was successful. When the president approved the order on 28 December 1967, Commerce retained the delegated authorities. The loss did not bother Fleming because, he said, he had the appropriations and "knew that the Commerce Department would never be able to implement" the order and its coordinative framework, an expectation that proved to be correct.[127]

The order provided a rather elaborate yet general set of instructions to the secretary of Commerce and the cochairmen about their roles and relationships. Further, it established the Federal Advisory Council on Regional Economic Development. Chaired by the secretary of Commerce, it consisted of the heads of several departments and agencies and was assigned general, advisory, and consultative responsibilities.[128] No doubt in part because of a secretarial transition in Commerce, implementation of the order was slow in coming. Indeed, the first meeting of the council was not held until 22 October 1968 near the end of Johnson's presidency.[129] The mechanism established by the order, as Derthick says, was "wholly ineffective."[130]

Conclusions

Despite publicly expressed enthusiasm and support, it is evident that joint multistate administrative regionalism and the establishment of water resources, Appalachian, and economic development commissions as components of the American administrative state were forced on the Johnson presidency. The commissions, especially the last two, were tolerated but unloved foster children in the Great Society family. The Bureau of the Budget did not like them for a variety of budgetary, administrative, and constitutional reasons, all having to do with, from its perspective, the imperative of protecting national power from expropriation by the states. Its antagonism was not offset by any discernible enthusiasm for the commissions in other presidential quarters, except for whatever political benefits their existence earned. State demands with strong congressional support for greater participation proved to be too potent to reject altogether. The real driving forces in the establishment of the economic development and Appalachian commissions were distributive politics and greater access to and control over federal funds. Joint multistate regionalism proved to be less a means for planning and governmental innovation along regional lines than an attractive format in which states could set forth distributive claims. With the benefits clear and attractive and the costs dispersed, the administration, more particularly the Bureau of the Budget, could only press for the best results it could obtain through negotiation.

A key decision was to accept the joint commission idea for water resources planning. In this case, the bureau could not mobilize sufficient support for national commissions, and it feared the joint compact alternative. Faced with the proposal for a mixed corporation for Appalachian development, the administration seized upon the river basin planning model as being more tolerable, even though no special program at all was preferred. The Appalachian commission then became the model for those who sought similar advantage for other parts of the country. The bureau responded in 1965 with the weakest possible reflection of the model, but it was forced by Congress to accept a somewhat stronger version. Then in 1967, building from the base established in 1965, incremental adjustments further strengthened not only the Appalachian and Title V commissions but also the role of states in determining the fate of federal funds and programs.

The role of the president and his White House aides in shaping multistate commission arrangements was limited but important. Ultimately, the president, seeing political advantages to be gained, did promote the Appalachian idea with some vigor, thus strengthening its advocates in Congress and in the states. It was his agents who made commitments to members of Congress during consideration of legislation for Appalachia in 1964 that later made commissions in other regions inevitable. The president's agents also mediated differences between the bureau and PARC on both the original Appalachian and economic development bills, sometimes siding with BOB and sometimes not. Perhaps the single most important effect of the White House on the commissions centered on Appalachia and Califano's decision, with Johnson's assent over BOB objections, not to submit draft legislation in 1967. This made it easier for supporters of the commission to increase its independence of Commerce and to enlarge its influence over grant expenditures. Changes in ARC arrangements, in turn, made it easier to strengthen Title V commissions. In this presidential involvement, one clearly sees the tension between immediate and focused political interests of the president and the more comprehensive and long-term perspective of the institutional presidency, at least as it was manifest in BOB at that time.

The bureau's apprehensions about the place of joint multistate commissions in the American administrative state proved to be well-founded. In both Appalachian and Title V operations, tension arose almost immediately between authentic regional development planning and securing and spending federal funds, and planning suffered as a result. Opening the door to state involvement in both cases led to pressures for more program independence, with implications for still larger state influence and pressure for increased funding. Finally, because of their unique features, the commissions were difficult to fit into the governmental structure either to provide some degree of overhead direction and control or to mesh systematically their operations with those of line departments and agencies. The problem, it should be noted, was not just in the centrifugal instincts of the commissions and their backers and in the state presence. It was also located in conflicting bureaucratic constituencies, philosophies, and program concepts at the national level and in bureaucratic disinterest in working collectively in settings such as interagency committees. As in other areas, a limited central management capacity in the presidency compounded difficulties.

A serious but flawed effort to solve these governance problems was stimulated in the White House in 1967, and it produced a structure for coordination, direction, and control in an executive order.

However, inertia and disinterest below negated the effort. Governance of the multistate commissions carried over as an agenda item for the Nixon administration.

Presidents and their aides are often frustrated in matters of government organization and unsuccessful in establishing administrative arrangements that satisfy presidential objectives. At least in the Johnson presidency, the regional development commissions presented an especially knotty challenge, one that was not overcome, in no small part because of their distinctive and innovative intergovernmental features. The uneasy juncture of the nation and the states as reflected in the commissions was the source of constitutional, political, and administrative quandries that were not readily solved by conventional coordination techniques.

6. The Revenue Sharing and Block Grant Options

Although the categorical grant-in-aid was the main device employed in further development of the American administrative state during the Johnson presidency, at times national policymakers considered alternative forms of assistance to subnational governments. Among the options were revenue sharing, or distribution of a portion of federal tax revenues to states and localities with few or no strings attached, and block grants structured with sufficient breadth to give recipients rather broad latitude to make their own categorical determinations. These options would have meant simpler administrative arrangements, more discretion for state and local governments, and less power in national bureaucracies. The revenue sharing option was rejected, as was the block grant concept in most instances. However, the Partnership for Health Act of 1966 consolidated a number of categorical grants into block form, and the Omnibus Crime Control and Safe Streets Act of 1968 established a new block grant to states in law enforcement and criminal justice. In 1968 the administration proposed block grants to states for vocational education, but Congress reintroduced categorical elements into the legislation before enactment. Ironically, in this same year Congress converted the administration's juvenile delinquency program, which was built around categorical grants, into one with distinct block grant features.

The means chosen for programmatic linkages between the center and the periphery are obviously of the utmost consequence for the geographical distribution of power. Although by their very nature categorical grants involve sharing national power with subnational units, their choice also reflects the presumption that the national role should be substantial in setting priorities and in program implementation. Categorical grants, whether national-state or national-local, might be described as controlled centralization. The degree of control is determined by the conditions, fiscal and programmatic, or by the requirements for accounting and auditing that attach to the grant. In contrast, the national role is reduced, and the discretion of recipients is enlarged in revenue sharing and, to a lesser extent, in block grants. Here there is a devolution from the national government to subnational units, and the latter have greater authority over the allocation of public resources. Although the term "decentralization" as applied to fiscal federalism is sometimes difficult to define with precision, revenue sharing and block grants are generally described as far more decentralizing than categorical grants.

Examination of the consideration of noncategorical options during the Johnson presidency provides insight into the dominant perspective that led to a distinct preference for categorical grants that accentuated the national role in intergovernmental administration.

The Rejection of Revenue Sharing

Before the Johnson administration's experience with revenue sharing is examined, a very brief look at history may be in order. In 1803 Congress earmarked 5 percent of the proceeds from the sale of public lands for distribution to the states in which the land was located.[1] The funds were expected to be used by the states for education and transportation, but there were no conditions attached. Then during the Jackson administration, the Treasury began to accumulate embarrassing surpluses, both from the sale of public lands and from a relatively high tariff. The national debt had been retired and the "serious inconvenience of an overflowing Treasury" occasioned Congress to adopt, in 1836, the Surplus Distribution Act. Payments were made to the states in 1837, until the panic that year eliminated the surplus. The total payments to the states amounted to $28 million.[2]

For many decades thereafter there was some sporadic interest in the possibility of the federal government sharing revenue with the states, but not until the 1950s were serious proposals introduced in Congress; the first of these was by a Republican member of the House, Melvin R. Laird of Wisconsin, in 1958.[3] A major feature of the Laird measure was its proposed substitution of general revenue sharing for an equivalent reduction in federal categorical aid.

The Heller Plan

The Johnson administration experience starts with Walter W. Heller, professor of economics at the University of Minnesota before becoming chairman of the Council of Economic Advisers under John F. Kennedy on 29 January 1961. He continued in that capacity until

15 November 1964. Heller, as an economist, had been interested for some time in revenue sharing and had suggested it as early as 1957.[4]

In the halcyon fiscal days of 1964, with a tax cut in place, the economy expanding, unemployment and inflation both under apparent control, and Vietnam impacts not yet apparent, the Council of Economic Advisers could safely predict that there would be future fiscal surpluses. On 12 May 1964 Heller, in a memorandum for the president, suggested that there was a "fiscal squeeze on State-local governments. . . . We should soon seize the initiative in the Federal-State-local fiscal relations issue. . . . By shared taxes, tax credits, specific or general grants-in-aid, or other devices, the Federal government can come to the rescue without imposing federal control or undermining 'states rights.'" The memorandum closed: "If we get a green light on this general idea, we'll push ahead with more specific approaches and proposals."[5] The president responded on 14 May: "Go ahead. Give me any more specifics you have. I am interested in it." Heller followed approximately two weeks later with detailed figures on federal, state, and local taxes as well as spending and debt, which the president could use "as evidence of the great fiscal pressure on state-local governments and your concern over them."[6] During this period the president's interest in revenue sharing was also confirmed in conversations with Heller.[7]

Heller made further public reference to the need for general federal fiscal assistance to state and local governments in a magazine interview in June 1964.[8] Then, in the summer of 1964, the administration established task forces to outline the possible legislative proposals for the anticipated postelection Johnson program. One of them, formed at Heller's initiative, was the Task Force on Intergovernment Fiscal Cooperation, chaired by Joseph A. Pechman, director of economic studies at the Brookings Institution.

As with all of the Johnson task forces, this one was charged to operate quietly, without consultation with outsiders or notice in the press. The principal reason for secrecy in this case, as in others, was to inhibit the organization of early opposition to or support for policy positions that the president might wish to accept, to accept in modified form after consultation with other advisers, or to reject. The task force report was not, in fact, released. The report recommended a new approach to intergovernmental fiscal relations—to channel a part of the "growing stream of Federal revenues to the States . . . to help assure an adequate level of public services in all States by mitigating the inequality of State resources."[9] The specific recommendation was the creation of a trust fund (outside the bud-

get) to receive 2 percent of the federal individual income tax revenues each year for distribution to the states on the basis of population or, alternatively, with some adjustments for personal income
levels and tax effort. At 1965 income levels, $5 billion would be dis-
tributed. The report stated that allocations should be made by the
states to their localities, but it did not specify the exact manner in
which this was to be accomplished. Such revenue distributions were
to supplement, not supplant, existing categorical aids.[10]

But before the report was completed, revenue sharing was caught
up in presidential politics. Senator Barry M. Goldwater of Arizona,
the Republican candidate in 1964, seized on intergovernmental fiscal relations as an issue. In doing so, Heller told the president, he
"beat us to the punch," although the Democratic platform did contain "the basic idea of more generous help to the States." Goldwater's plan, which echoed Laird's earlier proposal, was to give each
state a share of the income tax collected from that state and to provide supplementary grants to low-income cities and states. In exchange, approximately $10 billion in categorical grant programs
would be phased out. After noting the political liabilities in Goldwater's position and the provision in the Democratic platform, Heller
advised Johnson, "It is time to unveil our approach to the problem."[11]

That was soon to occur, but not in a way that advanced the cause
of revenue sharing. Starting in late September, Heller worked out a
set of brief position statements on economic and budget issues for
use in campaign speeches and press releases. One statement, following on the general commitment made in the Democratic platform
and informed by the work of the Pechman task force, focused on
strengthening the fiscal positions of state and local governments.
Heller knew that Johnson was sensitive to the state-local fiscal problems he had been describing. And to him, "Johnson seemed to be
particularly interested in having a plan that would distribute funds
on a more equitable basis" than Goldwater's.[12] It was on this perception that he proceeded. The statement approved by the president
through his closest aide, Walter Jenkins, contained a reference to un-
conditional grants. Later, Heller removed the specific reference,
which resulted in a rather ambiguous pledge of commitment.[13] Released on 28 October, it read in part: "The National Government, as
a constructive partner in a creative federalism, should help restore
fiscal balance and strengthen State and local governments by making available for their use some part of our great and growing Federal
tax revenues over and above existing aids. . . . Intensive study is now
being given to methods of channeling Federal revenue to States and

localities which will reinforce their independence while enlarging their capacity to serve their citizens."[14]

The implied promise of general assistance was compromised even as it was proffered, for on the same day the statement was released, there appeared on page one of the *New York Times* a story by Edwin L. Dale, Jr., describing in reasonably accurate detail the contents of the Pechman task force report. The headline above the story was "President Favors Giving the States Share of Revenue," and the first line read, "President Johnson endorsed in principle today a new plan for setting aside a fixed portion of the Federal income tax each year for automatic distribution to the states." The main source of Dale's story was an off-the-record interview with Heller, and, as Heller subsequently stated, he explicitly pointed out to Dale that the proposal had not yet been cleared with President Johnson. In Heller's view, he "was double-crossed."[15]

Presidential Decision

The task force proposal, as filtered through Dale's story, drew a mixed response. Two days after it appeared, Heller reported to Johnson that "the general idea of broadening the flow of Federal funds to States and localities seems to be getting *a very good reception.*" However, people in government, including Secretary of Labor W. Willard Wirtz and Assistant Secretary of Health, Education, and Welfare Wilbur Cohen, questioned the transfer of funds to the states with no strings attached. They were joined in their reservations by AFL-CIO officials.[16] In fact, Heller later said, Dale's story led George Meany, president of the AFL-CIO, "to explode."[17] Undergirding the negative reactions, according to Heller, was a desire for tight control over spending at the state level "to nail down" its uses, suspicion of state legislatures, and a fear that revenue sharing might reduce support for other grant programs. Heller's own support for revenue sharing remained unabated, however. He advised Johnson that the task force report would deal effectively with these criticisms.[18]

Revenue sharing in the Johnson presidency lingered on for a few more weeks until suffering, in Heller's words, "death by premature exposure."[19] After the election, on 14 November Heller sent Johnson a detailed, vigorous rebuttal to six major criticisms of revenue sharing. Two days later they reviewed the matter, and Johnson's apprehensions were evident. Unwilling to endorse revenue sharing, he expressed interest in a national commission to study it, causing Heller to develop plans for implementing the idea.[20] Shortly before the end

of November, the president discussed the topic in a telephone con-
versation with California governor Edmund G. (Pat) Brown, during
which, according to Brown, Johnson pointed to "a number of major
conceptual and political problems" in the revenue sharing idea.
(Brown, incidentally, thought they could be overcome.)[21]

Some believe that Johnson rejected revenue sharing simply because it was leaked and leaked at an especially inconvenient time—
just before the election.[22] But the record indicates that the president
did not reject the option automatically simply because the work of
the task force became public. An alternative thesis is suggested by
his response to a letter from a Washington acquaintance. The letter
applauded an interpretation of revenue sharing proffered by colum-
nists Rowland Evans and Robert Novak: that it was primarily a
means to get around the church-state problem in aid to education.
Revenue sharing would be used by the administration, they said, to
funnel money to the states for the support of education, both public
and parochial depending on state preferences, thus circumventing
the congressional impasse on the issue.

Johnson was not amused. The column, his response stated, was
"as is so many of their columns, inaccurate." Denying any approval
on his part, he characterized revenue sharing as "an idea advanced
by a study group but an idea not yet scrutinized in any way by responsible people in this Administration." His quintessential assessment of the situation, scrawled as he went over the draft response,
was "Already the gossip people have practically aroused enough opposition from labor et al. to guarantee its defeat."[23] In sum, revenue
sharing was kept off the policy agenda in 1964 not by the leak per se,
but by strong reservations in the Johnson administration, in Congress, and in key constituent groups. After the election Johnson considered instituting a national commission to examine revenue sharing, but the idea was dropped. Furthermore, the leak aside, it should
not be surprising that an extremely decentralizing initiative should
be passed over in the aftermath of an election in which a nationalist
sense of public purpose triumphed, one that ratified ambitious national policy goals.[24] The administration's official position in opposition to revenue sharing finally was made public at a background
press conference in mid-December.

The Issue Persists

Although rejected in 1964, revenue sharing persisted as a nagging
threat to specific and focused Great Society grant programs throughout the remainder of Johnson's presidency. The governors were its

strongest supporters. Among them, Republicans were quite vocifer-
ous in their advocacy, contributing something of a partisan edge to
debate, especially so since their party compatriots in Congress were
also attracted to the issue. Consequently, whenever the subject of
revenue sharing arose, the Johnson administration displayed political sensitivity as well as substantive wariness.

That sensitivity was tested as a National Governors' Conference
meeting neared in mid-summer 1965. Approximately two weeks before the meeting, the Republican governors served warning that they
would try to score political points with the revenue sharing issue.
They released a report that stoutly chastised Johnson for rejecting
revenue sharing on grounds of "personal peevishness" and "pique"
rather than on its merits.[25] Heller, scheduled to address the meeting
in Minneapolis, was attuned to presidential feelings on the matter.
He assured Johnson prior to his appearance that he had agreed to
speak only on the understanding that he would not discuss revenue
sharing in his remarks or in response to questions.[26] As it turned out,
revenue sharing caused no political wounds at the meeting. Buford
Ellington, then Johnson's liaison to the governors, attended the conference and reported to the president on 2 August 1965: "None of
the governors tried to put me on the spot regarding the Heller proposal. However, as you know, they favor any proposal that would
give the States a share of Federal taxes. I think we should devise
some plan to offset the big drive for the Heller proposal that will be
instigated by the Governors during the coming years."[27]

Ellington's prophecy about a "big drive" proved to be correct. With
considerable effort the administration managed to block proposed
hearings on revenue sharing by a subcommittee of the Joint Economic Committee later in 1965.[28] Pressure for revenue sharing grew
in 1966 even as the fiscal projections that contributed to its emergence as an option in 1964 were turning sour. Stanley S. Surrey, assistant secretary of the Treasury, captured the situation in his response early in the year to the Midland, Michigan, city council's
resolution in favor of tax sharing. "As you know, requirements for
Vietnam have increased the demands on the Federal budget and it is
not known what the financial needs of the Government will be for
Vietnam beyond the next year. For the time being, the Federal Government has no 'surplus revenues,' and the proposals made in this
context are not timely."[29]

Nevertheless, the political attractiveness of revenue sharing continued to draw adherents. By December 1966, as Heller put it, "the
pot" was "obviously boiling," and there were signs of concern in the
White House.[30] Presidential aides developed ideas for countering Re-

publican promotion of revenue sharing.[31] From the Treasury and the Council of Economic Advisers came protective talking points for the president to use in conversations with governors and others. They emphasized the large amount of assistance already going to state and local governments and the need to study carefully any sweeping innovations in intergovernmental fiscal relationships prior to action.[32] Ironically, on the same day Johnson received the talking points, Heller wrote to him on the need for a positive Democratic response to the growing interest in revenue sharing. Among other steps, he urged the president to make clear "that while it is premature in the light of Vietnam to earmark another big chunk of revenue for State and local governments, *work is going forward on additional programs to strengthen both the financial base and the independence of State and local governments.*"[33] The president apparently was not moved by Heller's plea. At about the same time it reached him, he asked Gardner Ackley, Heller's successor as chairman of the Council of Economic Advisers, "for all the arguments against federal tax sharing with state governments." The first of the eleven supplied by Ackley was the most telling: "We obviously can't afford it now or any time soon."[34]

All the arguments that might be mustered by Johnson's economic advisers could not stem the growing popularity of the revenue sharing idea in 1967 and 1968. There was fairly extensive public discussion. For example, Richard A. Musgrave, an economist and member of the Pechman task force, published a moderately favorable article in *The Nation*, and Pechman himself wrote more strongly in support of the idea for *The New Republic*.[35] In 1967 the Advisory Commission on Intergovernmental Relations (ACIR) took a strong stand favorable to revenue sharing.[36] Of greatest importance, a politically potent coalition of interest groups emerged in support of the concept. Based upon the realization that revenue sharing could be broadened to include localities, the advocacy of the National Governors' Conference and the Council of State Governments was joined by that of the National League of Cities, the U.S. Conference of Mayors, the National Association of Counties, and the International City Management Association.[37] A major step was taken when revenue sharing came under active consideration in Congress in 1967. Representative Martha Griffiths of Michigan, chairing a subcommittee of the Joint Economic Committee, held nine days of hearings on revenue sharing and its alternatives, featuring testimony by both Heller and Pechman.[38]

Despite growing support, the Johnson administration's opposition to revenue sharing did not waver. But this innovative approach to intergovernmental fiscal relationships, which could not find a place in "creative federalism," although it was endorsed in the 1968 Democratic platform, was ultimately welcomed into Richard M. Nixon's "new federalism," and revenue sharing became a reality in 1972. Other innovations that promised greater latitude for grant recipients were devised by the Johnson administration, however. The block grants enacted in 1966 and 1968 were striking exceptions to the commitment to categorical forms.

Block Grants and Categoricals

Grants-in-aid can change the distribution of political and economic resources within a federal system. The grantor patterns of the Office of Economic Opportunity attempted to give more political power to the poor. Model Cities, on the other hand, strengthened the fiscal and political resources of mayors. Grants may be allocated through formulas that redistribute economic resources from rich to poor states. Where grants are general in their purposes, with few "strings" attached, decision authority is transferred from the national government to the grantees—states or local governments or nonprofit agencies.

There is probably no choice in intergovernmental relations in the American administrative state that exposes more clearly the issues in fiscal resource allocation, the roles of professionals and political officials in the public sector, and the location of political power than the choice between block or categorical grants-in-aid. That which appears on the surface as a simple administrative election between different types of grants, in fact, involves a host of economic and political considerations, all intermeshed with the traditional conflicts that are inherent in multilevel government. Discussion of this choice in the Johnson presidency will be simplified by a preliminary sketch of the complexities.

Complexities

Categorical grants require applications and a heavy bureaucratic overlay in processing the applications, with accompanying delays and corresponding complaints by grantees. Grant simplification, by way of block grants, is a perennial demand of governors, mayors, and, indeed, many grantee agencies. The typical block grant features an entitlement determined by a formula spelled out in the statute. The formula will vary from grant to grant, but if states are the grantee jurisdictions, the state's share might be determined by factors such as population and relative state per capita income. If the eligible jurisdictions are cities, as is the case with the current program for community development block grants, small cities might be excluded, and the formula to determine a specific city's share of the entitlement might include housing conditions, income, and population.

Block grants, as they emerged during the Johnson administration and later in the Nixon, Ford, Carter, and Reagan administrations, carried with them a planning requirement. Once the jurisdiction's share is determined, it must submit a proposal for use of the funds. When the grant goes to the state, there may be a requirement for pass-through to local jurisdictions—municipalities or substate regions. This, in turn, may require the local jurisdiction to submit a proposal for the use of funds, which will be reviewed and integrated in an overall state plan.

Whether it is a state plan or a local plan that is required, that plan will be written in terms of specific projects or programs that the jurisdiction intends to implement within the guidelines in the statute, supplemented by the grantor agency's regulations. In the following year, if this system of intergovernmental administration works as intended, the grantor agency will review the prior year's performance under the grant before authorizing additional funding. State or federal auditors have the responsibility for assuring that the granted funds were, in fact, used for the purposes that had been authorized, and, in some cases, will undertake a performance audit directed at the outcomes of the program.

That which starts as a block grant, as the grantor agency responds to the state-local initiative, becomes in implementation a project-by-project grant. The significant difference is that the initial selection of the projects is the primary responsibility of the state or local jurisdiction, not the responsibility of the grantor agency. However, there are several points at which this kind of decentralization can, in fact, be very much influenced by central review and control—by the interpretation of regulations or mandates, by postaudit, or simply by informal advice and counsel to the recipient jurisdiction from either Washington or field offices of the grantor agency.

New programs may be initiated as block grants, or when categorical grants are consolidated, the result may be a block grant. In either case, block grants pose an interesting issue with respect to fiscal outcomes for grantees. A block grant with almost no restrictions on the use of funds, such as general revenue sharing, is a polar case. Here the program outcomes cannot be ascertained at the grantee level; that is, the grant comes into the state or local jurisdiction's treasury without earmarking. Being fungible, it is combined with all other jurisdictional general revenue, and since there are no radioactive tracers on the dollars, it is not possible, particularly after the first year's impacts, to ascertain whether the grant funds are used for reducing own-source revenue or whether jurisdictional outlay for police, fire, health, and similar services is increased as a result of the general purpose grant.

It is also possible that even when block grants are earmarked for special projects by jurisdictions, they will still be fungible, particularly when they are continued over a period of years. For example, a specific local government program for neighborhood health centers might have been undertaken in the absence of the grant for health centers and financed from own-source revenue. Thus, the grant appears to finance the health centers, but, in fact, the health grant is also fungible. The "true" fiscal outcome of the grant is to hold down own-source revenue or possibly to leave own-source revenue unchanged with larger outlays on other programs such as police, fire, and sanitation. In short, the program and tax burden outcomes of multilevel finance are very difficult to estimate, but this does not prevent students of public finance from making the attempt.[39]

Decentralization

There are other complexities in block grants. A significant number of scholars and political leaders favor the decentralization of choice on projects and programs. Choices made by lower-level jurisdictions, these scholars and leaders argue, will come closer to reflecting the tastes and preferences of the citizenry in the affected jurisdiction than if programs and projects are determined at the national level to reflect national preferences. Wallace E. Oates has presented this argument, in formal terms, as the "decentralization theorem."[40] Decentralized decision making will attain a more efficient allocation of resources. Here, efficiency is defined in terms of the welfare of the citizenry as reflected in their preferences. Thus, block grants with few conditions attached are superior to nationally-determined categoricals on "purely" economic grounds.

But there are a number of difficulties with a welfare economics approach to the choice between block grants and categoricals. The decentralization theorem overlooks the fact that one jurisdiction may have a preference ordering that favors private rather than public goods or that favors public education over sewage disposal. The reali-

zation of such preferences may impose external costs on other jurisdictions when, for example, downstream water supplies are affected
by inadequate sewage treatment.

A second difficulty with the decentralization approach is that
some interest group configurations, which, after all, are an expression of citizen preferences, may have greater influence at one level of
government than at another. It has often been observed that civil
rights advocates and those who support affirmative action and programs for the disadvantaged may have more influence at the national level than in state or local jurisdictions. The rhetoric of states'
rights and home rule is, no doubt, an important part of our political heritage, but both national and subnational interests must be
served.[41] Apprehension that the former may be slighted is a common
argument against block grants.

There are further implications in the transfer of decision authority from the national to state or local governments as block grants
are substituted for categoricals. Narrow and specific federal categorical grants are generally presumed to strengthen the professional
guilds that integrate national-state-local bureaucracies. Furthermore, the "iron triangles" composed of the guilds, congressional
subcommittees and their staffs, and the interest groups that support
the categorical program are similarly strengthened. "Special interests" structured into governmental processes are strengthened relative to the diffuse and unstructured "national interests," a matter of
deep concern to a number of political scientists for some time.[42]

When categoricals are consolidated into block grants, the Washington-level professionals and bureaucracies they serve lose power
and influence; and, in the case of block grants to states, governors or
their budget office or one of their departments may well gain power
and influence, depending on the nature of administrative arrangements. If governors and their immediate staffs have control over resource allocation in a block grant program, the generalists have
gained power at the expense of the professionals. If, as in the case of
a block grant for education, the state department of education were
to have responsibility for resource allocation, there is simply a substitution of one set of specialized interests at the state level for a set
of specialized interests at the national level. At the same time, the
governor, the governor's staff, or the responsible state agency must
make the difficult and frequently unpalatable decisions on resource
allocation.

Viewed in administrative terms, there can be no doubt that block
grants extended to states or municipalities on the basis of a formula
entitlement reduce the grantee's workload associated with grant ap-

plications and the grantor's workload associated with review and approval, as compared with the typical complex of categorical grants. However, as noted, block grants do not eliminate grantee obligations for adequate financial accounting or the grantor's obligation for audit. Nor do block grants eliminate the necessity that the grantee comply with the national "cross-cutting" requirements, such as affirmative action, equal opportunity, community participation, and the necessity for paying prevailing wages (Davis-Bacon). In short, block grants do not eliminate all the red tape that is the frequent target of critics of intergovernmental administration.

Finally, block grants of the type that are directed to states but require the integration of a state plan with substate plans require a high level of state-local coordination. Substate planning districts for health and for air pollution abatement may not be coterminous. Though water resource planning and land use planning are closely related as functional programs, they may not be jurisdictionally related within any one state. Further, the mechanics of generating the required local plans and their subsequent discussion and review by state planning agencies in such areas as health or criminal justice may be time-consuming and expensive.

In short, there is no magic in block grants; they are not the Holy Grail that untangles the intricacies of intergovernmental administration. They do not eliminate the political environments that influence intergovernmental programs and their administration. They decentralize such environments, weakening some interests and strengthening others. For such reasons, the choice between categorical and block grants is generally a contentious one in which the political values and interests of decision makers are likely to be more influential than considerations of administrative efficacy.

Partnership for Health

The health care programs of the Great Society were not only an integral part of the war on poverty, but they also reflected changes in societal attitudes toward the national government's role in health and, in turn, set in motion a confluence of political and economic interests that have kept health care on the national domestic policy agenda since that time. Although the national government had been involved for years in health programs at the state and local levels, Great Society initiatives significantly expanded that involvement. The programs also stimulated increased public and private expenditures at state and local levels by quasi-public medical care organizations and by the consumers of health care.

The enhancement of the public role in health care, in major part attributable to new federal programs, is underlined by the fiscal data. In 1960 public programs accounted for one-fourth of the nation's per capita expenditures on health. By 1969 public programs accounted for 40 percent of per capita expenditures. In this period national outlays for health increased fourfold.[43]

It was noted in chapter 2 that even the most significant of the Great Society health programs—Medicare—was a national undertaking, although third parties administered reimbursements. All other health programs adopted during the Johnson presidency were importantly intergovernmental, with financing through grants-in-aid to states, local governments, or nonprofit organizations.[44] The health programs had major programmatic dimensions. Medicare and Medicaid, for example, filled—at least partially—major gaps in the nation's social insurance system. These, together with the comprehensive health center program and an expanded maternal and child health program, were designed to provide increased access for the poor to health care facilities that had long been available to middle- and upper-income groups.[45]

In its programmatic, political, and administrative dimensions, health care and the public role in it involve issues that are extraordinarily complex and far beyond the scope of this volume. Viewed as an "industry," the provision of health care is most difficult to analyze and deal with in policy terms because of problems in data and measurement.[46] From the standpoint of the consumer of health care, Herbert E. Klarman describes the system as a collection of "complex, apparently irrational arrangements in health services . . . that stem from certain unique and peculiar circumstances of medical care."[47] In important respects, the Comprehensive Health Planning and Public Health Service Amendments of 1966, or the Partnership for Health Act, as the administration called the legislation, was an effort to deal with the complexities that had developed in the provision of public health services.

Origins

The Partnership for Health legislation was conceived and enacted in a political context described in general terms by S. Douglass Cater, special assistant to President Johnson on health and education. He wrote, "In the politics of modern America a new form of federalism has emerged, more relevant to the distribution of power than the old. . . . New subgovernmental arrangements have grown up, by which much of the pressing domestic business is ordered. Health has become such a subgovernment."[48] Cater suggests that there are five major operatives in this subgovernment: political executives, career bureaucrats, key committeemen in Congress, interest group professionals, and public interest elites. Their power derives from their continued interest and involvement and the priority that they attach to health policy over competing areas of governmental concern. Cater also predicted that the future politics of health would likely be as chaotic as in the past.[49]

In this complex of issues and political arrangements, the Partnership for Health legislation of 1966 and 1967 might appropriately be viewed as relatively insignificant. Nevertheless, from the standpoint of intergovernmental administration, Partnership for Health was the first successful effort to consolidate categorical grants into a block grant. Several project grants were also consolidated. As such, the law set a precedent for subsequent experiences with grant consolidation.

The Great Society health programs were initiated by Johnson in a message to Congress on 10 February 1964.[50] This message included legislative proposals on Medicare, health facilities, health manpower, mental retardation, health protection, and medical research. Of the major measures, Medicare was not then enacted, but significant changes were made in the Hill-Burton Act, which authorized construction funds for medical facilities.

The 1965 legislative program was, of course, Johnson's own, and it was considerably more ambitious than that of the previous year. In addition to Medicare and other carry-over bills, it included proposals drawn from the recommendations of the Commission on Heart Disease, Cancer, and Stroke and proposals from an outside task force chaired by Dr. George James, commissioner of health of the City of New York.[51]

Beginning with a strong plea for enactment of Medicare, the president's health message that year featured an extensive list of categorical grant programs on which action was sought.[52] Even as the message was being developed, however, the efficacy of the growing number of categorical grants for health services was being questioned. An early draft of the message, apparently prepared in the Department of Health, Education, and Welfare (HEW), contained language proposing an evaluation of existing program structures.[53] An attached discussion of policy issues raised by the draft, probably of BOB origin, made clear that evaluation would mean consideration of the block grant option.[54] The final version of the president's message, after noting the important role played by states and communities in health matters, stated, "General and special purpose grants have proved an effective means of strengthening the Federal government's partnership with them in improving the public health." The secretary of Health, Education, and Welfare, it continued, was directed to "study these programs thoroughly and to recommend to me necessary legislation to increase their usefulness."[55]

This was not the first instance of concern, some of it presidential, about the form of public health service grants. After a critical assessment by the Hoover Commission, the Truman administration unsuccessfully sought some consolidation, as did the Eisenhower administration. In the early 1960s, the National Commission on Community Health Services advocated a comprehensive, as opposed to a fragmented, approach to planning, organizing, and delivering services. Among its recommendations was a block grant for public health services. Although the commission's reports were not published until 1966 and 1967, the ideas it generated received considerable prior attention, especially in 1965 when Congress, following the president's recommendation, extended for one year the life of the categorical formula grants for public health services while the study he requested in the message was completed.[56]

In late August 1965, one task force named to work on the following year's legislative program focused on health care. Its chairman was Wilbur Cohen, under secretary of HEW, and Douglass Cater was the White House representative. Less than two weeks later its proposals, estimated to cost approximately $10.5 billion over a five-year period, were ready for consideration. Accounting for almost half the proposed expenditure was a vastly expanded commitment to maternal and child health care. Additional emphases included modernization of obsolete hospitals and other medical facilities, more beds for long-term care, development of home care as an option to institutionalization, and training for health care personnel.[57]

The work of the task force was not well received. Charles Schultze of the Bureau of the Budget complained to Califano that its product was a "very poor report." "Everybody," he continued, "including top HEW people agree." In his view, the core weakness of the report was the absence of an "overall framework." He followed with a number of specific points for consideration that differed markedly in some respects from the concerns of the task force. One of these was the "bewildering array of categorical health programs. . . . The major fault of the . . . report is that it does not come to grips with the problem." Schultze suggested that HEW secretary John Gardner be asked to review the matter over the coming year. "One specific alternative to be considered," the director continued, "is the substitution of *block community health grants* (subject to an approved community plan) for the existing host of categorical grant programs." Schultze asked for a White House meeting with Gardner to review this and other possibilities in the health care area. Held three days later, it involved Gardner, Schultze, Califano, Cohen, Cater, and Larry Levinson of Califano's staff. Initial decisions were made that gave the president's subsequent health proposals their distinctive and innovative cast.[58]

In Congress

A presidential message on health and education went to Congress on 1 March 1966, but as early as mid-December the content of the health segment was firmly in place. At that time, Cater received an outline of HEW's Partnership for Health program that featured the ideas of health services planning and grant consolidation.[59] Schultze's suggestion for an additional year of study had been transformed into a commitment to immediate action. The completed message began by acknowledging "20 landmark measures" in health enacted by the Eighty-eighth and Eighty-ninth congresses and the doubling of health care appropriations. Yet much more remained to be done to achieve the nation's goal of "good health for every citizen to the limits of our country's capacity to provide it."[60] Meeting health care needs, the president observed, "requires the cooperation of many agencies, institutions and experts—of state and local governments, of doctors, nurses and paramedical personnel." "A winning strategy" in the war on health problems "demands coordinated use of all the resources available."[61] That strategy, as outlined in the message, consisted of two basic elements. The first was comprehensive health services planning in order to identify and prioritize the distinctive needs of states and substate areas as a basis for devising a coordinated program of action to address those needs. The second element was increased flexibility in the established public health service grant programs to facilitate the matching of resources to needs.

The following day Senator Lister Hill (D-Ala.) introduced the administration's bill to amend the Public Health Service Act.[62] Three new planning grants were proposed. Another section of the bill contained the block grant provision consolidating nine existing categorical formula grants to the states into one formula block grant.[63] A state plan approved by the U.S. surgeon general was required for eligibility. The bill further stipulated that at least 15 percent of the funds be allocated to mental health programs and that at least 70 percent of the total grant amount be expended for services at the local level.[64] The mental health reservation aside, state expenditures under the block grant were not restricted to the subjects of the categorical grants it replaced. Finally, the bill proposed to consolidate seven existing project grants into one to be administered by the Public Health Service in HEW. The grants were open to state and local health agencies and nonprofit organizations for a variety of health service purposes.[65]

Generally speaking, the two central concepts contained in the legislation, comprehensive planning and greater flexibility in the health services grant system, did not encounter serious opposition in Congress. The idea of state planning in the health area was not new. For example, Hill-Burton grants for hospital construction were conditioned by annual inventories of facilities done by states and by state planning for the establishment of priorities.[66] Furthermore, members of Congress who were especially interested in health matters were aware of and sensitive to criticisms of inadequate planning and of fragmentation in health service programs. And although there was some opposition, the bill was strongly supported by several influential interest groups, notably the American Public Health Association, the Association of State and Territorial Health Officers, and the National Association of State Mental Health Program Directors.

In Senate and House hearings, administration spokesmen placed great emphasis on the complementary relationship between planning and grant consolidation. Comprehensive planning was a tool to be used by states in meshing a variety of old and new health programs and in playing the expanded leadership role required by new programs established in recent years. A block grant, together with consolidated project grants, would add substantially to flexibility and would enhance the ability of states to match resources to the needs identified in plans.

The administration obtained most of what it wanted in the bill passed by the Senate, but difficulties were encountered in the House. The authorization period was cut and levels were reduced. The House also excised two provisions that were intended to aid in resolving conflicts over priorities. One, in the administration's bill, mandated that starting in FY 1971 block grant services must be included in comprehensive state health plans. Because the bill as amended did not extend to 1971, what was intended to be only an interim requirement—the provision that block grant services be in accord with state plans—was retained. This less compelling requirement remained the standard even after reauthorization the following year. The other provision removed by the House had been added in the Senate and directed the secretary of HEW to prepare national health goals and guidelines to aid the states in planning.

Even as Johnson signed the act on 3 November 1966, work was underway on preparing next year's health program, which, of necessity, would include proposals to establish planning and grant consolidation on a more durable foundation. The task force working on health matters and others involved in policy decisions remained quite favorable to comprehensive planning and grant consolidation. As the 1967 program developed, the only real issue was the level of funding. The task force sought vast increases in financial commitment: nearly $290 million for FY 1968, including $170 million for the new grants, and a total of $2.248 billion over a five-year period.[67] By the end of December, however, the Bureau of the Budget had decided that a total of $170 million for the several Partnership for Health activities was a more reasonable figure. The president's request reflected BOB's position, meaning that there would be only a modest enrichment of the grant programs in the coming year. Congress made minor changes, and the legislation passed without major difficulty.

In summary, the primary origins of the consolidation of several categorical grants into a formula block grant for health services were located in the public health community's dissatisfaction with the rigid and fragmented program structure that had evolved over the years. It is not known whether HEW's initial 1965 legislative recommendations, thoroughly in the categorical mode and oblivious to the president's earlier directive to seek simplification, indicated basic satisfaction with the status quo in the U.S. Public Health Service bureaucracy. It is clear, however, that acceptance of the fragmentation critique by the Bureau of the Budget, Secretary Gardner, and the White House was the critical factor leading to presidential endorsement and ultimate approval of the Partnership for Health concept. Unquestionably, this block grant experiment was an authentic, albeit anomalous, progeny of the Johnson presidency.

The Ongoing Debate

Consideration of the block grant idea, as well as other approaches to grant consolidation, occurred periodically during Johnson's presidency. Early task forces considered block grants or general, noncategorical aid for elementary and secondary education, public assistance, and urban services. The categorical option won out in each case, however. The Partnership for Health program was a break in the pattern. Its precedent notwithstanding, in the administration there continued to be evidence of an ambivalence tilting toward antagonism to block grants, while in Congress they were somewhat, though not consistently, more popular. In each of the subsequent debates over the block form, the administration and Congress invariably took opposite sides of the issue.

There were four major conflicts in Congress that involved a choice between block and categorical approaches. In 1967 the administration fought off strong efforts in Congress to convert categorical grants in four titles of the Elementary and Secondary Education Act of 1965 into a single block grant to the states. The major reason for its opposition to consolidation was a conviction that state educational bureaucracies, if given authority and discretion, would be neither inclined nor competent to aim resources at improving the education of the disadvantaged and to spark innovative breakthroughs in educational concepts and techniques. These were the act's most important objectives.[68] But in the aftermath of this intense struggle, Johnson's 1968 education message asked Congress to enact the Partnership for Earning and Learning Act of 1968, which made basic changes in vocational education programs. It would, the message avowed, "give new flexibility to our system of matching grants, so the States can concentrate their funds where the need is greatest."[69] The key recommendation was to consolidate twenty-three categorical grants into a single block grant to states. It reflected a continuing interest in HEW and the Bureau of the Budget in grant consolidation in this area. At a White House meeting in late 1966 in which vocational education legislation for 1967 was considered, Charles Schultze of BOB questioned, according to meeting notes, "whether money shouldn't go by unrestricted grants to States and let States decide what to do."[70] The decision to seek only modest increases in 1967 and to save a major push for 1968 put off until then a mature block grant proposal. When it acted in 1968, Congress severely limited the discretion of states by specifying seven authorizations and three additional earmarkings. The law, Norman C. Thomas says, "was a congressional rather than executive branch product," heavily influenced by the American Vocational Association, local and state officials, and vocational educators.[71]

The enactment of new juvenile delinquency legislation and the Omnibus Crime Control and Safe Streets Act came in 1968. The two measures featured categorical programs in the administration's versions, but Congress substantially converted both into block form. Because the safe streets legislation was such a sharp departure from tradition and practice, it and its antecedents require close examination.

In the act the national government greatly extended its activities in an area that hitherto had been dominated by state and local jurisdictions. Their dominance notwithstanding, the national government had played something of a role. Over the years, prohibition of the transportation of certain items in interstate commerce was often intended to assist state and local law enforcement. Modest tangible assistance was given to state and local law enforcement as an off-shoot of the national government's law enforcement efforts in its own domain. The Juvenile Delinquency and Youth Offenses Control Act of 1961 provided direct assistance to states, but it emphasized the social and preventive dimension of the problem, not law enforcement. However, the Law Enforcement Assistance Act (LEAA) of 1965 and its successor, the 1968 legislation, brought policing—then, entire criminal justice systems throughout the country—within the reach of Washington. The safe streets legislation contained a comprehensive grant-in-aid program that gave the states major responsibilities for planning, for allocating funds to action projects, and for program administration. It went far beyond the 1961 and 1965 enactments.

Safe Streets

Enlargement of the national role in law enforcement was approached by policymakers with more trepidation than its enlargement in other areas. The police power is at the core of state prerogatives in the federal system. Over the years, certainly one of the strongest points of consensus in the American federal arrangement has been that there should be no national force invested with comprehensive policing powers. Even a perceived substantial national influence over the work of state and local law enforcement agencies was thought by many to be politically dangerous.

First Steps

Ironically, one of the most vocal contemporary opponents of national intrusion into state and local affairs was a major contributor to an enlarged national role in state and local criminal justice systems. Sensing public alarm about crime in the streets and urban unrest, in the 1964 campaign Goldwater made frequent statements on the "breakdown in law and order." In contrast to revenue sharing, where his endorsement had a negative effect, his position on law and order contributed to making law enforcement a national political issue and to rising pressures on the Johnson administration to act.

There was an initial presidential reluctance to respond. Alarmed by Goldwater's success in exploiting the crime issue, Democratic Party officials sought a dramatic countermove that would wrest it away from the contender. Specifically, they pressed for a mid-campaign White House conference on law enforcement, but without success.[72] The best they could obtain was a statement by the president on 26 September that focused on urban riots. After summarizing a Federal Bureau of Investigation (FBI) report on their causes, the statement announced several modest initiatives, the last of which was to call "at an appropriate time . . . a conference of State and city officials to discuss ways in which the Federal Government can continue to be of assistance in this whole area."[73]

That conference was never held. Instead, the most important policy effect of Goldwater's campaign rhetoric was to cause administration officials to begin to think systematically about program options in the law enforcement area. One official was Arnold Sagalyn, director of the Treasury Department's Office of Law Enforcement Coordination, whose ideas drew Cater's attention in September.[74] Sagalyn's basic thesis, put against the backdrop of obvious problems in law enforcement, was that "local and state police departments are in urgent need of help and assistance which can come only from the national level." It was his view that "the Federal government can provide leadership, training and other types of assistance without in any way doing injury to the established Federal-state relationships in this area." He envisaged a technical assistance program much like that provided to developing countries featuring an emphasis on training. With Cater's encouragement, Sagalyn began to work with Department of Justice officials on an assessment of law enforcement training resources. The scope of involvement broadened as work extended into the fall. By early December, Justice and HEW had produced a draft message on crime and delinquency. The purpose, a Justice official told Bill D. Moyers in the White House, was "to indicate what kind of message might result—perhaps next spring—if the President were to direct the Attorney General to begin now to consult with State and local enforcement officials and others and to develop a federal program."[75]

The president did wish to develop a program. He said in the State of the Union message in January 1965:

> Every citizen has the right to feel secure in his home and on the streets of his community.
>   To help control crime we will recommend programs:
> —to train local law enforcement officers;
> —to put the best techniques of modern science at their disposal;
> —to discover the causes of crime and better ways to prevent it.[76]

Johnson announced that he would assemble a panel of experts to search out answers to the national problem of crime and delinquency and that, in the meantime, he would welcome the recommendations and constructive suggestions of Congress.

On 8 March 1965 Johnson dispatched to Congress the first crime message by any president. In content it was quite close to that of the December Justice-HEW draft. The premise of the message, and the basis on which proposals were set forth, was that "crime is a national problem."[77] There had to be "a national effort to resolve the problems of law enforcement and the administration of justice—and to direct the attention of the nation to the problems of crime and the steps that must be taken to meet them."[78]

While asserting crime to be a national problem requiring increased efforts by the national government in combating it, the message was careful to recognize that "the basic responsibility rests on local authorities."[79] No "threat to the basic prerogatives of State and local governments" were to be read into the president's proposals.[80] These proposals recognized the "burdens" borne by state and local law enforcement agencies, and the national efforts prescribed were "to assist them in bearing these burdens successfully."[81] In addition to these assurances, the message spelled out in considerable detail national policy objectives and the various ways in which national agencies in the past were involved in law enforcement at state and local levels.[82] In the aftermath of the message, several administration bills bearing on federal law enforcement were introduced. The President's Commission on Law Enforcement and the Administration of Justice (Crime Commission) was established on 23 July 1965 by executive order. On 26 July, Attorney General Nicholas de B. Katzenbach was appointed chairman, and eighteen other members were named.[83]

Later that year, on the recommendation of the administration and with very little hesitation, Congress passed the Law Enforcement Assistance Act. There was an authorization of $7.2 million for grants-in-aid administered by the Office of Law Enforcement Assistance in the Department of Justice. Categorical grants were to go to state and local governments for a variety of experimental programs in all phases of law enforcement. Although resources were limited, the Advisory Commission on Intergovernmental Relations nonetheless observed that the act "was a pioneering attempt by the Federal Government to encourage State and local jurisdictions to improve their law enforcement and criminal justice systems."[84]

The administration's program for 1966 built upon the initiatives of the previous year. There was little that was new, although a near doubling of LEAA funds was recommended by the president. It was imperative, Johnson proclaimed, to "mobilize all of the resources of our creative federal system if we are to repel the threat of crime to our common well-being. The problems of crime bring us together. We must make a common response. There is no other way."[85]

Program Expansion

With the Law Enforcement Assistance Act now being implemented and, according to Katzenbach's report to the president, "already producing wide-spread action to improve virtually every phase of criminal justice," work began on an expanded anticrime program late in the summer of 1966.[86] Initial discussions involved Katzenbach, James Vorenberg, executive director of the Crime Commission, and James Gaither of Califano's staff. Over the next few months there would be several White House meetings involving these officials, Califano, and others to sift Crime Commission recommendations and form a set of presidential initiatives.[87]

The first meeting was on 18 August 1966. There appeared to be a general expectation that the 1967 program would be much more ambitious and far-reaching than those of the past two years. According to the minutes of the meeting, the policy planners were told that the Crime Commission would recommend that "most of the expenditure will be in support of state or local programs to improve the caliber of personnel, communications systems, treatment programs, etc." The commission would propose to rely heavily on state planning to guide the allocation of resources.[88]

Following this meeting, an inside task force was established to prepare concrete proposals. It was headed by Katzenbach, then later by Ramsey Clark when he became acting attorney general. Aided by Crime Commission staff, the task force had proposals ready for review by mid-November. They were submitted to the White House with proposals from a separate juvenile delinquency task force.

The Crime Commission was arguably the most ambitious and thorough of any public commission during the Johnson presidency. It had a professional staff of 40 who were assisted by 450 consultants and advisers; its products included nine task force reports, five field survey reports, forty-one consultant papers, and a final report of 340 pages. The commission's report, *The Challenge of Crime in a Free Society*, was filed in January 1967 and identified eight areas in which national assistance was needed: state and local planning, education and training of personnel, advisory services to criminal justice agencies, development of a national crime information system, demonstration projects in criminal justice agencies, research and development programs, institutes for research and training, and grants-in-aid for innovations in operations at state and local levels. Although the commission did not put price tags on its program recommendations, it did discuss the need for the expenditure of several hundred million dollars over the next decade.[89] A major thematic emphasis was on viewing the problem of crime in systemic terms and recognizing the critical interconnections among policing, the courts, corrections, and other components. The commission's work made an important contribution to task force considerations.

From the perspective of intergovernmental relations, the most significant of all the ideas in the joint report of the law enforcement and juvenile delinquency task forces was the recommendation for establishing a broad program of aid to support state and local law enforcement and criminal justice systems. There were a number of components. Several were to be administered by the Department of Justice. However, according to the task force report, "The major part of federal assistance would . . . be administered through operational grants-in-aid matched by state funds and used according to plans prepared by . . . state commissions in concert with local agencies and approved in conformity with federal guidelines. This aid would be used to institute innovations in the operation of criminal justice systems . . . where they were needed in a particular state."[90] In the initial years, the emphases were to be on planning and demonstration projects. Appropriations of $25 million to $50 million a year would be required. Later, as action programs were developed, costs would range from $500 million to $750 million per year.

Although the task force report was somewhat vague about the particulars of grant-in-aid arrangements, a Bureau of the Budget analysis indicates that it had in mind essentially a block grant approach. There were to be formula grants to states, then state agency allocations to state and local programs, with appropriate matching, based upon state plans. In 1968 Congress would insist on this type of arrangement, but it was not what the president proposed.[91] As introduced in the Congress in 1967, the administration's legislation was for the most part what ACIR has called "direct federalism"—categorical project grants to state agencies and to local jurisdictions or combinations thereof.[92] The switch from a block to a categorical approach was especially curious in light of public statements of the president in September and October 1966 to a group of governors and at a meeting of representatives of state law enforcement and criminal justice committees. These statements heralded in unqualified terms the key role of the states in the fight against crime.[93]

The change in approach was the product of four White House meetings in late November and December 1967.[94] Although the meetings were attended variously by a fairly sizable number of department, agency, White House, and BOB officials, the major players in them were Clark, Fred Vinson, in charge of the criminal division in the Justice Department, Katzenbach, now at the State Department, Vorenberg, Charles Haar of the Department of Housing and Urban Development, Gaither, and Califano. In considering the task forces' major proposals, the group began to think in terms of categorical programs instead of block grants. Toward the end of the first meeting, a question arose concerning the impact of task force proposals on the "consumers" of crime, the general public. This led to consideration of the possibility of legislation that might provide immediate and visible benefits in protecting individuals against crime. Specific means and specific programs were suggested, including improved street lighting, alarm systems, and better public telephone access to police. Although this approach was criticized by some on the grounds that it would put the president "on the line for making safe streets" and that "gadgets are not the answer to crime," it was attractive to others. Vorenberg and Haar agreed to develop more fully the safe streets idea as it had emerged during the meeting.

Vorenberg's paper, circulated prior to the next meeting, thoroughly delineated numerous specific project grants that might fit into a safe streets framework. Ultimately, however, he argued that the approach was unsound. It focused not on crime as a complex, systemic problem requiring a long-term program for its control; rather it emphasized the short run and the quick, fragmented fix. Consequently, the safe streets approach as it was then conceived, with a host of categorical programs focused on very specific anticrime measures for the immediate protection of individuals, was defective. There could be enormous costs, yet there was little or no evidence that the specific measures under consideration would have beneficial results. Finally, Vorenberg felt, there was a danger of creating the perception that the president and the national government had taken direct responsibility for contending with crime in the streets.[95] Vorenberg's critique was apparently effective for a short time. At that meeting, on 3 December, a more broadly conceived approach was the center of attention, although the safe streets idea, in the form of a package of categorical grants, continued to be of interest to some.[96]

The final decisions on the crime program were made by the group on 10 and 12 December. It had before it a new outline prepared in the Department of Justice. Various options were considered. Most of the discussion concerned two types of grants. One was a basic no-strings grant to local law enforcement agencies keyed to an increase in the local law enforcement budget, in effect a block grant to localities. The other was a program of project grants to state and local agencies for particular purposes such as training, crime laboratories, and information systems development.[97] The following specific issues were on the table at this point:

1. Whether, from an administrative point of view, the original task force proposal for a single block grant to the states would not be preferable to categorical grants in view of the large number of prospective recipients around the country.

2. Whether the national government should offer categorical assistance or, as Justice proposed, general assistance directly to local police departments.

3. The relationship of comprehensive state and local plans to grant proposals and awards.

4. Whether eligibility should be limited to only the larger local jurisdictions.

5. Whether grant funds could be used to pay salaries.

6. The appropriate balance to be struck in allocating resources to policing versus courts, corrections, and prevention of crime.

7. Whether the program should be administered by Justice or HUD.[98]

The idea of block grants to the states received no more support within the group now than at its first meeting. Nor was general assistance to local governments for law enforcement a popular alternative. The notes indicate an acute suspicion of local law enforcement agencies, apprehension about how general purpose grant funds might be misused, and an interest in national control over funds. At the same time, the notes reveal considerable anxiety about Washington's ability to control effectively the actions of hundreds, if not thousands, of state and, especially, local agencies. Consequently the group rejected general assistance in favor of categorical grants. Comprehensive state and local planning requirements would serve, it was hoped, as a tool in aiding the control function and in promoting the overall program's basic objectives of increasing investment, innovation, and effectiveness in anticrime efforts. Restricting eligibility to states and large cities also reduced the control problem and made the realization of program objectives somewhat less problematic. Placing limits on the use of grant funds for salaries would also contribute to this end. The problem of balance in the support of police and functions such as corrections was not resolved at this time.

What was retained from the task force's work was a systemwide perspective to be reflected in planning and in the administration of the program by the Department of Justice.

The working group's recommendations were approved by the president on 19 December, previewed in his State of the Union address, and presented in full to Congress in a special message on 6 February 1967.

The 1967 Message and Its Aftermath

Once more, care was taken to alleviate sensitivity to national involvement in local law enforcement. In the State of the Union address, Johnson said, "The idea of a national police force is repugnant to the American people. Crime must be rooted out in local communities by local authorities." Further, "The National Government can and expects to help."[99] In the crime message there were also strong assurances.[100]

The proposal sent to Congress was not complex. For the first year, the administration sought an authorization of $50 million, which was expected to rise to $300 million in the second, and four types of grants-in-aid. In the bill as introduced, the attorney general was authorized to make categorical grants to state and local agencies of up to 90 percent of the costs of planning improvements in law enforcement, courts, and corrections. Categorical action grants of up to 60 percent of program costs were authorized; state and local recipients were required to show a 5 percent annual increase in the expenditure of their own funds and to have comprehensive plans. Local eligibility was limited to single or combined jurisdictions with a population of at least 50,000, reduced from 100,000 only in the last draft of the message. The remaining two grant programs were for research and for the construction of physical facilities, such as crime laboratories, on a metropolitan or regional basis.

By this time, congressional receptivity to Great Society programs was diminished.[101] Hearings on the legislation in 1967 did not go smoothly in either the House or the Senate. The proposed bypass of the states and governors through the authorization of direct grants to cities was particularly controversial. Among the features attacked were the requirement of a local population minimum of at least 50,000 and the requirement that recipient outlays be increased at an annual rate of 5 percent. In addition, some in Congress expressed concern that vesting authority to award grants in the attorney general would subject state and local law enforcement to undue national influence.

Administration spokesmen countered the criticisms as best they could. The rationale offered for not channeling all grants through states was that crime in the streets was essentially an urban, local problem and that, in general, the states had little experience, expertise, or administrative capacity in this area. Population limits were defended on administrative grounds and as a means to stimulate regional and metropolitan approaches to law enforcement. The states would have a special role in working with and assisting less populous areas in the development and administration of programs under the proposed legislation, as well as in efforts focusing on courts and corrections. The 5 percent requirement was justified by the proposition that state and local expenditures in law enforcement and criminal justice systems needed to increase substantially.

The measure passed by the House on 8 August 1967 differed from the administration's proposal in important respects. Major changes were incorporated by the House Judiciary Committee to protect state and local interests. Provision was made for gubernatorial review of all project applications. The 50,000 population standard and the 5 percent requirement were dropped. The attorney general's discretion was limited in several small ways, and funds were authorized for only one year and by title in place of the open-ended authorization in the administration's bill.

Major blows were delivered on the House floor, where the administration's categorical approach was reshaped into block form by a coalition of Republicans and conservative Democrats. In essence, the amendment adopted provided that both formula planning and action grants would go to state planning agencies for further distribution at the state and local levels. This was, at root, the original approach recommended by the Katzenbach task force but rejected by the White House working group. The bill was passed by the House as amended on 8 August 1967, but the year ended without Senate action.

As 1967 drew to a close, the debates in Congress showed the overall position of the Johnson administration in its law enforcement initiatives to be precarious and somewhat uncomfortable. Crime clearly was a national issue. Since 1965, summers had been marked by scores of riots in major cities and hundreds of minor incidents of unrest. Crime was constantly in the spotlight for other reasons, including the Johnson administration's rhetoric and proposals. Consequently, each year seemed to require a more energetic and ambitious response than the last. Yet the fact of state and local preeminence in law enforcement and other criminal justice functions strictly limited what could be done by the national government on its own.

There were proposals for national action. While important, most of them, such as immunity legislation to make it easier to compel testimony, bail bond reform, and unifying federal corrections functions in Justice, would not in any direct sense make streets and homes safer. And the few initiatives that were more immediately related to the crime problem, such as gun control, were highly controversial and difficult for Congress to accept. The imbalance between rhetoric and action was noted by the president's 1967 task force on crime, chaired by political scientist James Q. Wilson of Harvard University. In preparing a legislative program for 1968, the task force acknowledged the limitations of national effort up to that time.[102]

Spurred by the Wilson task force report, the failure of Congress to enact legislation in 1967, and the prospect of a reelection campaign, the administration's policy planners outlined the most extensive anticrime program to date for presentation in 1968. A top priority was enactment of the legislation pending in Congress to which new provisions for law enforcement education and training were now attached. The appropriation requested for grants was $100 million, twice the amount sought the previous year. More than twenty additional executive initiatives and legislative proposals for national action were announced in the message that went to Congress on 7 February 1968.[103]

Even though the 1968 message was the president's fourth on crime, apprehension was still evident about the relationship between the national government and state and local law enforcement. Early in the process, the White House commissioned a paper from the Justice Department on the constitutional responsibilities of the state and national governments in controlling crime and domestic violence. The point stressed by Justice's analysis was that "the primary responsibility for control of crime and domestic violence belongs, under our constitutional system, to the state and local governments."[104] Providing the national leadership urged by the task force in view of constitutional and political realities called for striking an exceedingly fine balance.

The president's personal concern was such that he asked Associate Justice Abe Fortas of the U.S. Supreme Court, for years a close adviser, to review a draft of the crime message. Fortas had two fundamental criticisms. The draft, he asserted, did not "come to grips with the problems of safe streets and safe homes in simple, specific terms. It is this problem that bothers people," he said. By and large, the measures proposed would have an unclear and indirect effect on the safety of individual citizens. Furthermore, the draft message did not "sharply, clearly, pungently deal with the federal-state-local jurisdictional problem." It was muddled on the responsibilities of the various levels of government, especially as to the role of the national government.[105]

He put forth two options. One was to infuse the message with language that emphasized state and local responsibility for dealing with the crime problem and that forthrightly admonished officials at those levels to meet their responsibilities. The other option was to propose national measures that would hit directly at crime. Fortas specifically mentioned laws providing for gun registration, making use of an unregistered gun in commission of a felony a federal offense, and making it a federal crime "to injure, in the course of committing a felony, any person engaged in work or business affecting interstate commerce." Such measures, he admitted, were "necessarily drastic and constitutionally dubious."[106] Presidential staff working on the message acted on the justice's advice and added language reflecting his first option in a number of places.[107]

Emphasis on state and local government notwithstanding, the administration continued to insist upon its approach to safe streets legislation, an approach based upon the categorical grant device that would give the national government considerable influence in state and local law enforcement. The problem was to convince Congress that this was the correct approach. Since the House passed a measure in 1967, in 1968 the center of action was in the Senate. In the Senate Judiciary Committee there was notable concern about national influence in law enforcement, and it came to be focused on two major issues: organizational arrangements for administering the safe streets grant programs and, of course, the form the grants would take. The administration's position was rejected on both points. In the Judiciary Committee and on the Senate floor, the administration was able to repulse an effort to deny any administrative authority to the attorney general. However, it was forced to accept the location of operating responsibility in a three-member, bipartisan Law Enforcement Assistance Administration (LEAA) appointed by the president and subject to the general authority of the attorney general instead of in a single administrator. As Harold Seidman points out, this was a significant violation of administrative orthodoxy, which requires that cabinet officers have undiluted responsibility for the organization of their departments.[108]

The bill reported by the committee included the administration's categorical grant proposals. However, an amendment was inserted on the floor of the Senate providing for a block grant scheme quite similar to that passed by the House the previous year. Subsequently, the House accepted the Senate version, and the bill was signed by the president on 19 June 1968, 500 days after it was first proposed.

The 1968 legislation provided states with block grants for both planning and programs. First, planning grants (Title I) would go to each state at a minimum level of $100,000, with additional planning funds distributed on the basis of population. Forty percent of each state's grant was to be passed through to local jurisdictions. Federal funds for planning were to be matched by the states with a 10 percent contribution. Second, 85 percent of the action or program grant funds (Title II) were to be allocated to the states in accordance with population, and 75 percent was to be passed through to local jurisdictions. State agencies would decide how program grant funds would be used. The remaining 15 percent of the funds were to be allocated at the discretion of LEAA. Program grants were to be matched on a sixty-forty basis. The appropriations for fiscal 1969 were divided into $19 million for planning grants and $25 million for program grants.

Categorical grants were also authorized by the legislation. The national government would cover 75 percent of the cost of projects directed at organized crime and riot control and 50 percent of construction projects. Finally, Washington would fully fund grants for research, demonstration, and training programs. Modest amounts were appropriated for these purposes.

In examining the safe streets legislation as an intergovernmental innovation, the ACIR was struck by "the Act's heavy reliance on State governments as planners, administrators, coordinators, and innovators. . . . The State's overall role is to act as a catalyst in bringing together previously isolated components of the law enforcement and criminal justice system and coordinating, directing and supporting their efforts in a comprehensive attack on crime." [109] The significant role that Congress accorded to the states over the administration's opposition reflected a concern about national encroachment on local law enforcement agencies—the national police force issue. But there were other factors at work, and it is not easy to untangle the diverse forces that influenced Congress to alter the administration's proposal. During this period there was continued pressure from governors to reverse the pattern of direct grants to local governments and, in general, to give the states a larger role in intergovernmental programs. Further, there was mounting pressure for decentralization that would give states and local jurisdictions greater freedom from central control over the conditions and administration of grants-in-aid. And there seems always to be the feeling on the part of many that red tape and bureaucracy will be reduced by the transfer of authority from Washington to the field, to regional administrative structures, to states, or to local jurisdictions. Perhaps it is that part of the American psyche holding that Washington "doesn't know what goes on" or "doesn't know what is best" for regions, states, and communities—a belief that was to become much more forceful and pervasive in future years—that made an important contribution to the selection of block rather than categorical grants in law enforcement and related areas. Here, localism was a significant consideration.

Conclusions

In the Johnson presidency there clearly was minimal taste for block grants and even less for revenue sharing—approaches that, if widely employed, would have changed the American administrative state in major ways. What little enthusiasm there was for block grants was most evident in the 1966 task force on law enforcement and in the views of the Bureau of the Budget on public health and vocational education programs. The bureau's preference seemed principally animated by an institutional interest in administrative streamlining rather than by federal values that favored decentralization. This enthusiasm was set within a broader concern for program fragmentation that will be discussed in the following chapter.

Philosophical, political, and budgetary considerations undergirded the administration's coolness toward the block grant and revenue sharing options. Of greatest importance, the decentralization inherent in them was in basic contradiction with a leadership that was proactive and nationalist in character, one premised on the most generous definition of national problems and significantly affected by perceptions of illiberal tendencies and inadequacies in state and local governments. The categorical model was available and familiar. Powerful national bureaucracies were committed to it and were not inclined to back alternatives that would weaken them. Moreover, there was also a partisan political dimension. Many state and local jurisdictions were under Republican control. To endow Republican officials with generous discretionary resources would risk distortion of Democratic policy objectives. It would also limit the credit for action and initiative that could be claimed by a Democratic administration. Republican officials realized this full well in their press for revenue sharing, and no doubt so did Lyndon B. Johnson. For these reasons, there appeared to be a general feeling within the administration that if the Great Society were to be built, it must be engineered in Washington, in addition to being conceived there. There was also the fiscal situation. Revenue sharing and block grants on a large scale would be expensive. Their incremental yearly growth would perhaps be difficult to contain, a disturbing thought as budgetary pressures intensified starting in 1966. The categorical approach involving a large complex of programs, many of them small, inexpensive, and with limited constituencies, could make a political mark; yet, at the same time, costs could be more easily limited.

In the revenue sharing case, the administration was able to prevail because of the fiscal situation, the inbred congressional preference for categorical grants, the limited constituency that revenue sharing first attracted, and the strong constituencies for established categorical programs. As the constituency for revenue sharing grew, the task of resistance became more difficult. Probably only the conclusion of Johnson's presidency saved it from ultimate capitulation.

The interesting point about the block grant struggles is that the position of the administration prevailed only when it was supported by the key state officials, interest groups, and their congressional allies. That, ironically, was the case in the Partnership for Health legislation, one of two instances in which it pushed a block grant proposal. Indeed, it can be said that this was less a distinctive initiative of Johnson's presidency than a ratification of a conclusion previously reached within the influential public health community. In losing on a block grant proposal in vocational education and in its resistance to block grants for juvenile delinquency and safe streets, the Johnson presidency was no match for the dominant constituency interests in those policy arenas. These outcomes illustrate the complex and diverse influences that shape the American administrative state.

7. Repairing the Intergovernmental Administrative System

The Economic Opportunity Act, the Model Cities program, multistate commissions, block grants, and other consequences of Johnson's presidency with important intergovernmental dimensions were the products of complex forces and shifting sets of decision makers. These enactments did not derive from a grand plan to change intergovernmental relations in the American administrative state in certain planned, distinctive ways. As one analyst puts it, the various measures were "drafted on a case-by-case basis, tailored to each program's particular combination of objectives and political constraints."[1] To a limited extent during, but more particularly after, the deluge of legislation between 1964 and 1966, however, considerable attention was given to their administrative consequences and to devising correctives that transcended particular programs. Major emphasis was placed on strengthening government at state and local levels, especially general purpose units and their elected leaders; strengthening program coordination in the field; and streamlining the grant-in-aid system. An improved system for presidential policy management and central coordination was in the wings awaiting attention in the final months of Johnson's presidency.

Coming to the President's Agenda

Basic issues in intergovernmental administration were rarely addressed in the first part of Johnson's presidency. A major task force on government organization chaired by Don K. Price of Harvard University reported in late 1964. Focusing on departmental organization, it largely ignored intergovernmental administrative relationships, although its suggestion of departmental reorganization along functional lines had important implications for program coordination.[2] Early efforts to spark serious presidential interest in confronting general issues in intergovernmental administration were unsuccessful. For example, early in 1965 a Senate subcommittee headed by Senator Edmund S. Muskie (D-Maine) held hearings on legislation that eventually became the Intergovernmental Cooperation Act of 1968. It was drafted by the Advisory Commission on Intergovernmental Relations (ACIR), which had sought without success to have the measure accepted as part of the president's legislative program.[3] Eventually, when the bill was under consideration in the Senate, the Bureau of the Budget (BOB) endorsed it after certain revisions were made. It easily passed the Senate but languished in a House committee. Its supporters sought help from Harry McPherson in the White House. When he asked Henry Hall Wilson, who was in charge of liaison with the House, about the bill, Wilson replied, "I never heard of this one before."[4] In early July McPherson made further inquiries and learned that Wilson and Bill D. Moyers "cannot see pressing . . . on the intergovernmental bill as a priority item."[5]

First Steps

Lack of interest in the ACIR-Muskie legislation at this point did not indicate hubris about intergovernmental program administration at the presidential level. There was, as preceding chapters have shown, a recognition of administrative deficiencies in intergovernmental programs, particularly in the poverty area. Interest in remedial action dealing with administrative problems in general terms began to grow in August 1965 when Charles L. Schultze, director of the Bureau of the Budget, established a task force on intergovernmental program coordination. It was chaired by Stephen K. Bailey of Syracuse University.[6] The starting points of the task force's December report were the recent proliferation of programs and the finding that their purposes were "too often . . . lost in a maze of interagency and intergovernmental procedures, overlaps, delays, and jurisdictional disputes."[7] The task force's first recommendation was for strengthened central coordination through either BOB or an Office of Community Program Coordination in the Executive Office of the President.[8] The second was for a study of federal field organization as a prelude to decentralization.[9] Several recommendations concerned coordination among federal field offices and with state and local governments. A number of them focused on enlarging the coordinating capacities of state and local chief executives.[10] The report concluded with several recommendations for immediate action. They included limiting jurisdictional overlaps in local and regional planning required by federal programs, reducing discrepancies in grant-in-aid matching and other requirements, and broadening categories of aid to give recipients more discretion.[11]

During the next year, interest in intergovernmental program administration mounted steadily in and about the White House. The first major step taken after the Bailey task force reported, however, was an uncertain one. In his 1966 State of the Union message, the president announced: "I propose to examine our Federal system— the relation between city, State, Nation, and the citizens themselves. We need a commission of the most distinguished scholars and men of public affairs to do this job. I will ask them to move on to develop a creative federalism to best use the wonderful diversity of our institutions and our people to solve the problem and to fulfill the dreams of the American people."[12] The prospect of a commission and the challenge posed by Johnson sparked the interest of many. They included those whom Richard R. Warner characterizes as "professional intergovernmental reformers" on the staffs of the Advisory Commission on Intergovernmental Relations, Congress, the Bureau of the Budget, associations of state and local governments, and in universities.[13] Other interested parties included staff in the White House and, of special importance, Senator Edmund Muskie.

Although the Bailey task force reported just as work on the State of the Union message began in December 1965, the commission proposal had other origins. It was the result of Secretary of Defense Robert McNamara's proposal for a study of the entire governmental system and another offered by Kermit Gordon, former head of BOB, who suggested a presidential commission to spearhead a concerted effort at governmental modernization.[14] Schultze opposed a public commission on federalism. Just a few days before the president's message was delivered, he summarized his argument for Joseph C. Califano, Jr., who was inclined to support the commission idea. A public commission would be under heavy pressure to endorse revenue sharing, Schultze asserted. It would also be inappropriate. Such commissions are useful, he said, when answers are known and need blessing, "but in this case, . . . [we] don't have the answers ourselves yet. The major problem is a very complicated Government organizational problem going deep into the roots of the Federal system." Consequently, it was best to give the assignment to an internal group; then when basic directions were decided, a commission could be considered to generate public support.[15]

After the president's intention was announced in January 1966, debate over the proposed commission continued into the spring. Senator Muskie's view was that a commission would be a blow to

ACIR, which, he thought, should be given the responsibility for conducting the study and to which a new chairman should be appointed
to reinvigorate what all agreed had become a rather stodgy organization.[16] There was some division among Johnson's advisers as to the
role ACIR might play, and the pros and cons of various options were
weighed carefully.[17] After extensive discussion tentative agreement
was reached on a compromise: ACIR would examine problems in
the relationships between states and cities and federal field operations, and a presidential commission would examine the executive
branch in Washington. Although still favoring ACIR, Muskie indicated that he would be content with any presidential decision.[18] Apparently the president was not persuaded that the compromise was
sound, and no action was approved at that time. The ACIR study was
never undertaken, but an analysis of executive branch organization
was initiated several months later.

Stimuli and Transition

Although Muskie's advice on the conduct of the study was rejected—
before, during, and after 1966—the senator nonetheless stimulated
the Johnson administration to address questions of intergovernmental administration. Muskie was in the forefront of congressional
concern for intergovernmental administration, and he felt strongly
that some type of general legislation was needed. In every year of the
Johnson presidency, his Subcommittee on Intergovernmental Relations of the Senate Committee on Government Operations held
hearings on intergovernmental affairs and related legislative proposals. Federal, state, and local government officials, representatives
of public interest groups, and many others testified before the subcommittee. At minimum, it served as a forum for the airing of difficulties that were being experienced by the recipients of the Great
Society grants-in-aid. The subcommittee hearings certainly served
as a continuous prod on the executive establishment—and particularly on the Bureau of the Budget and major grantor departments and
agencies—to improve administrative performance. Muskie and his
able staff not only produced first-rate subcommittee reports but also
explored the philosophic bases of a complex system of intergovernmental relations. Senator Muskie's influence was further enhanced
by his service during these years as a member of the Advisory Commission on Intergovernmental Relations.

   The ACIR was established by Congress in 1959 to serve as a source
of analysis and recommendations for improving intergovernmental
relations. During Johnson's presidency, its role was both peripheral

and stimulative. It was peripheral in that the president and his aides were wary of a close, working association with it and did not rely directly on the commission for major assistance in addressing problems in intergovernmental relations. One important reason was that ACIR was not a presidential agency. The president appointed twenty of twenty-six members. Three members from the House and three from the Senate were named by the leaders of those bodies. Fourteen members represented state and local governments. Although they were appointed by the president, he was required to select from lists of nominees submitted by associations of state and local officials. Partisan balance was required in legislative and state and local appointments. Only in naming three members from the executive branch and three citizen members did the president have full discretion.

In the White House this membership structure caused the commission to be perceived as an unreliable instrument for pursuing presidential purposes. Not only was it unwieldy because of its size, but state and local interests held a majority of the seats, and there was significant Republican representation.[19] The perception of unreliability was reinforced from time to time by policy stances that contradicted the administration's. Endorsement of revenue sharing was a case in point, as was criticism of the Model Cities proposal by the commission's executive director in 1966.[20]

More often than not, however, ACIR's general orientation to intergovernmental relations fit well with that of the Johnson administration, and its studies influenced presidential actions. Muskie's advocacy of its recommendations was an important factor. From the commission's founding to mid-1966, several policy themes ran through its work. First and foremost, ACIR was concerned with strengthening state and local governments and improving relations between and among them. Most of its published reports addressed problems in these areas. Correcting governmental problems in metropolitan areas and strengthening the decision-making roles of elected officials were notable subthemes. Few commission studies, however, directly addressed specific problems in the administration of federal grant-in-aid programs. The ones that did, especially those examining public assistance and public health programs, stressed the importance of flexibility and broader discretion for recipients.[21]

In the aftermath of Johnson's ill-fated announcement of a commission on federalism in January 1966, public attention continued to be drawn to the general state of intergovernmental relations. In March Muskie delivered a widely noticed speech on creative federalism in which he discussed an extensive range of administrative problems.[22]

He began new hearings on the proposed Intergovernmental Cooperation Act that same month. Some elements of this legislation were
now supported by the administration. In April ACIR released a major
study of intergovernmental relations in the poverty program.[23]

A number of administration initiatives were also important in
raising awareness of systemic administrative problems. The field
visits sponsored by the President's Committee on Manpower in the
summer of 1966 were discussed in a previous chapter. Also during
that summer, the Bureau of the Budget undertook in-depth program
management surveys in several cities that were quite revealing.[24] In
the fall several task forces examined and reported on problems in
state and local personnel systems and various administrative limitations in the war on poverty.

Congressional attention to intergovernmental matters heightened
as 1966 drew to a close. Senator Abraham A. Ribicoff (D-Conn.) conducted extensive hearings on urban problems. In October Muskie initiated hearings on creative federalism. By this time, the Bureau of
the Budget had developed a basic perspective on issues in intergovernmental program administration. It was reflected in testimony
that Schultze presented to Muskie's subcommittee in November.
His views are worth quoting in some detail:

> Recent legislation has inaugurated a new range of programs
> whose characteristics create a new dimension for Federal man-
> agement and for intergovernmental relations. Under these pro-
> grams the Federal Government—
>
> Directly participates in special projects in States and
> communities;
> Acts as a coequal partner with State and local governments in
> carrying out those projects;
> In many cases works with a number of local governments orga-
> nized into special groups.
>
> Moreover, and very important, these programs usually require
> action by many Federal agencies, rather than a single one.[25]

He continued:

> To be effective we must decentralize. To decentralize is inevi-
> tably to allow great room for diversity and even for inconsis-
> tency. If we want the benefits of effective decentralization, we
> must be prepared to accept irreducible quotas of anomalies and
> errors which inevitably accompany decentralization.

It is this multi-jurisdictional approach to doing business that—as much as anything else—describes creative federalism. It is not conventional federalism in the old style, and because it is different, we have been slow and sometimes clumsy in changing our habits and developing new methods of working together with other levels of government. For their part, the States and cities have been equally slow in adapting their machinery and style to take full advantage of the new programs.

At the same time, it would be surprising if everything clicked smoothly in the wake of an immensely productive period of legislation.[26]

Schultze went on to point out that Congress and the executive could have bypassed the state and local governments in devising new programs. Programs could have been established as direct national operations, but he argued that this would be contrary to our whole national history as a federal system and would not have led to effective solutions. Most of the problems that these programs attacked were not the same nationwide, and solutions were available in the context of widely different local conditions and requirements. "In short," he noted, "the formidable managerial and intergovernmental problems of the new programs reflect this complexity of the social needs they are designed to meet and our determination to utilize the federal system of government in meeting them. Programs could have been formulated which are far simpler administratively—but in the end, far less effective."[27]

The director identified the following as the specific problems that preoccupied the administration and served as the grist for remedial steps:

1) Federal assistance is being provided through too many narrow categorical grant and loan programs.
2) A second major problem arises from the fact that certain of the planning requirements necessarily required as a condition of grants may be overlapping.
3) A similar problem relates to planning boundaries and jurisdictions, and shortages of personnel.
4) The information necessary for effective use and coordination of Federal grant-in-aid and loan programs is not always available in up-to-date, easily accessible form.
5) The Federal field structure needs improvement in order to make possible effective coordination in certain areas.

6) There is a great uncertainty regarding the availability and timing of Federal funds.

7) Severe shortages of qualified manpower in some areas make State and local recruitment for federally assisted programs sometimes difficult or impossible.

8) Federal actions are sometimes taken and regulations are prescribed without sufficient consideration of State and local laws, government structure, financial and administrative capabilities and ongoing programs.[28]

Later in his testimony Schultze said, "We do not have all of the answers, by a long shot. But we are making progress and will, I believe, continue to do so."[29]

As 1966 drew to an end, a basis was being established for more focused attention to systemic problems in intergovernmental program administration than at any prior point in Johnson's presidency. Schultze's testimony was a general culmination of a number of ad hoc initiatives and inquiries undertaken by the administration. It presented a relatively coherent view of problems and a general strategy for attacking them.

Richard R. Warner argues that an underlying development was the emergence of a meaningful concept of creative federalism at about this time. For a period during Johnson's presidency, he worked in the Bureau of the Budget, where, Warner later wrote, although a "believer," he was "confused about the precise meaning of 'creative federalism.'" Nevertheless Warner was "certain that it meant something important."[30] This confusion led him to undertake an exhaustive and extremely valuable study aimed at defining Johnson's creative federalism in conceptual terms. Warner concludes that in its first usage in the president's Ann Arbor speech in 1964 and for a period thereafter, the term was merely a slogan employed for political effect.[31] By the summer of 1966, it "had come to mean almost anything."[32] Not long afterward, Warner concludes, there was a change. Creative federalism came to be a generally accepted "strategy for reform of the Federal system which holds that both policy and administrative decisions on all multifunctional domestic programs must be made jointly by generalists at all levels of government, each level increasing its power substantially without diminishing the power of any other level."[33] Whether or not the conceptual agreement that Warner describes did in fact develop, it is clear that in 1966 administration officials began to give a great deal of thought to issues in intergovernmental program administration.

Schultze's testimony coincided roughly with two important and related political occurrences. One was the November elections, in which the Democratic party sustained serious losses. The other was the public expression of dissatisfaction with the current state of intergovernmental relations by a number of Democratic governors. In terms employed by John W. Kingdom in his analysis of agenda formation, the three major process streams—problem, policy, and political—were coupling, creating the possibility of "significant movement" on problems in intergovernmental relations.[34]

In January 1967 Johnson commented on intergovernmental matters in both his State of the Union address and the budget message. He also initiated the visits to state capitals by aides and began to be personally more accessible to state and local officials. The special message on the quality of government followed in mid-March. It gave substantial but not exclusive attention to intergovernmental relations. Three basic factors then affecting the federal system were emphasized: problems were increasingly national in scope, requiring national strategies that could be adapted to local needs; policy implementation required the interaction of many agencies at all levels of government; and problems transcended traditional governmental boundaries. Although some remedial actions had been initiated, as the president noted, several additional improvements were needed. These included better communications among levels of government, consolidation of grant-in-aid programs, improved consistency and coordination in implementation, and efforts by state and local governments to enlarge their administrative capacities.[35] In broad outline, action in these areas was at the core of subsequent efforts to confront the disarray and to smooth the rough edges of the new elements incorporated into the American administrative state in the mid-1960s. Most of the ideas reflected in the initiatives were not new. Some were implemented administratively, while others required legislative action, such as those contained in the Intergovernmental Cooperation Act that became law in 1968.[36]

The Problem of State and Local Administrative Capacity

Administrative deficiencies at state and local levels were generally recognized and were of considerable concern. Many grant-in-aid programs contained provisions intended to enlarge administrative capacity in a particular context. More general strategies were also considered.

Personnel

Strengthening the personnel resources of state and local governments was a major priority for some officials in Washington. Early in 1966 the president recommended to Congress that the Civil Service Commission (CSC) be authorized to provide fellowships for training state and local government employees as well as grants to prepare plans for training. The measure did not pass at that time. Later in the year, the nature of the personnel problem was captured succinctly by an outside presidential task force: "The manpower crisis facing State and local governments has both immediate and longer-term aspects. At this moment the development and implementation of Great Society programs is being obstructed by the absence of highly talented men and women who can get the job done."[37] This conclusion was supported by references to existing personnel shortages and to a very substantial growth in state and local employment needs projected for the next decade. Among specific limitations listed by the task force were low pay, rigid personnel policies, impediments to career mobility, inadequate attention to governmental manpower needs on the part of the educational community, and low prestige.[38]

The task force made a number of recommendations for improving state and local personnel systems. It sketched a role for the national government that would use cooperation, technical assistance, and grants to foster modernization, on the one hand, and give the president authority to set personnel standards for grant programs, on the other. Approaches were suggested for promoting personnel exchanges among all levels of government and with the private sector. Another recommendation was to enlarge the talent pool for attacking domestic problems through new working relationships, coordinated by the federal government, between state and local governments and educational and research institutions. Finally, several steps, including grants and fellowships, were suggested for improving education and training for the public service.

The work of the task force was supplemented by the subsequent efforts of an interagency group led by O. Glenn Stahl of the Civil Service Commission. Based upon these analyses, two proposals for legislative action were presented in the quality of government message.[39] One was for a Public Service Education Act funded by a $10 million authorization for the Department of Health, Education, and Welfare (HEW) to establish fellowships and training facilities for public administrators. A revised version of this proposal was eventually enacted as part of the Higher Education Act Amendments of

1968.[40] Johnson's 1966 recommendation for the support of training by state and local governments was put forward again as the Intergovernmental Manpower Act at an authorization level of $25 million. Although quickly passed by the Senate, the measure did not become law until 1970.[41]

Management

The 1966 task force on personnel also expressed concern about the overall management capacities of state and local governments. It believed that formal restrictions on executive authority and categorical grants that bypassed chief executives were major barriers to effective administrative leadership in intergovernmental programs. In addition, a majority of the task force cited limited funds for central management purposes as a source of problems and recommended grants to chief executives to alleviate this condition.[42]

General management incapacity was also worrisome to administration officials. Not long after the task force report was submitted, presidential aide S. Douglass Cater provided Johnson with a summary of comments from cabinet members "on how the Federal Government can contribute to more efficient local administration."[43] The suggestions contained in Cater's summary were quite varied, ranging from a comprehensive study of the problems of state and local governments to improved intergovernmental coordination in Washington. On several points the views of cabinet members echoed those expressed by the intergovernmental manpower task force. For example, Secretary of Housing and Urban Development (HUD) Robert Weaver and several of his colleagues urged that "consideration . . . be given to a new program of matching grants to state and local governments designed to improve the general governments' capability at the state and local level for organizing, managing, and coordinating diverse, complex and expanding programs."[44]

The proposal for general assistance to chief executives received an additional boost early in 1967 shortly before the quality of government message went to Congress. The source was Frederick M. Bohen, executive secretary of the Task Force on Government Organization, chaired by Ben W. Heineman. Bohen was responding to a request for suggestions on the means for addressing the problems and "bitches" of governors in the context of pressure for revenue sharing, a factor that also contributed to Cater's concern. He suggested the possibility of "small block grants to governors" to create modern executive offices that would allow them to play an enlarged role in the federal system. He noted, however, that most governors had not taken ad-

vantage of the resources available for their own purposes under existing federal programs.[45]

Several months later, general grants to chief executives were under
serious consideration in the White House. On 14 August 1967, Califano asked Schultze for BOB's assessment of this approach to improving the "organization, management, and systems analysis capabilities" of state and local governments.[46] Drawing upon an extensive
staff report, Schultze concluded that there was "no compelling
need" for such a program. He recognized that there were administrative deficiencies and that new federal programs exacerbated them.
However, he argued, there were many existing programs that could
be tapped to aid in planning and in the performance of other executive functions. Schultze noted in the course of his response that the
bureau soon planned to allow central administrative expenditures to
be counted as allowable costs in grant financing. This would enlarge
the flow of grant money for central administrative purposes from
substantive programs. Finally, Schultze pointed to a fatal limitation
in the influence that the national government could exert in such
matters. The basic problem was poor organization, which federal
funds alone could not correct. In his view, "We have no choice but to
rely on local initiative to get this job done."[47]

The bureau's negative stance killed any prospects for an ambitious
and comprehensive approach to strengthening state and local administration. Subsequently, however, some small steps were taken
toward that end. Encouragement was given to demonstrations in
planning, programming, and budgeting systems (PPBS) applications
at state and local levels and in the use of modern information management technologies in city government.[48] The Intergovernmental
Cooperation Act of 1968 contained a provision that could be used to
compensate for administrative and other limitations hampering state
and local governments. It authorized federal agencies to provide technical and specialized assistance to them on a reimbursable basis.

Chief Executives

Expanding the influence of elected state and local officials, especially chief executives, in the administration of grant programs was
addressed in a variety of ways. The significance of the 1967 amendments to the Economic Opportunity Act and the Model Cities program in this respect has been discussed. The Intergovernmental Cooperation Act of 1968 contained two provisions of some relevance.
Upon request, federal agencies were required to notify governors and
legislatures of grant awards in a state. It also allowed governors to

depart from the single state agency requirement for the administration of grant programs. As will be seen later, there were other relevant initiatives undertaken in the context of improving field coordination.

An effort was also made to enlarge the influence of chief executives in national program decisions, thus indirectly strengthening them in their own jurisdictions. BOB's Circular A-85 was issued on 28 June 1967. The sequence of events culminating in the circular began with a memorandum from the president to the major federal grantor agencies on 11 November 1966. "The basis of creative federalism is cooperation," the president stated. "To the fullest practical extent I want you to take steps to afford representatives of the Chief Executives of State and local government the opportunity to advise and consult in the development and execution of programs which directly affect the conduct of State and local affairs."[49] The memorandum asked the director of BOB, the ACIR, and the organizations representing state and local governments to work with federal departments and agencies in implementing its provisions. Bohen later wrote that the memorandum did not produce "revolutionary changes in attitude or approach in the federal bureaucracies, or a reliable pattern of follow-up." His sources in state government awarded the president "high marks for his concern and intentions" but gave the federal government "fairly low marks for action."[50]

Circular A-85 went beyond Johnson's memorandum and formalized procedures in an effort to make them more meaningful. Federal agencies were directed to submit proposed regulations affecting federal assistance programs to ACIR for distribution to the National Governors' Conference, the Council of State Governments, the International City Management Association, the National Association of Counties, the National League of Cities, and the U.S. Conference of Mayors. These, in turn, would presumably contact at least some of their membership. The intent of A-85 was to involve state and local elected officials more fully in the advance review of federal assistance regulations about which they so often complained. This, by indirection, might both reduce the influence of the professional groups that were often thought to be responsible for the complicated regulations that accompanied grants-in-aid and expand the influence of chief executives, although their involvement in the actual development of regulations was not mandated, and agencies were not required to make changes to meet their criticisms.[51]

Unfortunately, the implementation of A-85 was not an unmitigated success. Agencies did not always send their proposed regulations to ACIR; BOB frequently exempted agencies from the A-85 requirement; the public interest groups did not always respond; the agencies, in turn, were frequently deaf to the responses that were made.[52]

Clearly, national policymakers were reluctant to confront directly and aggressively the administrative deficiencies of state and local governments. No dramatic steps were taken to improve personnel systems and management practices or to vastly strengthen the position of chief executive. They were somewhat more adventurous in addressing problems of program interrelationships in the field.

Problems in Field Coordination

A major underlying contributor to administrative disarray, of course, was fragmentation that hampered pursuit of multifunctional approaches to problems in which joint decision making was required. At state and local levels the main causes of fragmentation were weak chief executives and a multitude of often overlapping local governments. These included, in addition to general-purpose units, thousands of special districts and authorities with more particular responsibilities. Although not the principal cause of fragmentation, some federal grant programs contributed to this condition by encouraging the location of responsibility for certain functions, such as urban redevelopment and transportation, in organizations set apart from general purpose local governments. Fragmentation at the state and local levels was joined by fragmentation in federal program structures composed principally of categorical grants and in field organization in which the regional boundaries of departments and agencies were idiosyncratic and in which programs were administered with a great deal of independence. Officials in Washington were especially concerned with the defects in the structure of government at the local level and in federal regional office arrangements.

The fragmentation of local government, particularly in metropolitan areas, was a familiar problem for governmental reformers. Analysts had long pointed to its costs, including neglect of areawide problems, disparities among jurisdictions within metropolitan areas in the services provided, foregone economies of scale in governmental operations, and deficiencies in the allocation of fiscal resources.[53] Numerous options for reform were widely discussed and advocated, ranging from radical change, such as governmental consolidation, to milder adaptations, such as the assignment of extraterritorial powers to cities.[54] In the 1960s attention to the horizontal dimension of the problem was supplemented by attention to its vertical dimension, especially to the role and impact of federal programs on local arrangements and intergovernmental program processes in metropolitan and, to an extent, nonmetropolitan areas.[55] The strategic challenge to policymakers and others interested in the problem was to devise ways to employ federal programs to counter centrifugal forces at the local level. New schemes for coordination in discrete program areas such as manpower promised at best only a limited impact on the general condition. Strengthening the role and capacity of general purpose local governments and their chief executives was a partial answer but did not attack jurisdictional multiplicity. During the 1960s a reformist theme evolved that seemed more generally promising: the promotion of areawide or regional institutions and processes within the states for planning and for federal program implementation.

Substate Regionalism

A connection between local areawide plans and federal programs was accentuated by section 701 of the Housing Act of 1954, which authorized a grant-in-aid program to support comprehensive planning. Between 1954 and the early 1960s, the new program, enlarged by Congress at several points, gave regional planning a considerable boost across the country.[56]

As indicated in Table 7, during Johnson's presidency major federal programs embodying the theme of substate regionalism increased from four to eighteen. They were not cut from a single pattern. In thirteen instances areawide use of the program was optional in that there were no sanctions or penalties for nonparticipation, while in five instances there were sanctions such as ineligibility for certain grant funds. In all cases, when programs were instituted, they were required to be organized on an areawide basis. Some programs contemplated the incorporation of a number of functional elements in the scope of activity, as in economic development planning, but most involved only a single function.

Areawide structures, as James L. Sundquist puts it, were to serve as "coordinators . . . responsible for bringing together the various agencies or jurisdictions or public and private groups that might be concerned with individual projects and for bringing separate projects into relation with one another."[57] There was considerable variation in the mechanisms provided. The most important of these was planning on an areawide basis, some form of which was required in all except two of the eighteen programs.

Three types of planning were associated with federal grant programs: first, project planning for a specific action, such as construction of a waste treatment facility; second, functional planning for

Table 7. Operational Approaches of Federal Areawide Programs, 1968

Program	Areawide Use of Program	Special Areawide Organizational Requirements	Functional Components of Areawide Programs Other Than Land Use	Areawide Coordinative Mechanisms Used			
				Required Plan	Coordinating Council	Areawide Authority to Veto Funding	Federal Funding Channeled through a Single Areawide Agency
Air Pollution Control (1967)	Optional	Yes	Single	State	No	No	No
Appalachian Local Development District Assistance (1965)	Optional	Yes	Multiple	State and Area	Yes	No	Yes
Areawide Comprehensive Health Planning (314b) (1966)	Optional	Yes	Single	State and Area	Yes	No	Yes
Areawide Comprehensive Planning Assistance (701) (1954)	Required	Yes	Multiple	Area	No	No	Yes (except some inter-states)
Community Action (1964)	Optional	Yes	Multiple	Area	Yes	Yes	No
Economic Development Planning (1965)	Optional	Yes	Multiple	Area	Yes	No	Yes

Program							
Law Enforcement Planning (1968)	Required	Yes	Single	State and Area	Yes	Yes	No
Manpower Planning (CAMPS) (1968)	Optional	Yes	Single	State and Area	Yes	No	Yes
New Communities (1965)	Optional	No	Multiple	None	No	No	No
Open Space (1961)	Optional	No	Single	Area	No	No	No
Regional Medical Program (1965)	Required	Yes	Single	Area	Yes	Yes	Yes
Resource Conservation and Development (1962)	Optional	Yes	Multiple	Area	Yes	Yes	Yes
Solid Waste Planning Grants (1965)	Optional	No	Single	None	No	No	Yes
Urban Mass Transportation Planning (1964)	Optional	No	Single	Area	No	Yes	Yes
Urban Transportation Planning (1963)	Required	Yes	Single	Area	Yes	Yes	Yes
Water/Sewer Facilities (1965)	Optional	No	Single	Area	No	No	No
Water and Sewer Planning for Rural Communities (1965)	Required	No	Single	Area	No	No	Yes
Water and Waste Disposal Systems for Rural Communities (1965)	Optional	No	Single	Area	No	No	No

Source: Adapted from Advisory Commission on Intergovernmental Relations, *Regional Decision Making: New Strategies for Substate Districts,* vol. 1 (Washington, D.C.: GPO, 1973), pp. 169 and 180–181.

limited developmental objectives, such as an improved system of urban mass transportation; third, comprehensive or general planning in which the needs and resources of an area were assessed; the goals, objectives, and policies for long-range physical, economic, and human resource development were delineated; and specific plans and programs were devised for action. Project planning was involved in many of the areawide programs. Functional planning was required in all but four programs. In eight, either comprehensive or general planning was required, or activities had to be consistent with a comprehensive plan. In addition to planning, in some instances coordination was strengthened through provision for a council of affected organizations and interests, giving areawide organizations a veto over program funding in their jurisdictions, and channeling federal funding through one areawide organization. Funding through a single organization meant that there would be no competition for funds or multiple funding, for example, in comprehensive health planning.

The program coordination potential of areawide arrangements emphasizing planning was offset by a number of factors. One was their proliferation in a short period of time, along with the proliferation of grant programs out of the conventional mold. Looking back from the perspective of 1973, the ACIR discerned the emergence of some major problems caused by proliferation. In a number of program areas, prospective sponsors competed for authority and funds in the context of ambiguous federal and state policies. Further, inconsistencies in organizational prescriptions were felt to "confuse" attempts to "consolidate regional effort."[58] Major sources of confusion were disparate and overlapping boundary lines. In a particular geographical area, as many as ten regional programs might be operative concurrently, no two of which necessarily reflected the same concept of region in their geographic scope. The condition was exacerbated by a growing number of state-sponsored regional planning districts.

There was some awareness of these limitations even as the number of areawide programs was increasing. A problem arose in Georgia in 1966. The Office of Economic Opportunity (OEO) withdrew its support from districts created under state authority in order to employ multicounty community action agencies whose boundaries were quite different from those of organizations doing related work.[59] Complaints were raised. The ACIR responded with several recommendations. One was that other states follow Georgia's lead and create their own planning and development districts. When such districts existed, the ACIR urged that they be used for implementing federal areawide programs where feasible. If separate organizations were required, boundaries should conform to those of state planning districts, and checkpoint procedures should be established to assure coordination with the state organizations and the maximum use of their resources in advancing federal program purposes.[60]

In September 1966, a few months after the ACIR put forward its views, President Johnson transmitted a memorandum that partially implemented them. It directed the heads of departments and agencies assisting state and local development planning to work with state and local planning agencies by employing consistent planning data bases and sharing resources. The boundaries of federally assisted planning and development districts were also to be the same as those of state districts unless there were sound reasons for divergence. BOB was assigned responsibility for coordinating the implementation of the memorandum.[61]

The bureau's formal follow-up was the issuance in early 1967 of Circular A-80, entitled "Coordination of Development Planning for Programs Based on Multi-jurisdictional Areas." It established guidelines and specifications for meeting the objectives stated by the president. Governors were given an opportunity to review and comment on the designation of districts by federal agencies. The agencies, in turn, were asked to review established boundaries for inconsistencies and to correct them. When possible in the future, designations were to conform to the boundaries of state districts. Although federal agencies subsequently did not redo established boundaries, the circular had some effect on lines drawn after it was issued.[62] The circular also sought to advance coordination in planning through consistency in planning bases, assumptions, and projections; improved communication among state and local agencies planning with federal assistance; and joint funding of related planning projects.

Interest in more effective planning went considerably beyond the question of boundaries and the other matters addressed in A-80. The character and implementation of plans were also on the administrative reform agenda. Historically, metropolitan or regional planning focused on land use, facilities location, and economic and social trends and forecasts. The Department of Housing and Urban Development, with primary responsibility for federal links to urban planning, made a concerted effort in the 1960s to supplement traditional concerns with a more pronounced emphasis in planning on budgeting and resource allocation in urban areas, on program administration, and on developing programs to resolve social problems. There was a related interest in making planning a less passive and a more active force in intergovernmental program coordination and implementation.[63] These objectives were the source of two reform subthemes. One concerned the organizational features of metropolitan planning structures and the other their powers.

In several decades of experience prior to the 1960s, various types of urban planning organizations were employed on a voluntary basis by local governments.[64] They included county, city-county, and multijurisdictional agencies. Often they were headed by a citizen board, and typically they did not have impressive means at their disposal for the implementation of the plans they devised, especially in regard to major development decisions by government agencies. The divorce of planning from government action was not an uncommon occurrence.

Such inadequacies were treated in a BOB paper entitled "Programs to Achieve Planned and Coordinated Metropolitan Development," completed in late 1965. Its premise was that it was in major urban centers "that our most important social, economic and physical development goals and objectives must be met. . . . Federal, state and local interests, responsibilities and efforts all converge in the metropolitan area."[65] The paper went on to argue cogently for improved planning and planning associated with action. It went so far as to recommend that each major urban area be required to establish a metropolitan action (not planning) agency with both comprehensive planning and program operation responsibilities.

That precise approach was not adopted, but steps were taken that fit with its objectives. The foundation for one of these was laid in 1965 when the 701 program was amended to make councils of governments (COGs) in metropolitan areas eligible for funding. Distinctive features of the councils were that membership was voluntary and that participating governments were represented by their chief elected officials. The first COG was established in the Detroit area in 1954. By 1965 there were 35; and, stimulated by the 1965 legislation and considerable support and encouragement from HUD, the number reached 103 in 1967. Three years later there were about 450.[66] Also in 1965 Congress authorized a total of $230 million for 701 programs, up from $75 million in 1961. Although the actual appropriation level was far less, the amount provided indicated an increased emphasis on planning. Another step was taken in section 204 of the Model Cities legislation passed in 1966. It required that all state and local applications for federal development loans or grants be reviewed by metropolitan or regional planning agencies, building generally on the review concept adopted previously in a few particular programs. It was further provided that if proposed projects were consistent with plans, applicants would receive an incentive bonus of 20 percent of their share of project costs. However, the bonus arrangement was not funded.

The purpose of section 204 was to give planning and other regional bodies headed by elected officials, such as COGs, broader access to development decisions. A major presumption underlying sponsorship of regional councils was that the direct involvement of local officials in areawide problems would result in more viable policies and better program coordination because of the political legitimacy incorporated in council decisions. Review by planning bodies or COGs would contribute to better and more active planning and stronger interrelationships in the implementation of federal programs.

Changes in 701 and enactment of 204 were major stimuli for the extension of what ACIR called "regional confederalism."[67] Growth in the number of regional councils was accompanied by growth in the number of regional planning commissions. The number of planning bodies increased from 43 in 1960 to 248 in 1969. More than half of these were in metropolitan areas. The distinction between the functions of the two types of organization was not clear-cut. In some instances, councils were designated as comprehensive agencies for federal program review purposes, and in some cases regional planning bodies were converted to councils. In many instances both types of organizations operated in the same geographical area. Even when this was the case and the planning agency performed the formal review function, there was broad planning of a different sort when COGs considered regional problems and concerns. The typical council received and administered federal grants on an areawide basis. Many also undertook their own independent cooperative activities, such as providing technical assistance to member governments, joint purchasing, forging mutual aid agreements in protecting public safety, and personnel training. All of these activities required planning of one type or another.

As a new dimension in the intergovernmental system, councils of government added to regional capacities for planning and coordination. They were also a source of some confusion. In remarks at a Baltimore workshop in late September 1967, William Brussett of the Bureau of the Budget commented, "COGs are a new animal in that they go in for something new in comprehensive planning. Everything is comprehensive planning now but this is comprehensive, comprehensive planning, or as some, who don't like redundancy, call it, policy planning. This is the kind of planning that . . . provides a canopy of policy within which the various functional activities can be related." But, he continued, COGs presented difficulties. "Our problem is that because the animal is so new no federal agency is quite sure how to relate its programs to a council."[68]

The bureau and others were attempting to deal with the confusion.[69] A planning coordination committee, with the participation of BOB and other agencies, was established by HUD to work on problems created by the proliferation.[70] On 11 April 1967 the bureau issued Circular A-82, setting out procedures for the review of state and local applications for assistance by planning agencies designated by HUD pursuant to section 204. By June 1968 review agencies existed in all 233 standard metropolitan statistical areas.[71]

The problem was further addressed in Title IV of the Intergovernmental Cooperation Act of 1968, which gave the president broad authority over the formulation, evaluation, and review of federal development programs. Building on the president's memo on development planning, Congress strongly endorsed the proposition that federal aid not only advance but also be consistent with state, regional, and local objectives and comprehensive plans. In addition, federal agencies were directed to coordinate their own development planning with one another and with local comprehensive plans and to give preference to units of general local government in the provision of assistance.

The Bureau of the Budget had responsibility for the implementation of Title IV but moved rather slowly.[72] According to its administrative history, Title IV was "extremely broad in its implications and its language could support a wide variety of procedural, organizational, and institutional innovations in intergovernmental relations. For this reason, its implementation must be approached with great care."[73]

In fact, BOB's implementation effort did not actually begin until the Nixon administration with the issuance in July 1969 of Circular A-95, superseding A-82. It was "a regulation designed to promote maximum coordination of Federal and Federally assisted programs and projects with each other and with State, areawide, and local plans and programs." Review requirements were extended to many more federal programs than had been covered previously.[74] Some of this carry-over beyond the Johnson presidency may be reported briefly. A-95 established the Project Notification and Review System (PNRS) to provide the means for state, regional, and local governments to review and comment on proposed applications for federal grants. There was to be a similar review of direct federal development projects. Authority was extended to governors to review and comment on functional state plans before their submission to federal agencies, and states were encouraged to establish substate districts to implement PNRS.

From the issuance of A-80 through the preparation of A-95, the national government followed a conceptual course that, although imprecise and capricious in some of its particulars, sought improved order in intergovernmental relations through coordination keyed to substate planning. Meanwhile, another dimension of the intergovernmental administration system also drew attention. That was the field structure linking Washington to states and communities.

Federal Field Organization

From the perspective of their own program operations, individual federal agencies continually grapple with problems in field administration. Johnson's administration was no exception. The efforts of the Department of Labor, for example, to reorganize its field offices were discussed in a previous chapter. Other agencies had similar experiences.[75] But there were systemwide concerns as well that produced initiatives. One was to make regional offices more effective instruments of multifunctional program coordination at that level, then at state and local levels. To this end, two major reforms were considered by the Johnson administration. One was to harmonize the regional structures of federal agencies, and the other was to establish a central executive presence in the field with Bureau of the Budget staff. These options will be considered in the context of regional coordination arrangements put into place during Kennedy's presidency.

In 1961 some major cities had informal organizations of federal officials designated as federal business associations or federal agency councils.[76] These were useful in information exchange, but they had no official standing and no established channels of communication with Washington or with the states. In short, they were not truly a part of the system of intergovernmental administration.

In 1961 the Bureau of the Budget, the Civil Service Commission, and a special assistant to the president, Frederick G. Dutton, organized a series of White House regional management conferences. Out of these conferences the general conclusion emerged that there were pressing needs for improved communication with Washington and better interagency cooperation in the field. Recommendations were discussed with the Executive Officers Group in Washington; the members were departmental assistant secretaries for administration. On 10 November 1961 President Kennedy, by presidential memorandum, created ten federal executive boards (FEBs) composed of federal officials in major cities "to improve internal Federal management practices and to provide a central focus for Federal participation in civic affairs in major metropolitan centers of Federal activity."[77]

By January 1962 the ten FEBs were functioning; two more were added in 1963 and an additional three in 1966. The cities where FEBs were located were usually the sites of a number of federal regional offices. These fifteen continued in existence through the Johnson presidency and were provided with Washington-level guidance jointly by the chairman of the Civil Service Commission and the director of the Bureau of the Budget. A central clearinghouse for information was established in the CSC.[78] Each year the chairmen of the FEBs met in Washington, and the chairman of the CSC annually provided a formal report on their activities to the president.[79]

The FEBs were intended to give federal executives in the field an increased awareness of presidential program interests requiring interagency cooperation and intergovernmental collaboration. They were to be activated by the participation of federal senior departmental and agency officials in the involved cities.[80] Board members were designated by the heads of their agencies, but there was no additional funding for the FEBs, and neither representatives of the CSC nor the BOB regularly attended FEB meetings.[81]

After the Watts riots in the summer of 1965 the FEBs were given additional responsibilities. In October 1965, CSC chairman John W. Macy, Jr., asked each board to identify five to ten critical urban problems that required cooperative federal action, to establish a task force for each problem, and to involve state and local government officials in the search for solutions.[82] Generally, the task forces directed their efforts toward minority and ghetto problems. In the spring of 1966 a Washington counterpart group—the Critical Urban Problems Committee—was organized with representatives from OEO and the Departments of Commerce, HUD, HEW, and Labor. Somewhat later, representatives from Justice, the Small Business Administration, the Equal Employment Opportunity Commission, and the U.S. Commission on Civil Rights joined the committee. The Washington-level group served as a coordinating body for the problems that had been identified locally by the FEBs.

As might be expected, the range of critical urban problems that were identified by the FEBs was very broad, and it varied from city to city.[83] In San Francisco a task force was organized for a special study of Oakland. Many FEBs organized crime control conferences. The New York City FEB worked on apprenticeship standards. The Denver FEB organized a counseling program for felony offenders. The FEBs sponsored federal information centers, organized summer recreation projects, and arranged for contributions to Red Cross blood banks. Of greater importance, the FEBs were expected to work closely with the neighborhood service centers organized by OEO and with the Model Cities organizations.[84]

President Johnson continued to give support to the FEBs during his tenure in office. Chairman Macy's annual reports on the activities of the boards were typically acknowledged from the White House with substantial praise for the effort. In Johnson's major message on the quality of government in March 1967, he set forth an agenda for intergovernmental reform that was supportive of the efforts of the boards.[85]

Nevertheless, when the chairman of the Civil Service Commission proposed in September 1968 that the FEBs be formalized by executive order, the proposal met with resistance, particularly from BOB:

> We see no pressing need to formalize the FEB structure by an Executive Order now. However, it is hard to muster strong objections to such an action. . . . The FEBs have not, it seems to us, been particularly successful in coping with Critical Urban Problems in a programmatic sense, despite high level Washington exhortation. At best, FEBs and their Critical Urban Committees (CUCs) have been able to mount some useful programs in their cities, but after two years of effort, it is clear to us that FEBs and CUCs are not going to make a significant contribution to improving the coordination and delivery of Federal services.[86]

Other observers close to the scene at the time were equally critical. Seidman writes, "The federal executive boards proved totally ineffective in dealing with critical urban problems because they were given a job they were inherently incapable of accomplishing and which was wholly alien to the purpose for which they were organized."[87] Seidman concludes that as long as the FEBs confined their activities to equipment sharing and joint training projects, they made a valuable contribution. Their failure to help solve critical urban problems flowed from the inability of an interagency committee to resolve conflicts about agency priorities, the disparities in the degree of authority delegated by the federal agencies to their field office staffs, and the press of the regular program duties assigned to FEB members. Field coordination was often regarded as extraneous to these duties.[88] The Advisory Commission on Intergovernmental

Relations similarly reported, "They ultimately proved unable to deal with the serious problems of interagency coordination for aided urban services, as had been hoped."[89]

Beyond efforts to strengthen coordination in selected cities through the FEBs, during the Johnson presidency many proposals were made for rationalizing the field structure of departments and agencies and placing regional headquarters in the same cities. In his message on quality of government, Johnson observed that the cause of intergovernmental cooperation was "poorly served" when the geographical boundaries of field offices were inconsistent. He continued, "I have asked the Director of the Bureau of the Budget to undertake a comprehensive review of the Federal field office structure and to develop a plan to assure the most effective use and location of these offices."[90]

Several months later, the Heineman task force in its final report suggested boundaries for ten regions, with common headquarters for OEO and the Departments of HEW, HUD, and Labor.[91] On 23 December 1967 the director of the Bureau of the Budget proposed creation of eight multistate regions with common boundaries for OEO and the three departments, plus the Small Business Administration. A memorandum containing these recommendations went to Califano, who forwarded it to the president with a recommendation that the regional changes be authorized so that next steps could be planned. Johnson marked the box labeled "disapprove" and added, "Hell no! Not this year."[92]

This seems to have marked the termination of the president's interest in common boundaries and in the location of regional headquarters in the same cities; he was undoubtedly concerned about congressional opposition to the proposal. It did not mark the end of action by BOB and the White House staff, both of which continued to press for change. In May 1968 proposals for common regional boundaries were transmitted by Phillip S. Hughes, assistant director of the bureau, to Califano and then from Califano to the president.[93] Again, approval was withheld. In December 1968 a final effort was made. Califano wrote to the president: "The structure of federal regions and field offices in the Nation is today a patchwork that is incapable of meeting the challenge of the great domestic programs which you have sponsored. This problem was studied by the Heineman Task Force which strongly endorsed this reform. The new Administration will find it difficult to institute such change during the next year and therefore it would seem proper and beneficial for it to be an accomplishment of your Administration."[94] Califano added that the recommendation was supported by Charles Zwick, who had succeeded Schultze as director of BOB. The president remained negative. It was left to President Richard M. Nixon to take the next step. This occurred on 27 March 1969 in a directive that established standard regions and headquarters cities for five departments and agencies.

One of the pervasive difficulties with federally sponsored regional decentralization is in the lines of administrative and programmatic responsibility. The regional field office of a federal department is responsible to its headquarters in Washington. Although the degree of regional "autonomy" varies from department to department, program directives do come from Washington—from the parent department. They are often shaped by negotiations among the parent department, presidential staff agencies, and the subcommittees of the authorizing and appropriations committees of Congress. Thus, at the regional level there is a strong tendency for the vertical responsibilities to Washington headquarters to be more important than the horizontal relationships with other departments and agencies in the region. Consequently, impaired interagency coordination in Washington is reflected in the field.

To alleviate this condition, the Bureau of the Budget, with the backing of the president, sought congressional approval for the establishment of its own field offices. During World War II, BOB maintained four field offices; these were abolished in an economy move during the Eisenhower administration in 1953.[95] But the possibility for BOB field offices emerged and re-emerged several times during the Johnson presidency. In 1964 BOB surveyed its staff members to ascertain their views on field offices and found that internal opinion was sharply divided.[96] Early in January 1965 Charles Schultze, then assistant director of BOB, weighed the pros and cons for Hayes Redmon, an assistant to Bill Moyers in the White House. Schultze's view was "that we ought not to establish regional representatives of the Executive Office as coordinators, expediters, or troubleshooters." The fundamental obstacles to coordination were located in Washington, and until these were dealt with effectively, an effort to compensate for them in the field would be of limited success at best. Schultze did feel that it was important to improve two-way communication between the Executive Office of the President and the field. Thus, he recommended experimentation with BOB regional field representatives. Their functions would involve oversight, liaison, and reporting, not direction and decision making.[97] In general, along with Schultze, the "front office" of BOB was continuously supportive of a BOB presence in the field. It took steps in this direction as early as August 1965 when more BOB personnel began traveling to the field to provide better information on intergovernmental administration.[98]

The field office concept was also considered outside BOB. In 1965 the Bailey task force recommended that the possibility of field offices "be examined." The Heineman task force in its final report recommended that BOB field offices be created. ACIR in 1967 observed that during the period from mid-1965 to mid-1966 "the Bureau's focus began to shift significantly to the problems of the Federal System and the need to improve intergovernmental as well as interagency coordination. To further this purpose it supported a "field staff" for BOB but not "field offices."[99]

In the summer of 1966 William D. Carey, formerly executive assistant director, was assigned responsibility in BOB for interagency relations in the Great Society programs and for intergovernmental relations.[100] Also at this time, BOB was engaged in a serious internal evaluation of its role and organization, an evaluation that culminated in a reorganization in 1967.[101] Thus, consideration of the establishment of field offices occurred at a time when the bureau was engaged in internal reorganization and an attempt to redefine its role in relation to the White House staff and the president. It was also a time when intergovernmental relations, as typified by the complexities of the grant-in-aid system, were under strong criticism from governors, mayors, public interest groups, and Congress.

In this atmosphere Phillip Hughes, deputy director of BOB, appeared before a subcommittee of the House Appropriations Committee on 21 March 1966 to request an appropriation increase of $1.1 million for the addition of forty-nine new positions, twenty-seven of which would be assigned to six small proposed field offices.[102] Hughes testified that field offices were necessary "to strengthen communications with and between managers of local programs, so that information can flow freely through well-established channels . . . to permit a coordinated Bureau evaluation of Federal programs in the field."[103] The field offices would not be a basic extension of the bureau but would perform a new kind of function in the field.[104] Hughes failed in his attempt to convince the subcommittee that BOB field representatives would be "catalysts" and not "czars," and the request for field offices was denied, a judgment in which the Senate concurred. Again, the members of Congress exhibited a concern for "too much" executive office presence in their states and congressional districts. Field offices were not authorized, but BOB was permitted to expand its Washington staff by twenty-two positions.

In 1967 Schultze returned to the subcommittee with a proposal to strengthen BOB's capacity to deal with intergovernmental relations through still more Washington staff.[105] The request was for twenty-one additional positions, but the House approved only six. The Senate was more generous, and ultimately all of the requested positions were allowed, along with a warning by the conference committee that none of the money was to be used for the establishment of field offices.

A BOB presence in the field might have made a salutary contribution to the coordinated implementation of federal programs. However, it would not have directly affected the major source of administrative difficulty—the complex nature of the grant-in-aid system itself and several systemic problems associated with the burgeoning number of grant programs.

Streamlining the Grant System

One obvious approach to streamlining grant programs was to reduce their number. Beyond consideration of specific block grants, some attention was given to methods of consolidation, but little was achieved. In his quality of government message, President Johnson asked BOB to develop legislative plans for consolidating categorical programs. There was study, but no specific recommendations emerged from the bureau. The 1967 version of Muskie's proposed Intergovernmental Cooperation Act contained a controversial title that was added the previous year. It authorized the president to prepare plans for grant consolidation to be submitted to Congress. The procedure was comparable to the long-standing presidential authority to present plans for the reorganization of federal departments and agencies—reorganization plans that go into effect unless vetoed by Congress. Consolidation through executive action was never endorsed by the president, however, and BOB adopted a neutral position. As the bill moved to passage in 1968, the provision for grant consolidation was removed. Also in 1967, the BOB developed and the administration proposed the Joint Funding Simplification Act. It allowed grant recipients to pool applications for funds from several categorical grant programs into a single package, an approach similar to that used in the Model Cities program. Although hearings were held in both houses on this measure during Johnson's time in office, enactment did not come until 1974.[106] Efforts to improve the administration of established grant programs were somewhat more successful.

Fiscal Aspects

Some of the fiscal requirements associated with grants were trouble-some to grantees, and several steps were taken to adjust them. For example, in 1965 BOB issued Circular A-73, providing for the sim-plification and coordination of audit procedures. In 1968 A-87 was produced to provide for uniformity in determining allowable costs in grant programs. The Intergovernmental Cooperation Act con-tained other provisions that simplified accounting procedures for recipients.

Disparities between the fiscal calendars of grant recipients and the congressional budget process were often a source of trouble. Uncer-tainty as to when and in what amounts funding would be available complicated the program and budget planning of prospective grant recipients. BOB conducted an extensive study of the general prob-lem and, with HEW, specifically of the problems in education pro-grams, where the uncertainties were especially vexing.[107] The presi-dent addressed the matter in his 1967 message on education and health in which Congress was asked to act promptly on appropria-tions. Subsequently, amendments to the major education laws pro-vided for one-year advance funding and two-year authorizations for some programs.[108] Although widely discussed and examined in some depth by the Bureau of the Budget at the president's direction, an ap-proach first advocated by Governor Nelson A. Rockefeller of New York was not implemented. The governor suggested that states and cities be allowed to finance initially the national share of project costs—in the construction of municipal waste treatment facilities, for example—and then later be reimbursed when federal funds were available.[109]

Processing

Administrative deficiencies in processing grant applications at-tracted greater and more sustained presidential interest. Problems pertaining to a particular application were often brought to the at-tention of the White House, addressed on a case-by-case basis, and handled as "case work" much like members of Congress deal with constituent problems. But in at least two instances broader correc-tive efforts were sponsored.[110] The first concerned the coordinated administration of the several water, sewer, and waste treatment grant and loan programs. The second was to reduce the time re-quired to process grant applications in a larger number of programs.

In October 1965 Secretary of Agriculture Orville Freeman brought coordination problems in water and related areas to the attention of Harry McPherson in the White House. Freeman pointed out that in addition to the Department of Agriculture, there were partially overlapping water, sewer, and waste treatment programs in the Housing and Home Finance Agency and in the Departments of HEW, the Interior, and Commerce. McPherson, in relaying Freeman's comments to Califano, concluded, "There may be reasons for this, but I can't see what they are." He suggested that BOB be asked to look into the matter.[111]

The reasons for a multiplicity of programs, of course, had to do with the intersection of departmental and congressional committee interests in tailoring programs to special constituency targets. BOB was aware of the problems encountered by many applicants in determining where their applications ought to be sent, and these problems often resulted in complaints to members of Congress. Based upon the work of an interagency committee, early in January 1966 BOB prescribed a preapplication form to be filed with any of the funding agencies. The recipient of the form would then determine which agency had jurisdiction to accept and process an application.

Not long after Freeman's complaint, Muskie brought the multiplicity of water, sewer, and waste treatment programs and other awkward administrative arrangements to the president's personal attention. Johnson in turn asked Milton P. Semer of Califano's staff to explore the situation. In his report to the president, Semer noted, "In theory, everything is worked out. Budget designed a plan, approved forms, and designated Commerce to chair an interagency task force. It is the talk of the town, however, especially on the Hill, as well as in the departments, that there is no coordination in practice." Muskie had suggested that the administrative model used to coordinate the accelerated public works program in 1962 and 1963 be considered. In that model BOB staff members served "as the anonymous link between the President and the bureaucracies" in order "to get people to do what they are supposed to do and have agreed to do." Semer thought that the approach had promise and so did Johnson. He told Semer to "move in on this."[112]

Semer moved quickly. Within a few days he had secured the services of two officials who had been involved in coordinating the accelerated public works program, luring one out of retirement.[113] In mid-June 1966 Johnson received a report of substantial progress from Semer. A reporting system was now in place that tracked individual grant applications and provided "a solid foundation for coordinating four separate programs." In addition, Semer suggested, the approach could be applied to other areas, such as education, health, recreation, and public works. The president indicated that he wanted to continue with the water, sewer, and waste treatment effort and to extend it to other program spheres.[114]

Management of the project now moved from the White House to BOB, where it was soon terminated, although Semer continued to feel that the system and the information it generated had great promise as an instrument for central program management and coordination.[115] The bureau was less optimistic. In its view, the key problem in the water, sewer, and waste treatment programs was setting priorities to guide decisions on awards in the context of limited fiscal resources. But, Schultze told Semer in October 1966, "Priorities have proved difficult to determine technically and, some fear, impossible to live with politically." Consequently, he felt that decisions should be left to the several agencies and should not be managed or coordinated through a central system. The bureau's view was that the only real answer to the coordination problem was program consolidation. Furthermore, Schultze said, the bureau "is not in a position to provide a permanent administrative crutch which will make the separate clientele-oriented organizations work." The reporting system was of limited value to BOB and not worth the investment of staff time. It would be discontinued unless Semer could persuade the departments to continue it with their own resources.[116]

They did, with the Department of Housing and Urban Development playing the lead agency role. Reports on grant processing continued to be prepared.[117] A common application form was developed, and processing time was shortened further.[118] However, the potential of a system, linked to the presidency, that would go beyond processing problems to more basic issues in interagency coordination in water, sewer, and waste treatment programs was foregone. Nor was its potential tested for use in other program areas.

Streamlining the administration of grant programs was still on the agenda in late 1966, however. Further action was stimulated by complaints of slow processing that were received in the White House from the likes of Richard C. Lee, the Democratic mayor of New Haven who enjoyed a national reputation for urban leadership and for massing federal resources for urban development. He sent Califano a forthright message on the point in mid-November 1966.[119] In the March 1967 message on quality of government, the president instructed the director of BOB to form a federal-state-local task force on simplifying grant programs. It was to report in thirty days. Although Schultze was ready to name task force members soon after the message was delivered, the president had second thoughts about this approach, and the task force was abandoned.[120]

Instead, the problem of processing time was to be handled internally. A few days after rejecting Schultze's task force proposal, Johnson asked BOB to look into delays in HUD. He received a report on 7 April 1967.[121] On the same day, he sent a letter to Secretary of HUD Robert Weaver about complaints of delay and asked him to "take a close look at the situation."[122] Califano followed with a meeting with Weaver and other HUD officials on the processing issue. Not long thereafter, Johnson talked about grant administration problems at a cabinet meeting. According to one of his aides, "The President cited a particular weakness, as he sees it, and that is state and local officials contend many times that they can't get decisions on their applications under Federal programs. He said that apparently, in some cases, applications sit around for months and, in some cases, years. He told the Cabinet that we have to put a stop to this."[123]

A top-level task force on grant administration was to follow. On 10 May 1967 Schultze reported to Johnson on the findings of a special interagency task force that explored administrative problems in Chicago, presumably the source of major complaints. There were, in fact, extensive delays. Federal agencies employed "*extremely elaborate review procedures.* Also, because agencies *delegate too little responsibility to their field offices,* applications bounce back and forth between the field and Washington." The underlying problem was that processing procedures antedated "today's emphasis on interagency *joint* action on *multipurpose projects.* Unless procedures can be dramatically overhauled, with more discretion delegated to the field," Schultze warned, "we will build up serious problems." He was particularly concerned that unless changes were made, programs such as Model Cities and neighborhood centers "simply won't get off the ground."[124]

Schultze recommended that Johnson instruct the secretaries of HUD, HEW, and Labor and the director of OEO to establish a joint administrative task force to reorganize processing procedures, to delegate more authority to the field, and to reduce processing time by 50 percent. The next day the president issued a memorandum that put in effect Schultze's recommendations. In it he said, "I regard this project as urgent and immediate."[125]

The task force was chaired by Dwight A. Ink, HUD's assistant secretary for administration, who was joined by his counterparts from the three other organizations. In late July it submitted an interim report to the White House that Califano summarized for the president. At Johnson's direction, Califano immediately sent a memorandum of support to the principals.[126] Another report, which was given to

Johnson on 30 September 1967, focused on four key program areas: Model Cities; neighborhood centers; manpower training; and water, sewer, and waste treatment grants. The report specified administrative changes that could meet the president's target of a 50 percent reduction in processing time. The president directed that implementation of the changes begin immediately, that the task force continue and expand its work to include other intergovernmental programs within the members' jurisdictions, and that all other departments and agencies duplicate the work of the task force in examining their own programs.[127]

In December the task force reported on implementation steps taken since its September submission. A final report was prepared in March 1968. It outlined problems, specific remedial actions to be taken in sixty-two programs, and projected that after full implementation there would be an overall decrease in processing time of 53 percent.[128] Concurrently, Johnson received a similarly promising report from Califano dealing with forty-six additional programs. Despite the positive nature of the reports, the president refused to make them public, commenting, "I don't like to advertise . . . these delays," even though two weeks before he had announced that he would not seek reelection.[129] Subsequently, White House attention to the problem waned, and progress on reducing grant processing time became dependent on the initiatives of program administrators. Thus the Johnson administration only tentatively came to grips with the systemic problems in grant administration that were presented in the tremendous growth it spawned in the number of intergovernmental programs.

One underlying factor contributing to a limited record of achievement in this and other areas was the absence of a strong organizational center for attacking administrative deficiences in a forceful and concerted manner. There was nothing akin to a National Intergovernmental Affairs Council in the Executive Office of the President that Muskie advocated for a time.[130] In the absence of such a center, a variety of devices were thrown into the breach. Numerous flawed mechanisms for program coordination have been discussed. Most had limited resources, no authority, and broad charters lacking a sharp focus on intergovernmental administration. An Executive Officers Group, consisting of departmental assistant secretaries for administration and their agency counterparts, worked sporadically with BOB on administrative problems.[131] The Bureau of the Budget played an important independent role, and in 1967 it went through a reorganization in major part to increase its ability to deal with intergovernmental administrative problems.[132] Late in 1967 a group of several departmental under secretaries began to address specific administrative issues.[133]

The bases for a much more ambitious initiative were on Johnson's desk from June 1967 onward. They were in the recommendations of the Heineman task force. Two of its proposals were especially promising as means for addressing administrative problems in intergovernmental programs. One was for an Office of Program Development located in BOB to manage legislative program development. The other was for an independent Office of Program Coordination with staff in the field to address problems in administration, especially those arising in intergovernmental relationships.[134] Whether in another term these would have been established and joined with a clear working concept of creative federalism is, of course, a question that cannot be answered.

Conclusions

Promoting and putting into place new domestic programs consumed a vast proportion of the Johnson administration's energies. But starting in late 1965 and early 1966, and building on through 1967 and into 1968, a fair amount of attention was given to the broad administrative implications of the programmatic initiatives. The task was a formidable one. Complex program structures were already in place, and others were emerging out of relatively independent program development streams. New programs altered patterns of power and other aspects of the American administrative state, but they did so in a way that confused more than clarified intergovernmental relations and the roles of the several levels of government.

Emergent confusion, plus the strains and tensions caused by rapid and profound change in domestic program arrangements, caused reactions by some state and local officials. The most notable were those of Democratic governors in the aftermath of the 1966 elections and of certain big-city mayors. An opportunity was created for intergovernmental reformers to move systemic issues onto the policy agenda. A very general concept of creative federalism inhering in the pronouncements and stances of the Bureau of the Budget, the Advisory Commission on Intergovernmental Relations, and the Department of Housing and Urban Development, in particular, may have provided a vague guide for action. It emphasized multifunctional and areawide approaches to domestic problem solving and the role of generalists, such as state and local chief executives and planners, in decision making. Schultze's testimony before Muskie's subcommittee was perhaps the most complete summary of the action agenda for harmonizing administrative relationships that derived from the concept of creative federalism.

The record of accomplishment was mixed at best. By and large, the extensive recommendations of the Heineman task force were ignored. Legislative proposals that might have had a major impact, such as placing grant consolidation authority in the president, went nowhere. Such legislative successes as there were came late and were quite modest in their potential effects. Little was done through either legislative or executive action that had a major positive impact on the overall administrative capacities of state and local governments and their chief executives, although weaknesses in these areas were considered to be major problems. Efforts to streamline the administration of grant programs either faltered or were only in the beginning stages of implementation in the final months of the Johnson presidency. Although action was not taken to rationalize federal regional arrangements or to establish a BOB presence in the field, other important steps were taken in the interest of improved field coordination. The promotion of substate regionalism resulted in the spread of a new set of governmental institutions across the country. These were intended to be settings for multifunctional program coordination on an areawide basis through both planning and administrative relationships that crossed individual functional program lines. However, these new institutions suffered from many limitations, not the least of which was their number and variety in type and scope.

8. From the 1960s Onward

The presidency of Lyndon B. Johnson was cut short by turmoil surrounding the Vietnam War. For most of the time he served, his aides and advisers operated on the assumption that there would be another term. Thus, what was left in early 1969 was not what was intended to be the full legacy of established programs, administered and coordinated effectively and functioning smoothly. The nature of Johnson's legacy in intergovernmental administrative relations will be explored after an overview of the Johnson period and an examination of the responses of subsequent administrations.

Overview

Johnson's Great Society enterprise was animated by a spirit that can be described as reformist in character. The focus was on policy, not administration. Yet the configurations of the American administrative state were tested and, in important respects, altered during Johnson's presidency by his policy and program initiatives. National power extended more broadly and deeply into subnational levels, and the intergovernmental mosaic was more intricate. In the end, however, a national bureaucracy remained at the core, stronger, in fact, as a result of Johnson's efforts. Yet it now faced across the federal divide state and local bureaucracies whose power was also enlarged by many new programs and the larger flow of dollars from Washington. A number of options were considered that had at least the potential for directly challenging and limiting national bureaucratic power. Most of those with reconstitutive shadings were either rejected or forced upon Johnson and his policymakers, producing incongruities in the pattern of administrative arrangements. Those rejected included revenue sharing and a guaranteed income approach to the problem of poverty, as opposed to an assistance and social service approach. Multistate commissions in which states genuinely shared in the exercise of national bureaucratic power were stoutly but not always successfully resisted. The block grants in law enforcement were a project of the states and their allies in Congress. Although willingly put forth by the administration, the block grant in public health was more a reflection of a consensus among health professionals than the product of a commitment on the part of national policymakers to this particular type of grant reform. Other block grant proposals fell as a result of the Johnson administration's distinct preference for the categorical variety.

By and large, the task forces that played such an important role in policy development, including those staffed from outside the government, evidenced no great antagonism toward national bureaucratic power. The major exception was the group that devised the war on poverty; some members sought alternative arrangements. The notion of a multifunctional approach to poverty principally orchestrated at the local level by community action agencies had clear reconstitutive possibilities. Although it challenged national bureaucratic power to a degree, in the end this approach proved to be overmatched. The Model Cities experiment was a milder and distinctly less threatening approach to multifunctional program activity at the local level.

In the context of the development of the American administrative state, this volume has explored three major characteristics of intergovernmental relations in the Johnson presidency. The first was the major programmatic and fiscal expansion of government in the national interest, implemented almost entirely through grants-in-aid. The second was the belated recognition of the large and serious administrative problems that emerged in relations among federal departments and agencies and in relations with states, local governments, and nongovernment agencies. These problems included the coordination difficulties that occurred in Washington, in states, and in urban and rural areas in consequence of the Great Society programs. The third consisted of a multitude of attempts to devise solutions to these intergovernmental administrative problems. The "creative federalism" of the Johnson presidency brought no detailed grand design or basic institutional reformulation of the intergovernmental system. To be sure, the legislative legacy in the range of enactments is impressive; the legacy is less impressive in regard to smoothly functioning administrative structures and processes.

The programmatic and fiscal expansion of the period was documented in previous chapters and need not be reviewed here. But the intergovernmental administrative problems that arose and the attempts to resolve them by ad hoc solutions raise a number of issues that should be addressed.

Perhaps the first, and almost naive, question is why the Johnson presidency did not administer more Great Society programs as national programs, without attempting to involve the states and local government. In addition to its grant-in-aid initiatives, many major New Deal programs were national. The Civilian Conservation Corps, the National Youth Administration, and the Works Progress Administration were administered under national government auspices, not by way of grants to subnational jurisdictions. In addition to these emergency programs, there were others, such as social security and the regulation of securities and other aspects of the economy, which are still administered nationally.

The precise answer is elusive, but the historical record provides a basis for some comment. Officials associated with the Johnson presidency may not have had an organizational philosophy, as some scholars have concluded, but they seemed to share two basic organizational dispositions. One emphasized national policy leadership leavened by substantial decentralization in administration involving expanded forms of intergovernmental relationships. What at first glance seems incongruous—pursuing national policy objectives through intergovernmental means—may, in actuality, have coherence. This disposition is akin to Douglas Yates's pluralist democracy model premised on the view that "governmental authority is and ought to be divided within the national government and between national and local governments."[1] As a theme, it was repeatedly enunciated in major presidential statements, including the commencement address at the University of Michigan in May 1964 and the message to Congress in 1967 on quality of government. It was emphasized again and again as Johnson signed important domestic legislation or addressed meetings of governors and mayors. Although some new programs, such as Medicare, were administered nationally, almost all of Johnson's major initiatives easily fit the pluralist democracy model.

It is by no means clear that Johnson or his advisers ever made a conscious general policy choice between administering Great Society programs as national programs or decentralizing their administration to state and local jurisdictions with grants-in-aid, although the options were weighed in some instances. The preference for intergovernmental arrangements seemed foreordained for several reasons. One was a governmental system still formally of federal design. The organizational philosophy reflected in the American federal

arrangement, although leavened by almost two centuries of development, helped shape pragmatic choices in the 1960s. Intergovernmental models were readily available, and many of the new programs were naturally linked to established grant programs. Greater
centralized control might well have encountered serious political
opposition in Congress, and President Johnson was certainly sensitive to this consideration. The artifact of federalism as political
philosophy, historical precedents, and pragmatic political considerations led almost inevitably to an organizational disposition that favored the selection of intergovernmental program formats.

The decision to decentralize administration can, of course, be justified on a number of grounds. No president savors the responsibility
for major increases in federal payrolls. Transfer payments are easier.
As has often been quipped, Washington is very efficient at writing
checks. Once the check is written to fund a grant-in-aid program,
the grantee assumes the administrative responsibility. Another justification could be found in the hope, partially realized in some programs such as community action, that the private, nonprofit sector
could be utilized in conjunction with state and local efforts for the
conduct of public programs, creating new and vital kinds of intergovernmental partnerships at the subnational level. Finally, as
Charles L. Schultze so often emphasized, particularly by 1966, the
new social programs were not only complex, but their outcomes
were also uncertain; in its implementation, social legislation must
be adapted to variations in local needs and resources and to variations in local administrative capability.

Thus, there were obvious administrative and political advantages
in the kind of cooperative patterns that were put together under the
vague rubric of creative federalism. They gave the appearance of sensitivity to the economic, social, and governmental diversity that is
endemic in our complex order. But, ironically, an intergovernmental
approach that recognized diversity undermined the possibility of
well-ordered program administration, at least in the short run.

Once the Johnson administration framed Great Society legislation
principally in intergovernmental terms, all manner of intended and
unintended consequences followed. As described in the preceding
chapters, new constituencies emerged, new and powerful interest
groups appeared, state and local bureaucracies were strengthened as
a function of new and expanded programs, community participation
became a reality, and the states were drawn to become more concerned with urban problems than had hitherto been the case. The
explosion of new programs strengthened the subcommittees of Con-

gress and, indeed, modified congressional behavior in that intergovernmental programs became of prime political interest. As David R.
Mayhew comments, in the aftermath of the 1960s, "across policy
areas generally the programmatic mainstay of congressmen is the
categorical grant" as they came to realize the electoral benefits presented by such programs.[2]

In regard to administrative consequences, a large number of complex, troublesome, and intertwined relationships surfaced that, when
taken as a whole, were not readily described by the conventional distinctions between intergovernmental and intragovernmental arrangements, or between centralization and decentralization, as the
terms were used above. There were varied areas of difficult inter-
organizational interaction. First were the programmatic and management linkages between the president and the Executive Office of
the President, on the one hand, and departments and agencies on the
other. Beyond this, there was the necessity for working out agreements and cooperative administrative arrangements among departments and agencies in Washington in which the Executive Office of
the President was often required to play a part. The experiences of
the Office of Economic Opportunity are sharply illustrative of these
complexities. Particularly important were the relations between
Washington and its field offices, especially where departments were
responsible for major grant-in-aid programs. In addition, there were
administrative transactions in the field—in urban areas, in states,
and in bounded regions such as watersheds, airsheds, and planning
areas—as national programs impinged upon one another, involving
all levels of government and the competing bureaucracies within
governments. These transactions were beset with a number of complexities that impinged on administration. They included, among
other things, the necessity of accommodating national goals and
standards to subnational interests, priorities, and capacities; coordinating program overlaps and interrelationships; and mediating
clashes among various participants in program implementation.

Ursula Hicks has pointed out that "the path of federalism is no
more likely to run smooth than the path of true love."[3] Clearly, the
experience of the Johnson presidency in intergovernmental program
administration was no exception to her rule. The problems experienced were caused by a variety of factors, not the least of which was
the magnitude of a sudden onslaught of new programs and the relatively brief time available to sort through and deal with their administrative implications. But there was a contradiction in its approach
to administration that could not be resolved easily. One theme is

suggested by notes prepared by Harry McPherson in November 1968 for a presidential speech, never given, on intergovernmental relations. These notes are worth quoting at some length:

> I want to talk tonight about a problem that has wracked this nation for 35 years; the role of the Federal government in relation to State and local government and to the private sector.
>
> . . . I could not accept the liberal dogma that the Federal government had all the answers. It seemed obvious to me that local needs could best be served by local leadership, and that even Federal programs would be more successful if such local leadership were given a strong role. Furthermore, it seemed to me that vigorous State and local leadership was in accord with our traditional distaste for centralization. And I believe that we can diminish the sense of apathy and impersonality and separateness that people inevitably feel in a huge and complex society, if they could enjoy a strong sense of participation at the local level. . . .
>
> . . . I could not share the view of some liberals that the private sector could not be counted on to serve public purposes. I had ample reason to know that the vast resources of talent and energy and institutional strength in the private sector could be tapped in the service of the nation.
>
> . . . We got past rhetoric to the concrete, down-to-earth problems of Federal-State relations. Some of these problems are highly technical and will require years of determined effort to resolve. But they can be resolved, if the man in the White House cares enough to keep the pressure on. We must have a systematic re-examination of grants-in-aid programs, a review of the decentralization of Federal operations and so on. Those are technical subjects, and rather dull. But they must be attended to if we care about the continued vitality of this society.
>
> . . . We still have a long, long way to go in shaping mutually satisfactory relations between the Federal government, State and local government, and the private sector. I sometimes think we need a new set of Federalist Papers, but unfortunately political philosophers are in short supply.[4]

The commitment to a pluralist approach in program design comes through quite clearly. A frustration with the way programs worked is equally apparent.

This frustration is in part rooted in another of the administration's organizational dispositions. It was a recipe for good administration similar to what Yates terms the administrative efficiency model, one conceived at a time when the tasks and processes of government were simpler than they had become in the 1960s. Among the major elements he includes in the model are appointment to position on the basis of merit; expertise, professionalism, and specialization of functions in bureaucratic structures organized hierarchically; an emphasis on planning and fiscal management; and direction and co-ordination by strong chief executives and their agents.[5] To this might be added the organization of functions along appropriate departmental, areal, or regional lines. To the extent that correctives to administrative problems were sought by the Bureau of the Budget and others, such as those discussed in the previous chapter, they were basically compatible with the prescriptions of the administrative efficiency model. One qualification needs to be entered. It concerns the reluctance during Johnson's tenure, presumably based at least in part on political considerations, to systematically enlarge institutional capacity for the exercise of management or executive leadership in the presidency, a key aspect of the administrative efficiency model.

As Yates points out, the pluralist democracy and administrative efficiency models are in basic conflict on a number of points.[6] Of special importance, the pluralist democracy model provides for the dispersal of power, whereas the other calls for its concentration. Rather than an absence of organizational philosophy, the Johnson administration was plagued instead by a commitment to two concepts of organization that could not be easily accommodated. Powerful, dispersed pluralist forces that were built into Johnson's intergovernmental programs overwhelmed the objective of administrative direction and control. These forces created political imperatives that were dealt with largely in political terms, as in the liaison relations with governors and mayors, in order to protect the president's political interests. Management imperatives were of less concern at the presidential level. Near the end of Johnson's tenure a sharper recognition of the problem began to emerge.[7] The recommendations of the Heineman task force for strengthening the institutional capacity of the presidency to supply unity, consistency, and coherence in governmental operations, especially in regard to intergovernmental programs, and for bringing about administrative reform in Washington and in the field represented an effort to ameliorate contradictions, although it is not clear that they would have done so if implemented.

This is not to say that corrective measures such as those discussed in previous chapters were inappropriate or without possible benefit. Rather, they were inadequate for bringing order to a sprawling intergovernmental administrative system and for moderating the unruly bargaining and negotiation in decision making that were apparently endemic to pluralist arrangements.[8]

In the end, several paradoxes mark the development of the American administrative state during Johnson's presidency. One was that, although policymakers were driven by a sense of national problems and purposes, intergovernmental programs were chosen for the most part as the instruments for addressing those problems and attaining those purposes. And there is an irony locked in the paradox. Giving impetus to the proclivity to define problems as national in character was a strong sense of the limitations of state and local governments, and in many quarters in Washington there was an antipathy to these subnational units.

A second paradox was that the increased scope and penetration of national power at subnational levels had generally decentralizing effects. Michael D. Reagan makes the case for decentralization, arguing that "the shift to creative federalism does not (at least in all ways) represent a further centralization. Rather, it constitutes the epitome of decentralization, in the sense that the federal government not only does not hire its own civil servants to run the programs . . . , but it even reaches below the states to local governments, to semi-public organizations, and to private business firms to administer 'its' programs. Furthermore, it is not entirely a matter of administrative decentralization; it is also very substantially a question of policy making decentralization."[9]

Perhaps the soundest hypothesis is that Great Society programs were *both* centralizing and decentralizing. This is the conclusion reached by Richard R. Warner in a most useful study. Johnsonian federalism—creative federalism, as it came to be designated—was decentralizing, he suggests, in that it expanded the capacities of subnational governments and employed them in policy determinations involving problems perceived to be national in character. It was centralizing in that it augmented the national role in governmental policymaking and propelled the national government much more deeply than before into the administrative processes and decisions of subnational units.[10] In Stephen Skowronek's terms, power concurrently became more concentrated and more dispersed, and there was increased penetration of the periphery by the center and, in a certain sense, of the center by the periphery.[11]

A third paradox was that although the features of certain Great Society programs challenged established bureaucratic structures, processes, and perspectives at all levels, those structures, processes, and perspectives in many instances were reinforced, if not strengthened. Processes of policy formulation and program development were further centralized in the presidency to serve as an antidote to bureaucratic influence on policy content and to precipitate ideas that transcended bureaucratic imagination and interests. Efforts were made to strengthen the hands of mayors and governors in intergovernmental program administration and to empower citizens in their relations with administrative officials. Program concepts and coordination devices were adopted that attempted to expand bureaucratic vision beyond narrow functional areas of responsibility and limited geographical jurisdictions. There was an emphasis on applying new types of intellectual skills that were more analytical, critical, and innovative than those commonly perceived to be found in large amounts in the typical bureaucratic operation. To an extent, these efforts had their desired effects. But in the end they were muted by reliance on established bureaucratic structures and processes for program implementation, which gave the organizations added resources, and by the inherent difficulty of producing change quickly in bureaucratic settings.

A fourth paradox was that although the complex of Great Society programs was the product of a strong presidency—indeed, it was evidence of the office's great strength—those same achievements contributed significantly to impairing presidential ability to lead and govern. In its domestic aspects, the presidency became more than a national office. It became a federal office—a federal presidency in the sense that national administrative authority works through states and their political subdivisions. It was a presidency in which expectations of national leadership remained high. It was also a presidency that not only had to contend with a "permanent government" at the national level but also had to work with a multitude of elected officials and bureaucracies at subnational levels, located far from the president's vision or constitutional reach and possessed of considerable political influence of their own. As Erwin C. Hargrove and Michael Nelson put it, "The problems of presidential control of federal agencies pale in comparison with the effort required to exercise authority over multitudes of state and local organizations charged with carrying out federal programs." [12] During Johnson's presidency, the problems were exacerbated by a weak, overloaded central management apparatus.

In the Aftermath of the Great Society

Debate over the performance of the intergovernmental administrative networks erected during Johnson's presidency and their paradoxical features has played a significant part in the nation's politics since he left office. In varying degrees, each of his four successors in the past two decades has sought alterations in the intergovernmental arrangements he sponsored. In some spheres the arrangements were extended. In others there were efforts to reform or even remove them. These efforts were stimulated by critical assessments of the effectiveness of intergovernmental programs in attaining policy objectives. They were further stimulated by a general shift in the national political climate, a shift that came in part because of perceived deficiencies in the Great Society enterprise.

As Henry J. Aaron forcefully points out, the Johnson administration's promotion of systematic policy analysis and program evaluation has had important effects on its reputation.[13] Critical assessments of the effectiveness of intergovernmental programs were produced even while it was in office. Subsequently, some broadly negative assessments from both the political left and right attribute flawed Great Society program results partially to reliance on intergovernmental bureaucracies in implementation.[14] Other general analyses paint a mixed picture of flawed and successful administration.[15] Studies of individual intergovernmental programs in education, health, community action, Model Cities, and other areas present similar results.[16] Most analyses underscore the especially knotty problems faced in attempts to attain national policy objectives through intergovernmental program arrangements and the acute design problems to be overcome if they are to work well. They emphasize the problematical prospects of limiting the discretion of state and local officials in program administration and the conflicts that may arise between national and subnational interests.[17] Paul E. Peterson, for example, has written persuasively about the barriers to attaining national redistributive objectives through city governments, a goal so evident in the war on poverty programs, because the dominant interests of cities unavoidably are developmental in nature. Redistributive efforts are not easily accommodated.[18]

Sober professional assessments of government programs ordinarily do not have direct and wide-ranging political effects. Parallel public perceptions that do may emerge, however. In the aftermath of the Great Society initiatives there was clearly a political reaction that helped fuel challenges to a variety of intergovernmental programs. There is no simple explanation. Allen J. Matusow, for example, points to a decline in social cohesion since the 1960s reflected in an "uprising against liberalism" by counterculture advocates, the new left, black nationalists, opponents of the war in Vietnam, and others alienated by or disappointed in Johnson's policies and programs.[19]

William A. Schambra posits a similar thesis. He argues that the central underpinning of Great Society programs was the liberal idea shared by many decision makers in Washington that the United States was a national community. In 1964 and 1965, especially, this idea was the basis for a "summons to national oneness" through attacks on inequality and efforts to integrate marginal groups into the community.[20] The commitment to the pursuit of nationalist objectives through the intergovernmental program means described in chapter 2 is congruent with Schambra's characterization. Not long afterward, he argues, disaffection set in partly because programs "failed to provide . . . the sense of community promised."[21] As the force of the national community idea eroded, there was an increase in the ranks of those who came to see the national government "as a distant, alienating bureaucratic monstrosity, ceaselessly spawning intrusive, insensitive, and expensive programs."[22] This disaffection, when added to the traditional opponents of the expansion of the national government's role through intergovernmental programs or otherwise, contributed to the elections of Richard Nixon, Jimmy Carter, and, especially, Ronald Reagan to the presidency. This changed political climate was reflected in the stances they took on nation-state-local relationships.

Nixon, Ford, and Carter

The arrival of the Nixon administration did not result in a complete and abrupt change in the presidential stance on all matters pertaining to intergovernmental relations. There was a measure of continuity in that several of its administrative initiatives bearing on intergovernmental programs had clear connections to the Johnson period. But the basic attitude was quite different. It was that the national government, especially its bureaucratic component, had become too powerful in many respects. Several courses of action were followed by Nixon and his aides in order to correct what they viewed as the excesses of the Johnson presidency. One, largely frustrated by a Democratic Congress, was to limit spending for social programs. Another was to shift power from the national to the subnational levels. Finally, institutional changes were sought in order to improve policy and program operations, including those of an intergovernmental character.[23]

Nixon's major statement on "new federalism," which was his alternative to creative federalism, came in a nationally televised speech in August 1969. It was to be, he said, "a new and dramatically different approach to the way in which government cares for those in need, and to the way . . . responsibilities are shared between the States and the Federal Government."²⁴ Specifically, authority was to be decentralized, even devolved, for programs in areas such as education, social services, job training, and law enforcement, where conditions and needs varied widely from community to community. On the other hand, according to Nixon, there were situations in which the national government should play a dominant role. For example, where there were externalities associated with government action or inaction, as in environmental pollution, a national response was in order. When national uniformity was required, as in the case of transfer payments for welfare or health insurance, national programs were the appropriate vehicles. When experimentation or demonstrations were necessary to produce innovations in policies and programs and to stimulate action on a broad front, as in the case of drug abuse prevention, national action was justified.

The relative clarity of the organizing principles notwithstanding, Nixon was largely unsuccessful in reshaping the American administrative state. Although "the idea," according to Richard P. Nathan, "was to weaken the federal bureaucracy," its power arguably increased substantially during Nixon's time in office.²⁵ In some instances, the accretions of power were sanctioned by new federalism criteria. New and expanded programs that preempted state authority, such as in environmental regulation, could be justified by the externality principle. In the interest of national uniformity, national programs replaced grant programs for the provision of aid to the aged, blind, and disabled. Another national program, providing a guaranteed annual income to replace aid to families with dependent children and other intergovernmental welfare programs, failed in Congress.

In areas where Nixon felt the states and localities ought to be in the forefront, his efforts fell far short in reducing the role of the national government. Proposals to terminate grant programs usually failed. The most ambitious plan to lessen the power of the national bureaucracy was revenue sharing, both general and special. Nixon first proposed general revenue sharing in 1969, but Congress did not act. A second plan was unveiled in 1971. One part called again for general revenue sharing with states and general purpose units of local government. The other part combined approximately 105 grant programs into six special revenue sharing programs in education, community development, transportation, rural development, law enforcement, and manpower. In special revenue sharing, funds were to be distributed to states and localities unfettered by planning, matching, and other requirements. General revenue sharing became law in 1972, but the special variants went nowhere.

Congressional opposition to special revenue sharing contributed to renewed interest in block grants and other forms of grant consolidation. Here the Nixon administration was somewhat more successful, but not spectacularly so. Its proposals for grant consolidation in various areas, such as health, were generally rebuffed by Congress, as was a request for presidential authority to consolidate grants subject to congressional review. Two new block grants were created, however. In 1974 the Comprehensive Employment and Training Act partially put into law Nixon's proposal to collapse various manpower programs into a block grant.[26] Later that year Congress passed the Housing and Community Development Act. Building upon the 1971 special revenue sharing program for community development and supplanting Johnson's Model Cities program, by then funded at about $500 million per year, the administration consolidated ten categorical programs into the community development block grant program for cities.[27] These programs notwithstanding, congressional commitment to categorical grants remained strong and usually determinative during Nixon's time in office.

Attempts to allow state and local governments more discretion and to reduce the weight of the national bureaucracy through means such as grant consolidation and revenue sharing were complemented by several organizational and administrative undertakings.[28] One emphasis involved better equipping the presidency to manage the sprawling executive establishment. First steps were modest and included an office to deal with intergovernmental relations under the direction of the vice-president and the Urban Affairs Council headed by a counselor to the president. The Bureau of the Budget was converted into the Office of Management and Budget (OMB) and reorganized in an effort to strengthen it as a presidential instrument for harnessing the bureaucracy and to place greater emphasis on program management. At the same time, the Domestic Council was created. With a staff far in excess of Califano and his small group, it was to serve as the type of central presidential mechanism for domestic policy development recommended to Johnson by the Heineman task force.[29]

Nixon's most controversial reorganization proposal was to abolish seven departments and a number of agencies and to reassemble their programs into four new departments—natural resources, community development, human resources, and economic affairs. Administrative streamlining through a rational arrangement of program responsibilities was one objective. Another was to disrupt and thereby weaken the political alliances linking program administrators, congressional committees, and interest groups that were perceived as obstacles to realization of Nixon's substantive policy objectives. As it turned out, the strength of the alliances outweighed the president's, and departmental reorganization was soundly rejected.

Numerous less dramatic initiatives were mounted in the interest of further decentralizing program administration and smoothing intergovernmental program implementation. Many of them had roots in the Johnson presidency and in the Intergovernmental Cooperation Act passed in 1968. In 1969 Nixon directed that a federal assistance review program be instituted. Led by OMB and involving the major domestic departments and agencies, its purpose was to decentralize, standardize, and simplify intergovernmental programs. Each of the participating organizations examined its own programs for the purpose of improving their administration. Based upon the group's recommendation, Nixon implemented the common regional boundaries concept. Inconsistencies in planning requirements, financial management, and procurement regulations were addressed, and a number of administrative circulars were issued by OMB. Building upon an experiment initiated late in Johnson's presidency, the Nixon administration established federal regional councils. The councils engaged in a wide variety of activities aimed at simplifying and coordinating processes for applying funds from several grant programs to single projects, improving communications among levels of government, and dealing with special regional problems.[30]

OMB developed a project notification and review system, first called for in the Demonstration Cities and Metropolitan Development Act of 1966, then in the Intergovernmental Cooperation Act. The basic purpose of the system was improved coordination of programs at state and local levels. OMB's Circular A-95 spelled out the procedures. Prospective applicants for grants were required to file notice of their intent with state and local clearinghouses, which would then circulate the notice to other agencies for review and comment and assist in working out any problems revealed by the process. Comments went to the granting agency with the application. The circular also addressed several other aspects of planning coordination.

Johnson's legislation to allow for the integrated administration of grant programs failed, but OMB continued to work on the idea as an alternative to grant consolidation. In 1972 it initiated an experimental program that led in 1974 to the enactment of the Joint Funding Simplification Act.[31] The law required the president to promulgate regulations to guide agencies in devising ways to facilitate bringing a number of programs together in support of a single project.

There were no notable changes in direction during the Ford or Carter presidencies.[32] Ford generally followed the course set in the Nixon period. He continued to ask Congress for grant consolidations, but except for vocational education in 1976, he was unsuccessful. Carter returned intergovernmental liaison responsibilities to the White House. Although once a governor, he did not appear to have a major interest in questions about the division of power among levels of government or in intergovernmental issues beyond generalized complaints about the national bureaucracy evident in the 1976 campaign and the first phase of his presidency. For a time he was engaged in welfare reform that potentially had some significant implications for intergovernmental relations, but his plan died aborning. In energy and other areas, there was further preemption of state authority, and the participation of state governments in revenue sharing was ended in 1980. Carter introduced a "new partnership" theme in 1978, calling for targeting community development and other funds on the poorest areas of cities. On the whole, however, his domestic policy agenda contained few new initiatives and none that truly challenged the established order.

On Reagan Eve

As the 1980 presidential election approached, much of the Great Society's intergovernmental program edifice remained in place. It was now embellished by revenue sharing, a few new block and consolidated grant programs, and many new categorical programs. State and local dependence on federal funds stood at an all-time high, with 26.3 percent of subnational expenditures funded by grants.[33] In addition, there were both new and expanded regulatory programs that, although containing intergovernmental components, included in them substantially extended national power. Despite generally unfavorable evaluations and presidential antipathy, the Appalachian Regional Commission and the other multistate economic development commissions were still operating.[34] There were casualties, however. Community action was now tamed, and its radical organizational and political potential long forgotten. The Model Cities program, after a promising start, was gone. The health, safe streets, and juvenile delinquency block grant programs also received favorable initial reviews, but Congress persistently burdened them with categorical features that reduced recipient discretion.[35]

Although administrative turbulence in intergovernmental relations was not as pronounced as in the 1960s, serious problems remained. Grantees still complained of an absence of coordination in Washington, red tape, delayed funding, conflicting and changing interpretations of requirements, and other administrative deficiencies.[36] Problems were exacerbated in the 1970s by a tremendous increase in national policy requirements attached to grants to promote nondiscrimination, environmental protection, health, and safety. In addition, administrative and fiscal requirements had become more elaborate.[37]

At the conclusion of her survey of intergovernmental relations in the 1970s, Martha Derthick states: "One never knows whether to stand in awe of the endless adaptability of American government—the headlong, innocent, unabashed pragmatism of it all—or to be appalled by the disorder and indifference to doctrine. As much as any set of domestic developments since the New Deal, the history of intergovernmental relations in the 1970s invites this wholly ambivalent reaction."[38]

Others were more certain in their position. In 1981 the Advisory Commission on Intergovernmental Relations, after reviewing the same developments, painted a rather depressing landscape in which "the overextended role that the national government now occupies in the federal system" was emphasized.[39] There were, it found, "increasingly prescriptive and intrusive" national policies tied to grants.[40] Consequently, "The spirit of intergovernmental cooperation has been replaced by rising levels of intergovernmental antagonism."[41] "The extreme intergovernmentalization of nearly every well-intentioned public endeavor" threatened to "transform an overresponsive system into an unaccountable, inequitable, inefficient, and economically unfeasible morass."[42] Obviously, precise critiques of the state of intergovernmental relations such as this had no direct bearing on the 1980 electoral results. There was, however, a general dissatisfaction with the contemporary condition of the American administrative state, now so laden with intergovernmental programs that they were seen by many as ineffective burdens and the sources of problems rather than solutions to them. The ground was prepared for the presidential initiatives of Ronald Reagan.[43]

The Reagan Presidency

The Great Society was built upon principles embodied in what James Ceaser labels the "liberal theory of governance." Since its inception, he says, "the core of the liberal idea has been to expand the purview of government—and in particular the federal government—into new domains in society in order to prohibit, modify, stimulate or create certain activities and forms of behavior."[44] As a governor, as a candidate for president, and in the presidential office, Ronald Reagan rejected this theory. Nowhere was his rejection stated more directly and clearly than in his first inaugural address. "In this present crisis," he said, "government is not the solution to our problem; government is the problem."[45] The crisis to which Reagan referred was in part an economic one in which the country was beset by high unemployment, high interest rates, and high inflation as well as a crisis in popular confidence in government, the "malaise" associated with the Carter presidency. Reagan's solution to the crisis was simple: he wanted, as he often said as a candidate, to get the government off the people's backs.

In Reagan's view, getting government off the people's backs meant, first, reducing federal spending and the taxes needed to sustain it. High taxes, he argued, stifled the national economy by reducing incentives for work, savings, and investment. Getting government off the people's backs also meant taking reconstitutive steps, including returning power to the states and localities—power that the federal government had assumed in the 1960s and 1970s. Devolving power was closely related to the goal of a general reduction in the scope of federal activity. "It is my intention," Reagan proclaimed in 1981, "to curb the size and influence of the federal establishment and to demand recognition of the distinction between the powers granted to the federal government and those reserved to the states or to the people."[46] Respect for the federal division of powers, devolution, and the reduction of federal spending were core goals of Reagan's "new federalism."[47] Because the expansion of national power was based largely in the initiatives of the Great Society, they were obvious targets for change.

One strategy for change focused on the budget. Upon entering office the Reagan administration proposed cutting social program expenditures by almost $75 billion by fiscal year 1985, or by about 17 percent of what had been appropriated the previous year.[48] He did not realize all of his budgetary objectives, but he had a major effect on grant-in-aid outlays. After a period of expansive growth, they reached a peak of $91.5 billion in fiscal year 1980, but by fiscal year 1985 they had fallen to $81.1 billion, measured in 1980 dollars.[49]

In association with spending reductions, the Reagan administration sought to restructure the intergovernmental program system by eliminating, consolidating, or reassigning responsibilities for various of its components. Approximately sixty programs, most of them quite small, were abolished in 1981. By the end of 1984 more than

one hundred programs had been dismantled.[50] The multistate commissions for economic development and water resources planning
were abolished, and revenue sharing for local governments was ended
in 1983. Several programs funding substate regional activities were
also terminated.[51] Despite the intensive efforts of the administration, Congress refused to eliminate either the Appalachian Regional
Commission or the Economic Development Administration.

The Reagan administration placed particular emphasis on grant
consolidation in ways that emphasized the importance and power of
states as opposed to local governments. In 1981 seven new block
grants were proposed to replace eighty-five categorical programs.[52]
Although called block grants, they were more in line with Nixon's
special revenue sharing concept in that there were no matching or
maintenance-of-effort conditions, and administrative requirements
were minimal. Congress enacted nine block grants but gave the president much less than he requested. Only fifty-four categorical programs were affected, and four of the new "block" programs were
built upon only a single categorical grant.[53] The following year a
block grant for job training was added to the roster. Several additional proposals were sent to Congress in 1983 and 1984 but to no
avail.

In 1982 Reagan proposed an ambitious and systematic shift of program responsibilities. One portion, the "swap," called for the national government to assume sole responsibility for Medicaid, and in
return the states would assume sole responsibility for aid to families
with dependent children and food stamps. In addition, there was to
be a "turnback" of other programs to the states. The plan was fairly
complex, but essentially from forty to sixty programs in areas such
as health, transportation, and education, involving well over one
hundred separate grants-in-aid, were to be transferred to the states.
Certain taxes would be relinquished to help states fund the programs. After a time, states would be free to use or not use the new
revenue resources as they saw fit—to continue to fund the programs,
to spend for other purposes, or not to spend at all. The plan received
a flurry of attention, much of it negative, and soon it passed into political limbo.[54]

Reagan was unable to secure congressional approval for many of
his recommendations aimed at reshaping intergovernmental arrangements, but his command of the executive branch enabled him to
loosen central controls in the implementation of grant programs.[55]
Among the steps taken were exempting certain grant programs from
OMB circulars, revising other circulars in order to liberalize requirements, and abolishing the A-95 review and comment process, fed-

eral regional councils, and OMB's intergovernmental program staff. Efforts were also made to soften the regulatory and national policy mandates imposed on grant programs through permissive enforcement.[56] The basic purpose underlying these adjustments, of course, was to restrain the power of the national bureaucracy and to widen the discretion of grant recipients.

The overall record of the Reagan administration suggests that at least for a time it was successful in arresting or slowing certain trends of previous decades. Among these were the increasing dependency of state and local governments on federal funds; exclusive reliance, for all practical purposes, on categorical grants; and more and more stringent and uniform national standards and requirements governing program administration.[57] But analysts who closely examined the cumulative impact of the Reagan presidency on federalism and intergovernmental relations conclude that it has been relatively modest. Despite a weakened sense of national community, the Reagan administration was unable to articulate a revised view of federalism that attracted sufficient support from the public, politicians, and bureaucrats to serve as a basis for fundamental changes. Arrangements forged in the 1960s and 1970s continued to enjoy the support of state and local officials and members of Congress, Republicans and Democrats alike. As John E. Chubb puts it, there remains "a bias for centralization rooted in contemporary American elections"—Reagan and an eroded sense of national community notwithstanding—"that shows little signs of changing."[58]

The Intergovernmental Legacy

After twenty years, despite shifts in public mood and the antagonism of Johnson's successors toward many achievements of his presidency, the effects of the Great Society undertaking on the American administrative state are still evident and significant in a variety of ways.

The first and most important element of the legacy is that, although there have been additions, subtractions, repackaging, and redirection, the intergovernmental program structures of the Great Society remain largely in place. Intergovernmental administration continues to occupy an important place in the American administrative state and to serve as a major alternative to direct national program administration. Though somewhat muted in the 1980s, prodigious power over these programs, many of them involving categorical grants, still inheres in a national bureaucracy based in Washington. This bureaucracy was given additional weight in the 1970s

by an extension of nationalized functions through several new intergovernmental programs, most of which were products of first steps
taken by the Johnson administration. In addition, national policy requirements were increasingly attached to grants, a practice that began in earnest during Johnson's time in office.

Another part of the legacy is that in the complex of intergovernmental relations, state and local governments are stronger in administrative capacity than during the 1960s. This capacity was strengthened by increased program responsibilities and the resources and
prodding accompanying them.[59] Great Society emphases associated
with sound administration—planning, for example—remain a part
of implementation routines. The radical restructuring of local government envisioned by some Great Society planners did not come to
pass, but a new strata of substate institutions for planning, coordination, and in some instances program operations now span the
country.

A transformed presidency may also be included in the legacy. The
challenge of coordinating intergovernmental programs that were
created in the 1960s contributed to strengthening the institutional
presidency in the 1970s. Further, issues in intergovernmental administration have persisted as a staple on the presidential agenda.
The enlarged impact of the national government at state and local
levels and the attendant dependencies raised the level of expectations projected on to the presidential office.[60] The problem is not an
entirely new one, but it has become more acute since Johnson's time
in office. In the short run, Johnson may have added to the problem by
exaggerating claims for Great Society programs. At the same time,
as noted previously, presidents and their aides have limited control
over the performance of intergovernmental programs in meeting expectations. In a certain sense, a national presidency is joined with
a pronounced federal dimension. Johnson's presidency "of all the
people" became, in addition, a presidency of all the governments, including state and local units over which there is no constitutional
authority and which are beyond a president's ability to command.
Governors, mayors, and other subnational officials are not subject to
a president's executive prerogative. Yet the chief executive's fortunes are now tied in a meaningful way to their performance or lack
thereof.

A final part of the Johnson legacy is in the politics of intergovernmental relations that shapes program structures and administration.
Patterns of participation and influence changed, according to most
close observers. Participation increased on the part of minority

groups, and their political skills, stimulated by new civil rights laws and war on poverty programs, were sharpened. Associations of state and local officials became more active and important, especially an energized "big six": the National League of Cities, the U.S. Conference of Mayors, the National Association of Counties, the International City Management Association, the National Governors' Conference, and the Council of State Governments. A host of new interest groups came into existence to serve narrow constituencies with stakes in particular interests and programs, such as aid for the handicapped, family planning, and mental health.[61] The role of professional policy analysts and entrepreneurs became much more pronounced. Partially in response to growing national bureaucratic power since the 1960s and the stimulation of the new variety of interest group, the federal judiciary became a much more active participant in intergovernmental policy and program matters.[62] A more complex political environment, in which the interests of state and local governments, as well as others, are vigorously represented, now envelops intergovernmental programs and their administration.

One result is constraints on the ability of presidents to provide decisive leadership in intergovernmental matters. David B. Walker identifies interest groups, especially those serving narrow constituencies, as the central actors in "a pulverizing pluralistic, highly variegated pattern of . . . politics," a pattern that is the source of demands for new and enlarged programs and the stout defense of established ones that complicate the intergovernmental order.[63] Cynthia Cates Coella and David R. Beam, in their discussion of intergovernmental relations, underscore the influence of policy entrepreneurs in Congress who are "no longer disciplined by Constitutional, political or institutional constraints." The result, they assert, is "responsiveness to almost all conceivable stimulus [*sic*] whether large, small, important, trivial, or of national or local interest."[64] Others see intergovernmental policy and politics as dominated by networks incorporating bureaucratic, technocratic, and interest group elements in particular policy and program spheres cutting vertically through levels of government and horizontally through executive and legislative branches.[65] Donald F. Kettl discerns the development of a segmented pattern in which the politics of resource distribution are centered in Congress, the politics of program substance are dominated by state and local officials restrained by regulatory and judicial forces, and the politics of execution feature the third parties that state and local governments rely on for implementation.[66] The national executive voice is dampened in all three areas.

On Contemporary Federal Life

In *The Federalist* No. 46, James Madison wrote, "If . . . the people should in the future become more partial to the federal than to the State governments, the change can only result from such manifest and irresistible proofs of a better administration as will overcome all their antecedent propensities."[67] Whether because of a perception "of a better administration" or not, public expectations over the years have produced an increasingly active national government in domestic matters. At the same time, the states and their governmental subdivisions have been assigned important roles in the implementation of programs originated at the national level.

S. Rufus Davis's lament about the historical obscurity of "the facts of federal life" was alluded to in chapter 1. It is certain that, although obscure, they differ now from those of the founding period. The experience of Johnson's presidency and subsequent developments suggest a number of observations, if not facts, about the contemporary American governmental system and perhaps about "federal life." One observation is that the appeal of what Samuel H. Beer terms "the national idea" is persistent and continuing, although its strength may vary from one decade to another.[68] In the Johnson presidency it produced a nationally driven but pragmatic approach to the allocation of functional responsibilities. The result was an expanded group of intergovernmental programs that varied considerably in their particular characteristics and subscribed to no consistent pattern. Another observation is that the intergovernmental program structures of the past provide the models for the present and future. As demands for national action arise, an almost instinctive response of policymakers is to adapt the familiar to the new problem, though there may be shifts in emphasis such as between categorical and other types of grants. Still another observation is that despite their extensive use in pursuit of national policy objectives, intergovernmental programs are imperfect means for realizing those objectives. In part this is because of the inherent complexities in intergovernmental administration exacerbated by interrelated administrative deficiencies that may be found at all levels of government.

A final observation relates to complexity: there is still present unresolved tension between centralizing and decentralizing tendencies in the American system, leading to intergovernmental programs in which both are manifest. The abstract principles of the American Constitution about which Madison wrote attempted a resolution that could not withstand the pressures of 200 years of national development. Contemporary efforts to resolve the tension, such as those of Richard Nixon, fail to gain broad acceptance. In the notes for a speech by Johnson on federalism, quoted earlier in this chapter, it was said, "I sometimes think we need a new set of Federalist Papers, but unfortunately political philosophers are in short supply." Absent political philosophers, decisions about governmental structures and processes will normally continue to be made in a largely incremental manner by pragmatic public officials and policy experts in the executive and Congress in the manner of the presidency of Lyndon Baines Johnson.

Notes

1. The Intergovernmental Mosaic

1. On the concept of the administrative state, see Fritz Morstein Marx, *The Administrative State: An Introduction to Bureaucracy* (Chicago: University of Chicago Press, 1957); and especially Paul P. Van Riper, "The American Administrative State: Wilson and the Founders," in Ralph Clark Chandler, ed., *A Centennial History of the American Administrative State* (New York: The Free Press, 1987), pp. 3–36.

2. Van Riper, "The American Administrative State," p. 7.

3. Arthur M. MacMahon, ed., *Federalism: Mature and Emergent* (New York: Doubleday, 1955).

4. Deil S. Wright, *Understanding Intergovernmental Relations* (North Scituate, Mass.: Duxbury Press, 1978), p. 44. See also Harry N. Scheiber, "Federalism and Legal Process: Historical and Contemporary Analysis of the American System," *Law and Society Review* 14 (Spring 1980): 683–689.

5. Morton Grodzins, *The American System* (Chicago: Rand McNally, 1966); Daniel J. Elazar, *The American Partnership* (Chicago: University of Chicago Press, 1962).

6. Edward S. Corwin, "The Passing of Dual Federalism," in Robert G. McCloskey, ed., *Essays in Constitutional Law* (New York: Vintage Books, 1957), p. 205.

7. Samuel H. Beer, "In Search of a New Public Philosophy," in Anthony King, ed., *The New American Political System* (Washington, D.C.: American Enterprise Institute, 1978), p. 7.

8. David B. Walker, *Toward a Functioning Federalism* (Cambridge, Mass.: Winthrop Publishers, 1981), p. 81.

9. James T. Patterson, *The New Deal and the States* (Princeton, N.J.: Princeton University Press, 1969), p. 207.

10. For further insight into intergovernmental relations during this period, see Jane Perry Clark, *The Rise of a New Federalism* (New York: Columbia University Press, 1938); and V. O. Key, Jr., *The Administration of Federal Grants to States* (Chicago: Public Administration Service, 1937). On emergent national-local relations during the 1930s, 1940s, and 1950s,

see Roscoe C. Martin, *The Cities and the Federal System* (New York: Atherton Press, 1965).

11. Wright, *Understanding Intergovernmental Relations*, p. 49.

12. Walker, *Toward a Functioning Federalism*, p. 83.

13. James L. Sundquist, *Politics and Policy: The Eisenhower, Kennedy, and Johnson Years* (Washington, D.C.: The Brookings Institution, 1968).

14. Wright, *Understanding Intergovernmental Relations*, p. 54.

15. "Address before a Joint Session of the Congress," 27 November 1963, "Annual Message to Congress on the State of the Union," 8 January 1964, *Public Papers of the Presidents of the United States: Lyndon B. Johnson, 1963–1964* (Washington, D.C.: GPO, 1965), p. 8 (hereafter cited as *Public Papers*).

16. "Annual Message to Congress on the State of the Union," 8 January 1964, *Public Papers*, p. 112.

17. "Remarks at the University of Michigan," 23 May 1964, *Public Papers*, p. 704.

18. Ibid., p. 706.

19. P.L. 88-352. The Civil Rights Act was primarily a national program to protect voting rights, but it also had some reasonably important intergovernmental dimensions. Title IV provided for grants or contracts to colleges and universities to train personnel to deal with desegregation problems. Title VII established the Equal Employment Opportunity Commission with responsibility, among other things, to work with state and local agencies in compliance. Title X established a community relations service to aid communities in resolving discriminatory practices disputes.

20. *Congressional Quarterly Almanac: 1967* (Washington, D.C.: Congressional Quarterly Service, 1968), p. 1282.

21. "The President's News Conference at the LBJ Ranch," 10 November 1966, *Public Papers*, p. 1358.

22. "Annual Message to the Congress on the State of the Union," 10 January 1967, *Public Papers*, p. 2.

23. Ibid.

24. Ibid., p. 4.

25. "Annual Message to the Congress on the State of the Union," 17 January 1968, *Public Papers*, p. 25.

26. "Annual Message to the Congress: The Economic Report of the President," 28 January 1965, *Public Papers*, p. 103.

27. "Annual Message to the Congress: The Economic Report of the President," 27 January 1966, *Public Papers*, p. 96; "Annual Message to the Congress: The Economic Report of the President," 26 January 1967, *Public Papers*, pp. 72–73.

28. "Annual Message to the Congress: The Economic Report of the President," 1 February 1968, *Public Papers*, pp. 126–127.

29. *Special Analyses, Budget of the United States Government, Fiscal Year 1980* (Washington, D.C.: GPO, 1980), p. 254.

30. For general characterizations of the period, see Wright, *Understand-*

ing Intergovernmental Relations, pp. 53–58; and Walker, *Toward a Functioning Federalism,* pp. 100–104.

31. James L. Sundquist with David W. Davis, *Making Federalism Work* (Washington, D.C.: The Brookings Institution, 1969), pp. 3–6.

32. Donald H. Haider, "The Intergovernmental System," in Richard M. Pious, ed., *The Power to Govern* (New York: Academy of Political Science, 1981), p. 24.

33. Martha Derthick, *Between State and Nation* (Washington, D.C.: The Brookings Institution, 1974), p. 207.

34. See Sundquist and Davis, *Making Federalism Work,* pp. 17–27. We do not at this point take up the notion of partisan mutual adjustment, the idea "that people can coordinate with each other without a dominant common purpose and without rules that fully prescribe their relations to each other." Charles E. Lindblom, *The Intelligence of Democracy* (New York: The Free Press, 1965), p. 3.

35. Harold Seidman, *Politics, Positions, and Power* (New York: Oxford University Press, 1976), p. 179.

36. Stephen Skowronek, *Building a New American State: The Expansion of National Administrative Capacities, 1877–1920* (Cambridge, England: Cambridge University Press, 1982), p. 20.

37. Ibid., pp. 24, 31.

38. Ibid., p. 4.

39. Ibid., p. 290.

40. Theodore J. Lowi, "Europeanization of America? From United States to United States," in Theodore J. Lowi and Alan Stone, eds., *Nationalizing Government* (Beverly Hills, Calif.: Sage Publications, 1978), p. 25.

41. Wright, *Understanding Intergovernmental Relations,* pp. 53–58; Daniel J. Elazar, "The American Partnership: The Next Half Generation," in Daniel J. Elazar, ed., *The Politics of American Federalism* (Lexington, Mass.: D. C. Heath, 1969), pp. 218–219; Richard H. Leach, *American Federalism* (New York: W. W. Norton, 1970), pp. 15–16.

42. Beer, "In Search of a New Public Philosophy," p. 17.

43. Walker, *Toward a Functioning Federalism,* p. 16.

44. Ibid., chap. 7.

45. Wright, *Understanding Intergovernmental Relations,* p. 445.

46. See, for example, *A Presidency for the 1980s* (Washington, D.C.: National Academy of Public Administration, 1980).

47. Rufus Davis, *The Federal Principle* (Berkeley: University of California Press, 1978), p. 205.

48. Deil S. Wright, "A Century of the Intergovernmental Administrative State: Wilson's Federalism, New Deal Intergovernmental Relations, and Contemporary Intergovernmental Management," in Chandler, ed., *A Centennial History of the American Administrative State,* p. 234.

49. Scheiber, "Federalism and Legal Process," p. 712.

2. Policy Nationalization and Subnational Administration

1. "The President's Toast at a Dinner for the Governors," 18 March 1967, *Public Papers of the Presidents of the United States: Lyndon B. Johnson, 1967* (Washington, D.C.: GPO, 1968), p. 375 (hereafter cited as *Public Papers*).

2. Doris Kearns, *Lyndon Johnson and the American Dream* (New York: Harper and Row, 1976), p. 212.

3. James L. Sundquist with David W. Davis, *Making Federalism Work* (Washington, D.C.: The Brookings Institution, 1969), p. 10.

4. Martin Landau, "*Baker* v. *Carr* and the Ghost of Federalism," in Glendon Schubert, ed., *Reapportionment* (New York: Charles Scribner's Sons, 1965), p. 246.

5. Samuel H. Beer, "The Modernization of American Federalism," *Publius* 3 (Fall 1973): 54.

6. Theodore J. Lowi, *The End of Liberalism* (New York: W. W. Norton, 1979), p. 274.

7. Samuel H. Beer, "In Search of a New Public Philosophy," in Anthony King, ed., *The New American Political System* (Washington, D.C.: American Enterprise Institute, 1978), p. 9. See also William M. Lunch, *The Nationalization of American Politics* (Berkeley: University of California Press, 1987).

8. James L. Sundquist, *Politics and Policy: The Eisenhower, Kennedy, and Johnson Years* (Washington, D.C.: The Brookings Institution, 1968), especially chap. 10.

9. Sundquist and Davis, *Making Federalism Work*, p. 12.

10. Ibid.

11. Information on Kennedy's legislative program is mainly drawn from *Congress and the Nation: 1945–1964* (Washington, D.C.: Congressional Quarterly Service, 1965).

12. Sundquist, *Politics and Policy*, pp. 85–91.

13. For views on Johnson's political pragmatism and policy values, see Robert A. Caro, *The Path to Power* (New York: Alfred A. Knopf, 1982); Paul K. Conklin, *Big Daddy from the Pedernales* (Boston: Twayne Publishers, 1986); and Rowland Evans and Robert Novak, *Lyndon B. Johnson: The Exercise of Power* (New York: Signet Books, 1966).

14. Lyndon B. Johnson, "Interdependence," *National Civic Review* 53 (Jan. 1964): 5.

15. Kearns, *Lyndon B. Johnson and the American Dream*, p. 216.

16. Lyndon B. Johnson, *The Vantage Point* (New York: Holt, Rinehart and Winston, 1971), p. 104.

17. Hugh Davis Graham, *The Uncertain Triumph: Federal Education Policy in the Kennedy and Johnson Years* (Chapel Hill: University of North Carolina Press, 1984), p. 162.

18. See generally James E. Anderson and Jared E. Hazleton, *Managing Macroeconomic Policy: The Johnson Presidency* (Austin: University of Texas Press, 1986).

19. See, for example, memo, Schultze to president, 20 September 1966, Ex FA 3, WHCF, LBJ Library.

20. Memo, Schultze to president, 6 April 1967, Ex FA 3, WHCF, LBJ Library.

21. Memo, Schultze to president, 7 November 1966, Ex FI 4, WHCF, LBJ Library. According to one analyst, Schultze's resignation in early 1968 was provoked by the "general disgust at the disarray of Johnson's policy of guns— and—Great Society." Graham, *The Uncertain Triumph*, p. 186.

22. Emmette S. Redford and Marlan Blissett, *Organizing the Executive Branch: The Johnson Presidency* (Chicago: University of Chicago Press, 1981), p. 11.

23. Emmette S. Redford and Richard T. McCulley, *White House Operations: The Johnson Presidency* (Austin: University of Texas Press, 1986), p. 2.

24. Untitled talking points, 2 July 1964, Ex FG 600, WHCF, LBJ Library.

25. Among them are Graham, *The Uncertain Triumph*; Nancy Kegan Smith, "Presidential Task Force Operation during the Johnson Administration," *Presidential Studies Quarterly* 15 (Spring 1985): 320; Redford and McCulley, *White House Operations*, chap. 5; and Norman C. Thomas and Harold L. Wolman, "The Presidency and Policy Formulation: The Task Force Device," *Public Administration Review* 29 (Sept./Oct. 1969): 459. This section relies heavily on these sources.

26. Graham, *The Uncertain Triumph*, p. xx.

27. Memo, Gordon and Heller to Moyers, 30 May 1964, Ex LE, WHCF, LBJ Library.

28. Untitled talking points, 2 July 1964, Ex FG 600, WHCF, LBJ Library.

29. Calculated from data in Redford and McCulley, *White House Operations*, p. 81.

30. Ibid., p. 88.

31. Ibid., pp. 88–92. Interest in Johnson's task forces perhaps causes the policy contributions of public commissions to be underestimated. See Thomas R. Wolanin, *Presidential Advisory Commissions: Truman to Nixon* (Madison: University of Wisconsin Press, 1975), pp. 228–239.

32. Department of the Interior, "Executive Branch Comments on Report of the Task Force on the Preservation of Natural Beauty," 18 November 1964, 7, attached to memo to president, 2 December 1964, Ex FG 600/Task Force on Preservation of National [sic] Beauty, WHCF, LBJ Library.

33. Department of the Interior, "Resource Policies for a Great Society," December 1964, p. 4, Task Force on Natural Resources file, task force collection, box 2, LBJ Library.

34. William D. Carey, "Presidential Staffing in the Sixties and Seventies," *Public Administration Review* 29 (Sept./Oct. 1969): 451.

35. Memo, Gordon and Heller to Moyers, 30 May 1964, Ex LE, WHCF, LBJ Library.

36. The issue papers are in Task Forces on the 1965 Legislative Program: Issue Papers folder, box 94, files of Bill Moyers, LBJ Library.

37. Task force issue paper, "Education," undated, p. 1, ibid.

38. Task force issue paper, "Natural Resources," 17 June 1964, p. 15, ibid.

39. Task Force on Education, "Report," 14 November 1964, p. i, task force collection, box 1, LBJ Library.

40. Task Force on Metropolitan and Urban Problems, "Report," 30 November 1964, p. 1, task force collection, box 2, LBJ Library.

41. Robert C. Wood Oral History Interview, 19 October 1968, p. 12, LBJ Library.

42. Task Force on Metropolitan and Urban Problems, "Report," p. i.

43. Wood Oral History Interview, p. 26.

44. Task Force on Metropolitan and Urban Problems, "Report," p. 1.

45. Task Force on Health, "Report," 6 November 1964, p. 4, task force collection, box 1, LBJ Library.

46. Task Force on Income Maintenance, "Toward Greater Security and Opportunity for Americans," 14 November 1964, p. ii, task force collection, box 1, LBJ Library.

47. Charles M. Haar Oral History Interview, 14 June 1971, p. 19, LBJ Library.

48. Task Force on Environmental Pollution, "Report," 9 November 1964, p. 3, task force collection, box 1, LBJ Library.

49. Task Force on Metropolitan and Urban Problems, "Report," p. 1.

50. Quoted in Graham, *The Uncertain Triumph*, p. 6.

51. Task Force on Education, "Report," p. ii.

52. Ibid., p. 4.

53. Haar suggests that the Task Force on Natural Beauty was an exception, for example, in its questions about pollution to the department officials: "How do you work with it? Do you put a sanction? Do you hit them over the head? Do you try incentives? What things move people certain ways?" Haar Oral History Interview, p. 18.

54. Task Force on Metropolitan and Urban Problems, "Report," p. ii.

55. Ibid., p. vi.

56. "Special Message to the Congress: 'Toward Full Educational Opportunity,'" 12 January 1965, *Public Papers*, p. 26.

57. "Special Message to the Congress on the Nation's Cities," 2 March 1965, *Public Papers*, p. 233.

58. "Special Message to the Congress on Law Enforcement and the Administration of Justice," 8 March 1965, *Public Papers*, p. 270.

59. "Special Message to the Congress on Area and Regional Economic Development," 25 March 1965, *Public Papers*, p. 323.

60. Draft education message attached to memo, Califano to Gardner et al., p. 4, E SP 2-3/1968/ED Education 2/5/68, backup V, WHCF, LBJ Library.

61. Task Force on Cities, "Report," 7 July 1967, p. i, task force collection, box 4, LBJ Library.

62. Task Force on Education, "Report," 30 June 1967, task force collection, box 4, LBJ Library.

63. The Bureau of the Budget was quite supportive of these new regulatory programs and at times played an important advocacy role. For example,

a memorandum to the president in September 1965 began with the statement, "For some time the Bureau of the Budget has been working on a program for an expanded and aggressive federal role for highway safety." Memo, White to president, 5 September 1965, Ex SA 2, WHCF, LBJ Library. A similar stance was evident in other areas.

64. Haar Oral History Interview, p. 12.

65. Charles J. Zwick Oral History Interview, 1 August 1969, tape 2, p. 12, LBJ Library.

66. A program to use federal properties as sites for urban development, including low-income housing, was initiated on the basis of presidential authority and also bypassed existing intergovernmental housing programs. It never got underway. See Martha Derthick, *New Towns In-Town* (Washington, D.C.: The Urban Institute, 1972).

67. Notes, "Cities" meeting, 19 November 1966, Cities folder, box 380, files of James Gaither, LBJ Library.

68. On housing policy during this period, see Leonard Freedman, *Public Housing: The Politics of Poverty* (New York: Holt, Rinehart and Winston, 1969); and Harold Wolman, *Politics of Federal Housing* (New York: Dodd, Mead, 1971).

69. Memo, Levinson to president, 7 September 1967, C.F. HS 3, WHCF, LBJ Library.

70. Task Force on Housing, "Draft Report," 1968, pp. 17–19, task force collection, box 2, LBJ Library.

71. The program was announced in "Special Message to the Congress— 'To Earn a Living: The Right of Every American,'" 23 January 1968, *Public Papers*, p. 46.

72. Gardner Ackley, "Basic Issues in Income Maintenance," 29 November 1966, Ex WE 6, WHCF, LBJ Library. For a general review of policy issues during the period, see Gilbert Y. Steiner, *The State of Welfare* (Washington, D.C.: The Brookings Institution, 1971).

73. Task Force on Public Assistance, "Report," 10 September 1965, task force collection, box 11, LBJ Library.

74. Working Group on a Negative Income Tax, "Report," 3 September 1965, Ex FI 11-4, WHCF, LBJ Library.

75. "Remarks at the Social Security Administration Headquarters in Baltimore," 12 October 1966, *Public Papers*, p. 1141. Califano later promised Johnson that he would ensure that the task force recommendations on social security would "go beyond anything the Republicans suggest." Memo, Califano to president, 22 November 1966, Ex WE 6, WHCF, LBJ Library.

76. Task Force on Income Maintenance, "Summary Report," 9 November 1966, p. 6, task force collection, box 16, LBJ Library.

77. Ibid., p. 11.

78. Ackley, "Basic Issues in Income Maintenance," 29 November 1966, Ex WE 6, WHCF, LBJ Library.

79. Notes of White House meeting, 29 November 1966, p. 7, Task Force on Income Maintenance file, task force collection, box 16, LBJ Library.

80. Zwick Oral History Interview, tape 2, pp. 15–16.

81. "Special Message to the Congress Proposing Programs for Older Americans," 23 January 1967, *Public Papers*, p. 32.

82. "Special Message to the Congress Recommending a 12-Point Program for American Children and Youth," 8 February 1967, *Public Papers*, p. 150.

83. *Economic Report of the President* (Washington, D.C.: GPO, 1967), p. 17. By this time such ideas were receiving considerable public attention. See Milton Friedman, *Capitalism and Freedom* (Chicago: University of Chicago Press, 1962), chap. 12; Robert Theobald, *Free Men and Free Markets* (Garden City, N.Y.: Doubleday, 1963); Robert Theobald, ed., *The Guaranteed Income* (Garden City, N.Y.: Doubleday, 1966); and Sar A. Levitan, "The Pitfalls of Guaranteed Income," *The Reporter*, 18 March 1967, p. 12.

84. Daniel P. Moynihan, *The Politics of a Guaranteed Income* (New York: Random House, 1973), p. 58.

85. "Statement by the President upon Signing the Social Security Amendments and upon Appointing a Commission to Study the Nation's Welfare Programs," 2 January 1968, *Public Papers*, p. 14.

86. Memo, Okun to Califano, 3 July 1968, Ex FG 654; and memo, Okun to president, 22 July 1968, Ex LA 8, WHCF, LBJ Library.

87. See, for example, Lester M. Salamon, "The Presidency and Domestic Policy Formulation," in Hugh Heclo and Lester M. Salamon, eds., *The Illusion of Presidential Government* (Boulder: Westview, 1981), p. 182.

88. The Bureau of the Budget was a major force in the development and promotion of these devices.

89. For example, in the Ninetieth Congress much of the legislative activity bearing on education involved consolidating and adjusting authorities and dealing with administrative problems. Norman C. Thomas, *Education in National Politics* (New York: David McKay, 1975), p. 104.

90. Henry J. Aaron, *Politics and the Professors: The Great Society in Perspective* (Washington, D.C.: The Brookings Institution, 1978); Daniel P. Moynihan, *Maximum Feasible Misunderstanding* (New York: The Free Press, 1969).

91. Wood Oral History Interview, p. 25.

92. Zwick Oral History Interview, tape 2, p. 14.

93. See, for example, Redford and McCulley, *White House Operations*, pp. 92–95 and 158–162.

94. The generalizations about congressional actions are based on two major sources. One is the enrolled legislation files containing BOB memoranda to the president analyzing bills presented for his signature. These are in the LBJ Library. The other is *Congress and the Nation: 1965–1968* (Washington, D.C.: Congressional Quarterly Service, 1969).

95. In a few instances Congress expanded national authority over states to a greater extent than sought by the administration. Examples include highway and motor vehicle safety.

96. The categorical character of most of the grant programs proposed also contributed to legislative success and interest group support. The potential benefits were clearly defined in the legislation. Many of the programs by de-

sign initially carried low price tags that facilitated acceptance. According to Zwick, "The legislative technicians, and I include . . . the President and Califano and Wilbur Cohen, were of the school that you take what you can get and run. . . . They would . . . say 'Oh, you start it with five million or ten million a foot in the door.'" Zwick Oral History Interview, tape 2, p. 16, LBJ Library. In the process, constituencies were created that would actively provide future support. See Totton J. Anderson, "Pressure Groups and Intergovernmental Relations, *The Annals* 359 (May 1965): 116; Suzanne Farkas, *Urban Lobbying: Mayors in the Political Process* (New York: New York University Press, 1971); and Donald Haider, *When Governments Come to Washington: Governors, Mayors, and Intergovernmental Lobbying* (New York: The Free Press, 1974).

97. Although it was not unusual for state and local officials to bring policy and program problems directly to the White House, their major contact points were the departments and agencies. These, of course, were extensive. A rough check made in response to a presidential inquiry showed that in 1966, in addition to formal communications, there were two to three thousand visits, telephone calls, or other contacts between top department and agency officials and governors and their aides. Memo, Bryant to Merdent, 20 December 1966, Ex ST/MC, WHCF, LBJ Library. The White House was generally kept informed about department liaison activities and major meetings with groups of state and local officials, such as a HUD meeting with state officials on urban problems to listen to their complaints and urge their greater involvement in urban matters. Memo, Califano to president, 9 February 1967, Ex FI 4/FG 170, WHCF, LBJ Library.

98. "Remarks to State Governors after President Kennedy's Funeral," 25 November 1963, *Public Papers*, p. 4. His basic substantive point was the importance of national cooperation with state governments and working together "for the common good." Ibid., p. 5.

99. Many departments and agencies had their own liaison offices that were loosely linked to policy and program operations and presidential liaison activities.

100. Buford Ellington Oral History Interview, 2 October 1970, interview I, p. 48, LBJ Library. Civil rights was one of his major priorities. Early in his tenure, he and Luther Hodges, former governor of North Carolina and then head of the Department of Commerce, visited thirty-four governors on civil rights matters. Ibid., p. 43.

101. The data are contained in an undated paper sent to files on 20 March 1967, Ex ST/MC, WHCF, LBJ Library.

102. The White House always watched the Republican governors with a wary eye. For example, late in 1967 presidential aide John Roche advised Johnson, "With Republican governors in office in the most populous urban states . . . we can anticipate a massive effort to blame the plight of the cities on the federal government." Memo, Roche to president, 17 November 1966, Ex ST/MC, WHCF, LBJ Library. Not long thereafter serious consideration was given to a proposal for the president to confer regularly with councils of governors established to consider policy issues in a variety of areas. It was

268   *Notes to Pages 52–58*

rejected. One White House aide opposed the idea because he believed "the Republicans such as Rockefeller and Romney would use the meetings for publicity on the 'steps of the White House.'" Memo, Kintner to president, 15 December 1966, Ex ST, WHCF, LBJ Library.

103. For example, Johnson was seriously criticized by some Democratic members of Congress from Ohio for his expressions of regard for James A. Rhodes, the Republican governor of that state. In reference to one such incident, a member complained, "This does not win friends among Democrats when Rhodes is out to discredit you and defeat the men you need in Congress." Note, Moeller to president, circa 23 September 1966, Ex ST/MC, WHCF, LBJ Library. In the midst of a later incident, Bryant commented to Johnson, "There is a basic conflict between Congressmen and Governors which I see no way to resolve." Memo, Bryant to president, 28 April 1967, Ex ST, WHCF, LBJ Library.

104. Among the complaints were an absence of a voice in policymaking, administrative complexity, education program guidelines, civil rights enforcement, and cutbacks in the distribution of highway funds ordered by Johnson earlier in the year as part of an effort to reduce inflationary pressures. Memo, Bryant to president, 20 December 1966, Ex ST/MC, WHCF, LBJ Library.

105. "The President's News Conference at the LBJ Ranch," 21 December 1966, Public Papers, p. 1447.

106. Memo, Markman to Watson, 20 December 1966, Ex PL 2, WHCF, LBJ Library.

107. Endicott Peabody Oral History Interview, 4 March 1969, p. 26, LBJ Library. Peabody was assistant director of OEP in 1968 and a former governor of Massachusetts. On 31 August 1968 Johnson signed Executive Order 11426, formally making liaison with states a part of OEP's mission. In October, legislation was enacted that changed OEP's name to the Office of Emergency Preparedness. P.L. 90-608.

108. Aaron, *Politics and the Professors*, p. 28.

3. Administrative Arrangements for Attacking Poverty

1. "Special Message to the Congress Proposing a Nationwide War on the Sources of Poverty," 16 March 1964, *Public Papers of the Presidents of the United States: Lyndon B. Johnson, 1963–1964* (Washington, D.C.: GPO, 1965), p. 377 (hereafter cited as *Public Papers*).

2. Ibid., p. 380.

3. For an excellent account of congressional reaction to the administration's initial proposals as well as the continuing impact of Congress on the poverty program, see William C. Selover, "The View from Capitol Hill: Harrassment and Survival," in James L. Sundquist, ed., *On Fighting Poverty* (New York: Basic Books, 1969), p. 158.

4. Daniel P. Moynihan, *Maximum Feasible Misunderstanding* (New York: The Free Press, 1969), p. 23.

5. Ibid., p. 25.

6. "Inaugural Address," 21 January 1961, *Public Papers*, p. 1.

7. Quoted in James L. Sundquist, *Politics and Policy: The Eisenhower, Kennedy, and Johnson Years* (Washington, D.C.: The Brookings Institution, 1968), p. 112.

8. The best known of these is Michael Harrington, *The Other America* (New York: Macmillan, 1962).

9. Sundquist, *Politics and Policy*, p. 113.

10. Ibid., pp. 113–114.

11. Paper, Frederick M. Bohen, "The OEO: Origins, Experience, Future," p. 6, filed with memo, Bohen to members of the President's Task Force on Government Organization, 30 November 1966, The OEO: Origins, Experience, Future folder, files of James Gaither, LBJ Library.

12. Sundquist, *Politics and Policy*, pp. 136–137.

13. Ibid., p. 137.

14. William B. Cannon, "Enlightened Localism: A Narrative Account of Poverty and Education in the Great Society," *Yale Law and Policy Review* 4 (Fall/Winter 1985): 12.

15. Sundquist, *Politics and Policy*, p. 137.

16. Cannon, "Enlightened Localism," p. 16.

17. Ibid., p. 8.

18. Ibid., p. 7.

19. Ibid., pp. 7–9.

20. Harold Seidman, *Politics, Positions, and Power* (New York: Oxford University Press, 1976), p. 171.

21. Sundquist, *Politics and Policy*, pp. 137–138.

22. Moynihan, *Maximum Feasible Misunderstanding*, p. 78.

23. Lyndon Baines Johnson, *The Vantage Point* (New York: Holt, Rinehart and Winston, 1971), pp. 73–74.

24. Cannon, "Enlightened Localism," p. 19.

25. C. Robert Perrin Oral History Interview, 10 and 17 March 1969, tape 2, p. 17, LBJ Library.

26. Johnson, *The Vantage Point*, p. 75.

27. Moynihan, *Maximum Feasible Misunderstanding*, p. 143.

28. Jack Conway Oral History Interview, 14 June 1982, p. 22, LBJ Library.

29. Moynihan, *Maximum Feasible Misunderstanding*, p. 142.

30. Cannon, "Enlightened Localism," p. 25.

31. On these and related matters, see Emmette S. Redford and Marlan Blissett, *Organizing the Executive Branch: The Johnson Presidency* (Chicago: University of Chicago Press, 1981), chap. 4.

32. Moynihan, *Maximum Feasible Misunderstanding*, p. 93.

33. Cannon, "Enlightened Localism," p. 24.

34. "Annual Message to the Congress on the State of the Union," 8 January 1964, *Public Papers*, p. 114.

35. Sar A. Levitan, *The Great Society's Poor Law* (Baltimore: Johns Hopkins University Press, 1969), p. 59.

36. The administration proposed only the VISTA veto. Congress added the additional authority.

37. Sec. 205 (a).

38. Moynihan, *Maximum Feasible Misunderstanding*, p. 87.

39. Perrin Oral History Interview, tape 2, p. 16.

40. Richard Blumenthal, "The Bureaucracy: Antipoverty and the Community Action Program," in Allan P. Sindler, ed., *American Political Institutions and Public Policy* (Boston: Little, Brown, 1969), pp. 137–142.

41. Cannon, "Enlightened Localism," p. 32.

42. Ibid., pp. 52–53.

43. On the point, see generally Robert A. Levine, *The Poor Ye Need Not Have With You* (Cambridge, Mass.: M.I.T. Press, 1970).

44. Memo, Ellington to president, 15 June 1965, Ex WE 9, WHCF, LBJ Library.

45. Memo, vice president to president, 2 December 1965, filed with memo, Valenti to president, 7 December 1968, Ex WE 9, WHCF, LBJ Library.

46. John C. Donovan, *The Politics of Poverty* (New York: Pegasus, 1967), p. 45.

47. William F. Haddad, "Mr. Shriver and the Savage Politics of Poverty," *Harper's* 231 (Dec. 1965), p. 44.

48. Letter, McKeldin to president, 20 January 1965, filed with memo, Moyers to files, 26 January 1965, Office of Economic Opportunity folder 1 of 2, files of Bill Moyers, LBJ Library.

49. Memo, Shriver to Moyers, 2 February 1965, Ex WE 9, WHCF, LBJ Library.

50. As of 30 September 1965, sponsorship of community action programs was as follows: cities, 7.0 percent; counties, 7.6 percent; multicounty, 2.1 percent; states, .04 percent; and private nonprofit organizations, 72.9 percent. Advisory Commission on Intergovernmental Relations, *Intergovernmental Relations in the Poverty Program* (Washington, D.C.: GPO, 1966), p. 28.

51. Office of Economic Opportunity, *Administrative History*, vol. 1, pt. 1, undated, pp. 86A–90, LBJ Library.

52. Mayor William G. Walsh, Senate Committee on Government Operations, *Creative Federalism: Hearings before the Subcommittee on Intergovernmental Relations*, 90th Cong., 1st sess., 1967, p. 734. Another "classic" controversy arose with Mayor Richard J. Daley of Chicago over the participation of the poverty population in program decisions. Mayor Daley was generally victorious in this contest—a consequence of President Johnson's intervention. Moynihan, *Maximum Feasible Misunderstanding*, pp. 144–145.

53. Office of Economic Opportunity, *Administrative History*, vol. 1, pt. 1, p. 192. Mayor Yorty would subsequently charge that community action personnel incited the Watts riot later in 1965. OEO's response was that they had helped to calm the situation. Ibid., p. 193.

54. Robert A. Levine Oral History Interview, 26 February 1969, tape 1, p. 18, LBJ Library.

55. Bernard Boutin Oral History Interview, 17 March 1977, p. 6, LBJ Library.

56. Memo, Schultze to president, 18 September 1965, Ex WE 9, WHCF, LBJ Library.

57. Memo, Shriver to president, 6 November 1965, Ex WE 9, WHCF, LBJ Library.

58. Memo, vice president to president, 2 December 1965, Ex WE 9, WHCF, LBJ Library.

59. Office of Economic Opportunity, *Administrative History*, vol. 1, pt. 1, pp. 202–203. Congress ratified OEO's position. The 1966 amendments to the act required that one-third of community action agency board members must be representative of the poor.

60. Memo, Califano to president, 1 June 1966, Ex WE 9, WHCF, LBJ Library.

61. Letter, Shriver to president, 8 August 1966, Ex WE 9, WHCF, LBJ Library.

62. For example, telegram, Yorty to president, 29 November 1966, Gen FG 11-15, WHCF, LBJ Library. Around this time Shriver was meeting with governors who were members of the federal-state relations committee of their conference. Letter, Shriver to president, 10 September 1966, Ex FG 11-15, WHCF, LBJ Library.

63. Perrin Oral History Interview, tape 1, p. 43.

64. Moynihan, *Maximum Feasible Misunderstanding*, p. 157.

65. P. L. 89-794.

66. Advisory Commission on Intergovernmental Relations, *Intergovernmental Relations in the Poverty Program*, p. 96.

67. Memo, Ellington to president, 2 August 1965, Ex ST/MC, WHCF, LBJ Library.

68. Memo, Jacobsen to president, 29 July 1965, Ex ND 19/CO 312, WHCF, LBJ Library.

69. Roger H. Davidson, "The War on Poverty: Experiment in Federalism," *The Annals* 385 (Sept. 1969): 5.

70. Letter, president to Connally, 10 June 1965, Ex WE 9, WHCF, LBJ Library.

71. Office of Economic Opportunity, *Administrative History*, vol. 1, pt. 1, pp. 168–169.

72. Ibid., p. 167.

73. Advisory Commission on Intergovernmental Relations, *Intergovernmental Relations in the Poverty Program*, pp. 84–93.

74. Perrin Oral History Interview, tape 2, pp. 2–3.

75. "The President's News Conference at the LBJ Ranch," 21 December 1966, *Public Papers*, p. 1454.

76. Perrin Oral History Interview, tape 2, p. 1.

77. Ibid., p. 2.

78. During the session Governor Nelson E. Rockefeller of New York addressed the nagging underfunding problem in EOA programs. He said, "The culmination of this was last week when we were visited by 1000 poverty families. They were led by Federal Agents financed by the Federal Govern-

ment and when we asked them about this, they said, 'Well, this is part of community action.'" Rockefeller continued, "We like the Federal Government taking initiative. We think this is one of the greatest programs in the community. But I can't think that the President of the United States, nor his representatives, has the right to arouse hopes, aspirations, make promises which then they are not in a position to deliver." Transcript of White House briefing, 18 March 1967, p. E-3, Ex ST, WHCF, LBJ Library.

79. Memo, Bryant to president, August 1967, Ex ST, WHCF, LBJ Library.

80. "Special Message to the Congress: America's Unfinished Business, Urban and Rural Poverty," 14 March 1967, *Public Papers*, p. 331.

81. Memo, Shriver to president, 13 October 1967, Ex FI 4/FG 11-15, WHCF, LBJ Library.

82. A complete history of the Green amendment is contained in Office of Economic Opportunity, *Administrative History*, vol. 1, pt. 2, pp. 598–607. Even while the amendment was being considered, new grant actions once again raised the ire of Yorty and Daley. Califano to president, 2 June 1967, Ex FA; memo, Cohen to president, 24 August 1967, C.F. FA, WHCF, LBJ Library. There was also widespread public discussion of the possible role of community action agencies in urban riots during the summer. Memo, Shriver to president, 25 August 1967, C.F. Subject Reports, OEO, WHCF, LBJ Library. Although OEO apparently attempted to execute the Green amendment conscientiously, few mayors opted to bring agencies under their direct control. Less than 5 percent of local governments took advantage of the new power provided by the amendment. James L. Sundquist with David W. Davis, *Making Federalism Work* (Washington, D.C.: The Brookings Institution, 1969), p. 39.

83. P.L. 90-222.

84. This is not to suggest that there were no more difficulties. For example, it was not long after reauthorization that OEO was under attack again from Mayor Daley for funding a project to work with youth gangs in Chicago. Memo, Harding to president, 18 April 1968, C.F. Subject Reports, OEO, WHCF, LBJ Library.

85. Bertrand M. Harding, interview with Jesse Burkhead, Washington, D.C., 20 April 1979.

86. Levine Oral History Interview, tape 1, pp. 28–29.

87. Ibid., p. 29.

88. Moynihan, *Maximum Feasible Misunderstanding*, p. 4.

89. Report, Presidential Involvement, Economic Opportunity Act Amendments of 1967 folder, box 34, files of Joe Califano, LBJ Library.

90. Although there was a great deal of individual interaction between state and city officials and Shriver and his aides, there was little in the way of institutionalized relationships. Not until 1967 did OEO sponsor a conference in Washington for state officials. Office of Economic Opportunity, *Administrative History*, vol. 1, pt. 1, p. 177. A public official advisory council was created in 1966, but it was never particularly active.

91. See James E. Anderson, "Administrative Politics and the War on Pov-

erty," in Dorothy Buckton James, ed., *Analyzing Poverty Policy* (Lexington, Mass.: Lexington Books, 1975), chap. 6.

92. "Annual Message to the Congress on the State of the Union," 14 January 1969, *Public Papers*, p. 1266.

93. Comptroller General, *Review of Economic Opportunity Programs*, 91st Cong., 1st sess., 1969, p. 10.

94. Arthur P. Solomon, "A Summary of Problems of Organization and Administration in the Federal Government's Manpower Programs," 1966, p. 2, Labor-Manpower folder, box 17, files of James Gaither, LBJ Library.

95. Ibid., p. 3.

96. Task Force on Urban Employment Opportunity, "Report," 1966, pp. 73–74, task force collection, box 5, LBJ Library.

97. Sec. 612.

98. Sec. 211.

99. Sec. 611 (a) (3). Early drafts of the act placed their authority in the director. James L. Sundquist Oral History Interview, 17 April 1968, p. 45, LBJ Library.

100. Sec. 611 (a) (2) (b).

101. Sec. 604.

102. "Report of the President's Task Force on the Los Angeles Riots, 11–15 August 1965," 17 September 1965, pp. 3–4, task force collection, box 10, LBJ Library.

103. Letter, Collins to Califano, 8 October 1965, Ex WE 9, WHCF, LBJ Library.

104. Memos, Guffey to Seidman, 1 January 1965 and 17 March 1965, E 1-17/65, Record Group 51, National Archives.

105. Task Force on Intergovernmental Program Coordination, "Report," 22 December 1965, p. 3, task force collection, box 3, LBJ Library. BOB had asked for a more thorough review than it got. Memo, Schnoor to Guffey, 10 September 1965, Record Group 51, National Archives.

106. U.S. Conference of Mayors, "Special Report: The Office of Economic Opportunity and Local Community Action Agencies," attached to memo, vice president to president, 2 December 1965, p. 3, filed with memo, Valenti to president, 7 December 1965, Ex WE 9, WHCF, LBJ Library.

107. Ibid., p. 102.

108. Quoted in Sundquist and Davis, *Making Federalism Work*, pp. 15–16.

109. Advisory Commission on Intergovernmental Relations, *Intergovernmental Relations in the Poverty Program*.

110. Memo, Wirtz to Califano, 3 January 1965, Ex WE 9, WHCF, LBJ Library.

111. Task Force on Urban Employment Opportunities, "Report," 14 July 1967, task force collection, box 5, LBJ Library.

112. Memo, Schultze to Califano and Moyers, 26 July 1966, Ex FG 11-15, WHCF, LBJ Library.

113. Ben W. Heineman Oral History Interview, 16 April 1970, p. 28, LBJ Library.

114. President's Task Force on Government Organization, "The Organization of the War on Poverty and the Future of the Office of Economic Opportunity," p. 4, attached to memo, Califano to president, 15 December 1966, Heineman Task Force folder, box 43, files of Joe Califano, LBJ Library.

115. Quoted in Office of Economic Opportunity, *Administrative History*, vol. 1, pt. 1, p. 135. At the start of the antipoverty program, preparation and annual revision of the five-year plan was intended to contribute to certainty of policy and to coordination. The mechanism failed as immediate problems monopolized the attention of officials. Perrin Oral History Interview, tape 2, p. 7.

116. Office of Economic Opportunity, *Administrative History*, vol. 1, pt. 2, p. 409.

117. Quoted in Frederick M. Bohen, "Program Transfer into a Revitalized HEW: Manpower Development and Poverty Programs," undated, p. 6, Federal Government Manpower Program folder, box 3, files of Frederick M. Bohen, LBJ Library.

118. Memo, Hughes to Califano, 6 August 1966, Ex LE/WE 9, WHCF, LBJ Library.

119. Memo, Schultze to president, 7 November 1966, Ex FI 4, WHCF, LBJ Library.

120. Stanley C. Ruttenberg Oral History Interview, 25 February 1969, tape 1, p. 13, LBJ Library.

121. Office of Economic Opportunity, *Administrative History*, vol. 1, pt. 2, p. 406.

122. Ibid., p. 402.

123. Memo, Staats to Califano, 3 December 1965, Task Force on Adult Work Programs, task force collection, box 10, LBJ Library.

124. Office of Economic Opportunity, *Administrative History*, vol. 1, pt. 2, p. 409.

125. Ruttenberg Oral History Interview, tape 1, p. 13.

126. Memo, Feldman to president, 23 October 1964, attached to document, "Office of Economic Opportunity Delegations of Authorities," approved by the president 24 October 1964, Ex FG 11-15, WHCF, LBJ Library.

127. Perrin Oral History Interview, tape 1, p. 34. In addition to the formal delegations, OEO negotiated about 150 interagency agreements in the first two years of operation. Michael S. March, "Coordination of the War on Poverty," *Law and Contemporary Problems* 31 (Winter 1966): 126–128.

128. Sundquist Oral History Interview, p. 11.

129. Task Force on Agriculture, "Report," 15 November 1964, p. 17, task force collection, box 1, LBJ Library.

130. Sundquist Oral History Interview, p. 60.

131. Letter, Freeman to vice president, 4 October 1965, attached to memo, McPherson to Califano, 12 October 1965, C.F. FG 11-15, WHCF, LBJ Library.

132. Sundquist and Davis, *Making Federalism Work*, pp. 141–144.

133. Memo, Schnittker to Califano, 8 December 1965, Agricultural and Rural Life folder, box 1, files of Harry McPherson, LBJ Library.

134. "Special Message to the Congress Proposing a Program for Rural America," 25 January 1966, *Public Papers*, p. 80.

135. Memo, Carey to McPherson, 15 February 1967, Ex SP 2-3/1967/WE 9, backup III, WHCF, LBJ Library.

136. Memo, Shriver to Califano, 2 March 1967, Ex SP 2-3/1967/WE 9, backup XV, WHCF, LBJ Library.

137. Memo, Freeman to Califano, 28 April 1967, attached to letter, Califano to Freeman, 4 May 1967, Ex AG 6, WHCF, LBJ Library.

138. See generally Sundquist and Davis, *Making Federalism Work*, pp. 163–166.

139. R. Sargent Shriver Oral History Interview, 27 April 1977, p. 38, LBJ Library.

140. Ibid., p. 39. Otis A. Singletary, Jr., the first head of the Job Corps, provides an interesting insight into the spontaneous way the poverty program was put together. "Right after the election I flew out to the ranch with Shriver to brief Johnson about what we were doing—in the prepping of the Poverty Program, which . . . he placed great stock in early in the game. It was a pretty long day for me because Johnson really zeroed in the way he can do. He's a very intense man, as you know. He asked me a whole flock of questions about the Job Corps and then took me in at lunch and sat me next to him and continued all through lunch.

"On the way back to Washington that night, Sarge and I were flying in that Jet Star . . . , Shriver said to me—and I assume you want it the way he said it—being the devout Catholic he is, he said: 'Jesus Christ, when did you decide all that!'

"I said, 'Just sitting there answering those questions.'" Otis A. Singletary, Jr., Oral History Interview, 12 November 1970, p. 3, LBJ Library.

141. Perrin Oral History Interview, tape 1, p. 28.

142. Ibid., p. 29. On balance, Perrin was quite positive about Shriver's leadership.

143. Bernard Boutin Oral History Interview, 17 March 1977, p. 18, LBJ Library. For a discussion of appointments to upper-level OEO positions, see Richard L. Schott and Dagmar S. Hamilton, *People, Positions, and Power: The Political Appointments of Lyndon Johnson* (Chicago: University of Chicago Press, 1983), chap. 6.

144. Bertram M. Harding Oral History Interview, 20 November 1968, p. 3, LBJ Library. Leaks were endemic. "There was no such thing as loyalty. Everybody had his own line to some reporter. . . . And the President would get furious when stories would be leaked around him of things he knew nothing about." Herbert J. Kramer Oral History Interview, 10 March 1969, p. 22, LBJ Library. Kramer was director of public affairs at OEO for a time.

145. Perrin Oral History Interview, tape 1, pp. 39–40.

146. Memo, Janis to Weaver, 15 May 1967, attached to memo, Weaver to Califano, 17 May 1967, Ex WE 9, WHCF, LBJ Library.

147. Sundquist Oral History Interview, p. 58.

148. Harding Oral History Interview, p. 10. The proclivity of OEO staff to

take all credit for program successes was also a source of tension. Kramer Oral History Interview, p. 7.

149. Sundquist Oral History Interview, p. 44.

150. Ibid., p. 42.

151. Sundquist, "Co-ordinating the War on Poverty," *The Annals* 385 (Sept. 1969), p. 43.

152. Memo, Perrin to Shriver, 27 December 1966, Poverty—2 folder, box 7, files of Joe Califano, LBJ Library.

153. The term is used in a slightly different context by Harding. Harding Oral History Interview, p. 25.

154. Perrin Oral History Interview, tape 2, pp. 3–5.

155. Office of Economic Opportunity, *Administrative History*, vol. 1, pt. 1, p. 127. Other coordinative structures also fared poorly. For example, one Labor Department official reported in 1968 that the President's Committee on Manpower was "in limbo." It had not met for over a year. Thomas I. Royals Oral History Interview, 4 November 1968, p. 7, LBJ Library.

156. R. Sargent Shriver, "Paper on Background and Future Organizational Alternatives for OEO," p. 12, OEO Background Materials folder, box 2, files of Federick M. Bohen, LBJ Library.

157. Bohen, "Program Transfers into a Revitalized HEW," p. 16.

158. Shriver Oral History Interview, pp. 41–42.

159. Eli Ginzberg and Robert M. Solow, eds., *The Great Society* (New York: Basic Books, 1974), p. 217.

160. Bohen, "Program Transfers into a Revitalized HEW," p. 18.

161. Ibid., p. 19.

162. Memo, Wirtz to Heineman, 28 November 1966, Heineman Task Force folder, box 43, files of Joseph Califano, LBJ Library.

163. Ruttenberg Oral History Interview, tape 1, p. 7.

164. Bohen, "Program Transfers into a Revitalized HEW," p. 11.

165. Sundquist and Davis, *Making Federalism Work*, p. 74.

166. J. David Greenstone and Paul E. Peterson, *Race and Authority in Urban Politics* (Chicago: University of Chicago Press, 1976), p. 4.

167. Bohen, "Program Transfers into a Revitalized HEW," p. 18.

168. Shriver, "Paper on Background and Future Organizational Alternatives for OEO," p. 15.

169. Advisory Commission on Intergovernmental Relations, *Intergovernmental Relations in the Poverty Program*, pp. 72–73.

170. U.S. Conference of Mayors, "Special Report: The Office of Economic Opportunity and Local Community Action Agencies," p. 2.

171. OEO did not completely ignore preference requirements, nòr did the departments always ignore community action agencies. Bohen's comment about the neighborhood youth corps is suggestive. "While the program has not systematically boycotted or by-passed Community Action Agencies, it has not waited to be included in their plans or programs but has generally developed independently." Bohen, "Program Transfers into a Revitalized HEW," p. 9.

172. Ibid., p. 16.

173. Memo, Guffey to Seidman, 7 January 1965, Record Group 51, National Archives.

174. Levine Oral History Interview, tape 1, p. 26.

175. Perrin Oral History Interview, tape 1, p. 20.

176. Joseph A. Kershaw, *Government against Poverty* (Chicago: Markham, 1970), pp. 55–56.

177. Quoted in Office of Economic Opportunity, *Administrative History*, vol. 1, pt. 1, p. 138.

178. See Sundquist and Davis, *Making Federalism Work*, pp. 40–43. In FY 1967, 43 percent of OEO funds were earmarked. This declined a bit to 37 percent and 38 percent in the next two fiscal years. Ibid., p. 42. There is evidence that at least some OEO-Washington officials favored the earmarking as a stimulus to rapid program development. See John G. Wofford, "The Politics of Local Responsibility: Administration of the Community Action Program," in Sundquist, ed., *On Fighting Poverty*, pp. 92–93.

179. Charles E. Lindblom, *The Policy-Making Process* (Englewood Cliffs, N.J.: Prentice-Hall, 1968).

4. The Halting Search for Administrative Order in Poverty and Related Programs

1. Bertram M. Harding Oral History Interview, 20 November 1968, p. 29, LBJ Library.

2. Memo, Perrin to Shriver, 27 December 1966, Poverty—2 folder, box 7, files of Joe Califano, LBJ Library.

3. Memo, Carey to Ruttenberg, undated, Labor-Manpower folder, box 17, files of James Gaither, LBJ Library.

4. Memo, Califano to president, 13 March 1967, C.F. FG 160, WHCF, LBJ Library.

5. C. Robert Perrin Oral History Interview, 10 and 17 March 1969, tape 2, p. 29, LBJ Library.

6. C. Robert Perrin to Jesse Burkhead, 30 May 1979.

7. Memo, Carey to Gaither, 4 April 1968, Record Group 51, National Archives.

8. *Transition of OEO*, November 1968, Office of Economic Opportunity, Book 1, box 11, files of Charles Murphy, LBJ Library.

9. Perrin to Burkhead, 30 May 1979.

10. Memo from Wirtz, "Manpower Administration," attached to memo, Ruttenberg to Gaither, 21 December 1967, Labor-Manpower folder, box 17, files of James Gaither, LBJ Library.

11. Department of Labor, *Administrative History*, vol. 1, pt. 1, undated, pp. 3–9, LBJ Library.

12. Memo, Califano to president, 11 October 1968, attached to memo, Gaither to Levinson, 12 October 1968, Ex FG 160, WHCF, LBJ Library.

13. For details on the conflict, see Emmette S. Redford and Marlan Blissett, *Organizing the Executive Branch: The Johnson Presidency* (Chicago: University of Chicago Press, 1981), pp. 180–183.

14. Memo, vice president to president, 12 May 1965, Ex LA 2, WHCF, LBJ Library.

15. Memo, Schultze to Moyers, 14 June 1965, Ex FG 160-8, WHCF, LBJ Library.

16. Memo, vice president to president, undated, attached to Task Force on Summer Programs, "Report," 31 March 1966, task force collection, box 19, LBJ Library.

17. Memo, Perrin to Califano, 14 December 1966, C.F. FG 600/Task Force/S*, WHCF, LBJ Library.

18. President's Council on Youth Opportunity, "Report of the Chairman," undated, Ex FG 782, WHCF, LBJ Library.

19. On the general coordination problem and consideration of organizational change, see Redford and Blissett, *Organizing the Executive Branch,* pp. 88–106.

20. Memo, Cater to Moyers, 9 December 1964, Ex WE 9, WHCF, LBJ Library.

21. Memo, Shriver to Califano, 24 January 1965, Reorganization Proposals—S folder, box 95, files of Joe Califano, LBJ Library.

22. Memo, Shriver to president, 13 December 1966, attached to memo, Califano to president, 15 December 1966, Heineman Task Force folder, box 43, files of Joe Califano, LBJ Library.

23. The recommendation was changed in the task force's final report. Coordinating responsibilities were to be placed in a new Office of Program Coordination in the Executive Office of the President.

24. Memo, O'Brien to Califano, 3 January 1967, Poverty—2 folder, box 7, files of Joe Califano, LBJ Library.

25. Memo, Califano to president, 19 April 1968, Ex FG 11-15, WHCF, LBJ Library.

26. Memo, Cater to Moyers, 9 December 1964, Ex WE 9, WHCF, LBJ Library.

27. See Harding Oral History Interview, p. 9.

28. Memo, Schultze to Califano, 26 July 1966, Ex FG 11-15, WHCF, LBJ Library.

29. Robert A. Levine and Walter Williams, "Effective Administration of Manpower Programs for the Poor," 14 April 1967, p. 3, attached to memo, Harding to Califano, 25 April 1967, Ex LA 2, WHCF, LBJ Library.

30. Frederick M. Bohen, "Program Transfers into a Revitalized HEW: Manpower Development and Poverty Programs," undated, p. 17, Federal Government Manpower Program folder, box 3, files of Frederick M. Bohen, LBJ Library.

31. Jule M. Sugarman, interview with Jesse Burkhead, Washington, D.C., 20 April 1979. See also Jule M. Sugarman Oral History Interview, 31 January 1972, pp. 8–24, LBJ Library.

32. Memo, Cater to O'Brien, 1 February 1965, Ex WE 9-1, WHCF, LBJ Library.

33. Memo, Sloan to Shriver and Harding, 3 February 1967, C.F. FG 11-15, WHCF, LBJ Library.

34. The substance of this paper, prepared under government auspices, appears in Sar A. Levitan and Garth Mangum, *Federal Training and Work Programs in the Sixties* (Ann Arbor, Mich.: Institute of Labor and Industrial Relations, 1969).

35. Task Force on Urban Employment Opportunities, "Report," 14 July 1967, p. 69, task force collection, box 5, LBJ Library.

36. Perrin Oral History Interview, tape 2, p. 40.

37. Harding Oral History Interview, p. 10.

38. Perrin Oral History Interview, tape 2, p. 41.

39. Memo, Califano to president, 18 December 1965, Ex WE 9, WHCF, LBJ Library.

40. *Washington Post*, 25 December 1965, p. A1.

41. Memo, Schultze to Califano and Moyers, 26 July 1966, Ex FG 11-15, WHCF, LBJ Library.

42. Memo, Moyers to Califano, 5 August 1966, Ex FG 11-3, WHCF, LBJ Library.

43. Attached to memo, Wilson to Moyers, 12 September 1966, Ex WE 9, WHCF, LBJ Library.

44. Noted on ibid.

45. Memo, Califano to president, 15 February 1968, Ex FI 1-2, WHCF, LBJ Library.

46. Memo, Cohen to president, 9 March 1968, Ex FG 165, WHCF, LBJ Library.

47. Memo, Wozencraft to Temple, 1 April 1968, Ex FG 11-15, WHCF, LBJ Library.

48. "Remarks at Columbus Circle, Syracuse, New York," 19 August 1966, *Public Papers of the Presidents of the United States: Lyndon B. Johnson, 1966* (Washington, D.C.: GPO, 1967), p. 846 (hereafter cited as *Public Papers*).

49. Memo, Schultze to Califano, 27 September 1965, Ex FG 600/Task Force on Health, WHCF, LBJ Library.

50. Memo, Califano to Cater, 18 November 1965, Ex WE, WHCF, LBJ Library.

51. Joseph A. Califano, Jr., *A Presidential Nation* (New York: W. W. Norton, 1975), p. 33.

52. "One-Stop Neighborhood Centers, Explanatory Paper," 26 August 1966, attached to memo, Schultze to Califano, 30 August 1966, Ex WE 9, WHCF, LBJ Library.

53. Note, Shriver to Califano, undated, Ex SP 2-3/1967/WE 4, Older Americans, backup III, WHCF, LBJ Library.

54. Memo, Cannon to Cater, 24 February 1967, Ex SP 2/3/1967/ED, WHCF, LBJ Library.

55. "Special Message to Congress: America's Unfinished Business, Urban and Rural Poverty," 14 March 1967, *Public Papers*, p. 336.

56. Memo, Weaver to Califano, 3 March 1967, Ex SP 2-3/1967/WE 9, backup XII, WHCF, LBJ Library.

57. "The President and His Executive Office," 15 June 1967, Organiza-

tion and Management of Great Society Programs folder, box 248, files of James Gaither, LBJ Library.

58. Califano, *A Presidential Nation*, p. 33.

59. James L. Sundquist with David W. Davis, *Making Federalism Work* (Washington, D.C.: The Brookings Institution, 1969), p. 44.

60. Ibid.

61. Memo, Zwick et al. to President's Committee on Manpower, 4 March 1966, Labor and Manpower Programs folder, box 57, files of Joe Califano, LBJ Library.

62. Thomas I. Royals Oral History Interview, 4 November 1968, pp. 13–14, LBJ Library.

63. President's Committee on Manpower, "Report," p. 11.

64. Memo, Wirtz to president, 3 November 1967, Ex LA 2, WHCF, LBJ Library.

65. Memo, Allen to Gaither, 29 November 1967, Task Force on Manpower, task force collection, box 23, LBJ Library.

66. Task Force on Urban Employment Opportunities, "Report," p. 74, attached to memo, Schultze et al. to president, 14 July 1967, Task Force on Urban Employment Opportunities, task force collection, box 5, LBJ Library.

67. Memo, Wirtz to president, 30 January 1967, attached to memo, Califano to president, 31 January 1967, Ex LA 2, WHCF, LBJ Library.

68. Memo, Berry to Shriver, 4 April 1967, Ex LA 2, WHCF, LBJ Library.

69. Memo, labor-manpower branch to director, 21 May 1968, attached to memo, Carey to Gaither, 5 June 1968, CONC Empl. Prog. folder, box 17, files of James Gaither, LBJ Library.

70. "The FY 1969 Plan for the Concentrated Employment Program," 23 July 1968, attached to memo, Ruttenberg to Carey, 24 July 1968, CONC Empl. Prog. folder, box 17, files of James Gaither, LBJ Library.

71. Ibid., p. 7.

72. Memo, Radley to director, 11 November 1967, Task Force on Manpower, task force collection, box 23, LBJ Library.

73. Executive Order 11422, 15 August 1968, *Federal Register*, vol. 33, 3 Jan. 1968, p. 11739.

74. Letter, Cohen to Zwick, 1 August 1968, attached to memo, Gaither to Levinson, 6 August 1968, Labor-Manpower folder, box 18, files of James Gaither.

75. James C. Gaither Oral History Interview, 24 March 1970, tape 5, p. 31.

76. P.L. 89-754. The program became known thereafter as Model Cities. "Demonstration Cities" apparently evoked in the minds of some an unfavorable association with urban riots.

77. James L. Sundquist to Jesse Burkhead, 23 May 1979. The view is documented in Sundquist and Davis, *Making Federalism Work*, pp. 79–80.

78. Task Force on Metropolitan and Urban Problems, "Report," 30 November 1964, task force collection, box 2, LBJ Library, p. 39.

79. Memo, Reuther to president, 13 May 1965, attached to letter, Reuther to Goodwin, 4 June 1965, legislative background files, Model Cities 1966

folder, box 1, LBJ Library. Reuther's interest was stimulated by the earlier task force report shown to him by Mayor Jerome P. Cavanagh of Detroit, who was one of its members. Bernard J. Frieden and Marshall Kaplan, *The Politics of Neglect* (Cambridge: MIT Press, 1975), p. 38.

80. Charles Haar Oral History Interview, 14 June 1971, p. 45, LBJ Library.

81. Memo, Califano to Weaver, 27 August 1965, legislative background files, Model Cities 1966 folder, box 1, LBJ Library.

82. Notes on meeting of 15 October 1965, ibid.

83. Memo, McPherson to president, 9 December 1965, Ex LG, WHCF, LBJ Library.

84. Wood's comments on this experience are in Robert C. Wood Oral History Interview, 19 October 1968, pp. 18–23, LBJ Library.

85. "Special Message to Congress Recommending a Program for Cities and Metropolitan Areas," 26 January 1966, *Public Papers*, p. 83.

86. Ibid., p. 85.

87. Ibid.

88. Congressional Quarterly, *Congress and the Nation: 1965–1968* (Washington, D.C.: Congressional Quarterly Service, 1969), pp. 196–206. See also Sundquist and Davis, *Making Federalism Work*, pp. 79–82; and Advisory Commission on Intergovernmental Relations, *Improving Federal Grants Management* (Washington, D.C.: GPO, 1977), pp. 65–66. The progress from task force through legislation is traced in detail in Frieden and Kaplan, *The Politics of Neglect*.

89. Provision was made for the appointment of "metropolitan expediters" at the request of local officials. None were ever requested.

90. For an excellent discussion of the discretionary role of the bureaucracy, see Lawrence D. Brown and Bernard J. Frieden, "Rulemaking by Improvisation: Guidelines and Goals in the Model Cities Program," *Policy Sciences* 7 (Dec. 1976): 455.

91. The original scheme provided for only one year of planning. Funding on the order of $12 million was added at the suggestion of Senator Edmund S. Muskie (D-Maine) to allow more cities to participate. This was only one of several changes inserted in the bill as it moved through the Senate. Muskie's leadership was instrumental in the bill's passage. Memo, Califano to president, 26 December 1966, Ex FI 4/FG 170, WHCF, LBJ Library.

92. *Congress and the Nation: 1965–1968*, p. 197.

93. Department of Housing and Urban Development, *Administrative History*, vol. 1, pt. 1, chap. 5, p. 40, LBJ Library.

94. Ibid., p. 206.

95. Ibid., p. 209.

96. Ibid., p. 224.

97. Department of Housing and Urban Development, *Improving the Quality of Urban Life: Program Guide: Model Neighborhoods in Demonstration Cities* (Washington, D.C.: GPO, 1966), p. 11.

98. Sundquist and Davis, *Making Federalism Work*, pp. 85–86.

99. Department of Housing and Urban Development, *Administrative History*, vol. 1, pt. 1, chap. 5, pp. 18–19. The White House was kept in-

formed of the selection of the cities. For example, Johnson was informed in July 1967 about applicant cities and those that were likely to be accepted. Memo, Califano to president, 10 July 1967, Ex LG, WHCF, LBJ Library. In general, the archival material suggests no substantial presidential involvement in selection despite considerable awareness at HUD of the political stakes involved.

100. Robert C. Wood, "The Federal Role in Creative Federalism: The Next Step Forward," in Donald E. Nicoll, ed., *Creative Federalism* (Washington, D.C.: U.S. Department of Agriculture Graduate School, 1967), p. 36.

101. Memo, Kintner to president, 9 February 1967, Ex FI 4/FG 170, WHCF, LBJ Library.

102. Department of Housing and Urban Development, *Administrative History*, vol. 1, pt. 1, chap. 5, pp. 20–21.

103. Ibid., p. 35.

104. Memo, Lora to Califano, 9 March 1967, Ex LG, WHCF, LBJ Library.

105. Memo, Weaver to Califano, 12 December 1967, Ex LG/Los Angeles, WHCF, LBJ Library.

106. Department of Housing and Urban Development, *Administrative History*, vol. 1, pt. 1, chap. 5, p. 30.

107. Sundquist and Davis, *Making Federalism Work*, pp. 103–116.

108. Ibid.

109. Memo, Gardner to president, 29 March 1967, Ex LG, WHCF, LBJ Library.

110. For example, memo, Wirtz to Califano, 5 May 1967, Ex LG, WHCF, LBJ Library.

111. "Special Note on Model Cities," in Task Force on Model Cities, "Report," 5 July 1967, p. 171, task force collection, box 4, LBJ Library. The note also emphasized two other basic problems: disproportionate incentives for physical development and lack of knowledge about human and physical development, a deficiency not likely to be eliminated in a three-year experiment given the resources available.

112. "Interagency Relationships in Conducting Model Cities Programs," 7 December 1967, p. 3, legislative background files, Model Cities, Passage and Signature folder, box 2, LBJ Library.

113. Ibid.

114. Department of Housing and Urban Development, *Administrative History*, vol. 1, pt. 1, chap. 5, p. 34.

115. Robert C. Weaver Oral History Interview, 19 November 1968, tape 2, p. 7, LBJ Library.

116. For example, memo, Califano to Wirtz, 6 August 1968, Ex LG, WHCF, LBJ Library.

117. For example, letter, Blaisdell to Zwick, 7 August 1968, attached to letter, Califano and Zwick to Powers, 26 September 1968, Ex LG, WHCF, LBJ Library.

118. For example, letter, Califano to Cohen, 27 September 1968, Ex LG, WHCF, LBJ Library.

119. Memo to Clark, 17 September 1968, Ex LG; and memo, Califano to Wirtz and Weaver, 28 August 1968, Ex LG, WHCF, LBJ Library.

120. Sundquist and Davis, *Making Federalism Work*, p. 128.

121. Memo, Harding to Califano, 21 August 1968, Ex LG, WHCF, LBJ Library.

122. Letter, Weaver and Harding to president, 27 September 1968, attached to memo, Levison to Gaither, 27 September 1968, Model Cities folder, box 47, files of Joseph Califano, LBJ Library.

123. Sundquist and Davis, *Making Federalism Work*, p. 102.

124. Paul E. Peterson, *City Limits* (Chicago: University of Chicago Press, 1981).

5. Experiments in Multistate Administrative Regionalism

1. Advisory Commission on Intergovernmental Relations, *Multistate Regionalism* (Washington, D.C.: GPO, 1972), p. 169.

2. Advisory Commission on Intergovernmental Relations, *Regional Decision Making: New Strategies for Substate Districts* (Washington, D.C.: GPO, 1973), p. 2.

3. Advisory Commission on Intergovernmental Relations, *Multistate Regionalism*, p. 2. For an example of a more complex formulation, see Howard W. Odum and Harry Estill Moore, *American Regionalism* (New York: Henry Holt, 1938), pp. 14–17.

4. Advisory Commission on Intergovernmental Relations, *Multistate Regionalism*, p. 1. This section relies heavily on pp. 1–8 of this study and on the commission's *Regional Decision Making*, pp. 53–58.

5. Brooke Graves, *American Intergovernmental Relations* (New York: Charles Scribner's Sons, 1964), p. 617. Other general considerations of administrative regionalism may be found in James E. Fesler, *Area and Administration* (University: University of Alabama Press, 1949); Arthur Maass, ed., *Area and Power* (Glencoe, Ill.: The Free Press, 1959); Philip Selznick, *TVA and the Grass Roots* (Berkeley: University of California Press, 1949); and Martha Derthick, *Between State and Nation* (Washington, D.C.: The Brookings Institution, 1974).

6. Odum and Moore, *American Regionalism*, p. 4 and chap. 1.

7. Otis L. Graham, Jr., *Toward a Planned Society* (New York: Oxford University Press, 1976), pp. 52–56.

8. Advisory Commission on Intergovernmental Relations, *Multistate Regionalism*, p. 8.

9. "Remarks upon Signing the Appalachia Bill," 9 March 1965, *Public Papers of the Presidents of the United States: Lyndon B. Johnson, 1965* (Washington, D.C.: GPO, 1967), p. 271 (hereafter cited as *Public Papers*).

10. This section relies heavily on Advisory Commission on Intergovernmental Relations, *Multistate Regionalism*, chap. 4; and Derthick, *Between State and Nation*, chap. 6.

11. Quoted in Derthick, *Between State and Nation*, p. 13.

12. Ibid., p. 138.

13. Ibid.

14. Ibid.

15. For examinations of the origins of the Appalachian Regional Commission and its programs, see Advisory Commission on Intergovernmental Relations, *Multistate Regionalism*, chap. 2; Derthick, *Between State and Nation*, chap. 4; Monroe Newman, *The Political Economy of Appalachia: A Case Study in Regional Integration* (Lexington, Mass.: Lexington Books, 1972); Emmette S. Redford and Marlan Blissett, *Organizing the Executive Branch: The Johnson Presidency* (Chicago: University of Chicago Press, 1981), pp. 173–180; Donald N. Rothblatt, *Regional Planning: The Appalachian Experience* (Lexington, Mass.: Heath Lexington Books, 1971); and James L. Sundquist, *Politics and Policy: The Eisenhower, Kennedy, and Johnson Years* (Washington, D.C.: The Brookings Institution, 1968), pp. 97–105.

16. Newman, *The Political Economy of Appalachia*, p. 20.

17. Rothblatt, *Regional Planning*, p. 48.

18. Sundquist, *Politics and Policy*, p. 100.

19. Newman, *The Political Economy of Appalachia*, p. 28.

20. John L. Sweeney Oral History Interview, 14 November 1968, p. 14, LBJ Library.

21. President's Appalachian Regional Commission, *Appalachia* (Washington, D.C.: GPO, 1964), Appendix D.

22. Sweeney Oral History Interview, p. 14.

23. "Statement by the President Following a Meeting to Discuss the Eastern Kentucky Emergency Program" 13 December 1963, *Public Papers*, pp. 49–50.

24. Note to White, undated, attached to memo, White to president, 2 March 1965, Ex FG 203, WHCF, LBJ Library.

25. William L. Batt, Jr., Oral History Interview, 10 March 1967, p. 181, JFK Library.

26. Memo, White to president, 3 February 1964, Ex BE 5-5/Co1 (Appalachia), WHCF, LBJ Library.

27. Memo, White to president, 2 March 1964, Ex FG 203, WHCF, LBJ Library.

28. Sweeney Oral History Interview, p. 15.

29. Sundquist, *Politics and Policy*, p. 103.

30. Sweeney Oral History Interview, p. 15.

31. "Remarks at the Airport, Huntington, West Virginia, upon Departing for Washington," 24 April 1964, *Public Papers*, p. 547.

32. Sweeney Oral History Interview, p. 15.

33. Newman, *The Political Economy of Appalachia*, p. 1.

34. Rothblatt, *Regional Planning*, p. 52.

35. "Bureau of the Budget Views on Proposed Program of the President's Appalachian Regional Commission," 18 December 1963, attached to memo, Schultze to Sorenson and White, 18 December 1963, p. 1, Ex BE 5-5/Co1 (Appalachia), WHCF, LBJ Library.

36. Ibid.

37. Ibid., p. 2.

38. Memo, Seidman to director, 12 November 1963, attached to memo, Seidman to White, 5 December 1963, Ex BE 5-5/Co1 (Appalachia), WHCF, LBJ Library.

39. Attached to memo, Schultze to Sorenson and White, 18 December 1963, pp. 5–6, Ex BE 5-5/Co1 (Appalachia), WHCF, LBJ Library.

40. Memo, Seidman to director, 12 November 1963, attached to memo, Seidman to White, 5 December 1963, Ex BE 5-5/Co1 (Appalachia), WHCF, LBJ Library.

41. Attached to memo, Schultze to Sorenson and White, 18 December 1963, p. 7, Ex BE 5-5/Co1 (Appalachia), WHCF, LBJ Library.

42. Sundquist, *Politics and Policy*, p. 103.

43. Memo, Sweeney to president, 27 January 1964, Ex BE 5-5/Co1 (Appalachia), WHCF, LBJ Library.

44. President's Appalachian Regional Commission, *Appalachia*, p. vii. Governor William W. Scranton of Pennsylvania objected to its reinclusion. He also preferred a commission consisting of governors or their designees and a special assistant to the president. This assistant would head a council for Appalachia made up of representatives of federal agencies doing business in the region. His views were expressed in his own letter of endorsement. The eight Democratic governors signed another.

45. Memo, Gordon to president, 28 January 1965, Ex BE 5-5/Co1 (Appalachia), WHCF, LBJ Library.

46. Ibid.

47. Memo, Sweeney to president, 27 January 1964, Ex BE 5-5/Co1 (Appalachia), WHCF, LBJ Library.

48. President's Appalachian Regional Commission, *Appalachia*, p. 34.

49. Memo, Gordon to president, 28 January 1964, Ex BE 5-5/Co1 (Appalachia), WHCF, LBJ Library.

50. Memo, Sweeney to president, 27 January 1964, Ex BE 5-5/Co1 (Appalachia), WHCF, LBJ Library.

51. Memo, Roosevelt to president, 5 February 1964, Ex BE 5-5/Co1 (Appalachia), WHCF, LBJ Library.

52. Memo, Roosevelt to president, 13 March 1964, Ex FG 203, WHCF, LBJ Library.

53. Memo, Gordon to president, attached to memo, White to president, 7 July 1964, Appalachia 1964 folder, box 39, files of Bill Moyers, LBJ Library.

54. On 25 October the president established a committee to continue the planning process and named Sweeney chairman. "Executive Order 11186 Establishing the Federal Development Planning Committee for Appalachia," 25 October 1964, *Public Papers*, pp. 1433–1434. It was from this position that he oversaw passage of the legislation through Congress. See also Advisory Commission on Intergovernmental Relations, *Multistate Regionalism*, pp. 20–21.

55. Derthick, *Between State and Nation*, p. 108; Sundquist, *Politics and Policy*, 104–105; Advisory Commission on Intergovernmental Relations, *Multistate Regionalism*, pp. 58–59.

56. "Special Message to the Congress on Area and Regional Economic Development," 25 March 1965, *Public Papers*, p. 320.

57. Memo, Batt to White, 7 February 1964, Ex FG 155-4, WHCF, and memo, Dooley to Valenti, 19 May 1964, Ex FG 155-4, WHCF, LBJ Library.

58. For the details of previous and related legislation, particularly the Area Redevelopment Act of 1961, see *Congressional Quarterly Almanac* (Washington, D.C.: Congressional Quarterly Service, 1966), pp. 799–809.

59. Complicating the situation were the complaints of influential senator John Stennis that Mississippi was not getting its share of accelerated public works funds. In fact, as Secretary of Commerce Luther H. Hodges told the president, during the Kennedy years "participating agencies were instructed by members of the White House staff *not* to approve any projects for the State of *Mississippi*." Memo, Hodges to president, C.F. FI 4/FG 155-4, WHCF, LBJ Library.

60. Sar A. Levitan, *Federal Aid to Depressed Areas* (Baltimore: Johns Hopkins University Press, 1964).

61. "Area and Regional Economic Development," 12 November 1964, legislative background files, Appalachia folder E, box 1, LBJ Library.

62. Memo, Commerce and Finance Division to Schultze and Hughes, legislative background files, Appalachia folder E, box 1, LBJ Library.

63. "Area and Regional Economic Development," 12 November 1964, p. 8, legislative background files, Appalachia folder E, box 1, LBJ Library.

64. "Bureau of the Budget Changes in the Proposed 1965 Amendments to the Area Redevelopment Act," 26 January 1965, legislative background files, Appalachia folder E, box 1, LBJ Library.

65. Derthick, *Between State and Nation*, p. 111.

66. Memo, Sweeney to White, 11 February 1964, legislative background files, Appalachia folder E, box 1, LBJ Library. Batt argued strenuously the other way. Memo, Batt to White, 12 February 1964, legislative background files, Appalachia folder E, box 1, LBJ Library.

67. Memo, Commerce and Finance Division (R. S. Adkins) to Capron, 24 February 1964; and memo, Capron to White, 8 March 1965, legislative background files, Appalachia folder E, box 1, LBJ Library.

68. The situation in the House committee is described in memo, Capron to Wilson and White, 28 May 1965, legislative background files, Appalachia folder E, box 1, LBJ Library. The White House wanted the House Public Works Committee to handle the legislation rather than the more difficult Banking and Currency Committee, which had handled area redevelopment. White House aide Harry C. McPherson, Jr., reported to the president that the House parliamentarian gave assurances that this would be done. "It is now called the Public Works and Economic Development Act. No real substantive changes have been made. We just inserted 'public works' on an average of three times per page." Memo, McPherson to president, 30 March 1965, Ex LE/FA, WHCF, LBJ Library.

69. Memo, Watson to president, 9 February 1966, attached to memo, Foley to Watson, 9 February 1966, Ex BE 5-5, WHCF, LBJ Library.

70. President's comment, attached to memo, Simpich to Jones, 9 December 1966, Ex BE 5-5, WHCF, LBJ Library.

71. "Statement by the President on the Progress of the Appalachian Program," 12 March 1966, *Public Papers*, p. 309; memo, Valenti to president, 6 December 1965, Ex FG 203, WHCF, LBJ Library; memo, Valenti to president, 28 February 1966, Ex FG 203, WHCF, LBJ Library.

72. For a general analysis of presidential appointments in the Johnson period, see Richard L. Schott and Dagmar S. Hamilton, *People, Positions, and Power: The Political Appointments of Lyndon Johnson* (Chicago: University of Chicago Press, 1983).

73. Sweeney Oral History Interview, p. 24.

74. President's comment attached to memo, Moyers to president, 15 December 1966, Ex FG 203, WHCF, LBJ Library.

75. Memo, Watson to president, 12 June 1965, Ex FG 155-4, WHCF, LBJ Library.

76. Memo, Macy to president, 17 August 1965, Ex FG 282, WHCF, LBJ Library.

77. Memo, Watson to president, 4 May 1966, Ex FG 282, WHCF, LBJ Library.

78. Quoted in Jeffrey L. Pressman and Aaron Wildavsky, *Implementation* (Berkeley: University of California Press, 1979), p. 31.

79. Memo, Macy to president, 31 May 1966, Ex FG 155-20/A, WHCF, LBJ Library.

80. Memo, Schultze to Califano, Ex FG 155-21, WHCF, LBJ Library.

81. Derthick, *Between State and Nation*, p. 115. There are indications that political considerations were generally important in Economic Development Administration appointments. For example, in late 1965 Clifton C. Carter of the Democratic National Committee sent Watson a list of names for consideration as regional directors of EDA. Memo, Carter to Watson, 30 November 1965, Ex FG 155-20, WHCF, LBJ Library.

82. Joe W. Fleming II Oral History Interview, 19 February 1969, p. 42, LBJ Library.

83. Newman, *The Political Economy of Appalachia*, pp. 9–13.

84. Derthick, *Between State and Nation*, pp. 90–91.

85. Of course, recipients of grants—for highways, for example—were still bound by funding agency requirements.

86. Memo and attached materials, Schlei to president, 9 March 1965, Ex FG 670, WHCF, LBJ Library.

87. Derthick, *Between State and Nation*, p. 98.

88. Memo, McPherson to president, 11 March 1965, Ex FA 5, WHCF, LBJ Library.

89. Memo, Sweeney and Moynihan to McPherson, 10 March 1965, Ex FA 5, WHCF, LBJ Library.

90. Memo, Baker to Moyers, 27 February 1965, Ex FA 5, WHCF, LBJ Library.

91. Memo, Sweeney and Moynihan to McPherson, 10 March 1965, Ex FA 5, WHCF, LBJ Library.

92. Memo, McPherson to president, 11 March 1965, Ex FA 5, WHCF, LBJ Library. The "gov" reference is to Governor Edward T. Breathitt of Kentucky, who was deeply involved in the salvage effort.
93. Memo, McPherson to Shriver, 18 March 1965, Ex FA 5, WHCF, LBJ Library.
94. Memo, Sweeney to McPherson, 5 April 1965, Ex FA 5, WHCF, LBJ Library.
95. Memo, McPherson to president, 7 April 1965, Memos for the President (1965) folder, box 52, files of Harry McPherson, LBJ Library.
96. Memo, McPherson to Moyers, 19 April 1965, Ex FA 5, WHCF, LBJ Library.
97. Memo, McPherson to president, 8 June 1965, Ex FA 5, WHCF, LBJ Library.
98. Newman, *The Political Economy of Appalachia*, pp. 104–105.
99. Derthick, *Betweeen State and Nation*, p. 84.
100. Newman, *The Political Economy of Appalachia*, p. 106.
101. Ibid, p. 107.
102. Ibid., p. 109.
103. Sweeney Oral History Interview, p. 22.
104. Ibid., p. 23.
105. Fleming Oral History Interview, p. 27.
106. Memo, McPherson to Califano, 13 December 1965, Ex BE 5-5/Co1 (Appalachia), WHCF, LBJ Library.
107. Fleming Oral History Interview, p. 28.
108. Memo, McPherson to Califano, 4 January 1967, Ex LE/BE 5-5/Co1 (Appalachia), WHCF, LBJ Library; memo, Califano to president, 17 January 1967, Ex LE/BE 5-5/Co1 (Appalachia), WHCF, LBJ Library; memo, Schultze to president, 17 January 1967, Ex LE/BE 5-5/Co1 (Appalachia), WHCF, LBJ Library.
109. "Letter to the President of the Senate and to the Speaker of the House Recommending Extension of the Appalachian Program," 20 January 1967, *Public Papers*, p. 31.
110. Memo, Schultze to president, 26 January 1967, attached to memo, Califano to president, 27 January 1967, Ex LE/BE 5-5/Co1 (Appalachia), WHCF, LBJ Library.
111. The act also increased road construction mileage, revised the health demonstration program, established a housing development fund, and instructed the commission to study the impact of acid mine drainage. P.L. 90-103.
112. Letter, Connor to Schultze, 10 October 1966, Ex BE 5-5, WHCF, LBJ Library.
113. Derthick, *Between State and Nation*, pp. 113–114.
114. Department of Commerce, *Administrative History: The Area Redevelopment Administration and the Economic Development Administration*, undated, vol. 1, p. 32, LBJ Library.
115. Memo, Frey to Gaither, 3 March 1967, Appalachia folder, box 41, files of James Gaither, LBJ Library.

116. Ibid. Also memo, Office of Legislative Reference (Frey) to director, 3 April 1967, attached to memo, Gaither to Califano, 3 April 1967, Ex LE/BE 5-5/CO1 (Appalachia), WHCF, LBJ Library.

117. Extensive maneuvering involving top White House aides was required. Memos, Gaither to Califano, 13, 22, 23, and 26 June 1967, Appalachia folder, box 41, files of James Gaither, LBJ Library; memo, Califano to president, 10 July 1967, Ex LE/BE 5-5/CO1 (Appalachia), WHCF, LBJ Library.

118. Memo, Foley to Macy, 8 February 1966, attached to memo, Foley to Watson, 9 February 1966, Ex BE 5-5, WHCF, LBJ Library.

119. "Direction and Coordination of Federal Cochairmen and Regional Development Programs"; and memo, Gaither to Califano, 5 June 1967, Appalachia folder, box 41, files of James Gaither, LBJ Library.

120. "Letter . . . Recommending Extension of the Appalachian Program," 20 January 1967, *Public Papers*, p. 31.

121. "Direction and Coordination of Federal Cochairmen and Regional Development Programs"; and memo, Gaither to Califano, 5 June 1967, Appalachia folder, box 41, files of James Gaither, LBJ Library.

122. Memo, Gaither to Califano, 2 January 1969, Appalachia folder, box 42, files of James Gaither, LBJ Library.

123. Fleming Oral History Interview, pp. 35–36.

124. Memo, Califano to president, 5 October 1967, Ex LE/BE 5-5/CO1 (Appalachia), WHCF, LBJ Library.

125. Memo, Califano to president, 30 October 1967, Ex LE/BE 5-5/CO1 (Appalachia), WHCF, LBJ Library.

126. Ibid.

127. Fleming Oral History Interview, p. 36.

128. Executive Order 11386, 28 December 1967, *Federal Register*, vol. 33, 3 Jan. 1968, p. 5.

129. Memo, Dykman to Jones, 21 October 1968, Ex FG 657, WHCF, LBJ Library.

130. Derthick, *Between State and Nation*, p. 100.

6. The Revenue Sharing and Block Grant Options

1. Richard P. Nathan, Allen D. Manvel, and Susannah R. Calkins, *Monitoring Revenue Sharing* (Washington, D.C.: The Brookings Institution, 1975), p. 344.

2. Ibid., pp. 344–345. The definitive treatment of this experience is Edward G. Bourne, *The History of the Surplus Revenue of 1837* (New York: Burt Franklin, 1885).

3. Nathan et al., *Monitoring Revenue Sharing*, p. 347.

4. Walter W. Heller, "U.S. Budget Surpluses and Tax Policy," *Canadian Tax Journal* 5 (July–Aug. 1957): 321.

5. Memo, Heller to president, 12 May 1964, Ex ST, WHCF, LBJ Library.

6. Memo, Heller to president, 27 May 1967, Ex FI 11, WHCF, LBJ Library.

7. Erwin C. Hargrove and Samuel C. Morley, eds., *The President and the*

Council of Economic Advisers: Interviews with CEA Chairmen (Boulder: Westview Press, 1984), p. 213.

8. *U.S. News and World Report*, 29 June 1964, p. 59.

9. Task Force on Intergovernmental Fiscal Cooperation, "Report," 11 November 1964, p. i, task force collection, box 2, LBJ Library.

10. Ibid., pp. iv–v.

11. Memo, Heller to president, 18 September 1964, Ex PL 6-3, WHCF, LBJ Library.

12. Hargrove and Morley, eds., *The President and the Council of Economic Advisers*, p. 213.

13. Memo, Heller to president, 8 December 1964, C.F. FA, WHCF, LBJ Library.

14. White House Presidential Statement No. 6, Economic Issues, 28 October 1964, Ex FA, WHCF, LBJ Library.

15. Walter W. Heller to Jesse Burkhead, 18 June 1979. See also Hargrove and Morley, eds., *The President and the Council of Economic Advisers*, p. 214.

16. Memo, Heller to president, 30 October 1964, Ex BE 5, WHCF, LBJ Library.

17. Memo, Heller to president, 26 July 1965, C.F. FA, WHCF, LBJ Library.

18. Memo, Heller to president, 30 October 1964, Ex BE 5, WHCF, LBJ Library.

19. Memo, Heller to president, 18 December 1964, C.F. FA, WHCF, LBJ Library.

20. Memo, Heller to president, undated, C.F. FA, WHCF, LBJ Library.

21. Letter, Brown to Johnson, 1 December 1964, attached to letter, president to Brown, 10 December 1964, Ex FA, WHCF, LBJ Library.

22. Alan L. Otten and Charles B. Seib, "No-Strings Aid for States," *The Reporter*, 28 January 1965, pp. 33–35.

23. Draft letter, president to Meyer, 17 November 1964, attached to letter, president to Meyer, 28 November 1964, Ex FA 2, WHCF, LBJ Library.

24. Pechman was of the view that the rejection of revenue sharing reflected a preference to channel money to specific Great Society programs that Johnson favored, such as aid to education. Joseph A. Pechman Oral History Interview, 19 March 1969, pp. 14–15, LBJ Library.

25. *Washington Post*, 13 July 1964, p. A2.

26. He was also careful to inform Johnson that since November he had "refused to talk publicly—or conspire privately" on revenue sharing. "The so-called 'Heller Plan' is not being talked up—or about—by Heller." Memo, Heller to president, 26 July 1965, C.F. FA, WHCF, LBJ Library.

27. Memo, Ellington to president, 2 August 1965, Ex ST/MC, WHCF, LBJ Library.

28. Memo, Califano to president, 16 December 1966, Ex FA, WHCF, LBJ Library.

29. Letter, Surrey to city council, 25 January 1966, Gen FA, WHCF, LBJ Library.

30. Memo, Heller to president, 16 December 1966, Ex FA, WHCF, LBJ Library.

31. Memo, Markman to president, 15 December 1966, Ex ST, WHCF, LBJ Library.

32. Memo, Califano to president, 16 December 1966, Ex FA, WHCF, LBJ Library.

33. Memo, Heller to president, 16 December 1966, Ex FA, WHCF, LBJ Library.

34. Memo, Ackley to president, 20 December 1966, C.F. FA, WHCF, LBJ Library.

35. Richard A. Musgrave, "National Taxes and Local.Needs," *The Nation*, 16 January 1967, p. 78; Joseph A. Pechman, "Money for the States," *The New Republic*, 8 April 1967, p. 15.

36. Nathan et al., *Monitoring Revenue Sharing*, p. 351.

37. Samuel H. Beer, "The Adoption of General Revenue Sharing," *Public Policy* 24 (Spring 1976): 127–195.

38. U.S. Congress, Joint Economic Committee, *Hearings before a Subcommittee on Fiscal Policy*, 90th Cong., 1st sess., 1967.

39. For example, Stephen M. Barro, *The Urban Impacts of Federal Policies* (Santa Monica, Calif.: RAND, 1978), especially pp. 64–155; Roy Bahl, Jesse Burkhead, and Bernard Jump, *Public Employment and State and Local Government Finance* (Cambridge, Mass.: Ballinger, 1980), chap. 3.

40. Wallace E. Oates, *Fiscal Federalism* (New York: Harcourt Brace, 1972), especially chap. 3, Appendix A. See also Albert Breton and Anthony Scott, *The Economic Constitution of Federal States* (Toronto: University of Toronto Press, 1978).

41. Samuel H. Beer, "A Political Scientist's View of Fiscal Federalism," in Wallace E. Oates, ed., *The Political Economy of Fiscal Federalism* (Lexington, Mass.: Lexington Books, 1977), pp. 21–46.

42. See Theodore J. Lowi, *The End of Liberalism* (New York: Norton, 1969), especially pp. 214–239.

43. Estimates by Sar A. Levitan and Robert Taggart, *The Promise of Greatness* (Cambridge, Mass.: Harvard University Press, 1976), pp. 82–83.

44. See David C. Warner, "Fiscal Federalism in Health Care," *Publius* 15 (Fall 1975): 79–99.

45. For excellent brief summaries of Great Society health programs see David C. Warner, ed., *Toward New Human Rights* (Austin: Lyndon B. Johnson School of Public Affairs, 1977), pp. 143–236, especially Theodore Marmor with James Marone, "The Health Programs of the Kennedy-Johnson Years: An Overview," p. 157; Levitan and Taggart, *The Promise of Greatness*, pp. 82–99. For an appraisal that extends through 1975 see Karen Davis and Cathy Schoen, *Health and the War on Poverty* (Washington, D.C.: The Brookings Institution, 1978).

46. The seminal work on the economics of health is the 1932 final report, reprinted in 1972, of the Committee on the Costs of Medical Care, *Medical Care for the American People* (New York: Arno Press, 1972). A major effort

to bring health care into the mainstream of economic analysis was initiated by Kenneth J. Arrow, "Uncertainty and the Welfare Economics of Medical Care," *American Economic Review* 53 (Dec. 1963): 941.

47. Herbert E. Klarman, "Major Public Initiatives in Health Care," in Eli Ginzberg and Robert M. Solow, eds., *The Great Society* (New York: Basic Books, 1974), p. 123.

48. Douglass Cater and Philip R. Lee, eds., *Politics of Health* (New York: Medcom Press, 1972), p. 4.

49. Ibid., p. 6.

50. "Special Message to the Congress on the Nation's Health," 10 February 1964, *Public Papers of the Presidents of the United States: Lyndon B. Johnson, 1964* (Washington, D.C.: GPO, 1965), p. 275 (hereafter cited as *Public Papers*).

51. Task Force on Health, "Report," 10 November 1964, task force collection, box 1, LBJ Library.

52. "Special Message to the Congress: 'Advancing the Nation's Health,'" 7 January 1965, *Public Papers*, p. 12.

53. "Proposed Message," undated, Ex SP2-3/1965/HE Health 1/7/65, WHCF, LBJ Library.

54. "Policy Issues Raised by Recommendations in Proposed Health Message," undated, attached to ibid.

55. "Special Message to the Congress: 'Advancing the Nation's Health,'" 7 January 1965, *Public Papers*, p. 20.

56. Advisory Commission on Intergovernmental Relations, *The Partnership for Health Act: Lessons from a Pioneering Block Grant* (Washington, D.C.: GPO, 1977), pp. 5–9.

57. Task Force on Health Care, "Report," 10 September 1965, Ex FG 600/ Task Force on Health, WHCF, LBJ Library.

58. Memo, Schultze to Califano, 1 October 1965, Ex FG 11-1, WHCF, LBJ Library.

59. Memo, Huitt to Cater, 17 December 1965, Ex LE/FA5, WHCF, LBJ Library.

60. "Special Message to the Congress on Domestic Health and Education," 1 March 1966, *Public Papers*, p. 238.

61. Ibid., p. 239.

62. The discussion of congressional consideration of the legislation relies heavily on Advisory Commission on Intergovernmental Relations, *The Partnership for Health Act*, pp. 10–15.

63. The nine grant programs were for general health, tuberculosis, cancer, mental health, heart disease, chronic diseases and health of the aged, radiological health, dental health, and home health services. Two other related programs were omitted because they were not administered by HEW.

64. Singling out mental health in this manner was to ensure that state mental health agencies, typically independent of public health agencies to which the block grants would go because of the single state agency requirement, would receive a reasonable share of the funds.

65. The project grants to be consolidated were for tuberculosis, heart dis-

ease, cancer, radiological facilities, venereal disease, neurology, and home health care.

66. Klarman, "Major Public Initiatives in Health Care," p. 115.

67. "Agenda HEW meeting," 30 December 1966, Ex SP 2-3/1967/ED, backup VIII, WHCF, LBJ Library.

68. Hugh Davis Graham, *The Uncertain Triumph: Federal Education Policy in the Kennedy and Johnson Years* (Chapel Hill: University of North Carolina Press, 1984), pp. 149–155; Norman C. Thomas, *Education in National Politics* (New York: David McKay, 1975), pp. 74–91.

69. "Special Message to the Congress on Education: 'The Fifth Freedom,'" 5 February 1968, *Public Papers*, p. 168. In late 1967, Califano, after a meeting with Gardner, Cater, and others, recommended a general aid program for higher education, but the idea received no further serious consideration. Memo, Califano to president, 1 November 1967, Ex FA 2, WHCF, LBJ Library.

70. Notes, "Task Force on Education Meeting," 14 February 1966, legislative background files, Education Professions Development Act of 1967 folder, box 1, LBJ Library.

71. Thomas, *Education in National Politics*, p. 100.

72. Memo, Sagalyn to Cater, 9 September 1964, Ex JL 6, WHCF, LBJ Library.

73. "Statement by the President upon Making Public an FBI Report on the Recent Urban Riots," 26 September 1964, *Public Papers*, p. 1138.

74. "Lawlessness and the Police," attached to memo, Sagalyn to Cater, 9 September 1964, Ex JL 6, WHCF, LBJ Library.

75. Memo, Schlei to Moyers, undated, Ex SP 2-3/1965/JL Law Enforcement/3/8/65, WHCF, LBJ Library.

76. "Annual Message to the Congress on the State of the Union," 4 January 1965, *Public Papers*, p. 7.

77. "Special Message to the Congress on Law Enforcement and the Administration of Justice," 8 March 1965, *Public Papers*, p. 264.

78. Ibid., p. 271.

79. Ibid., p. 265.

80. Ibid., p. 270.

81. Ibid., p. 265.

82. Ibid.

83. For approximately a month during May and June, by letters and emissaries Johnson unsuccessfully attempted to recruit former prosecutor, New York governor, and Republican presidential candidate Thomas E. Dewey to head the commission. Letters, president to Dewey, 19 and 27 May 1965, Ex FG 999-5, WHCF, LBJ Library.

84. Advisory Commission on Intergovernmental Relations, *Making the Safe Streets Act Work: An Intergovernmental Challenge* (Washington, D.C.: GPO, 1970), p. 9.

85. "Special Message to the Congress on Crime and Law Enforcement," 9 March 1966, *Public Papers*, p. 292.

86. Letter, Katzenbach to president, 28 July 1966, Ex JL 6, WHCF, LBJ Library.

87. Gaither to files, 15 November 1968, legislative background files, Safe Streets and Crime Control Act of 1968, Background Summary folder, box 1, LBJ Library.

88. "Meeting on Crime—Justice—1967 Legislation," 18 August 1966, legislative background files, Safe Streets and Crime Control Act of 1968, 1966–67 Task Force on Crime II folder, box 1, LBJ Library.

89. President's Commission on Law Enforcement and the Administration of Justice, *The Challenge of Crime in a Free Society* (Washington, D.C.: GPO, 1967). For a discussion of the work of the commission, see Henry S. Ruth, Jr., "To Dust Shall Ye Return?" *Notre Dame Lawyer* 43 (1968): 811.

90. "Joint Report of the Task Force on Law Enforcement and the Administration of Justice and the Task Force on Juvenile Delinquency," legislative background files, Safe Streets and Crime Control Act of 1968, Report of the Task Force on Law Enforcement and the Administration of Justice 11/66 folder, box 1, LBJ Library.

91. Memo, Sutton to director, 24 November 1966, Task Force on Law Enforcement 1966, task force collection, box 17, LBJ Library.

92. Advisory Commission on Intergovernmental Relations, *Making the Safe Streets Act Work*, pp. 10–11.

93. "Statement by the President at a Meeting with a Group of Governors in Problems of Crime and Law Enforcement," 29 September 1966, *Public Papers*, p. 1087; "Remarks to the Delegates to the Conference of State Committees on Criminal Administration," 15 October 1966, *Public Papers*, p. 1206.

94. Memo, Gaither to files, 15 November 1966, legislative background files, Safe Streets and Crime Control Act of 1968, Background Summary folder, box 1, LBJ Library. Also in this file are rough meeting notes taken by Gaither, which are employed in the discussion of the working group deliberations.

95. Vorenberg to Califano, 2 December 1966, pp. 9–10, Task Force on Law Enforcement 1966, task force collection, box 17, LBJ Library.

96. Memo, Haar to Califano, 6 December 1966, Task Force on Law Enforcement 1966, task force collection, box 17, LBJ Library.

97. Memo, Clark to Califano, 9 December 1966, Task Force on Law Enforcement 1966, task force collection, box 17, LBJ Library.

98. Based on the meeting notes of 10 December and "Issues on Law Enforcement Grant Proposal," 10 December 1966, legislative background files, Safe Streets and Crime Control Act of 1968, 1966–67 Task Force on Crime I folder, box 1, LBJ Library.

99. "Annual Message to Congress on the State of the Union," 10 January 1967, *Public Papers*, p. 6.

100. "Special Message to Congress on Crime in America," 6 February 1967, *Public Papers*, p. 138.

101. Legislative background is drawn from Advisory Commission on Intergovernmental Relations, *Making the Safe Streets Act Work*, pp. 10–18;

Congress and the Nation: 1965–1968 (Washington, D.C.: Congressional Quarterly Service, 1969), pp. 317–318 and 321–326.

102. Task Force on Crime, "Report," 15 December 1967, p. 1, Ex FG 600/Task Force/C, WHCF, LBJ Library.

103. "Special Message to the Congress on Crime and Law Enforcement: 'To Insure the Public Safety,'" 7 February 1968, *Public Papers*, p. 183.

104. Memo, "Re: The Constitutional Responsibilities of the States and the Federal Government for *Control of Crime and Domestic Violence*," attached to letter, Wozencraft to Nimetz, 19 January 1968, legislative background files, Safe Streets and Crime Control Act of 1968, Background—1967–68 Task Force on Crime folder, box 2, LBJ Library.

105. Memo, "Crime Draft," attached to note, Muriel to Califano, 6 February 1968, Ex SP 2-3/1968/JL Crime Message 2/7/68, backup III, WHCF, LBJ Library.

106. Ibid.

107. Memo, Califano to president, 3 February 1968, legislative background files, Safe Streets and Crime Control Act of 1968, 1968 Crime Message #2 folder, box 6, LBJ Library.

108. Harold Seidman, *Politics, Positions, and Power* (New York: Oxford University Press, 1970), p. 87.

109. Advisory Commission on Intergovernmental Relations, *Making the Safe Streets Act Work*, p. 18.

7. Repairing the Intergovernmental Administrative System

1. Richard R. Warner, "The Concept of Creative Federalism in the Johnson Administration" (Ph.D. diss., American University, 1970), p. 263.

2. Task Force on Government Reorganization, "Report," 6 November 1965, task force collection, box 1, LBJ Library.

3. Letter, Bane to president, 23 November 1964, Ex LE/FA, WHCF, LBJ Library.

4. Memo, Wilson to McPherson, 18 June 1965, attached to memo, McPherson to Cikens, 7 July 1965, Ex LE/ST, WHCF, LBJ Library.

5. Memo, McPherson to Hays, 7 July 1965, Ex FG 11-1, WHCF, LBJ Library.

6. Other members were William Colman of ACIR, Herbert Kaufman of Yale University, James L. Sundquist of the Brookings Institution, Stephen B. Sweeney of the University of Pennsylvania, and Robert C. Wood of the Massachusetts Institute of Technology.

7. Task Force on Intergovernmental Program Coordination, "Report," 22 December 1965, p. 2, task force collection, box 3, LBJ Library.

8. Ibid., pp. 3–4.

9. Ibid., p. 6.

10. Ibid., pp. 8–10.

11. Ibid., pp. 11–12.

12. "Annual Message to the Congress on the State of the Union," 12 January 1966, *Public Papers of the Presidents of the United States: Lyndon B.*

Johnson, 1966 (Washington, D.C.: GPO, 1967), p. 7 (hereafter cited as *Public Papers*).

13. Warner, "The Concept of Creative Federalism in the Johnson Administration," p. 275.

14. Memo, Califano to president, 20 April 1966, Ex ST, WHCF, LBJ Library.

15. Memo, Schultze to Califano, 7 January 1966, Ex FG 600, WHCF, LBJ Library.

16. Memo, Semer to president, 12 April 1966, Ex ST, WHCF, LBJ Library.

17. Memo, Schultze to Califano, 3 April 1966, Ex ST, WHCF, LBJ Library; "Study on Intergovernmental Relations Alternatives and Approaches," attached to draft memo, Califano to president, 28 April 1966, Ex ST, WHCF, LBJ Library.

18. Draft memo, Califano to president, 28 April 1966, Ex ST, WHCF, LBJ Library.

19. These views are reflected in notes attached to memo, Schultze to Califano, 13 April 1966, Ex ST, WHCF, LBJ Library.

20. Memo, Weaver to Califano, 3 December 1966, Ex LG, WHCF, LBJ Library.

21. U.S. Congress, subcommittee on Intergovernmental Relations, Senate Committee on Government Operations, *Five-Year Record of the Advisory Commission on Intergovernmental Relations and Its Future Role*, document no. 80, 89th Cong., 2d sess., 1966. See also Deil S. Wright, "The Advisory Commission on Intergovernmental Relations: Unique Features and Policy Orientation," *Public Administration Review* 25 (Sept. 1965): 193.

22. *Congressional Record*, 25 March 1966, pp. 6833–6835.

23. Advisory Commission on Intergovernmental Relations, *Intergovernmental Relations in the Poverty Program* (Washington, D.C.: GPO, 1966), pp. 32–34.

24. Advisory Commission on Intergovernmental Relations, *Improving Federal Grants Management* (Washington, D.C.: GPO, 1977), p. 11.

25. U.S. Congress, Senate Committee on Government Operations, *Creative Federalism: Hearings before the Subcommittee on Intergovernmental Relations*, 89th Cong., 2d sess., 1966, p. 388.

26. Ibid., p. 389.

27. Ibid., p. 390.

28. Ibid., pp. 390–393 (italics in original).

29. Ibid., p. 394.

30. Warner, "The Concept of Creative Federalism in the Johnson Administration," p. 20.

31. Ibid., p. 251.

32. Ibid., p. 284.

33. Ibid., p. 359. Warner assigns great importance to the thinking of Robert C. Wood in the development of the concept of creative federalism, especially his essay "The Federal Role in Creative Federalism: The Next Step Forward," in Donald E. Nicoll, ed., *Creative Federalism*, (Washington, D.C.: U.S. Department of Agriculture Graduate School Press, 1967), pp. 29–39.

34. John W. Kingdom, *Agendas, Alternatives, and Public Policies* (Boston: Little Brown, 1984), pp. 20–21.

35. "Special Message to Congress: The Quality of American Government," 17 March 1967, *Public Papers*, pp. 365–368.

36. P.L. 90-577. For a history of congressional actions and a summary of testimony see *Congressional Quarterly Almanac 1968* (Washington, D.C.: Congressional Quarterly, Inc., 1969), pp. 505–509; *Congressional Quarterly Fact Sheet: Jan. 31, 1969* (Washington, D.C.: Congressional Quarterly, Inc., 1969), pp. 201–203.

37. Task Force on Manpower for State and Local Government, "Report," 17 December 1966, p. 10, task force collection, box 5, LBJ Library.

38. Ibid., pp. 4–5.

39. James Gaither and Califano were quite interested in the work of this group.

40. P.L. 90-575.

41. P.L. 91-648.

42. Task Force on Manpower for State and Local Government, "Report," p. 2.

43. Memo, Cater to president, 6 February 1967, Ex ST, WHCF, LBJ Library.

44. "Summary of Cabinet Views," sec. IV, attached to ibid.

45. Memo, Bohen to Jacobsen, 14 March 1967, Ex FG 749, WHCF, LBJ Library.

46. Memo, Califano to Schultze, 14 August 1967, C.F. FA, WHCF, LBJ Library.

47. Memo, Schultze to Califano, 2 October 1967, Record Group 51, National Archives. From time to time there was discussion of general management grants to state departments of education and labor, but they encountered substantial opposition on the grounds that such discretionary resources would be wasted by incompetent officials.

48. Warner, "The Concept of Creative Federalism in the Johnson Administration," p. 246.

49. "Memorandum on the Need for 'Creative Federalism' through Cooperation with State and Local Officials," 11 November 1966, *Public Papers*, pp. 1366–1367.

50. Memo, Bohen to Jacobsen, 14 March 1967, Ex FG 749, p. 2, WHCF, LBJ Library.

51. Harold Seidman, *Politics, Positions, and Power* (New York: Oxford University Press, 1976), pp. 184–185.

52. See Advisory Commission on Intergovernmental Relations, *Improving Federal Grants Management*, pp. 135–137.

53. Norman Beckman, "How Metropolitan Are Federal and State Policies?" *Public Administration Review* 26 (June 1966): 96.

54. Bernard J. Frieden, *Metropolitan America: Challenge to Federalism* (Washington, D.C: ACIR, 1966), pp. 86–113.

55. See, for example, Robert H. Connery and Richard H. Leach, *The Federal Government and Metropolitan Areas* (Cambridge, Mass.: Harvard Uni-

versity Press, 1960); and Roscoe C. Martin, *The Cities and the Federal System* (New York: Atherton Press, 1965).

56. For background on section 701, see Advisory Commission on Intergovernmental Relations, *Regional Decision Making: New Strategies for Substate Districts*, pp. 56–63.

57. James L. Sundquist with David W. Davis, *Making Federalism Work* (Washington, D.C.: The Brookings Institution, 1969), p. 196. See also Monroe Newman, *The Political Economy of Appalachia: A Case Study in Regional Integration* (Lexington, Mass.: Lexington Books, 1972), p. 100.

58. Advisory Commission on Intergovernmental Relations, *Regional Decision Making*, p. 186.

59. Sundquist and Davis, *Making Federalism Work*, p. 162.

60. Advisory Commission on Intergovernmental Relations, *Intergovernmental Relations in the Poverty Program*, p. 169.

61. Memo, president to secretary of commerce et al., 2 September 1966, Ex ST, WHCF, LBJ Library.

62. Advisory Commission on Intergovernmental Relations, *Regional Decision Making*, p. 192.

63. Department of Housing and Urban Development, *Administrative History*, undated, vol. 1, pt. 1, chap. 6, p. 15, LBJ Library.

64. For general background, see Advisory Commission on Intergovernmental Relations, *Regional Decision Making*, pp. 52–58.

65. Paper, "Programs to Advance Planned and Coordinated Metropolitan Development," filed 2 April 1966, p. 1, Ex LG, WHCF, LBJ Library.

66. The discussion of councils of government relies heavily on Advisory Commission on Intergovernmental Relations, *Regional Decision Making*, pp. 58–80; Nelson Wickstrom, *Councils of Government* (Chicago: Nelson-Hall, 1977); and National Service to Regional Councils, *Regionalism: A New Dimension in Local Government and Intergovernmental Relations* (Washington, D.C.: National Service to Regional Councils, undated).

67. Advisory Commission on Intergovernmental Relations, *Regional Decision Making*, p. 51.

68. National Service to Regional Councils, *Summary of Workshop Proceedings* (Washington, D.C.: National Service to Regional Councils, 1967), p. 9.

69. A part of the growing complexity was that after the amendment of 701 in 1965 and the enactment of 204 in 1966, general new regional planning programs were established in areas such as health and law enforcement. Further, in certain areas some comprehensive planning and review functions were being performed by economic development districts, also instruments of regional confederalism, not planning commissions or regional councils.

70. "Summary of Recent Activities to Promote Improved Intergovernmental Relations," 6 October 1967, p. 5, Gen SP 2-3/1967/FE, WHCF, LBJ Library.

71. Warner, "The Concept of Creative Federalism in the Johnson Administration," pp. 156–157.

72. "Intergovernmental Cooperation Act: 'The President's Memorandum to the Director of the Bureau of the Budget Delegating Authority under the Act,'" 8 November 1968, *Weekly Compilation of Presidential Documents*, 18 November 1968, vol. 4, p. 1592.

73. Bureau of the Budget, *Administrative History*, undated, supplement, enclosure 5, p. 8, LBJ Library. The act also sought to improve field coordination by requiring that federal agencies comply with local planning and zoning in the acquisition, use, and disposition of land.

74. For additional background specific to A-95 see Jerome M. Stam, "Office of Management and Budget Circular A-95: An Overview," U.S. Department of Agriculture, Economics, Statistics and Cooperative Services Staff Paper, August 1979, pp. 1–5.

75. In planning HUD's organizational structure much attention was given to developing a field organization that would facilitate program coordination. Emmette S. Redford and Marlan Blissett, *Organizing the Executive Branch: The Johnson Presidency* (Chicago: University of Chicago Press, 1981), pp. 41–42. For a time the department considered the establishment of metropolitan desks in Washington to facilitate coordination in particular cities. The model cities legislation provided for metropolitan "expediters" in cities, but there was no implementation. Robert A. Aleshire, "The Metropolitan Desk: A New Technique in Program Teamwork," *Public Administration Review* 26 (June 1966): 87.

76. Civil Service Commission, *Administrative History*, undated, vol. 1, pt. 2, chap. 11, pp. 1–2, LBJ Library.

77. *U.S. Government Organization Manual, 1979–80* (Washington, D.C.: GPO, 1979), p. 859.

78. The chairman of the Civil Service Commission was the central point of contact with the FEBs. This was confirmed by President Johnson in 1964. "Letter to the Chairman, Civil Service Commission, on Coordination of Federal Activities in the Field," 13 January 1964, *Public Papers*, p. 128.

79. See, for example, memo, Macy to president, 4 April 1966, Ex LG, WHCF, LBJ Library; and "Exchange of Letters between the President and Chairman John W. Macy, Jr., of the Civil Service Commission on Chairman Macy's Annual Report on Activities of the Boards," 4 September 1968, *Weekly Compilation of Presidential Documents*, 9 September 1968, vol. 4, pp. 1307–1308.

80. Civil Service Commission, *Administrative History*, vol. 1, pt. 2, chap. 11, p. 3.

81. As early as 1965 the chairman of CSC had also encouraged the establishment of federal executive associations in smaller cities. In May 1965 there were fifty-seven such associations and by December 1968 eighty-eight had been established. Information on federal business associations and federal executive associations is contained in Record Group 51, National Archives.

82. Civil Service Commission, *Administrative History*, vol. 1, pt. 2, chap. 11, pp. 5–6.

83. Ibid., pp. 8–14.

84. Memo, Macy to FEB chairman, 27 November 1967, Record Group 51, National Archives.
85. "Special Message to the Congress: The Quality of American Government," 17 March 1967, *Public Papers*, pp. 358–368.
86. Memo, Kugel to Hughes, 16 September 1968, Record Group 51, National Archives.
87. Seidman, *Politics, Positions, and Power*, p. 205.
88. Ibid., pp. 215–216.
89. Advisory Commission on Intergovernmental Relations, *Improving Federal Grants Management*, p. 183.
90. "Special Message to the Congress: The Quality of American Government," 17 March 1967, *Public Papers*, p. 367.
91. Task Force on Government Organization, "The Organization and Management of Great Society Programs," 15 June 1967, task force collection, box 4, LBJ Library.
92. Memo, Califano to president, 21 December 1967, Quality of American Government Study folder, box 205, files of James Gaither, LBJ Library. At this time the bureau was studying a number of other aspects of field organization, including the location, authority, and interrelationships of operating units subordinate to regional offices. "Summary of Recent Activities to Promote Improved Intergovernmental Relations," 6 October 1967, Gen SP 2-3/1967/FE Quality of American Government 3/17/67, WHCF, LBJ Library.
93. Memo, Califano to president, 17 May 1968, Government Organization folder, box 8, files of James Gaither, LBJ Library.
94. Memo, Califano to President, 3 December 1968, Ex FG 160, WHCF, LBJ Library.
95. Redford and Blissett, *Organizing the Executive Branch*, pp. 190–191.
96. Memo, Seidman to division and office chiefs, "Draft Report on Bureau Field Offices," 30 April 1964, Record Group 51, National Archives.
97. Memo, Schultze to Redmon, "Regional Coordination of Federal Programs," 19 January 1965, Record Group 51, National Archives.
98. Memo, Carey to Staats, "Bureau of the Budget Role in Federal Field Relations and Intergovernmental Relations," 11 August 1965, Record Group 51, National Archives.
99. Bureau of the Budget, *Administrative History*, vol. 1, pt. 4, p. 128.
100. Ibid.
101. Ibid., vol. 1, pt. 6, pp. 190–199; Larry Berman, *The Office of Management and Budget and the Presidency, 1921–1979* (Princeton: Princeton University Press, 1979), pp. 90–102. Additional information on BOB's internal self-survey is contained in Record Group 51, National Archives.
102. U.S. Congress, House Committee on Appropriations, *Department of Treasury and Post Office and Executive Office Appropriations for 1967: Hearings before a Subcommittee of the House Committee on Appropriations on H.R. 14266*, 89th Cong., 2d sess., 1966, p. 729.
103. Ibid., p. 730.
104. Ibid., p. 770.

105. U.S. Congress, House Committee on Appropriations, *Department of Treasury and Post Office and Executive Appropriations for 1968: Hearings before a Subcommittee of the House Committee on Appropriations on H.R. 7501*, 90th Cong., 1st sess., 1967, p. 662.

106. P.L. 93-510.

107. Memo, Hughes to Califano, 31 August 1967, attached to memo, Levinson to president, 2 September 1967, Ex FE 9, WHCF, LBJ Library.

108. Warner, "The Concept of Creative Federalism in the Johnson Administration," p. 238.

109. Memo, Hughes to Califano, 31 August 1967, attached to memo, Levinson to president, 2 September 1967, Ex FE 9, WHCF, LBJ Library.

110. Improvement was also sought in particular program spheres. For example, in 1966 HEW tried to get presidential support for legislation to allow statutory grant regulations to be waived in health programs in the interest of administrative efficiency. Memo, Lewis to Califano, 12 December 1966, Ex LE/HE 3, WHCF, LBJ Library.

111. Memo, McPherson to Califano, 12 October 1965, C.F. FG 11-15, WHCF, LBJ Library.

112. Memo, Semer to president, 5 April 1966, Ex HE 8-3, WHCF, LBJ Library.

113. Memo, Semer to Watson, 11 April 1966, Ex HE 8-3, WHCF, LBJ Library.

114. Memo, Semer to president, 18 June 1966, Ex FE 9, WHCF, LBJ Library.

115. Memo, Semer to Schultze, 25 July 1966, attached to memo, Semer to Astin, Ex HE 8-3, WHCF, LBJ Library.

116. Memo, Schultze to Semer, 22 October 1966, Ex HE 8-3, WHCF, LBJ Library.

117. Memo, Smith to Nobles, 17 February 1967, Ex UT 4, WHCF, LBJ Library.

118. Memo, Watson to president, 25 August 1967, Ex FI 5-7, WHCF, LBJ Library; and memo, Weaver to Califano, 26 September 1987, Ex HE 8-3, WHCF, LBJ Library.

119. Letter, Lee to Califano, 16 November 1966, attached to memo, Weaver to Califano, 23 November 1966, Ex HS 3, WHCF, LBJ Library.

120. Memo, Schultze to president, 22 March 1967, Ex FG 600/Task Force/S*, WHCF, LBJ Library.

121. Memo, Schultze to president, 7 April 1967, attached to memo, Kintner to president, 21 April 1967, Ex FA, WHCF, LBJ Library.

122. Letter, president to Weaver, 7 April 1967, Ex FA, WHCF, LBJ Library.

123. Memo, Panzer to Califano, 21 April 1967, Ex FA, WHCF, LBJ Library.

124. Memo, Schultze to president, 10 May 1967, Ex FG 600/Task Force/J*, WHCF, LBJ Library.

125. Memo, president to Gardner et al., 11 May 1967, attached to letter, Roberts to Daley, 12 May 1967, Ex FE 9, WHCF, LBJ Library. Upon signing the memorandum, the president directed that a copy be sent to Mayor Richard Daley of Chicago.

126. Memo, Califano to president, 27 July 1967, attached to memo, Califano to Wirtz, 28 July 1967, Ex FE 9, WHCF, LBJ Library.

127. Memo, president to Weaver et al., 27 October 1967, Ex FG 600/Task Force/J*, WHCF, LBJ Library.

128. Joint Administration Task Force, "Reducing Federal Grant-in-Aid Processing Time," March 1968, Ex FG 600/Task Force/Joint Administrative, WHCF, LBJ Library.

129. Noted on memo, Califano to president, 13 April 1968, Ex FG 160, WHCF, LBJ Library.

130. Earlier Muskie suggested to Johnson that he establish a National Council for Domestic Affairs patterned after the National Security Council. The council was to be chaired by the president and run on a day-to-day basis by an executive director who also would be a special assistant to the president. Muskie's advice was not wholly welcomed. Although McPherson reacted positively to his ideas, the Bureau of the Budget did not, he told the president. Memo, Muskie to president, 15 February 1966, attached to memo, McPherson to president, 15 February 1966, Memorandum for the President (1966) folder, box 52, files of Harry McPherson, LBJ Library.

131. See letter, Ink to Califano, 25 February 1966, Ex FG 202, WHCF, LBJ Library.

132. The president approved the reorganization in July 1967. Memo, Schultze to president, 22 July 1967, Ex FG 11-1, WHCF, LBJ Library.

133. See memo, Schultze to Califano, 11 December 1967, Ex LG, WHCF, LBJ Library.

134. For a more complete discussion of the work of the Heineman task force, see Redford and Blissett, Organizing the Executive Branch, pp. 195–209.

8. From the 1960s Onward

1. Douglas Yates, Bureaucratic Democracy: The Search for Democracy and Efficiency in American Government (Cambridge, Mass.: Harvard University Press, 1982), p. 12.

2. David R. Mayhew, Congress: The Electoral Connection (New Haven: Yale University Press, 1977), p. 129.

3. Ursala K. Hicks, Federalism, Failure and Success (New York: Oxford University Press, 1978), p. 12.

4. Notes for Speech folder, undated, box 6, files of Harry McPherson, LBJ Library. There is no mention of intergovernmental relations in the last State of the Union message and only brief mention in the last budget message.

5. Yates, Bureaucratic Democracy, pp. 23–30.

6. Ibid., pp. 32–33. See also the insightful essay by Robert D. Reischauer, "Government Diversity: Bane of the Grants Strategy in the United States," in Wallace E. Oates, ed., The Political Economy of Fiscal Federalism (Lexington, Mass.: Lexington Books, 1977), pp. 115–127.

7. Charles L. Schultze, The Politics and Economics of Public Spending (Washington, D.C.: The Brookings Institution, 1968), chap. 7.

8. See, for example, Helen Ingram, "Policy Implementation through Bargaining: The Case of Federal Grants-in-Aid," *Public Policy* 4 (Fall 1977): 499; and Jeffrey L. Pressman, *Federal Programs and City Politics* (Berkeley: University of California Press, 1975).

9. Michael D. Reagan, *The New Federalism* (New York: Oxford University Press, 1972), pp. 23–24.

10. Richard Warner, "The Concept of Creative Federalism in the Johnson Administration," (Ph.D. diss., American University, 1970), pp. 377–386.

11. Stephen Skowronek, *Building a New American State: The Expansion of National Administrative Capacities, 1877–1920* (Cambridge, England: Cambridge University Press, 1982).

12. Erwin C. Hargrove and Michael Nelson, *Presidents, Politics, and Policy* (New York: Alfred A. Knopf, 1984), p. 234.

13. Henry J. Aaron, *Politics and the Professors: The Great Society in Perspective* (Washington, D.C.: The Brookings Institution, 1978).

14. From the left, see Marrin E. Gettleman and David Mermelstein, eds., *The Great Society Reader: The Future of American Liberalism* (New York: Vintage Books, 1967). From the right, see Charles Murray, *Losing Ground: American Social Policy 1950–1980* (New York: Basic Books, 1984); and Lawrence M. Mead, *Beyond Entitlement: The Social Obligation of Citizenship* (New York: The Free Press, 1986).

15. Such analyses include Marshall Kaplan and Peggy Cuciti, eds., *The Great Society and Its Legacy* (Durham: Duke University Press, 1986); Sar A. Levitan and William Taggart, *The Promise of Greatness* (Cambridge, Mass.: Harvard University Press, 1976); David C. Warner, ed., *Toward New Human Rights: The Social Policies of the Kennedy and Johnson Administrations* (Austin: Lyndon B. Johnson School of Public Affairs, 1977); and John E. Schwartz, *America's Hidden Success: A Reassessment of Twenty Years of Public Policy* (New York: Norton, 1983).

16. Other studies come to negative conclusions. One of the most important of these, because of the influential perspective in intergovernmental program administration articulated there, is Jeffrey L. Pressman and Aaron B. Wildavsky, *Implementation* (Berkeley: University of California Press, 1973).

17. The implementation literature is insightful on these points. Examples include George C. Edwards III, *Implementing Public Policy* (Washington, D.C.: Congressional Quarterly Press, 1980); Erwin C. Hargrove, *The Missing Link* (Washington, D.C.: The Urban Institute, 1975); Daniel A. Mazmanian and Paul A. Sabatier, *Implementation and Public Policy* (Glenview, Ill.: Scott, Foresman, 1983); Robert T. Nakamura and Frank Smallwood, *The Politics of Policy Implementation* (New York: St. Martin's Press, 1980); Laurence J. O'Toole, Jr., and Robert S. Montjoy, "Intergovernmental Policy Implementation: A Theoretical Perspective," *Public Administration Review* 44 (Nov./Dec. 1984): 491; and Carl E. Van Horn, *Policy Implementation in the Federal System* (Lexington, Mass.: Lexington Books, 1979).

18. Paul E. Peterson, *City Limits* (Chicago: University of Chicago Press, 1981).

19. Allen J. Matusow, *The Unraveling of America: A History of Liberalism in the 1960s* (New York: Harper and Row, 1984), p. xiv.

20. William A. Schambra, "Progressive Liberalism and American 'Community,'" *Public Interest* 80 (Summer 1985): 37.

21. Ibid., p. 32.

22. Ibid., p. 42.

23. For a general review of developments during Nixon's presidency, see David B. Walker, "How Fares Federalism in the Mid-Seventies?" *The Annals* 416 (Nov. 1974): 17.

24. "Address to the Nation on Domestic Programs," 8 August 1969, *Public Papers of the Presidents of the United States: Richard M. Nixon, 1969* (Washington, D.C.: GPO, 1970), p. 638.

25. Richard P. Nathan, *The Administrative Presidency* (New York: John Wiley and Sons, 1983), p. 27.

26. P.L. 93-203.

27. P.L. 93-383. Most evaluations of the Model Cities program find that it produced positive results in the form of improved planning and coordination. Advisory Commission on Intergovernmental Relations, *Improving Federal Grants Management* (Washington, D.C.: GPO, 1977), pp. 76–77.

28. Discussion of developments during the presidency of Richard Nixon is based principally upon Advisory Commission in Intergovernmental Relations, *Improving Federal Grants Management*, and Nathan, *The Administrative Presidency.*

29. Deficiencies in the institutional presidency that led to Nixon's adaptations are discussed in two articles by William D. Carey. They are "Intergovernmental Relations: Guides to Development," *Public Administration Review* 28 (Jan./Feb. 1968): 22; and "Presidential Staffing in the Sixties and Seventies," *Public Administration Review* 29 (Sept./Oct. 1969): 450. Dilemmas in presidential policy management were examined extensively during the 1970s and early 1980s. Two illustrative examples are Richard Rose, *Managing Presidential Objectives* (New York: The Free Press, 1976); and Hugh Heclo and Lester M. Salamon, eds., *The Illusion of Presidential Government* (Boulder: Westview Press, 1981). A useful overview of the Domestic Policy Council and its successors is provided in Margaret Jane Wyszomirski, "A Domestic Policy Office: Presidential Agency in Search of a Role," *Policy Studies Journal* 12 (June 1984): 705. On the recent history of OMB see Peter M. Benda and Charles H. Levine, "OMB and the Central Management Problem: Is Another Reorganization the Answer?" *Public Administration Review* 46 (Sept./Oct. 1986): 379.

30. Federal executive boards continued to operate in a number of cities.

31. P.L. 93-510.

32. Martha Derthick, "Intergovernmental Relations in the 1970s," in Lawrence E. Gelfand and Robert J. Neymeyer, eds., *Changing Patterns in American Federal-State Relations during the 1950s, the 1960s, and the 1970s* (Iowa City: Center for the Study of Recent History of the United States, University of Iowa, 1985), pp. 49–59.

33. Paul E. Peterson, Barry G. Robe, and Kenneth K. Wong, *When Feder-alism Works* (Washington, D.C.: The Brookings Institution, 1986), p. 2.

34. Advisory Commission on Intergovernmental Relations, *Multistate Regionalism* (Washington, D.C.: GPO, 1972); Martha Derthick, *Between State and Nation* (Washington, D.C.: The Brookings Institution, 1974).

35. Advisory Commission on Intergovernmental Relations, *The Partner-ship for Health Act: Lessons from a Pioneering Block Grant* (Washington, D.C.: GPO, 1977); *Making the Safe Streets Act Work* (Washington, D.C.: GPO, 1970); and *Safe Streets Reconsidered: The Block Grant Experience 1968–75* (Washington, D.C.: GPO, 1977). See also B. Douglas Harmon, "The Block Grant Experience: Readings from a First Experiment," *Public Administration Review* 30 (Mar./Apr. 1970): 141; and David T. Stanley, "How Safe the Streets, How Good the Grant?" *Public Administration Review* 34 (July/Aug. 1974): 380. See also James Q. Wilson, *Thinking about Crime* (New York: Basic Books, 1975), pp. 198–209. Two more recent re-ports have been prepared by the Congressional Budget Office: *Federal Law Enforcement Assistance: Alternative Approaches* (Washington, D.C.: GPO, 1978); and *The Law Enforcement Assistance Administration: Options for Reauthorization* (Washington, D.C.: GPO, 1979).

36. Jerome J. Hanus, "Authority Costs in Intergovernmental Relations," in Hanus, ed., *The Nationalization of State Government* (Lexington, Mass.: Lexington Books, 1981), p. 19.

37. Ibid., pp. 14–16. See also Advisory Commission on Intergovernmen-tal Relations, *Regulatory Federalism: Policy, Process, Impact, and Reform* (Washington, D.C.: ACIR, 1984); and Donald F. Kettl, *The Regulation of American Federalism* (Baton Rouge: Louisiana State University Press, 1983).

38. Derthick, "Intergovernmental Relations in the 1970s," p. 59.

39. Advisory Commission on Intergovernmental Relations, *The Federal Role in the Federal System: The Dynamics of Growth* (Washington, D.C.: ACIR, 1981), p. 7.

40. Ibid., p. 95.

41. Ibid.

42. Ibid., pp. 30–31. Similar views are expressed in Daniel R. Beam, Tim-othy J. Conlan, and Daniel B. Walker, "Federalism: The Challenge of Con-flicting Theories and Contemporary Practice," in Ada W. Finifter, ed., *Po-litical Science: The State of the Discipline* (Washington, D.C.: American Political Science Association, 1983), p. 267; and David B. Walker, *Toward a Functioning Federalism* (Cambridge, Mass.: Winthrop Publishers, 1981). For more positive assessments, see Thomas J. Anton, "Decay and Recon-struction in the Study of American Intergovernmental Relations" (paper presented at the annual meeting of the American Political Science Associa-tion, Chicago, August 1983); and Peterson et al., *When Federalism Works*.

43. According to one analyst, Reagan's victory was caused not so much by a swing to the right as by a disaffection with the welfare state constructed by liberal Democrats. Everett Carl Ladd, "The Reagan Phenomenon and Pub-lic Attitudes toward Government," in Lester M. Salamon and Michael S.

Lund, eds., *The Reagan Presidency and the Governing of America* (Washington, D.C.: Urban Institute Press, 1984), pp. 221–249.

44. James W. Ceaser, "The Theory of Governance of the Reagan Administration," in Salamon and Lund, eds., *The Reagan Presidency*, p. 68.

45. "Inaugural Address," 20 January 1981, *Public Papers of the Presidents of the United States: Ronald Reagan*, 1981 (Washington, D.C.: GPO, 1982), p. 1 (hereafter cited as *Public Papers*).

46. Ibid., p. 2.

47. "Remarks at the Mid-Winter Congressional City Conference of the National League of Cities," 2 March 1981, ibid, p. 176.

48. John L. Palmer and Isabel V. Sawhill, "Overview," in Palmer and Sawhill, eds., *The Reagan Record* (Cambridge, Mass.: Ballinger, 1984), p. 13.

49. Peterson et al., *When Federalism Works*, p. 2.

50. Daniel B. Walker, "The Nature and Systemic Impact of 'Creative Federalism,'" in Kaplan and Cuciti, eds., *The Great Society and Its Legacy*, p. 206.

51. Ibid., p. 207.

52. Claude E. Barfield, *Rethinking Federalism: Block Grants and Federal, State, and Local Responsibilities* (Washington, D.C.: American Enterprise Institute, 1981), p. 29.

53. Nathan, *The Administrative Presidency*, p. 61. See also David R. Beam, "New Federalism, Old Realities: The Reagan Administration and Intergovernmental Reform," in Salamon and Lund, eds., *The Reagan Presidency*, pp. 423–427.

54. Nathan, *The Administrative Presidency*, pp. 65–68.

55. See generally Chester A. Newland, "Executive Office Policy Apparatus: Enforcing the Reagan Agenda," in Salamon and Lund, eds., *The Reagan Presidency*, p. 135.

56. Beam, "New Federalism, Old Realities," pp. 433–440. There is empirical evidence of loosened enforcement. See Jane Massey and Jeffrey D. Straussman, "Another Look at the Mandate Issue: Are Conditions of Aid Really So Burdensome?" *Public Administration Review* 45 (Mar./Apr. 1985): 292.

57. George E. Peterson, "Federalism and the States," in Palmer and Sawhill, eds., *The Reagan Record*, pp. 256–259.

58. John E. Chubb, "Federalism and the Basis for Centralization," in John E. Chubb and Paul E. Peterson, eds., *The New Direction in American Politics* (Washington, D.C.: The Brookings Institution, 1985), p. 274.

59. See, for example, Daniel J. Elazer, *American Federalism: A View from the States* (New York: Harper and Row, 1984), pp. 256–257; and Carl W. Stenberg, "States under the Spotlight: An Intergovernmental View," *Public Administration Review* 45 (Mar./Apr. 1985): 319.

60. The most vigorous statement of this view is Theodore J. Lowi, *The Personal President: Power Inverted, Promise Unfulfilled* (Ithaca: Cornell University Press, 1985).

61. Barfield, *Rethinking Federalism*, pp. 15–16.

62. David Rosenbloom, "The Great Society and the Growth of 'Judicial

Federalism'—Protecting Civil Rights and Welfare," in Kaplan and Cuciti, eds., *The Great Society and Its Legacy*, pp. 208–217.

63. Walker, *Toward a Functioning Federalism*, pp. 234–235.

64. Cynthia Cates Colella and David R. Beam, "The Political Dynamics of Intergovernmental Relations," in Hanus, ed., *The Nationalization of State Government*, p. 156.

65. Samuel H. Beer has written extensively on the new patterns in intergovernmental politics. See, for example, "The Modernization of American Federalism," *Publius* 3 (Fall 1973): 49; and "The Adoption of General Revenue Sharing: A Case Study in Public-Sector Politics," *Public Policy* 24 (Spring 1976): 127. Also insightful are Hugh Heclo, "Issue Networks and the Executive Establishment," in Anthony King, ed., *The New American Political System* (Washington, D.C.: American Enterprise Institute, 1979), p. 87; and H. Brinton Milward, "Policy Entrepreneurship and Bureaucratic Demand Creation," in Helen M. Ingram and Dean E. Mann, eds., *Why Policies Succeed or Fail* (Beverly Hills, Calif.: Sage Publications, 1980), p. 255.

66. Donald F. Kettl, "The Maturing of American Federalism," in Robert T. Golembiewski and Aaron Wildavsky, eds., *The Cost of Federalism* (New Brunswick, N.J.: Transaction Books), p. 73.

67. Willmoore Kendall and George W. Carey, eds., *The Federalist Papers* (New Rochelle, N.Y.: Arlington House, 1966), p. 295.

68. Samuel H. Beer, "The National Idea in National Politics" (lecture delivered to the faculty and officers of Boston College, Chestnut Hill, Mass., 21 April 1982). His basic views are spelled out in an earlier article, "Liberalism and the National Idea," *Public Interest* 5 (Fall 1966): 70.

Name Index

Sawhill, Isabel V., 306
Schambra, William A., 245, 304
Scheiber, Harry N., 22, 259, 261
Schoen, Cathy, 291
Schott, Richard L., 275, 287
Schubert, Glendon, 262
Schultz, George P., 107
Schultze, Charles L., 28–29, 42, 70,
　80, 82, 105, 108, 109, 151, 157,
　160, 161, 180, 181, 184, 200, 201,
　204–206, 207, 210, 225, 227, 230,
　231, 233, 238, 263, 271, 273, 274,
　278, 279, 280, 284, 285, 286, 287,
　288, 292, 296, 297, 300, 301, 302
Schwartz, John E., 303
Scott, Anthony, 291
Scranton, William W., 138, 285
Seib, Charles B., 290
Seidman, Harold, 18, 61, 142–143,
　195, 223, 261, 269, 273, 277, 285,
　295, 297, 300
Selover, William C., 268
Selznick, Philip, 283
Semer, Milton P., 229–230, 301
Shelley, John F., 69–70
Shriver, R. Sargent, 62–63, 68, 69,
　71, 75, 76, 83, 86, 87, 88, 89, 90,
　91, 93, 95, 100, 103, 104, 107,
　110, 154, 270, 271, 272, 275, 276,
　277, 278, 279, 280, 288
Sindler, Allan P., 270
Singletary, Otis A., Jr., 275
Skowronek, Stephen, 18–19, 242,
　261, 303
Smallwood, Frank, 303
Smith, Nancy Kegan, 263
Solomon, Arthur P., 273
Solow, Robert M., 93, 276
Sorenson, Theodore, 142, 284, 285
Staats, Elmer, 274, 300
Stahl, O. Glenn, 208
Stam, Jerome M., 299
Stanley, David T., 305
Steiner, Gilbert Y., 265
Stenberg, Carl W., 306
Stennis, John, 286
Stone, Alan, 261

Straussman, Jeffrey D., 306
Sugarman, Jule M., 106, 278
Sundquist, James L., 6, 15–16, 24,
　59, 86, 89, 90, 94, 114, 124, 125,
　139, 143, 213, 260, 261, 262, 268,
　269, 272–285 passim, 295, 298
Surrey, Stanley S., 171, 290
Sweeney, John L., 137, 138, 139,
　140, 143, 144, 145, 148, 150, 152,
　153, 154, 156, 157, 284, 285, 286,
　287, 288
Sweeney, Stephen B., 295

Taft, Robert, 40
Taggart, Robert, 291
Theobald, Robert, 266
Thomas, Norman C., 184, 263, 266,
　293
Truman, Harry S., 25

Valenti, Jack, 270, 273, 286, 287
Van Horn, Carl E., 303
Van Riper, Paul P., 1, 259
Vinson, Fred, 190
Vorenberg, James, 188, 190, 294

Walker, Daniel B., 306
Walker, David B., 4, 20, 255, 259,
　260, 261, 304, 305, 307
Wallace, George C., 73, 74
Walsh, William G., 270
Warner, David C., 291, 303
Warner, Richard R., 201, 206, 242,
　295, 296, 297, 298, 301, 303
Watson, W. Marvin, 149, 150, 151,
　268, 286, 287, 301
Weaver, Robert C., 109, 110, 115,
　120, 123, 209, 231, 275, 279, 281,
　282, 296, 301, 302
Whisman, John D., 136, 137
White, Lee C., 138, 142, 148, 284,
　285, 286
Wickstrom, Nelson, 298
Wildavsky, Aaron, 287, 303, 307
Williams, Walter, 278
Wilson, Henry Hall, 200, 279
Wilson, James Q., 194, 305

Subject Index

Accelerated Public Works Act of 1962, 146

Administrative efficiency, 240–241

Administrative regionalism, 129–131

Advisory Commission on Intergovernmental Relations, 7; and BOB, 211, 226; on categorical project grants, 189; and commission on federalism, 201–202; critique of intergovernmental relations, 250; on federal executive boards, 223–224; on governor's veto in poverty programs, 74; and Intergovernmental Cooperation Act of 1968, 200; on Law Enforcement Assistance Act of 1965, 187; on multistate regionalism, 132; on poverty programs, 81–82; on revenue sharing, 172; role and influence in Johnson presidency, 202; on substate regionalism, 128, 216

Advisory Committee on Water Resources Policy, 133

Aircraft noise control, 42, 43

Air pollution control, 10, 42, 49

Alabama, 73, 74

American administrative state: and cooperative federalism, 3–6; criticisms of, 250; definition, 1; development of, 18–20; and Economic Opportunity Act of 1964, 63–67; effects of Johnson presidency on, 19–20, 235–236; and grants-in-aid, 165–167; and intergovernmental programs, 253; and multistate commissions, 131–132, 162–164; paradoxes in, 242–243; and policy and program development, 199; presidency in, 125; and war on poverty, 97

American Municipal Congress, 27

American Public Health Association, 182

Appalachian Regional Commission, 140–141, 150–162

Appalachian Regional Development Act of 1965: enactment of, 9; and governors, 136–139; Johnson on, 132; negotiations leading to, 141–146; in 1965 legislative program, 40–41; origins of, 136–138; provisions of, 140–141; reauthorization of, 157–159; and regionalism, 128

Area Redevelopment Act of 1961, 26, 136, 137, 138, 146–147

Association of State and Territorial Health Officers, 182

Atlanta, 71

Baker v. Carr, 24

Baltimore, 68, 121

Block grants: compared to cate-

Interstate Conference on Water
Problems, 134

Job Corps, 17, 64, 70
Job Opportunities in the Private
Sector (JOBS), 44
Joint Administrative Task Force
(1967), 231–233
Joint Funding Simplification Act of
1974, 227, 248–249
Juvenile Delinquency Prevention
and Control Act of 1968, 10, 184
Juvenile Delinquency and Youth Of-
fences Control Act of 1961, 185

Kennedy administration: agenda of,
6–7, 25–26; and Appalachia,
136, 137; and Economic Opportunity Act of 1964, 57–60; and
federal field coordination,
221–222; intergovernmental programs in, 25–26; task forces in,
29–30; and Water Resources
Planning Act of 1965, 133
Kentucky, 136, 137

Law Enforcement, national programs in, 43
Law Enforcement Assistance Act of
1965, 9, 41, 185–187
Law Enforcement Assistance Administration, 195
Legal services, 72
Local governments: and Economic
Opportunity Act of 1964, 64; and
federal law enforcement assistance, 185; and Model Cities program, 119–126; and revenue
sharing, 172; and Safe Streets Act
of 1968, 185–197. *See also* Subnational governments
Los Angeles, 69, 121

Manpower Development and Training Act of 1962, 26
Manpower programs: and coordination problems, 77–79, 83–86,

111–113; Job Opportunities in
the Private Sector, 44; and na-
tional options, 26; reorganiza-
tion in Department of Labor,
101–102; spinoffs from OEO,
107; and state employment services, 94; work experience, 64.
See also Department of Labor;
Economic Opportunity Act
of 1964; Office of Economic
Opportunity
Meat and poultry inspection, 42
Medicaid, 9, 178
Medicare, 9, 26, 36, 43, 178
Migrant worker programs, 64
Milwaukee, 71
Mine safety, 42
Minimum wage, 25, 43
Minneapolis, 71
Model Cities program: basic concepts, 117; and citizen participation requirements, 121–122;
coordination, 120, 122–125;
and councils of governments,
218–219; and Economic Opportunity Act of 1964, 56, 114; enactment, 9; interagency team
visits, 121; and neighborhood
centers, 111; in Nixon administration, 247; origins, 37,
114–119; selection of cities,
119–120
Motor vehicle and highway safety,
42, 43
Multistate commissions, 131–132,
162, 164, 252
Multistate economic development
commissions, 146–149,
151–152, 158–159

Nation, 172
National Alliance of Businessmen,
44
National Association of Counties,
172, 255
National Association of State

Mental Health Program Directors, 182

National bureaucracy: categorical grants, 176, 197; challenges to, 20, 63–67, 126, 235–236, 246, 250–251; and cooperative federalism, 5–6; interagency conflict in war on poverty, 59–60, 83–88, 97; Johnson's legacy, 253–254; power of, 19–20, 24–25, 126–127; and task forces, 236. *See also* American administrative state

National Commission on Community Health Services, 180

National Defense Education Act of 1958, 25

National Endowment on the Arts and Humanities, 9

National Governors' Conference, 51–53, 73–74, 171, 172, 255

National League of Cities, 255

National programs; 26, 36, 43–44, 54, 237–238

National Resources Planning Board, 131, 133

National Youth Administration, 237

Natural resources, 43

Neighborhood centers, 72, 109–111

Neighborhood Youth Corps, 64, 70

New Deal, 4–5, 19–20, 25, 27, 237

New Republic, 172

New York Times, 169

Nixon administration: and federal regional organization, 225; and Intergovernmental Cooperation Act of 1968, 220–221; and intergovernmental relations, 245–249; and multistate commissions, 164; and revenue sharing, 173; and war on poverty, 77, 107

Office of Economic Opportunity (OEO): administrative characteristics of, 88–89, 93; and Appa-

lachian Regional Commission, 153–55; and check point procedure, 111; and community action programs, 93, 95–97; and concentrated employment program, 112; and coordination role, 77–92, 103–105; and guaranteed annual income, 45–46; and interagency conflict, 83–90; and Model Cities program, 121, 123–125; and neighborhood centers, 109–111; political problems of, 67–76; reauthorization, 10, 74–76; regional offices, 100–101; reorganization, 105–109; and substate regionalism, 216. *See also* Community action programs; Economic Opportunity Act of 1964; War on poverty

Office of Emergency Planning, 51–53, 68

Office of the Vice President, 51–53, 68, 69, 71, 86–87, 102–103

Oil pollution control, 43

Omnibus Crime Control and Safe Streets Act of 1968, 10

Partnership for Earning and Learning Act of 1968, 184

Partnership for Health Act of 1966, 9, 177–183

Philadelphia, 68

Planning: and administrative regionalism, 130–131; and Appalachian Regional Commission, 152; in block grant programs, 174, 182, 196; and community action programs, 93; and councils of governments, 218–220; federal assistance for, 87–88, 131, 213; in Model Cities program, 119–120; and multistate economic development commissions, 148; requirements for, 47; and substate agencies, 213–221

Planning-Programming-Budgeting System (PPBS), 210

Republican Party, 9, 168–169, 171, 185–188
Revenue sharing, 166–170, 246–247
River basin planning commissions, 42, 133–135, 149

Safe Streets Act of 1968: antecedents, 185–188; and Congress, 192–193, 195–196; development of proposals, 188–192, 194–195; enactment, 10; provisions, 196
St. Louis, 68–71
San Francisco, 69
Small Business Administration, 17
Social and Economic Development Council, 104
Social Security, 25, 36, 43, 45–46
Solid waste disposal, 42
State development, 18–19
State governments: and Appalachian Regional Commission, 152; assessments of, 26, 34, 36, 61, 184; and multistate economic development commissions, 146–148; and Partnership for Health Act of 1966, 181–182; preemption of authority, 41–43; presidential liaison with, 50–53; and river basin planning commissions, 134; and Safe Streets Act of 1968, 185, 189, 196; and war on poverty, 64, 72, 74–75, 93–94. *See also* Governors; Subnational governments
Subnational governments: administrative deficiencies of, 28, 34–36, 54, 59, 207–212; chief executives and intergovernmental programs, 50–53, 210–212; and Congress, 49–50; and cooperative federalism, 4–6; and creative federalism, 6–18; Johnson's legacy, 254; and Nixon administration, 246–247; and Reagan administration, 251; and substate regionalism, 213–221. *See also* Gover-

nors; Intergovernmental programs; Local governments; Substate regionalism
Subpresidency, 29–30, 54, 55
Substate regionalism, 213–221
Summer youth employment programs, 102–103
Syracuse, 69

Task Force on Agriculture and Rural Life (1965), 87
Task Force on Cities (1966), 41, 122–123
Task Force on Crime (1967), 194
Task Force on Education: in 1964, 32, 36, 37; in 1967, 41
Task Force on Environmental Pollution (1964), 36
Task Force on Government Organization (1966), 48, 78–79, 82–83, 93–94, 103–104, 107, 224, 226, 233, 241
Task Force on Government Reorganization (1964), 47, 199
Task Force on Health (1964), 37
Task Force on Health Care (1965), 180
Task Force on Income Maintenance (1964), 35–38
Task Force on Intergovernmental Fiscal Cooperation (1964), 47, 167–168
Task Force on Intergovernmental Program Coordination (1965), 47, 80–81, 200–201, 226
Task Force on Juvenile Delinquency (1966), 188, 189
Task Force on Law Enforcement and the Administration of Justice (1966), 188, 189, 197
Task Force on Los Angeles Riots (1965), 80
Task Force on Manpower for State and Local Governments (1966), 47–48, 208, 209
Task Force on Metropolitan and Urban Problems (1964), 35–39, 44,